CAPTIVE INSURANCE COMPANIES

British Library Cataloguing in Publication data
Bawcutt, Paul
   Captive Insurance Companies
   Insurance – 4th Ed.
   1. Insurance
   1. Title

ISBN 1 85609 130 9

CAPTIVE INSURANCE COMPANIES

*Establishment,
Operation and Management*

FOURTH EDITION

PAUL BAWCUTT

Managing Director, Risk and Insurance Research Group Limited

LONDON
WITHERBY & CO LTD
32–36 Aylesbury Street
London ECIR 0ET

First Published 1982
Published 1997

WITHERBY

PUBLISHERS

© Paul Bawcutt
1982 1987 1991 1997

ISBN 1 85609 130 9

Printed and Published by
Witherby & Co. Ltd.
32–36 Aylesbury Street
London EC1R 0ET
Tel 0171–251 5341
Fax 0171–251 1296
International Tel +44 171 251 5341
International Fax +44 171 251 1296

DEDICATION

When I was putting the finishing touches to this fourth edition, my friend Duncan Neil died suddenly. He had been generous enough to write the Foreword for the second edition of my book even though, at the time, has was heavily engaged in introducing insurance legislation in the Isle of Man and helping to make it a very successful offshore centre.

I used to see Duncan often, during the late 1980's when he was Insurance Supervisor and more recently when he sat on the Board of a number of the captives owned by my clients. He was always helpful, knowledgeable and took his responsibilities very seriously. He was good fun at social occasions, enjoyed a joke even when it was directed at him.

It seems inadequate to dedicate a book on captives to such a decent man but I do so with humility and great regret that I will never again have the pleasure of his company.

Those in the captive business sector will not forget Duncan and will greatly miss his erudition and companionship.

Paul Bawcutt
April 1997

PREFACE

to

First Edition

Captive insurance companies have become popular and a major topic of discussion in the insurance world over the last twenty-five years. Their history, however, goes back at least one hundred years and, arguably, many centuries before that. In a book on the early history of insurance published in 1926 in London, the author described the establishment of what today might be called an industry or association captive, where industrial groups joined together to establish organisations for which the principal objective was the provision of mutual indemnification against loss. This description referred to a method of mutual financial protection established in the year AD 779 by a trade guild. Subsequently, the first insurance policies were issued in the Middle Ages, most of these being produced by mutual groups, a practice which continued to be the main method of insurance protection until the late nineteenth century

If we trace the history of today's major insurers, we discover that most of them, including such companies as Guardian Royal Exchange and General Accident, were established by small groups of people who joined together either to provide financial protection for each other, as the trade guilds did in AD 779, or to improve on the insurance offered by the then-established insurance companies. This history, particularly the motives for the introduction of insurance, has relevance to the captive insurance company concept because many of the reasons coincide with those which have resulted in the establishment of captives and their significant growth in recent years.

In the nineteenth century the mutual groups were located in the country or area in which the individuals involved were domiciled. They were usually operated on a non-profit-making basis, the residual profit, if any, being reflected in either a return to the members or a reduction in future costs. The reason for domestic establishment was simply convenience, and was made possible by the fact that legislation covering such an operation was negligible. In addition, there were no taxation worries: tax did not operate or there was no profit to tax. As insurance companies developed, risks became greater and insurance became a major provider of service to the community, pressure for legislation and the need to spread the risk on a much wider basis became necessary and the insurance company environment that we see today became recognisable.

The evolution of insurance, from its origin as a form of mutual risk-spreading and financial protection to the insurance industry of today, with its mammoth premium volumes and contribution to world economy, has been a major development over a comparatively short period of time. The growth of captives has been, in many respects, a repeat performance of the history of the major worldwide insurers and, like those companies, captives are becoming an influential factor in the industrial insurance field.

The purpose of this book is to examine captives in their modern setting and to consider the advantages and disadvantages of their use by industrial corporations and the processes that need to be undertaken to decide whether a captive insurance company is feasible, how it should be protected by reinsurance and where it should be located and managed. The financial considerations that need to be taken into account if a captive is to be managed effectively and make a contribution to the owner's business performance are also examined. The final chapter will look at the possible future for captives, including the potential for them to develop outside business. This latter move may well complete the cycle for captives, as it did for the original insurance companies, so that as the retention of their own business declines, they will become part of the insurance establishment.

PREFACE

to

Fourth Edition

As with the previous editions it is difficult to keep up to date with the development and growth of the captive insurance sector. Since the third edition, captive formation has continued to grow at the rate of at least 10% per annum and interest in the captive concept continues to spread all over the world. From the traditionally open markets of North America, United Kingdom, Scandinavia and Australia we are now seeing new captives being formed by ship owners in Russia, pharmaceutical companies and ship owners in Germany, a wide range of businesses in France, Italy and Spain, newly privatised companies in the Far East, the overseas subsidiary operations of Japanese multinationals and a wide mix of companies based in Latin and South America. The growth of captives is always inextricably linked with the breaking down of international trading barriers and the deregulation of local insurance industries. This is a growing feature of corporate insurance and there are no signs that growth, as a result of these new freedoms to operate, will diminish.

Every edition of this book has reported on the increasing number of locations available for captive insurance company formation and the expected trend towards onshore formation (as distinct from the traditional establishment in low tax, offshore areas) has continued. This has been influenced by changes in the tax regimes of countries where many captive owners are based and also by insurance regulatory changes in particular, the introduction of the European Union freedom of services legislation which came into force, from a practical standpoint in 1996 and allows insurance companies in one member state to write insurance business into others. There has also been considerable growth in the development of new risk financing techniques. It appears that the rent-a-captive is now returning

ix

not just as a possible and often effective alternative to a captive but also as a reinsurance-type mechanism behind the captive itself. One of the most significant developments has been the emergence of financial insurance or reinsurance products (often, in a version particularly attractive to large corporate buyers, referred to as finite risk insurance) which can be utilised as a direct insurance mechanism or as reinsurance behind a captive.

As I write, there is beginning to be a development of mixed insurance and banking products designed primarily to help major corporations minimise or spread the effect of substantial losses on their profit and loss account and balance sheet. Apart from the continuing development of financial insurance products, quasi-insurance entities are now prepared to offer what one might call a "contingent preference share" concept which involves the "insured" paying a "premium" to a financial organisation that has agreed to purchase preference shares in the event of a catastrophe loss, and thereby inject capital at a time when it may be desperately needed. Subsequently, the shares are purchased back by the corporation as its position improves. There will be more and very significant developments in this sector. These concepts can be used in conjunction with captives but could also be a threat to them. However, this threat is likely to be one that impacts only the very largest corporations in the world and it is expected that captives will continue to grow and remain part of the risk financing armoury of an increasing number of companies in all parts of the world.

In the 1980's, when there was a sudden departure of insurance capacity with a resulting increasing in insurance premiums and the availability of insurance cover, there was considerable growth in the formation of mutuals and group captives, particularly in the liability insurance areas. Despite the fact that, since that time, the insurance market has not experienced any dramatic reductions in capacity, the interest in mutuals and group captives has continued to grow. As in the 1980's many of those that have survived have been established on the nineteenth century principles of mutuality typified by the structures developed by ship owners for their liability risks and known commonly as protection and indemnity or P&I Clubs. More recently a number of small industry captives have been established, most notably by a group of chemical companies to insure environmental risks in Germany and, again, this is a trend we may see developing over the coming years.

Every edition of the book has referred to the increasing interest of the taxation authorities in captives, as they grow and continue to spread into new territories. The number of tax court cases involving captive owners and the United States Internal Revenue Service has continued with the results, for captive owners, mixed but on balance becoming more favourable. Legislation aimed at controlled foreign companies, often with the captive insurer in mind, have been introduced in a number of new countries and refined in countries like the United Kingdom, Sweden, Australia and New Zealand where CFC legislation has impacted captives for many years. This trend will continue and there seems little doubt that many of the advantages of having a captive in a low tax area will largely disappear but the benefits of being in a location which is dedicated to the captive concept and has a regulatory and business infra structure specially devoted to it should continue.

The third edition reported a decline in the interest amongst captives of writing so called unrelated business, i.e. insurance business not connected to the owner of the captive. This change in strategy was mainly due to substantial losses made by a large number of, primarily North American, captives who entered the international reinsurance market with poor timing and inadequate expertise in order to mitigate the impact of USA tax legislation affecting captives. To a large extent this lesson seems to have been learned and there has been few signs of captives moving into conventional insurance or reinsurance; most now concentrating their strategies on using their captive insurer as an increasingly important part of their overall risk financing approach. In addition, many now use their captives to underwrite risks, such as environmental impairment or product recall, where insurance cover is either impossible to obtain or cannot be purchased without substantial cost.

The area where there has been a degree of expansion into unrelated insurance business is the underwriting of customer risks such as extended warranty on consumer products (e.g. washing machines, televisions, video recorders, refrigerators) and credit life insurance which provides insurance protection to customers if they are unable to repay outstanding debts due, for example, to illness, death, unemployment or redundancy. There are a number of captives that specialise in this area and have been very successful in helping to enhance the product which their owner produces or sells.

This new, fourth edition has been updated to reflect the significant changes that have taken place over the last five years. It puts increasing emphasis on areas such as the rent-a-captive, financial reinsurance, the increasing use of onshore captive locations and developments in the international taxation area. The final chapter looks at the future of captives and begins to question whether they still have a role to play and particularly whether they are being used effectively by their owners. In June 1996, at a conference in Luxembourg, I made a presentation entitled "Should You Close Down Your Captive?" – this caused headlines in the insurance and risk management press and, to some extent, the message that I was trying to convey was misunderstood. However, I believe strongly that if captives are to develop they need to have proper strategies and should play an increasing, and probably a different role, in the risk financing and insurance arrangements of their owners. Many captives have stagnated and without revitalisation could disappear. This would be a pity but the captive, like any other concept, needs to be regularly questioned, adapted to changing circumstances and look to the future and not the past. In a re-written format I have included the presentation that I made in June 1996 because without a regular review of the contribution that a captive is making, its future may be limited.

The number of captive locations continues to expand and the book again includes details of all of the known, credible locations. In the appendices, details, in summary form, of the legal requirements and special consideration for captives have been widened to include, compared to the third edition, Gibraltar, Switzerland, Panama and the British Virgin Islands. The fairly arbitrary list of captives has been updated to reflect the wider geographic spread of owners and demonstrate how captive formation has spread from the dominating position of the United States and the United Kingdom to today's situation where captives can be found in virtually all developed countries around the world.

I have also decided, in this edition, to embellish some of the more technical insurance, taxation and accounting issues by quoting from articles and papers that have appeared in Captive Insurance Company Review (a monthly newsletter published by my consultancy company Risk & Insurance Research Group Limited) so that the reader can gain a more detailed insight into the increasing importance of taxation and accounting matters on the captive scene. Naturally, full accreditation is given to those who wrote these articles and I am also grateful for the editor of CICR, the writers and presenters involved for allowing me to do this. The accounting treatment of captives and especially the way in which they are consolidated with their owners is becoming an increasingly important issue as accounting standards change and a common international approach to the accounting treatment of insurance companies develops. In a new insurance accounting environment, many of the advantages previously associated with captives will either decline or disappear and this is often not being recognised. I see this issue as one of the most important influences on the future of captives and it will affect whether they will survive in their existing form or be overtaken by some of the new risk financing ideas that are currently going the rounds.

It is my intention to provide a new edition which is larger than the previous three editions. It includes a great deal more information, is more detailed and technical and has a new bias towards the importance of captives developing and extending their roles. The edition naturally reflects the continuing growth of the captive sector over the last five years and where events have overtaken them, old concepts and ideas have been eliminated. Whilst it is difficult to keep up to date a book which is usually re-written every five years, I have done my best to anticipate future events so that those buying this edition in the next century will not find it too out of date or irrelevant.

As ever, I am reliant on clients, business colleagues and those who share my interest in the captive insurance concept for helping to continue to expand my knowledge of this topic; and of course, much of the new information included in this edition has been derived from consultancy projects, contacts, listening at conferences and reading the numerous journals which now devote a great deal of space to captives and related self-insurance mechanisms. I hope that this edition does some justice to those who have unknowingly, or in some cases inadvertently, helped me to complete this book, and I wholeheartedly thank them for their assistance.

P.A.B.
March 1997

ACKNOWLEDGEMENTS

I am pleased to continue with the acknowledgements made in the previous three editions of this book by reminding readers that the material was original based on workshops organised by Risk Research Group and subsequently my own consultancy company, Risk & Insurance Research Group Limited. My business partner in Risk Research Group, Jim Bannister, was almost entirely responsible for developing the early workshops in the 1970's and a great deal of his original ideas and concepts remain in the workshops run in the name of RIRG today. I am therefore pleased to continue acknowledging his help and ideas.

The workshops have, of course, developed over this period and my own role in them has diminished. The person now responsible for leading the workshops is my colleague Christian Dinesen and his influence on the workshops run today is reflected in this new edition. I would also like to acknowledge Christian's help with many of the tables which have been incorporated in the book, particularly as information gathering is always a major task when writing a new book or updating an old one. In addition my colleague Chris Best has continued contributing to my thinking and the research through his activity as the Editor of Captive Insurance Company Review, which monitors captive developments world-wide and reports on them succinctly and informatively each month.

A practical difficulty when writing books is to find someone willing and patient enough to put the whole thing onto the word processor. Angela Millard is such a person and did sterling work and helped retrieve my embarrassment at failing to meet a deadline agreed with the publishers. The new publishers also deserve a mention. Alan Witherby, who I have known for a quarter of a century, approached me to ask whether he could publish the fourth edition and this coincided with the previous publishers being taken over by an American firm that did not have much appetite for books that

ACKNOWLEDGEMENTS

would not sell an enormous number of copies. Alan is very committed to the insurance and risk management publishing business and the whole industry should be grateful to him for maintaining his independence, devotion to the business and, of course, his legendary business acumen.

Other friends in business were kind enough to allow me to reproduce charts, sample agreements, documents and articles and I have acknowledged this where appropriate. I apologise to anyone whose contribution I have omitted — this is not deliberate but almost certainly incompetence. As ever I must not overlook the debt that I owe to my clients; without whom I would not have gained the experience of captives that has gone into this book.

Finally, I continue to express gratitude to my family, Jean, Clare and Lucy who still put up with me and have, in the new parlance, given me "space" to sit at home and complete this latest edition.

PAB

CONTENTS

CONTENTS

5 Managing a Captive 173

Captive management requirements. Selecting the managers.
Captive set-up and operating costs. Management agreements.
Constitution of the captive board. Annex 5.1, Annex 5.2,
Annex 5.3.

6 Accounting, Taxation and Investment Needs 197

Accounting aspects. Taxation. The issue of captive residency.
Investment basics.

7 Loss Control and Claims 269

Loss control. Handling claims.

8 The Future Development of Captives 277

Market reactions to the captive. Legislation in captive locations.
Expanding into unrelated business. Captive pooling facilities.
Financial reinsurance. Re-location. Summary.

APPENDICES

CHAPTER 1

WHAT IS A CAPTIVE
AND WHY IS IT FORMED?

What is a Captive?

The purist definition of a captive is probably:

An insurance company that only insures all or part of the risks of its parent.

The key factor in this definition is that the insurance company is owned by the parent and therefore has its own 'captive' business.

Other definitions are available, and are probably clearer although less succinct. They include the following:

Insurance companies set up by industrial or commercial groups primarily to insure some of the risks of their parent(s).

A limited purpose wholly owned insurance subsidiary of an organisation not in the insurance business, which has as its primary function the insuring of some of the exposures and risks of its parent or the parent's affiliates.

Defining captives is difficult and becomes even more difficult as they develop into unrelated businesses. As we shall see later in this chapter, there is a myriad of captive types and once one moves away from the 'pure' captive owned by the parent and insuring only the

1

parent's business, relating the area to the pure definitions above poses problems. It would probably be more helpful to accept the origins of captives and move towards a situation where the word 'captive' disappears and where the captive as we know it becomes merely an integral part of the insurance industry or, at the very least, is referred to as an insurance affiliate of a corporation. This would cover not only those captives insuring the parent's own business but also those that have established as a major diversification and have become an important profit centre for the parent corporation.

If we look at recent captive history, we see that the early captives formed in the United Kingdom in the 1920s and 1930s were established as insurance companies operating on a co-insurance basis, usually in respect of property risks only. Among these early captives were Blackfriars Insurance, formed in 1937 by Unilever, and Imperial Chemicals Insurance Limited. These captives were essentially part of the market since they were taking a small share of their own risks and relied on market rating, complied with the appropriate domestic legislation and paid the corporation tax. In addition, elsewhere in Europe, in the 1920s Norsk Hydro were forming AS Industriforsikring domestically in Norway, and FL Smidth were forming Forenede Assurandorer in Denmark.

As interest in captives as a method of improving risk-financing techniques developed, parent companies looked towards offshore locations to avoid complex insurance legislation and high taxation. These developments in the early 1950s, particularly in the United States of America, were the starting-point of the real growth of captive insurance companies. Of the 3,000 captives in the world today, the vast majority were formed after 1950 and located away from the parent company's domestic environment. It is primarily the offshore captive, initially writing its parent's business, that is the subject of captive feasibility studies and establishment that we see today. There is, however, still sometimes a need for captive insurance companies to be established in the same country as the parent and to comply with local legislation and taxation requirements.

The last few years have seen an increasing move form formation in the traditional offshore locations to onshore areas who specialise in providing an attractive environment for captives. This has mainly been a result of many tax authorities becoming increasingly aggressive so far as the tax deductibility of premiums paid to captives is concerned and the taxing of profits made by the captive as though it is resident in the same country as its parent. For example, in the United States, the State of Vermont has become a major captive centre, and a serious competitor to offshore locations, with over 300 captives at the last count. This is due not only to tax considerations but the convenience of managing a captive in the same country as the parent, which often results in a reduction in operating cost and almost certainly a useful reduction in management time. Similarly, many mutuals established, for example, for professional indemnity exposures, have been established by accountants and lawyers in the United Kingdom instead of places like Bermuda, where they would have naturally been formed in the past. In the United States of America, we have also seen many state insurance commissioners developing specific legislation for captive insurance companies as they try to compete with the success of Vermont. There have been similar developments in Europe, where particular mention needs to be made of the Financial Services Centre in Dublin, Gibraltar (both of which open up the prospect of being able to write business direct from these locations into all countries of the European Union), Sweden, Luxembourg and also of Australia, where the primary insurance legislation and related regulations has been relaxed specifically to encourage the formation of captives in an attempt to dissuade Australian companies from forming their captives in Singapore, which has been the main area for Australian owned captive insurance companies.

However, regardless of location or complexity of government attitude, the criteria for establishing a captive insurance company remain the same. Wherever it is located it needs to be established properly and to be regarded as a properly instituted insurance company, meeting the financial and management criteria to which major insurers are expected to adhere.

The captive must also ensure that the business that it is writing is profitable. This will be linked closely to the risk-management capability of the parent company. Most captives have been formed by companies with above-average claims experience because the financial benefits are greater compared to the payment of conventional insurance market premiums. However, it is important that captive owners maintain this good loss history or, at least, ensure that the captive is not exposed, particularly in its early stages of development, when losses could seriously harm its financial base or affect the cost of its reinsurance protection.

Risk management loss prevention and control measures can therefore not be divorced from the captive insurance company concept. It can be argued that the captive is an important part of the risk-management process contributing to an effective risk-financing programme. It should certainly be regarded in this light by those companies establishing a captive to handle their own business otherwise its future could be short and expensive for the parents.

Captives Today — Worldwide Review

The majority of captive insurance companies in the world have been formed by US corporations. Each year Captive Insurance Company Reports, an American publication, produces a list of captives worldwide and although is not complete, because of the difficulty of extracting information in many captive locations, this does give an excellent picture of worldwide developments and the latest position in the captive movement.

In 1996 the Captive Insurance Company Reports Directory (published by Tillinghast — Towers Perrin) listed well over 3,000 captives world-wide. It estimated that captives located in the areas that account for most captives, e.g. Vermont, Bermuda, Cayman Islands, Barbados, Guernsey, Dublin, Luxembourg, Isle of Man and Singapore underwrote premiums in excess of US$ 15.5 billion, and had investable assets in the region of US$ 35 billion and, on a combined basis, have capital and surplus estimated at US$ (15.5 billion).

The premium throughput and assets of captives worldwide continues to grow and seems largely unaffected by the vagaries of the insurance market cycles. The total premium volume, orchestrated by captives, is now believed to approach 20% of all world-wide commercial insurance premium and is a very much bigger figure for captives owned by companies in the United States (perhaps 35%) and the United Kingdom (perhaps 30%). These figures make captives, as an insurance industry sector, one of the most important and many individual captives can compare in size, measured by investable assets, with many conventional insurance companies. This growth continues apace all over the world, and although there is dispute about the actual financial contribution and roles of captives and similar risk financing mechanisms, there seems little doubt that captives and similar facilities account for well over 30% of worldwide industrial insurance premiums and when self-insurance mechanisms, such as retrospective rating plans, are included this figure almost certainly rises above 40%.

United States of America and Canada

The size of the United States and its relatively free insurance environment has resulted in the majority of captives being owned by US parent corporations. Most of these captives are located in Bermuda, which is geographically convenient to the United States. There are probably over 900 captives located and managed in Bermuda and perhaps 80 per cent to 90 per cent of these are owned by US parents. The majority of these companies were set up in Bermuda in the 1960s and 1970s with considerable growth in this period and after. Formations dropped in the early 1980s owing to the soft insurance market conditions, but a resurgence of formation was seen in 1986. In 1978 the Bermuda authorities looked at the possibility of introducing insurance legislation, which had previously not existed, and in 1981 the Bermuda Insurance Act was introduced to provide a means of authorising and controlling insurance companies located in the islands.

Following the decision by a Harvard-based medical malpractice captive to form its insurance company in the Cayman Islands rather than in Bermuda, the Caymans grew significantly, particularly for group and association captives, in the late 1970s and early 1980s, and as a natural consequence of this growth also introduced their own insurance legislation with similar objectives and controls to those operating in Bermuda.

Perhaps the most significant development for American companies in recent years has been the questioning by the United States Internal Revenue Service of the tax status, and in particular, the tax deductibility, of premiums paid to captives. When this development was first mooted many captives felt that one way to avoid the problem was to enter into unrelated or non-parent business on the basis that at a certain level the tax authorities would regard the captive as a genuine insurance vehicle and grant tax deductibility. Unfortunately this hope has not been realised and tax deductibility, as will be seen later in the book, is an important issue for US companies contemplating using their captives as a self-insurance vehicle. In addition the tax position and the unavailability of products liability and medical malpractice capacity in the 1970s saw the growth of association and group captives with shared ownership rather than the single ownership common to most captive companies.

The development of captives in the United States and in particular growth among those formed within those states specialising in providing captive facilities has continued, as has the growth throughout the 1980s of association and group captives. Unlike many other parts of the world, captives ebb and flow in North America very much in line with insurance market conditions, with more formations and wider use of captives when capacity is short and premiums high and a drop in interest during the soft market cycles.

CAPTIVE INSURANCE COMPANIES

The onshore development which started in a small way with Colorado, Tennessee and, most importantly, Vermont has increased considerably.

Vermont now handles over 300 captives and many other States are now vying for a share of what is an increasing cake. In addition to the States mentioned, new-comers include Hawaii (which has been reasonably successful), Delaware, Georgia, Illinois, Puerto Rico and the US Virgin Islands.

Further north in Canada, British Columbia has entered the scene, providing special attractions for Canadian-owned companies wishing to avoid excise taxes and follow what may be an increasing trend to locate within the same country as the captive's parent. However, despite this many Canadian-owned captives use Barbados as their area of operations, mainly because of double tax treaty advantages.

Europe

Captive development within Europe was, until recently, dominated by United Kingdom companies, who have established in excess of 200 captives. These captives were originally located, during the late 1950's and early 1960's, in Bermuda and subsequently Guernsey when the imposition of exchange controls limited captive establishment, for all practical purposes, to the then scheduled sterling territories of the Channel Islands, Gibraltar, the Isle of Man and the Republic of Ireland.

As a result of this situation, Guernsey became, during the early 1970s, the most common location for UK-owned captives writing in those days mainly elements of their international property exposures. After a long period of gestation Guernsey introduced full insurance legislation in September 1986 and is highly regarded as an important area for captives and offshore reinsurance companies, with around 300 insurance companies licensed at the beginning of 1996.

Another very popular location for UK-owned companies has been the Isle of Man, which was for many years in a similar position to Guernsey so far as insurance legislation and taxation was concerned but which decided, after an abortive attempt to introduce legislation in 1981, to make an effort to provide competition to Guernsey. The Isle of Man introduced specific legislation in 1986 under an exempt insurance act which eliminated the normal corporate tax rate of 20 per cent where insurance companies writing non-Isle of Man business were established and put into place special insurance legislation designed to ensure proper supervision and control but to allow exempt companies to operate in a flexible environment.

One of the most important developments in recent years has been the establishment of Luxembourg as a captive reinsurance centre. Luxembourg, which provides attractions through the ability to defer tax due to generous allowance of technical insurance reserves, has become very popular with captives owned mainly by Swedish companies, but also for Belgium, German French, Spanish and, more recently, Japanese-owned insurance subsidiaries.

Another significant entrant to the captive scene is the Financial Services Centre in Dublin which was established, with European Union funds, to develop a financial services infra structure and improve employment prospects within the city. Dublin is of particular significance because one of the deficiencies of one of its main competitors, Luxembourg is the ability to establish direct insurance companies. This restraint can be overcome in Dublin where direct writing companies can be formed and provide the ability to write from the captive, direct insurance policies across borders into other European Union countries. This advantage will, in 1997, also be replicated within Gibraltar. Gibraltar has been a captive centre for many years but has only recently got its act together. However, through its links with the United Kingdom, it will be accepted as part of European Union insurance legislation which allows captive insurance companies located in one E.U. state to write direct policies into another.

Clearly the implementation of the third non-life directive and the influence of freedom of services legislation on the insurance market for large risks is of considerable importance to captive owners and to the insurance industry generally. The availability of captive locations within the European Union is potentially one of the most important developments in the history of European captives and could herald expansion of captives established and perhaps a diminution of European Union-owned captives located in the traditional low tax areas.

The use of a European Union-based location with the capability to write direct policies opens up the opportunity of issuing direct, so-called Euro-policies from the captive location to the individual subsidiaries of the company located throughout the Union and thereby avoid restrictions on the writing of non-admitted insurance and the related fronting and other handling costs that have previously been necessary in order to overcome local insurance legislation, insurance market tariffs, cartels and other obstacles.

European Union-captive development is at an early stage but promises to be an exciting development and may involve important changes in the way in which European Union captives are structured. It will also be influenced by freedom of services legislation and, the E.U. tax position on companies established outside of the E.U., in particular those established in low or nil tax areas.

As in most parts of the world, the extent of the development of captives within Europe is related very much to the position of the insurance market and the legislation in force in the individual countries. Because of the implementation of the Third Insurance Directives, the legislative playing field has become much more level and there is now a strong trend towards the formation of captives throughout Europe. However, there remains a tendency towards different applications of the captive concept depending on the cultural, legal and insurance market conditions as well as the insurance distribution systems and the level of expertise. There have been a number of European countries where captives have been established for decades. These have tended to be countries which have a relatively free insurance market and a distribution system in which retail insurance brokers dominate. Of particular note is the Netherlands, where, despite the fact that there is a system of tax relief for self-insurance available, (which allows credits to be taken for money that would otherwise have been spent on insurance premiums) there are a growing number of captives formed both domestically and offshore.

Offshore captives owned by Dutch parents have usually been located in the Netherlands Antilles, which has advantages for captives and specific and important benefits for the Dutch parent, because dividends distributed by the captive can be returned to the parent in The Netherlands without any payment of additional Dutch corporation tax.

Belgium is also a very competitive insurance market from the insurance viewpoint, and there are captives owned by Belgium companies. However, in view of the number of major companies with Belgium parentage, the potential is limited.

Germany is a growing and very important market for the formation of new captives. Historically most captives have been established within Germany and many of these would deny the term captive if it was suggested to them. Although captive establishment has been frustrated by the influence of the German insurance market on captive owners, including equity interest and Board representation, this has also been exacerbated by the perhaps unique concept of the captive broker which is commonly used and involves German companies forming insurance broking subsidiaries to earn insurance commissions on premiums paid to the insurance company with whom they place their business.

However, Germany is now beginning to acknowledge the role that captives can play in the risk-financing programmes of their major companies and despite many of the difficulties surrounding captive formation, in particular the insurance market influences and the attitude of the German tax authorities to insurance companies established in tax havens, developments are encouraging.

The development of the Financial Services Centre in Dublin has influenced the growth of German captives, particularly in the early stages of Dublin's existence when an attractive double tax treaty between Germany and Ireland provided a means of overcoming many of the tax difficulties normally associated with establishing a captive insurance subsidiary within a member state of the European Union. This benefit has largely disappeared but German interest in captives is accelerating but with a bias against establishment in tax havens (particularly those with sand and palm trees!) because of the feeling that there is something dubious about such areas. In addition to greater interest in captives, the insurance market in Germany is becoming much more competitive, the dominance of local insurers is disappearing and the new generation of risk managers are more inclined to consider new risk financing techniques.

Historically, France and Italy have also been difficult areas for captive formation due, in the early years, to a restrictive exchange control environment but more recently due to insurance market attitudes. However, like Germany this is a rapidly changing situation with many large French companies having formed captive insurers, particularly in Luxembourg. In addition, many large French insurance and reinsurance companies, as well as insurance brokers, have acknowledged the role that captives can play in corporate insurance and have established their own captive insurance management operations and, in some instances, their own overseas reinsurance entities. There is, therefore, growing interest and greater capability available to the French insurance buyer.

On a smaller basis Italy, and to a greater extent Spain, are also following the French example, and as exchange control regulations ease and the freedom of services legislation begins to have an impact, we can expect a more common approach to the use of captives in risk-financing programmes and the disappearance of the individual country postures which have for so long inhibited the availability of the captive concept to many large Continental European insurance buyers.

Outside of the European Union, Switzerland has a number of captives domestically and particularly offshore in well established captive locations such as Bermuda. There is also the opportunity to establish captives within Switzerland and this has been achieved in Zurich. Details of the use of Switzerland as a captive location is dealt with in the location section of this book. The image of Switzerland, the preferential tax treatment and a welcoming attitude towards captives, means that the country has potential as a growing captive location and, of course, has the advantage of being the home to many of the world's largest insurance and reinsurance operations.

In Scandinavia there are captives in Denmark, Norway, Sweden and Finland. In Sweden there are a number of domestic captives and a growing number of captives located offshore, particularly in Luxembourg but also in Bermuda and the Cayman Islands. In addition there is also an offshore industry captive involving the Swedish airline SAS and two non-Swedish airline corporations, KLM and Swissair. There has been a long debate on captives in Sweden, between industrial companies, the insurance industry and the government, linked both to the development of the insurance industry and the effect of captives on it and also to exchange control. Originally, permission was given by the Swedish government for two companies to insure their own business in respect of non-Swedish risks, with captives located in Sweden and managed by one of the Swedish insurance companies. Subsequently, a Swedish company was given the authority to underwrite Swedish risks in a new domestic captive formed by that company. It was also given permission to manage the company itself. This permission was given for a trial period and all subsequent submissions were held up by a moratorium established by the government. However, during this period the Swedish central bank relaxed exchange controls restrictions and it became possible for Swedish companies to apply for permission and usually get authority to export capital to form captive insurance companies externally. This happened in a number of cases, primarily in Bermuda and subsequently in Luxembourg. Although the restrictions on domestic establishment were still maintained by the moratorium, the subsequent reports (originally by a professor of economics at Stockholm University and subsequently by a government committee) accepted the principle of captive formation, and the previous inhibitions on permitting Swedish companies to form captives has disappeared.

Nowadays Sweden has the largest number of captive insurance companies per head of population than anywhere else in the world.

The last count of the number of Swedish-owned captives amounted to over eighty with the majority located in Luxembourg. However, since the beginning of 1990, Swedish captives have looked towards Dublin either for the establishment of new captives or for second captives which are able to underwrite business on a direct basis within the European Community. This is particularly important to Swedish-owned companies wishing to take advantage of the freedom of services legislation and underwrite business direct into Europe.

Apart from the captive locations already mentioned, other possible growth areas include Cyprus. Cyprus may be of interest to ship owners and/or companies with Middle East connections and was used by Australian owned captives to gain the benefit of double tax treaty and the omission of Cyprus from the list of territories where captives, owned by Australian companies, needed to gain approval from the Australian Tax Office. However, this position changed when the Australian accruals tax legislation came into force in the early 1990's and Cyprus is no longer as attractive for captive insurers emanating from Australia. However, Cyprus does have insurance legislation with a favourable tax rate and reasonable standards of financial management but it does remain time consuming to form an insurance company in Cyprus.

Malta is a relative newcomer to the captive scene, has introduced attractive insurance legislation and provides a concessionary low tax rate of 5% for captive insurances companies. It has a developing captive management infra structure and hopes to develop once Malta is admitted to the European Union.

Aaland is located near to Sweden but is part of Finland and operates under Finnish Insurance Law. It has proved attractive to a few Swedish owned captives and has the attractions of low capitalisation, a 17% corporate tax and credible supervisory structure which is overseen by the Finnish insurance regulatory body.

There is no doubt that Europe provides an important market for the growth of captive insurance companies. It is difficult to obtain full details of the number of European-owned captives as European multinationals tend to favour confidentiality in their operations in contrast to the more open environment that exists in the United States. There are, however, an estimated number of captives in excess of 300 and this is expected to grow to at least 500 over the next two years and could move up towards 1,000 over the next decade. The wider European market transforms the potential for captive formation, and combined with freedom of services in the insurance sector and the possibility of more European countries joining the European Union or at the very least developing economic ties, provides a market as large as that which exists in the United States of America. It is therefore reasonable to anticipate that over the next ten or twenty years the number of captives could equal that established by North America companies.

In addition to captive formation there are within Europe, a large number of medium-size companies which, while not large enough to establish their own captives, could well be interested in captive alternatives such as external risk funding or rent-a-captive facilities. We can therefore expect to see growth in these areas, where such facilities provide many of the captive benefits without the need for formal establishment and capitalisation.

Companies providing these risk-funding facilities are becoming more readily available and these are often managed offshore by major insurance companies or in some cases by insurance brokers or other captives. The funding concept could be as relevant in the European context as is the captive. For those considering these alternatives, the same criteria can, in general terms, be used for these programmes as can be used for the proper captive arrangements. In addition, where domestic legislation or exchange controls are prohibitive – and there are still a number of European countries where this is the case – they could well be an attractive and acceptable legal alternative to the captive for many companies.

Asia

The area with the most potential for captive formation is obviously Japan. Although there have been a number of Japanese captives established, many in Bermuda, the peculiarities of the Japanese insurance market have precluded significant growth of captives owned by Japanese corporations in more recent years. However, as Japanese corporations expand throughout the world and establish their own operations in Europe and elsewhere there is a growing tendency for these subsidiary companies to establish a captive insurance subsidiary. In very recent times Japanese-owned captives have been established in Luxembourg and the Financial Services Centre in Dublin, and this must be the beginning of an expansion of the captive concept for the overseas subsidiaries of Japanese corporations.

In Asia there are two good captive locations, Hong Kong and, Singapore. Hong Kong has probably lost its place as the major location for captives to Singapore in recent years, although it still has the ability to allow insurance companies writing non-Hong Kong business to avoid Hong Kong corporate tax and of course has a financial structure and business efficiency which is second to none among the world tax havens.

Hong Kong does not have specific captive insurance legislation and its high capitalisation requirements probably means that it would only be of great interest to a substantial company with a major insurance programmes. Looking forward, of course the transfer of Hong Kong to China may affect its credibility as a potential captive location due to concerns about political instability and the regulatory environment. However, given that a number of Chinese companies are showing an interest in captives this prognosis may be misplaced.

Singapore has specifically developed both insurance regulations and a low tax rate for captive insurance companies writing non-Singapore business and has become the favoured location among Australian-owned captives. This position is begining to wane as the new Australian Accruals Tax Legislation has an impact, but certainly so far as the Asia area is concerned, Singapore is the largest location in terms of number of captives, and is equally important because of the capability, infrastructure and the specialist captive management operations available.

Other parts of the world

Australia is probably the most competitive insurance market in the world and this has a significant impact on the relatively small formations of captive insurance companies. However, there are in the region of thirty captives owned by Australian companies and, as mentioned above, most of these are located in Singapore although a number exist in Bermuda, Cyprus and the Cayman Islands. Captives established offshore are being particularly hit by the Australian Accruals Tax Legislation which has the effect of taxing the profits of a captive as though it were resident within Australia and the future benefits of establishing a captive in a low tax area must be questioned, particularly given the Australian insurance market situation. However, the action of the Australian Insurance Commissioner in introducing special regulations for captives could mean that many Australian-owned captives will give up their offshore status and move onshore as this could, in many cases, be more effective than continuing to utilise low tax areas where the accruals tax legislation operates.

We are also likely to see the growing use of captives owned by Australian companies for the funding of contingent risks such as environmental impairment, and possibly the greater use of external risk-funding or rent-a-captive facilities.

The new tax legislation in Australia probably means the end of locations like Vanatua and Nauru which have been used in the past because of their exempt company benefits, relaxed or non-existent insurance legislation and nil taxation.

New Zealand has also introduced controlled foreign company legislation which severely inhibits the benefits of establishing offshore in territories other than a list of seven developed countries. The potential for significant captives formation from New Zealand is also limited due to the relatively small number of large companies. However, it is possible that New Zealand companies might consider Australia as a captive location because of the favourable regulatory environment towards captives and the fact that Australia is an approved country so far as the New Zealand CFC tax legislation is concerned.

Interestingly, New Zealand itself is now seen as a potential captive location because of the ease of establishing a captive insurer in the country due to the low capitalisation and regulatory requirements. Whilst the tax rates are high, for companies with harsh CFC legislation this may not be an inhibition because New Zealand has double tax treaties with most countries and allows a degree of equalisation reserving which could be beneficial.

One of the growing countries for captive formation is South Africa. A few years ago the South Africa government commissioned a study into captive insurance companies and their use by South African corporations and concluded that they be strongly discouraged. The conclusion of the enquiry by Judge Melamet was as follows: —

The Commission were able to identify South African owned captives and the method of operation advantages and disadvantages are considered. Captive premiums outward were calculated at between R200 million and R300 million but it was felt the real figure was much higher. The Commission recommends:

- that a stated part of the funds of each South African captive be returned to the parent companies in South Africa;
- that the Revenue consider whether unjustified claims are being made for tax deductibility of premium paid offshore and whether there are breaches of the Insurance Act (i.e. that captives are really carrying on insurance business in South Africa without

being licensed). Premiums paid overseas by captives should be disallowed for tax except premium ultimately paid to reinsurers;
- that annual returns are required for each captive each year and they be supervised by a committee covering insurance supervision, foreign exchange and overseas investment;
- the establishment of a limited insurance licence category for captives operating in and established in South Africa, with different tax treatment from that of ordinary insurers.

However, the recommendations of the enquiry were not accepted and the subsequent growth of captives owned by South African Corporations has been significant. This reflects the freedom of the insurance market, the quality of insurance skills and the domination of insurance broking firms. There have been over twenty captives formed in recent years with most of these being established in either the Isle of Man or Guernsey. However, there are a number of South African captives located elsewhere including Bermuda and the Cayman Islands. The major inhibition to the formation of captives is exchange control regulation but unlike many other countries with these restrictions, the South African Reserve Bank has given approval to many captives particularly those owned by major corporations with significant international activities or insurance exposures which require access to the international insurance market.

In the Caribbean area, locations come and go as politicians see the development of an offshore insurance sector as an important diversification from tourism and local industry. Barbados has been particularly successful over the last twenty years, mainly the result of an attractive double tax treaty arrangement with Canada and, early on, a treaty with the United States which enabled captive parents to avoid federal excise tax on insurance and reinsurance premiums. After much debate, Bermuda eventually negotiated a similar treaty but both treaties were ended at the beginning of this decade and this advantage for Barbados and then Bermuda disappeared.

The Bahamas has been a captive location since the early 60's and has continually tried to regain the position that it lost during this decade, when the government antagonised the captive community by threatening the introduction of a profits tax. Typically for countries in this situation, it has found it difficult to make up its position particularly as its timing was bad because the negative image occurred just as a substantial growth of captives formed by North American companies began to accelerate. However, it has made efforts in the last year or so, linked with a change of Government, to improve its image and get back in on the captive scene.

Other areas in the Caribbean include the Netherlands Antilles, the Turks and Caicos Islands, Antigua and the British Virgin Islands, all of which have their share of captives and varying degrees of success in attracting a reasonable level of offshore insurance business.

Further afield, countries such as Mauritius, Seychelles, Cook Islands and Western Samoa present themselves as potential offshore financial centres, but for most captives there is a strong tendency to utilise proven locations which have sensible legislation and controls, a good financial and banking infrastructure and, perhaps most importantly, a choice of good, capable insurance management facilities.

If we look at the captive scene today we see that it is growing very steadily with the growth spreading, from its origins in the United Kingdom and North America, throughout the world. As locations develop business they find the need to introduce legislation to control the 'bad apples'. In many respects this legislation enhances the status of the insurance environment because of the stability it creates and demonstrates the seriousness of both the captive movement and the people that are trying to attract and provide services to it.

The tax problems that have existed in the United States for many years are also beginning to spread as the growth of captives extends throughout the world. Tax problems not so much in the premium deductibility area but in the areas of transfer pricing and controlled foreign companies legislation, will be reflected in other parts of the world and create problems for captives. These will be overcome by many techniques, including expanding captives into full insurance companies, integrating captives into groups in order to spread risk exposure and expanding the captive's activity into wider ranges of the company's business, particularly if this can be achieved on a worldwide basis and can involve many of the parent's own subsidiaries. In addition, the reduction in the tax advantages concentrates attention on the role of the captive as an important element of a risk management programme and can help to make sure that it is recognised as a facility which has advantages which go far beyond those of a tax nature.

There is no doubt that the risk-financing concept, which is now being used in a very sophisticated way by major companies throughout the world, will remain and that the captive is an integral part of this approach.

Reasons for Captive formation

Meeting insurance needs

The main reason put forward by major corporations for forming captive insurance companies has been that the conventional insurance industry has not met their financial needs. This criticism can be broken down into the categories of price, cover, service and capacity.

Once a major corporation analyses its insurance programme, it realises that the purchase of insurance involves paying to the insurance company a significant mark-up to pay for expenses, profit and commission payments to brokers. In addition, the premium paid to the company is usually paid in advance. This means that the insurance company holds on to the premium until claims are paid back to the company and it earns investment income on this retained premium. It is also earning investment income on the profits made from the insurance transaction.

The most effective means of reducing this unattractive financial deal, without losing the benefits that the insurance industry provides in the form of catastrophe cover, is to retain more of the insurance within the business of the industrial company. The method usually employed to achieve this is to keep a deductible, whereby the company pays the first amount of each loss and obtains a discount from the insurance company for this retention.

The willingness of companies to retain more risk, particularly at the lower levels of exposure, is considerable, but they are often frustrated in their attempts to do this because the insurance industry will not offer them what they consider to be adequate discounts for the risks that they are taking. The question of adequate discount for deductibles has been argued for a number of years without significant success. The captive can help to solve this problem by putting the insurance buyer in the same position as an insurance company, enabling him to retain all of the risk within his own operation and then, by reinsurance cover, protecting him above the level that he does not wish to retain himself.

This technique usually enables the buyer to obtain a more attractive reinsurance discount or credit for his self-retention than he would from the direct insurance market. The main reason for the differential between these two parts of the insurance industry is that the direct insurer has very considerable expenses, most of which are funded by the premiums he receives from the low-level loss area. On the other hand the reinsurer has minimum expenses, since the services he provides are not as comprehensive as those which the direct insurer has to provide to his customers, and particularly to his private customers who need much greater attention and service than the major industrial buyer.

Providing a funding mechanism

Another reason for captive establishment is to provide a chronological funding mechanism without tax penalty. The rationale behind this is that it would be more convenient for the major company to fund within its own resources for losses which occur irregularly over, say, a five- or ten-year period, replacing premium payments by provisions to an internal fund. However, while premiums paid to insurance companies are tax deductible, funds developed for losses which have not occurred need to be established out of post-tax sources. This makes the internal fund option unattractive compared with the insurance premium payment method. However, if the company can form its own insurance company, the premiums paid (with the exception to some extent of the United States) will be deductible in the same way as they are to a normal insurance company. The premium payment can then be retained within the insurance company and funds can be developed to finance a major-loss that might occur over a cycle.

Reducing the price cycle

A further motivation for captive formation could be the use of the captive to develop muscle within the market to reduce the sometimes volatile cycle of insurance prices. By establishing your own insurance company you are able to price in relation to your own loss experience and, if this is stable and good, your pricing should be on a much more level basis than market pricing, which is subject to volatility due to the actions of others over whom the company has little influence. This is particularly relevant in areas such as aviation, where not only is there volatility in rating but the attraction of a stable insurance price over a long period is valuable in relation to financial control and the maintaining of competitiveness.

Inequity of rating

In looking at the reasons for captive formation it can be said that the inadequacy of the conventional insurance market in covering the needs of major buyers has resulted directly in captive growth. If these needs had been met the captive movement may not have been as successful as it has in the last twenty years.

One of the major criticisms of industrial buyers with above-average and, in many cases, very profitable insurance accounts has been that the premiums charged by insurers have not recognised these factors. In many cases companies with loss ratios on property risks of as low as 5 per cent of premiums paid are paying rates very similar to those of their competitors, who have loss ratios of ten times their own or, in some cases, well over 100 per cent. When the financial director analysing his insurance expenditure over a period often years sees that he has paid out premiums to the insurers of £10 million and has received back £500,000 in claim payments, there is a very strong motivation to find some alternative method of financing In this context the captive insurance company offers such a buyer the opportunity to reflect his loss experience more accurately and to retain the profits, which would otherwise have gone to the insurance company, within his own operation.

While one can understand the difficulties of the conventional insurer in this problem, because of the desire to attract business and spread losses over a wide span, the problem is not one with which the major corporation with a minimal loss experience can have much sympathy. The failure to take into account differences in experience is therefore one of the main reasons for captive growth.

Unavailability of cover

There have been a number of incidents, particularly in the products liability area, where insurance companies have not been prepared to provide buyers with the cover that they need. One of the most interesting examples was the development of a captive insurance company by Johnson & Johnson to provide cover for products liability on contraceptive pills. This captive called Middlesex Assurance was established to write this coverage before acceptance by the conventional market. Another example, on a group basis, was the establishment of Oil Insurance Limited by over twenty oil companies to provide liability cover for oil pollution.

There is little doubt that the volatility of insurance market conditions has been instrumental in persuading insurance buyers with capacity and coverage problems to seek other ways of handling risks particularly those in the casualty and liability areas. For example the difficult market conditions which existed primarily in the United States but also in other parts of the world in 1986 resulted in insureds and insurance brokers putting together structures which we might loosely call captives to provide capacity particularly at the high levels of catastrophe exposure. Examples of this development included a structure

WILLIS CORROON (BERMUDA) LIMITED

Table 1.1(a) Currently Trading — Liability/Casualty/Property & Miscellaneous

Company	Principle Backing	Shareholder Equity	Maximum Line & Minimum Attachment	Classes Written
ACE Group	Public Company	$1.5 billion	$200mm (Liabs) x/s $100mm $50mm (D&O) x/s $50mm $25mm (Space) Quota Share $50mm (Property) x/s $25mm	Finite/Liability D&O Space/Aviation Products Property
Chubb Atlantic Indemnity	CHUBB	$100 million ($4.5 million in assets)	Various	Financial/Liability/D&O E&O/Property
CODA	ACE	ACE	$25 million	D&O
Glencoe Insurance Company	Renaissance Re	$50 million	$5 million primary	Direct insurance & Facultative Reinsurance DIC/Cat perils only
Harrington International Insurance Limited	Swiss Re & Winterthur	$500 million	$100 million x/s $500,000	Property Captive R/I only
Lexington Bermuda	Lexington Boston	"Branch Office" status	$25mm x/s $25mm not stand alone	Excess Casualty — USA domiciled accounts only
Oil Insurance Limited	44 oil companies (35 from US)	$1,475 million	$225mm per occurrence	Property for Oil companies
SCUUL	Approximately 55 Colleges and Universities	$80 million	$25mm x/s $1mm or $10mm x/s $1mm for Public Schools (have been known to attach as low as $100,000)	Educators Legal Liability Public Liability Excess of Loss R/I
Sphere Drake Underwriting Management	Sphere Drake Insurance plc	$150 million	$5mm (Casualty) $2mm (Property)	Captive R/I
Starr Excess	AIG (24%), Gen Re, Quantum Fund, AON, Munich Re	$300 million $300 million "on call"	$150mm (Liabs) x/s $25mm $50mm (D&O) x/s $50mm	Liability D&O

Table 1.1(a) (cont'd)

Company	Principle Backing	Shareholder Equity	Maximum Line & Minimum Attachment	Classes Written
Tate & Lyle Re	Tale & Lyle plc	$61 million	$250,000	Property, Third Party Captive R/I or Direct
XL Insurance	Public Company	$2.006 billion	$150mm (Liabs) x/s $25mm $50mm (D&O) $100mm (Property) x/s $25mm or x/s $100mm (Chemicals) or x/s $10mm (Construction) $50mm (Prof) x/s $25mm $100mm (COAXL) x/s $25mm $100mm (Marine) x/s $25mm N.A. Legal Liabs. Or $15mm non-N.A. Legal Liabs. or $5mm other non-liabs.	Direct Insurance only, X/S Liability Property D&O Marine Finite Professional Indemnity
XL Re	XL Insurance	$250 million	$100mm XOL or Quota Share	Multi-line, multi year single aggregates

WILLIS CORROON (BERMUDA) LIMITED

Table 1.1(b) Currently Trading – Property Catastrophe Market

Company	Principle Backing	Shareholder Equity	Maximum Line	Classes Written
CAT Limited	Morgan Stanley, CHUBB, AT&T Pension Plan, Chemical Venture Partners, Zurich Reinsurance Holdings, Cnetre Re, Plymouth Rock, GM	$341 million	$15mm	Cat Prop
Global Capital Re	Goldman Sachs (19%) Johnson & Higgins (5%) 75% Publicly Owned	$496 million	$20mm	Cat Prop Traditional and Finite
IPC Re	AIG (25%), Gen Re	$434 million	$5mm (treaty) $15mm (program)	Cat Prop (treaty)
La Salle Re	Aon, CNA, Lazard Freres 30% Publicly Owned	$415 million	$20mm	Pro-Rata Cat Treaties Anything Short-tail Casualty clash Fidelity/Surety/Bond Political Risk
Mid Ocean Re	Marsh McLennan JP Morgan, XL (30%) 30% Publicly Owned	$969 million	$20mm/£10mm	Cat Prop (treaty)
Partner Re	Swiss Re Head & Company L.L.C.	$1,311 million	$50mm	Cat Prop (treaty)
Renaissance Re	USF&G, Warburg Pincus, GE Financial, 25% Publicly Owned	$526 million	$40mm	Marine & Aviation 97% Cat Prop (treaty)
Sphere Drake Bermuda	Sphere Drake Holdings Limited	$124 million	$5mm	Cat Prop (treaty)

Table 1.1(b) (cont'd)

Company	Principle Backing	Shareholder Equity	Maximum Line	Classes Written
Terra Nova (Bermuda) Insurance Company	Donaldson, Lufkin & Jenrette, Bishop Eastgate, Marsh Capital Corp., JP Morgan	$78 million	Varies by Class Largest to date $7.5mm	Multi Line Treaty Short tail liability Marine Property Political Risk Bond Business
Tempest Re	Gen Re ACE await approval from SEC to purchase company	$692 million	$10mm (US) Non-US >$10mm	Cat Prop

WILLIS CORROON (BERMUDA) LIMITED

Table 1.1(c) Currently Trading — Financial

Company	Principle Backing	Shareholder Equity	Maximum Line	Classes Written
Accord Re	CNA Financial (49%)	$20 million	Various In excess of $100mm	Financial
Centre Re	Zurich	$1,078 million	Various — net cannot exceed 10% of company's worth	Financial Multiple lines of coverage
Commercial Risk Partners	SCOR Western General Insurance	$212 million	Various	Financial Workers Comp., GL Blended Aggregate Covers Multi-year property
Exporters Insurance Co.	Group Captive	$23 million	$9.5 million	Export/Credit
Inter-Ocean	American Re plus others	$42 million	Up to $10mm unbundled prop $25mm liability or $25mm prop/liab combined	Financial
Scandinavian Re	Asea Brown Boveri Sirius International of Stockholm	$130 million	Various	Finite Risk All Property & Casualty plus Financial
Stockton Re	Stockton Holdings Co. ORIX (40%)	$250 million	$50mm largest to date	Specialty risks including both traditional and finite

24

called ACE put together by Marsh & MacLennan with a large number of US corporations and originally aimed at providing capacity in excess of US$100 million.

Another example is XL which was originally structured and promoted by Marsh & McLennan and Johnson & Higgins as a "Son of Ace" to provide cover in excess of US$50 million up to US$100 million. ACE and XL have been incredibly successful as providers of catastrophe liability business and are now amongst the biggest insurance companies in the world. In addition, they have established operations in other parts of the world including London, Dublin, Frankfurt and the Far East and are accepted as an important part of the catastrophe insurance market place.

These facilities and many others have mushroomed in recent years and table 1.1 provides a comprehensive list of the facilities currently available showing the cover provided, ownership, shareholder equity, capacity and the types of insurance underwritten. This survey which has been provided by Willis Corroon (Bermuda) Limited demonstrates the growth of these facilities and the contribution that they are making to providing capacity in the property, casualty and financial reinsurance areas.

There continue to be a number of facilities which provide group captive operations. These include facilities in the captive locations such as Bermuda and the Cayman Islands but also Risk Retention Groups located in domestic USA jurisdictions including Vermont, Illinois, Tennessee and Colorado. Those that have been particularly successful include: —

- Bank Insurance Company Limited ("BICL") which is owned by a number of commercial banks
- Corporate Officers & Directors Assurance ("CODA") — which provides Directors & Officers cover
- Oil Insurance Limited ("OIL") — which provides capacity for oil companies
- Railroad Association Insurance Limited ("RAIL") — which provides excess liability cover for railroads
- Associated Electrical & Gas Insurance Services Limited ("AEGIS") — liability including Directors & Officers cover for electric, gas and telephone utilities
- Energy Insurance Mutual ("EIM") — liability capacity for the electric and gas industry

These facilities are examples of the value of the captive concept in resolving market problems and hopefully providing continuity of coverage and sensible pricing designed to avoid the volatility of the insurance cycle.

Another area of market difficulty has been the refusal of insurance companies, because of restrictions imposed by regulatory authorities, to provide insurance policy wordings which are necessary for the buyer. An example of captive development in these circumstances was the formation of Arch Insurance Company by a group of United States contractors to provide cover against strikes, which had been refused by a number of state commissioners.

The ability to produce an insurance policy with your own wording and to cover risks which the conventional market finds unacceptable is another useful facility that the captive can offer.

Unacceptable rating

The development in the United States of group captives or pooling captives in recent years has resulted from the dramatic, and subsequently unjustified, premium increases for products liability risks. Many of these groupings were formed by a number of unrelated companies to provide coverage at rates that they felt were more rational. The alternatives for these companies would have been to pay very high premiums on what would probably have been a non-refundable basis until the market volatility eased and more acceptable costs were available or not to have any cover in a potentially damaging area. The establishment of captives and particularly group captives to beat the market cycle has been another factor in captive growth.

Inadequate service

Captives have sometimes been formed as a mechanism to replace inadequate services for which the cost is included in the basic premium structure. The captive can be used to finance the loss cost and enable the company to buy technical services particularly in the form of loss control and claims handled independently from an insurance service provider. In this way the combination of insurance protection and technical support can be of an overall higher standard than would be obtained from a normal insurance policy purchased in the market. This development has not been a significant reason for captive formation, but is often an ancillary reason so far as the buyer is concerned. It is interesting to note that in the last few years there has been some recognition of this development and also of the desire of many buyers to separate the purchase of insurance from technical and claims services. We now see many major insurers providing services, which were previously integrated on an individual basis, on a separate fee-related system of remuneration.

These are some of the reasons why captives are formed: price cover service and the capacity for risks with which the insurance market did not wish to get involved. There are non-captive ways to solve these problems but the captive does offer an overall financial facility that provides major companies with a mechanism that enables them to smooth variability in their earnings as a result of contingent events. In the past insurance provided this by enabling the company to allocate a fixed amount of money in its annual budget to provide for major losses through the use of insurance. As companies of good record have seen the trade-off between premium and loss become unacceptable and restrictions on coverage become more serious, the attraction of the captive to help solve this need, to smooth losses on a tax-beneficial basis and to break the insurance price cycle has been of paramount interest. It has also been a prime motivation in generating interest in the captive insurance concept.

Diversification

A currently unusual but growing reason for captive formation is as a diversification into insurance services. This can take the form of developing an insurance company which can either offer insurance services to customers and suppliers or which is a full open-market operation and thus more akin to a full conventional insurance company.

A number of insurance companies have been formed to provide insurance services to customers of the parent company. One of the major US insurers, Allstate, was originally formed by the US corporation Sears Roebuck to offer services to retail mail-order customers. In Europe an important manufacturer of contact lenses established a captive insurance company which provided coverage for loss or breakage of lenses with the insurance polices being sold through retailing opticians. In this way the customer is provided with an additional service but is tied to the manufacturer in the sense that in the event of breakage or loss, the claim is paid by the manufacturer. The manufacturer is then in a position to resell or repair the product, thus maintaining his connection with the customer and also benefiting from the increased sale plus profit from the insurance operation.

The establishment of insurance companies or the use of an existing insurance company to develop outside business is also a characteristic of the US position due primarily to tax difficulties. However, it is a development that would probably have occurred anyway as owners of captives reached the optimum position in relation to their own risks and looked towards the captive as an important financial diversification.

Advantages and Disadvantages of Captives

Advantages

Probably the most commonly accepted advantage of forming a captives insurance company is the ability to gain access to the reinsurance market. Reinsurers, as the wholesale market of the insurance industry, operate on much lower cost structures than direct insurers who need to provide primary service to both their industrial md their personal line customers. In addition, by forming a captive insurance company in order to place business with the reinsurance market the buyer can decide how much of the low-level claims he wishes to retain within his own operation and buy reinsurance coverage only above this level. In this way he can avoid the necessity to pay premiums which include the mark-up components of the direct insurer, such as expenses commission, investment income and profit. Any mark-up can be limited to that required by the reinsurer for the portion of the buyer's risk that the reinsurer is taking.

Another advantage is that the captive owner can select the risks that he wishes to retain within his insurance company. He can retain the more profitable part of his insurance programme leaving the less attractive part in the general insurance market. There may of course, be a market reaction to this approach but properly managed there is no reason why the buyer cannot develop risk selection to his advantage. This risk selection approach is applicable not only to different classes of risk but also to risks within an individual class, such as property exposures. It can also apply to the selection of a particular part of the risk within an individual class that is more attractive to the captive or more manageable within its financial capability. For example a company may own two major high-value factories and 100 retailing shops. It may make sense because of the spread of risk and the low probability of a high loss to retain the shops within the captive but to keep the major high-value factories in the conventional market. In this way the captive owner may be taking advantage of the market system of common rating in the particular industry for his higher-risk areas while retaining the low probability exposure within his own financial operation.

Reference has already been made to the captive's advantage in reducing insurance company costs. These costs include the following:

1. Insurance company clerical and accounting expenses, which would generally apply across the whole of the insurance company's portfolio other than being allocated on an as-used basis to the individual major buyer.
2. The costs that the insurance company allocates to acquisition of new business and that are not needed within the captive.
3. The insurer's other expenses and profits.
4. Perhaps most important is the advantageous cash flow from which the insurance company benefits while it retains the buyer's premium within its operation.

The captive insurance company also offers advantages from the taxation viewpoint because it enables the company to provide a mechanism for medium-term funding using premium payments from the parent which are tax deductible. The captive insurance company can thereby build up reserves through the mechanism of premium payments without the tax penalty that would apply in most countries on any internal funds held by corporations at the end of an accounting year.

Captive insurance companies can also play a very important role for multinationals by enabling them to have much greater control of their global risk-financial strategy. They can be particularly helpful in implementing the financial policies which incorporate local and central deductibles, gain wider overall coverage and a worldwide reduction of insurance expenditure.

For the major multinational there is usually a corporate desire to maintain as much risk within the company as possible in relation to its overall financial stature. For those multinationals that are decentralised from a management viewpoint, the central view on what the level of self-insurance should be will probably be very different from the view of the manager of a local country operation. Unless a mechanism is found to resolve this problem, the company will be paying much more for insurance globally than it needs to and its worldwide self-insurance policy will be unrelated to its financial capability.

The captive can play a part in centralising a worldwide risk-financing policy by obtaining business from the insurers handling the country's subsidiary programmes so that at the very least, the profits from the insurance transactions which were previously going to local insurance companies will accrue to the captive. This approach can be embellished substantially by the development of global insurance programmes using one insurer or a consortium of insurers. It is then possible to provide local coverage but to supplement this through global policies which retain much higher deductibles than those applying locally and also provide much higher coverage than that available in some countries where the multinationals operate. Although the global policy programmes provided by the conventional market help to solve this problem to a great extent, the captive offers additional flexibility, particularly where local technical difficulties arise such as local capacity problems, strict regulations of policy wordings and premium control.

One advantage of the captive already mentioned is its ability to insure risks for which the conventional market is unable to offer full coverage. In principle, the captive is able to create funds which can be used to pay for losses arising as a result of any contingent event. However, in such eases it is probably going to be necessary to establish that the premium charged for such risks bears some relationship either to the loss history or to a likely market premium if tax deductibility of the premium is to be allowed by the authorities. In addition, it will be necessary for the captive to issue a proper policy document. These aspects are very important in establishing a viable and prudent operation for insuring conventionally uninsurable contingent events.

As the captive grows and its reserves develop, it can extend its retention policy to include much more of the company's risks. It can also reduce the reinsurance protection it needs to buy in order to protect itself, provided, of course that its loss experience does not deteriorate to any significant extent. It can be seen that, when the captive reaches its optimum in relation to reinsurance pricing and retention of its own risk, it can then use its financial position to move into other areas of insurance and grow as an important profit centre for the company.

Disadvantages

The major direct insurance company has an advantage over the captive because its spread of risk is very much larger. Therefore its need for reinsurance is less but its ability to retain higher levels of risk on an individual basis is much greater than the captive could hope to achieve particularly in its early stages of development. For many potential captive owners the narrowness of their portfolios if they have a low spread of risk with very high levels of value may mean that the reinsurance cost will be so high that the amount left to fund the retention in the captive is unacceptable.

Where the captive is considering insuring risks for which cover is not available in the market, it may have difficulties in putting together statistics which can justify the premium payment. This may be particularly difficult for contingent risks that have not yet occurred, such as product recall, strikes, penalties for contract, patent suits and so on.

Another disadvantage is that, where the captive is being used to fund low-level losses, the company may have to provide its own services in the form of, perhaps, fire engineering, claims handling and document issue. It may be difficult to provide these on an economic basis in relation to the size of the captive's business.

For companies on the borderline of captive formation, the need to comply with regulations in the form of capitalisation requirements or reserving for high-level exposures may be disadvantageous. It also needs to be recognised that the reinsurance market tends to be experience-rated, so that the loss history of the captive will be directly related to the reinsurance cost. The company's loss control capability will be a crucial factor in this area and it could be that, where the trade-off between the risk retained in the captive and the residual premium left to pay for the losses is marginal, any significant loss in a year could change the position dramatically. In this case the residual amount would be inadequate or would disappear as a result of a poor claims record and the captive would fail.

The majority of captive owners establishing their insurance company for the first time will probably require co-operation from the market. This is likely to take the form of fronting facilities or engineering and claims facilities and, if the potential captive owner is operating in a difficult insurance market environment, he may find that this co-operation is either not available or is possible only at an exorbitant cost. In addition, if the risks being put into the captive are of an uninsurable nature in the conventional sense, reinsurance facilities to protect him against any catastrophic exposure may be difficult or impossible to purchase.

If the objective is to integrate, within the captive, insurances from overseas subsidiaries, there may be particular difficulties due to local company legislation. In particular, if the countries involved do not allow insurers who are non-admitted to operate, it may be difficult to obtain local market support in the form of fronting facilities. Inhibitions in the form of local legislation may prohibit adequate cessions or premium amounts to the captive. This will often be a problem if high reserves are required by local regulations or if there is control on reinsurance cessions outside the country. In these cases the use of a captive may not be worthwhile, since the premium available may be so small as to make the administrative effort counter-productive in relation to premium received and the risk taken.

Another factor that many multinationals come up against is the relationship between their political position in the market-place and the attitudes of the authorities to a large amount of their local insurance leaving the country in the form of reinsurance premiums. For the potential captive owner whose insurance interests are largely in such countries the captive answer may not be acceptable and a risk-financing programme on the more conventional basis may be the only prudent option available.

A further problem for the captive can be the government controls and returns in the country in which the captive is to be domiciled. Most developed countries have onerous control over insurance, including strict solvency requirements, high capitalisation, exchange control restrictions and the admissibility of assets in relation to reserves held. In addition there can often be considerable delay in actual formation of the company because of the requirement to supply on a continuing basis a considerable amount of information to the authorities in the form of statistical data on the captive company's performance, methods of calculating claims reserves, audit requirements and so on. Naturally, one of the methods used to resolve this particular problem is to establish the captive in an environment where it is less difficult to operate. For some countries however, it may not be possible to do this, owing to government control or restrictions on captive formation such as exchange control restrictions, reinsurance controls or the attitude of the insurance supervisory authorities.

One factor that is sometimes not taken into account when costing the feasibility of the captive is the amount of management time that will be required to run the company. Although many companies employ independent management companies to handle the actual captive activity, the establishment of the insurance company and management time on decision-making in relation to the current and future activities of the company can be costly. In some cases this may not be justified in relation to the return that the company can expect from the captive it is establishing. Other problems in the area of management may be pressures both internal and external in relation to premium rating and claims settlements. Some managers may feel that the establishment of an insurance company will mean that there will be a more favourable attitude towards claims settlements. This may be particularly true where the company is insuring liability covers in which the relationship with employees and customers may be a factor in deciding the amount of a claim that should be paid. The prudent captive owner will resist such pressures and operate the company at arm's length taking a commercial view of any claim being made.

This area of management reaction and involvement must be considered and decided upon before the company is actually established. The management may feel, particularly in overseas areas, that premiums should be reduced substantially and while there may be some justification for this in order to motivate loss prevention activity it is important that the premium payment bears a relationship to the market position. It is also important that the company takes into account the advantages of paying premiums offshore and the future development of the captive as a profit centre, through the reserves established with a view to extending its base in the future, in order to retain much more of the company's risk and reduce the overall expenditure of the group's activities.

Finally, there will be a major disadvantage so far as the captive is concerned if the loss control of the company deteriorates. If we assume that companies forming captives are those with good records, it is important to determine, both from the outset and on a regular basis that such experience is based on good management control and not simply on luck. If the loss control of the company is inherently bad the captive is likely to suffer over the long term, with results that may be more detrimental to the company than if it had stayed within the conventional insurance market.

Types and Choice of Captive

Although the basic definition of a captive that was suggested earlier related to companies writing their own business the actual position is more complicated. It is necessary to separate captives into a number of different groups according to their size and the choices that are available to the potential captive owner.

Classified according to size, captives fall into three principal categories:

1. Paper captives.
2. Small scale captives.
3. Full-scale captives.

Paper captives

A paper captive is an insurance company that has been established on a confidential low-key basis primarily to provide funding facilities for the risk exposures of the group. These companies are usually established on an exempt basis and located in areas where little or no legislation exists and where the taxation rates are minimal and probably of an annual nominal sum. They are often located in one tax haven and managed from another and may be used for contingent risk as well as for conventional insurable exposures. Such captives are cheap to run and would usually be managed outside the company possibly by an accountant or lawyer. They remain confidential so far as the outside world and particularly the government of the parent company are concerned and, while they have some place in the world of captives they remain very susceptible to legislation both from the domicile in which they are located and from revenue authorities who could regard some of the companies formed in this way as being devices to avoid taxation.

Small-scale captives

The small-scale captive is the normal captive in its early days, retaining relatively small risks of the company with a view to eventually becoming a full-scale captive or an insurance diversification of the parent. Small-scale captives may be located domestically or offshore but are generally offshore in order to obtain the benefits of legislative simplicity and low tax. They are normally managed outside the company by independent management companies, broking management companies or insurance company managers although some are handled by lawyers and accountants. Since the management services are shared with other captive owners, the cost of management will be relatively low and this type of captive is often the initial starting-point for the company that is deciding to move into the captive arena.

Small-scale captives are usually reliant on the insurance market for support in two respects. First they usually need fronting facilities for policy issue and technical services, and second, they are generally dependent on the market for reinsurance, which would play a major part in their overall financial programme. Small-scale captives probably make up at least 80 per cent of the captives throughout the world.

Full-scale captive

The full-scale captive is the captive which has been established for many years and which is considered by its owners to be a major financial diversification. It will be of a size that enables it to have its own management and will be largely independent of the market because of its high level of risk retention and its reduced need for reinsurance protection or fronting facilities. It can be located either domestically or offshore, depending on the needs of the parent, and, because of its independence and its own management structure, will have a much higher cost of operation.

A potential captive owner faces choices regarding the ownership of the captive, its required scope, the function to be carried out and the captive location. The following are the alternatives in each of these four categories:

(a) Single-parent or multiple.
(b) Pure or open-market.
(c) Direct or reinsurance.
(d) Domestic or offshore.

Single-parent or multiple captives

The first category is the captive that is owned entirely by the parent company or owned jointly with a number of other corporations or bodies.

A single-parent company is able to control its own affairs, decide on its own objectives and keep its activities reasonably confidential. The captive owned by a number of companies may involve a lower cost because the expenses of managing the captive can be spread across a number of owners, and it may save money in the reinsurance market because the spread of risk and premium volume will be much greater.

However, any joint operation suffers from the potential problem of conflict of interest, as partners disagree or as one of the partners produces a loss experience which increases costs for the remainder. Although the individual members' management cost of the joint venture is likely to be lower than that of the single parent, the company may be involved in much more time-consuming management discussion with the other partners.

The essentials of a successful mutual are to ensure that the partners selected are of the right category and are people with whom the company can work satisfactorily, and that the potential benefits of greater buying power, because of the size of the premium and risk spread available, are more beneficial to the company than operating as a single-parent captive. So far as the US position is concerned, the additional factor that needs to be taken into account is that the multiple approach may help to defend the individual company against attack from the Internal Revenue Service on premium deductibility, a defence which may not be possible with the single-parent-owned company.

Pure or open-market captives

The pure captive is the captive that is underwriting only its own business. It is likely that the company contemplating the establishment of a captive, other than for tax reasons, will start on this basis. A possible exception to this might be where the spread of risk and size of the exposure are so high that the only way that the parent company can improve upon its existing risk-financing programme is to join forces with others in a similar position, a position that has existed in aviation and marine industries in the past.

Apart from this example, however, the choice for the owner is between the company writing its own business or going into the market and writing other people's business on a fairly discriminating basis. Companies considering open-market business have a choice of two general approaches for obtaining business externally. First, they can participate in a pool, usually on reinsurance business, in which they have a share and which is managed by an underwriting agency or possibly another insurance company. This is a relatively easy way to participate in outside business since the underwriting and selection of risk is decided externally and the captive does not require any underwriting expertise of its own. However, the dangers of this approach are that the underwriting performance of the pool may not be good and the quality of underwriting may not be acceptable. In addition, it is important that, when deciding upon such an approach, the captive ensures that the benefits and business being written by the pool, in which it is participating, actually fits the overall financial and strategic objectives.

The other alternative to the open-market approach is to participate in reciprocal insurance exchange. This involves the captive passing a proportion of its own business to another captive or insurance company in exchange for the other company's business, on the basis of mutual profitability. The objective here is to try to expand the base of the captive so that profit benefits can be obtained by spreading risk into areas of similar profitability to that of the captive but for which the captive is limited because of its inability to retain more of its own risk. The danger here once again is that it might be necessary to have underwriting skill to make particular decisions and it is clearly necessary to ensure that the potential profitability of the company with whom you are reciprocally exchanging, is actually going to match the underwriting performance you envisage for your own business.

Direct or reinsurance captives

A direct captive insurance company is one that issues policy direct to its clients without any intervention from the conventional direct insurance market. Depending on the classes of business handled, the direct captive will be restricted to underwriting non-admitted business unless it has been established on an authorised basis domestically in the country where the risk exists.

Where the captive is writing on a direct basis in its country of domicile it is obviously going to need to be of a sufficient size to comply with both domestic legislation and documentation requirements if the effort is to be worth while. In addition, it will probably need to provide services and have a staff capable of issuing policies, handling claims and providing accounting and management services.

In most practical situations the direct captive is unable to operate, because of legislation, in countries where the risks of its parent exist and where an insurer is required to be 'admitted'. There are some countries including the United Kingdom where, for certain classes of risk, usually property, it is possible to underwrite risk on a non-admitted basis, but these are the exception rather than the rule. For this reason, the majority of captives are reinsurance captives that are participating in the risks of the parent by receiving reinsurance of their own risk from the company that is issuing policies on their behalf in the local country of operation. This system is called 'fronting'. Where the company is a multinational and it is necessary for the captive to retain risk for exposures in a whole variety of countries, the international needs and legislative restraints will be such that the reinsurance captive with a fronting facility will be the only answer to the problem.

Domestic or offshore captives

In principle there is no reason why a captive insurance company cannot be established in any country where insurance legislation permits insurance companies to operate. From a practical point of view domestic captives located in the country of origin of the parent, are usually subject to additional legislation, high capitalisation, high taxation and the onerous data requirements of the authorities. There may, however, be cases where for political reasons it is necessary to form the captive domestically particularly if the parent company is government-owned or where the government has a substantial shareholding.

One of the benefits of the domestic captive is that it is convenient from an operational point of view and can be managed within the operations of the parent corporation. A possible disadvantage, however, is that in some parts of the world the domestic captive may not be able to select the risks which would be most beneficial, since there may be some pressure from the authorities for it to participate in other classes. This is a particular problem in countries where there is a method of sharing sub-standard risks for compulsory insurances through the whole insurance community. The captive in this environment might be involved automatically in underwriting outside business of an undesirable underwriting nature.

Most captives are located offshore in an environment which is reasonably free of legislative restraints and with a low taxation position This offers clear benefits in relation to the build-up of reserves reduction of management time and the cost and speed of establishment. In many of these offshore locations it would be possible to form a captive within thirty days and to render information to the authorities on a very limited basis and in total confidence. It does need to be said, however, that even in these offshore locations tougher insurance legislation is being introduced. Such legislation is far less onerous than that which is likely to apply in the domestic environment of the parent, but it is a factor that needs to be taken into account when deciding on the best location so far as the parent company is concerned.

Summary

Premium figures developed by observers of the captive scene show that they have now become a very important part of the insurance market and may be involved with up to 30 per cent of industrial premiums throughout the world. Since those companies which have established captives have done so because they have been unable to obtain the necessary financial advantages from the insurance market the risk selection has been favourable and most remain profitable.

Another advantage of the captive is that like most forms of self-insurance it provides a very significant loss control incentive to the company and is particularly valuable in helping the company to implement its risk-management strategy. It remains a fact that most people worry much more about protecting their own property if they have to participate themselves in the losses than they would if they felt that the insurance industry would pay the claim regardless of their loss-control standards. Although this may be a shallow view since the cost is likely to be repaid to the insurance industry in the long term, it does remain a significant psychological barrier which is often difficult to overcome, particularly for multinationals who are trying to integrate the risk-management concept into their overall management philosophy.

The decision to establish a captive insurance company is a major one for the management and requires detailed consideration based on the understanding that it will be necessary for the company to acquire new skills to manage the company and obtain the real benefits that are available. Those companies that have established insurance subsidiaries on a prudent and considered basis have reaped considerable rewards in the form of reduced insurance expenditure and improved coverage. In many cases annual reductions in insurance costs exceed 30 per cent of previous premium expenditure per annum. The captive also offers an opportunity for the company to diversify into other areas in the future.

There is no doubt that the captive insurance company as an integral part of overall risk-financing policy is here to stay and that the financial benefits, from the point of view of both insurance cost and the protection of the assets of the company can be substantial. It should, however, be remembered that captives formed without care or adequate reinsurance protection and by companies with poor loss control will not decrease the risk-financing cost but could add substantially to it if the risk retention level or the reinsurance protection for the captive is over-ambitious or inadequate.

CHAPTER 2

CRITERIA FOR CAPTIVE FORMATION

The initial step in considering whether a company should establish its own insurance subsidiary is to carry out a feasibility study. Feasibility studies generally have two parts: the preliminary study and the in-depth study.

The preliminary study is primarily a strategic look at the company's existing insurance programme and record so that it is possible to judge whether, on the basis of premium volume, loss history, values at risk and overall objectives, it is worth while for a captive to be formed.

The in-depth study also deals with these areas but involves a detailed investigation of the risk exposures of the company. In particular, this study will attempt to evaluate, in specific terms, the values at risk and the adequacy of the loss prevention measures and to obtain detailed reinsurance costings, so that the trade-off between the existing programme, the formation of a captive and other alternatives can be evaluated before a decision is made. In evaluating the loss history of the company, the in-depth study will attempt to project losses forward, developing mathematical models or other scenarios which will test the stability of the captive and its reinsurance protection in a variety of situations. These situations will usually include the worst possible outcome over a period of, say, five to ten years. The mathematical evaluations will include the effects of cash flow and the volatility of the reinsurance cost in both positive and negative situations.

Components of a Feasibility Study

The first two requirements of the feasibility study are deciding what the real objectives of the company are in establishing its own insurance subsidiary and ensuring that the preconditions for captive formation are met. Once satisfactory answers can be given to these points, the next stage is to consider, in the light of the objectives and preconditions, whether there are alternatives to a captive which could produce similar benefits.

Identifying the company's objectives

Before carrying out the feasibility study, it is necessary to discuss with the company why they wish to consider the formation of a captive. The possible reasons that might be given often include the following:

1. To reduce existing insurance costs.
2. To improve existing coverage or to cover risks which are currently uninsurable.
3. To satisfy risk-financing needs.
4. To obtain adequate credit for more self-insurance.
5. To integrate the multinational insurance programme.
6. To improve cash flow.
7. To help to implement group risk management or risk-financing strategy.
8. To achieve diversification of the company and create an insurance profit centre.

The objectives of the company in establishing a captive will be crucial in relation to developing the feasibility study work. If the needs are related primarily to insurance costs, the objective and feasibility study become relatively simple and will involve developing a strategy which enables the company to overcome market restraints by gaining access to the reinsurance market. If the objective is to improve cover or to insure currently uninsurable risks, the task may be more difficult because of the necessity to obtain fronting facilities and reinsurance protection and to ensure that the techniques used are acceptable so far as the tax deductibility of the premiums is concerned.

The company that wishes to establish a captive for a number of reasons, including reduced insurance costs, implementations of global insurance programmes and risk management plans, will require much more detailed investigation, particularly in relation to the management approach and the countries in which it operates.

A company wishing to diversify by establishing its own insurance company falls into a separate category, and the approach will differ depending on whether the company wishes to diversify as a long-term strategy following the establishment of a captive to insure its own risk, or whether it wishes to set up its own insurance company as a separate, unrelated operation. It is not intended to deal with the second category here although the development of outside business on the back of an established captive operation is considered later in the book.

Captive preconditions

It is possible to separate the prime preconditions for captive formation into the following six categories:

1. Loss control.
2. Management commitment.
3. Retention capability.
4. Premium volume.
5. Market co-operation.
6. Management capability.

1. Loss control

The future of the captive's survival will depend on the ability of the company to manage its risks and to ensure that the loss experience does not deteriorate to a point at which the captive's financial viability suffers. It is important when looking at the historical loss experience of the company and its existing prevention methods that we differentiate between a good loss history and one in which the company has merely been lucky. This part of the feasibility study work is essential and needs to be faced frankly when the study is being undertaken. Although it may be possible, even in bad loss situations, to develop a short-term captive strategy which is almost fail-safe, the company commissioning the study must be made aware of the long-term implications if the loss history deteriorates and the financial position of the captive is placed at risk. Investigation of loss control capability will include not only engineering work on property and liability surveys but also an understanding of the management organisation, its standing in the market and the overall commitment of the company to the improvement or maintenance of its current loss standards.

2. Management commitment

Management commitment both to understanding the implications of establishing an insurance company and to its success is crucial. This is particularly important for multinational companies that may be operating in an environment where local management is autonomous in its operations and where a lack of support for the corporate objectives could seriously affect the financial position of the captive. It is also important that, centrally, the key financial decision-makers and the top management are deeply involved in the decisions that relate to retention of risk levels and reinsurance protection and have an understanding of how the insurance market works and the implications of the decisions that are made. Captives established at low level without the adequate involvement or commitment of top management have little chance of real success or, at the very least, optimising the financial benefits that can accrue from the development.

3. Retention capability

The attitude of the company towards retaining risk will be important when a decision is made on the reinsurance plan and the future of the captive's development. Attitudes towards risk retention capability vary from company to company and depend very much on their overall risk-taking attitude. Some companies will accept a very significant variability in earnings, of perhaps up to 5 per cent, in their commercial activities but take a very much more conservative view when it comes to insurable risk. A yardstick that is sometimes used is that a prudent or perhaps conservative approach would be to accept a variability of 1 per cent of earnings in relation to annual, aggregate, self-insurance levels plus premium savings.

Other rules of thumb which might be used to develop an annual aggregate retention include the following:

(a) *Working capital* — a range of from 1 to 5 per cent of working capital is often used. This reflects the liquidity of an organisation and its capability of handling current obligations.

(b) *Surplus/earnings* — another method is to take 1 per cent of the sum of the current year's earned surplus and the average of the last five years' earnings before tax. Each year's earnings should be discounted for inflation or to reflect patterns of growth.

(c) *Stockholders' equity* — a third method is to take 0.1 per cent of the most recent year's stockholders' equity as the maximum loss to be retained in any one occurrence.

(d) *Sales* — sales are also used as a basis for a rule of thumb. One suggestion has been to use 0.1 per cent of sales as the maximum loss per occurrence that the organisation should retain.

(e) *Earnings per share* — another method easily understood by management is to take 10 per cent of earnings per share. This is commonly called the 'threshold of pain'.

(The above summary is taken from an article in Risk Management Reports which dealt with corporate asset protection programmes.)

The captive's plan needs to reflect the risk-taking philosophy of the company. Clearly, with a higher risk-taking approach there is more opportunity to realise quicker returns in the captive than if a more prudent approach is taken and the company wishes, for example, to retain comparatively low 'stop loss' protection during the early years of development.

In addition, the retention levels will affect the capitalisation and reserve position of the company, and this needs to be related to a decision on the solvency margin level at which the company should be aiming, particularly in its early years of operation. If the company adopts a prudent approach of having a 50 per cent solvency margin (solvency margin being the ratio of capital and reserves to retained premium), the capital requirement may need to be relatively high if a high-risk-taking philosophy is adopted. Conversely, low retention will reduce the need for high capital but will also reduce the profit potential of the captive while reserves are being built up in the early years.

Another factor relevant to retention is the attitude of the local manager to local retention levels. This problem can be resolved by a two-tier deductible programme linked with a global insurance policy that enables the company centrally to retain much higher levels of deductibles than those that are applied locally in individual management budgets.

It is also necessary to look at the retention capability of the captive overall, rather than on an individual basis in relation to each class of risk. An aggregate of high-level retention on different classes could, in some situations, coincide with a single incident, and the captive could be severely damaged if such an event occurred. Indeed, participation in the whole range of classes or risks does have a number of dangers, particularly in the early stages of development, and special attention needs to be given to the effect of losses in one area on other classes and the combination or domino effect that this might have both on overall insurance costs and on the captive's reinsurance protection.

4. Premium volume
People often ask what the minimum level of premium needs to be before a captive insurance company can be formed. While premium levels of £750,000 are probably a reasonable answer to this question, it is not possible to be specific because the decision needs to be related directly to the classes of risk involved, the individual loss exposure and the residual amount left in the captive in relation to the risk it is retaining. Technically, it would be possible to establish a captive insurance company for levels of premium as low as £250,000, provided

that the risk exposure was low and that, after the deduction of management and set-up costs, there was still a good chance of the captive being profitable. However, for such classes of risk it would usually be possible to obtain adequate financial benefits from other alternatives, such as deductibles or retrospective rating, which would be less costly than captive establishment.

5. Market co-operation

Market co-operation in relation to the necessary fronting facilities, claims handling services, reinsurance and shareholding interest in the company is essential. For the reinsurance captive, adequate service locally at reasonable cost is necessary. It is also important for the company to have alternatives available, so that, if the original company is not able to match up to the services or becomes uncooperative over the period, changes can be made.

The company embarking on a captive for the first time will need considerable co-operation from the market, and it is important that this is recognised and that the relationships developed with the market are established on a good working basis, without animosity. A reasonable approach is required in the early stages to reinsurance costs and adequate provisions for services provided by the insurers. It would be foolish to try to reduce costs to the lowest level possible and to lose goodwill which may be necessary at a later stage of the relationship, especially if losses occur.

6. Management capability

The ability of the company's management to establish the captive and to understand its mechanics is crucial. In many cases it may be necessary for the company to employ external help from insurance companies, brokers or consultants to ensure that the feasibility study is carried out with competence, that the establishment of the captive is correct and that major problems are not overlooked. Where problems could exist over exchange control regulations, taxation or compliance with local insurance legislation, it is important that advice is sought in these areas before captive establishment is embarked upon. While companies should economise as far as possible in obtaining this advice, it is important that no short cuts are taken. The consequences of an error in a number of areas could not only be financially onerous, but could impinge seriously on the standing of the company in the eyes of its government, shareholders, customers and the market generally.

Alternatives to a captive

If the company's major objective is to improve its risk-financing policy by retaining more risk within the company's own operations, there are a number of budgetary and insurance solutions which might achieve this without the necessity to form a captive. It may even be possible to meet the needs on a more economic basis than through the captive method.

Operating budgets

One of the most effective methods of retaining within a company risks of low value and high frequency is to pay for losses out of operating budgets. The use of an operating budget for this purpose has a number of advantages.

First, losses set at the correct level in relation to local management budgets have the effect of pinpointing the effectiveness of management's loss control, since the results of their loss prevention activity will be readily recognised and rewarded if they can improve on their agreed budget performance. The psychological impact of losses appearing in budgets rather than as a fixed insurance premium can be very valuable in improving loss control effort. It also has the advantage of differentiating succinctly between good and bad management in this area.

Second, the financial benefit of paying for losses out of operating budgets is that the losses are paid for as they occur and not in advance, as they would be if they were paid for as part of an annual insurance premium. In addition, of course, no payment is made for losses that do not occur and so the profit performance is improved. Payment of losses as they occur is also advantageous for cash flow. Provided that the loss level is selected at a suitably low level, which avoids carry-over to future years, the losses paid will be tax deductible in the same way as insurance premiums. Problems in operating budgets arise only where the losses are of an infrequent and sizeable nature, and where such a loss would seriously harm the overall or local management profit performance in that year and act negatively rather than positively from a psychological and motivational standpoint.

Self-insurance and funding

If it were possible to operate a similar system to the operating budget approach for larger losses, by developing funds within the company to pay for losses that occur beyond a financial year, the same financial benefits would accrue to the company, since losses would be paid as they occurred, cash flow benefits would accrue and the psychological advantages of losses appearing in budget would be available. However, in most countries it is not possible to develop internal funds in such a tax-beneficial way because the fund would be reduced at the end of each year by corporation tax payments. Where funding without tax penalty is available, as in The Netherlands, this alternative is worth consideration. Where it is not, the captive solution offers substantial advantages, because the premiums paid to the captive can be tax deductible to the parent and can be held as reserves to pay for the major losses that might occur on an irregular basis.

Participative insurance
We can separate participative insurance into a number of areas. The following list is not exhaustive, but it does include most of the options that are available from the insurance market, although in some cases not as a general matter of course. The methods of participative insurance which seem to have most relevance in the context of alternatives to the captive approach are the following:

1. Deductibles.
2. Co-insurance.
3. Retrospective rating plans.
4. External risk funding.
5. Credit.

Deductibles. Deductibles or excesses are available from direct insurers in exchange for a discount from the base premium rate. The principle of the deductible is that the company can take out an insurance policy on the understanding that it will pay the first amount of each loss and that the discount allowed on the premium will be proportional to the size of the deductible taken and the frequency of the losses that are likely to occur. In addition, it may be possible to obtain aggregate deductible protection so that, if the multiple of each individual loss deductible exceeds a predetermined level the insurance company will pay the excess. The combination of an 'each loss' deductible and the aggregate deductible will result in a lower discount than the each loss deductible but may, in some circumstances, be beneficial to the company. An example of the application of an each loss deductible and the combination of each loss and aggregate deductibles is given in Table 2.1.

Table 2.1 Each loss and aggregate deductibles

Property insurance		
	Premium	£600,000
Deductible of £100,000 each loss	25% discount	£150,000
		£450,000

Trade saving of £150,000 plus interest against unlimited series of deductibles up to £100,000 each.

Table 2.1   (cont'd)

Introduce aggregate deductible of £200,000

		Premium	£600,000
Each loss deductible of £100,000 and aggregate deductible of £200,000 per year		20% discount	£120,000
			£480,000

Trade saving of £120,000 against maximum annual exposure of £200,000

The decision made regarding the deductibles alternative will be directly related to the discount that the insurance company is willing to give. So far as property insurance is concerned, it will often be found that, for the additional risk that the company is taking, the saving is not adequate, so that the trade-off, unless the company is highly confident that no losses will occur, is not acceptable. However, so far as liability insurance (including automobile cover) is concerned, it may be possible to obtain a beneficial discount which bears a direct relationship to the claims saving by the insurers. In these cases, when the investment income advantage of the premium reduction is taken into account, it may well produce a more attractive alternative than insuring from the ground up. The position with automobile and general liability insurance may be complicated by compulsory legislation, but it is often possible to come to an agreement with the insurance company whereby it provides full policy coverage but makes an allowance for the deductible discount within the overall premium costing.

Another important factor that needs to be taken into account when studying the deductible alternative is the accumulation of deductibles when multiple losses arise from one event. For example, if it is decided to retain £5,000 on damage to motor vehicles, it should be remembered that, in the event of a serious fire in which 100 vehicles are destroyed, the multiple of 100 £5,000 deductibles may reach a level which is unacceptable to the company in relation to its overall risk retention capability.

Co-insurance. The co-insurance technique is similar to the deductible technique except that, instead of the company retaining a specific amount for each loss, it retains a specific percentage for each loss that occurs. Co-insurance is seldom selected as a conscious decision to participate in an Insurance programme. It is more likely to be applied by the insurance company itself, because of its desire for the company to share significantly in losses where the company can influence the loss amounts or the occurrence of loss, for example fidelity insurance.

Retrospective rating plans. The use of retrospective rating is applicable primarily to liability insurances where a company wishes to have the payable premium related directly to the claims that occur. The principle of the retrospective rating plan is that, at the beginning of the year, the company pays a deposit premium plus the basic expenses of the insurance company, and then, perhaps a year later, pays an additional premium once the claims in that year are known or have been estimated. The objectives are to ensure that, as far as possible, premium payment claims are delayed and the appropriate cash flow benefits realised, and that the premium is proportional to the claims figures.

Restrospective rating plans can be very complicated in structure. From the point of view of the buyer, they should be developed in such a way as to optimise the cash flow benefits by ensuring that the premium payment is delayed for as long as possible with the optimum objective being to pay the premium to the insurance company only when a claim is settled. This is particularly important with liability claims, where settlements can often take up to ten years and where the investment income benefits that accrue to the insurance company can be substantial and far exceed the original premium cost.

An example of how claims settlement delays can affect the investment income benefits to an insurance company is shown in Table 2.2, which lists various classes of insurance and shows a cumulative interest rate of 10 per cent over the period that it takes for claims to be settled. It can be seen from Table 2.2 that, for motor insurance, the claims will probably all be settled within a comparatively short time and that the interest benefit above the initial premium payment is 18 per cent. This contrasts with employers' liability, where the period of claims settlements is very much longer and the insurers gain the

Table 2.2 The effect of claims settlement delays on investment income benefits

Class	Cumulative interest rate (10%)
UK motor	18.03
Non-marine 'short-term'	14.70
Non-marine 'all other'	71.69
Marine hull	36.33
Marine liability	63.70
Aviation hull	11.70
Aviation liability	51.71
UK fire	13.24
UK employers' liability	46.31
Reinsurance fire XS loss	9.58
Reinsurance accident XS loss	103.94
Marine reinsurance	45.91
Aviation reinsurance	61.80

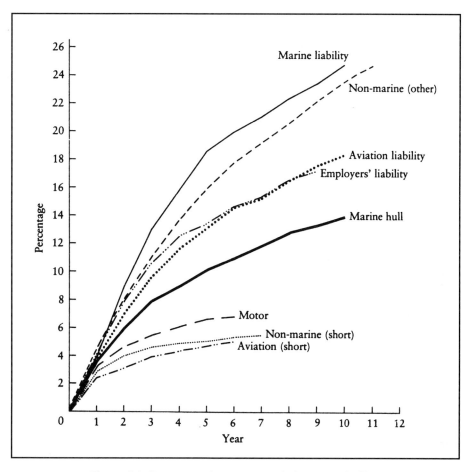

Figure 2.1 Investment income: cumulative annual effect

benefit of approximately half of the premium as investment income during the time that they hold the premium until the final claim payment is made. Figure 2.1 shows the same approach graphically, indicating the cumulative effect of interest rates and showing clearly the number of years that it takes for claims in different classes to be settled. It can be seen from this that the employers' liability claim total will remain outstanding for nine years whereas the motor claims total is settled after six years. With excess of loss reinsurance, it may take up to eleven years before the final results are known.

An example of a retrospective rating plan is shown in Table 2.3. In this example, in addition to a favourable method of claim settlement, the plan includes protection against the company having to pay in excess of a predetermined figure if, in a single year, the losses exceed

Table 2.3 Retrospective rating plan

Estimated annual premium			£500,000
		Deposit	125,000
		Expenses	10,000
		Initial payment	£135,000
Final claims cost			
Claims	£250,000		
Expenses	20,000		
	£270,000		
Insurer's profit			
and overheads say 10%	27,000		
	£297,000		
			£297,000
		Less deposit	125,000
		Extra payment due	£172,000

Note:

    (a) Programme would include minimum and maximum charge to protect insurer against inadequate revenue and insure against major exposure in a single year.

    (b) Optimum programme would accrue interest to deposit payment and pay balance as the claims are settled.

the expected amount. The normal approach on plans with this structure would be to agree to pay the insurer a minimum premium of 50 per cent of the estimated annual premium and to be protected by the insurance company automatically if the final claims cost exceeded 150 per cent of the estimated annual premium. Retrospective rating plans as an alternative to captives can be beneficial for risks such as liability, where the captive may not wish to become involved in long-term reserving problems and where the needs for compulsory insurance, particularly in claims handling, are onerous and expensive.

External risk funding. Risk funding has developed as a useful alternative to captives in recent years. It has the advantage of enabling companies that face restrictions on captives in their own countries or those with low premium volume to obtain many of the benefits without having to go to the bother of establishing their own insurance subsidiaries.

Risk funding does not require any capitalisation: the funds are held offshore by an insurance company which provides the mechanism to hold these funds usually under a separate account against which they hold premiums buy reinsurance in relation to the risk retention level agreed and pay claims.

Table 2.4   External risk funding mechanisms

Total premium to insurer	£300,000
Insurer retains 10%	
therefore premium to risk fund	£270,000
Reinsurance for fund:	
(a) excess of £200,000 per loss	
(b) excess of £400,000 any one year	
say 60%	£162,000
	£108,000
Reinsurance commission to fund at 20%	32,400
	£140,400
Plus Investment income	
Less Management costs	

Table 2.4 gives an example of how an external risk fund operates. It accrues investment income on the premium retained within the fund pending claims payments. The surplus of the funds at the end of the year can be held as reserves and added on to the following year's fund, until the company decides to extend the base of the retention programme, to reduce the reinsurance protection or release the money for other purposes.

Risk funding is a very credible captive alternative where the company is only interested in reducing its insurance costs or is unable to establish its own captive insurance company. Like the captive, it involves management agreements with the sponsoring insurance company and will almost certainly require a degree of fronting facility and technical service provisions. It does, however, provide access to the reinsurance market which would not be available to the company through its insurance on a direct basis.

Although the example in Table 2.4 is for a property account, it is technically possible to develop risk-funding techniques for liability insurance. In these cases it would be possible to use the claim-reserving skills of the fronting insurer to ensure that the fund is kept at the right level, that adequate protection is obtained and that substantial investment income benefits are gained.

In addition to the external risk-funding concept which involves structures or facilities developed in conjunction with the conventional insurance market, there are other schemes, sometimes called rent-a-captive programmes, which link premium participation and loss experience to the structure of the rent-a-captive, often through preference share arrangements. An example of this is the insurance profit centre which is operated by Mutual Indemnity Limited from a base of operations in Bermuda (see the case study, at the end of the chapter).

The important considerations with external risk funding or rent-a-captive concepts are the wording of the management agreement, the effect of the structure on tax deductibility, repatriation of surplus funds or replacement of any deficit, and the security and credibility of the insurance vehicle that is being used. These programmes offer a valid alternative to the captive, particularly for companies with low premium volume or who are located in countries where exchange control prohibits the establishment of a captive offshore. In addition they can provide an intermediate step between conventional insurance and a captive, and the development of the funds may enable a captive to be capitalised at a future date in the location where the funding facility is domiciled.

Credit. The final alternative is to obtain from bankers the promise of standby credit in the event of a major loss. The simplest option is to have a predetermined agreement with the bank, for which an annual fee is payable, stipulating that, in the event of a major loss, the bank will lend money to the company to pay for the loss, charging an interest rate of, say, 1–2 per cent above the lending rate at the time of the loss occurrence.

Standby credit for contingent risks was popular many years ago but has come into disrepute because it was used by companies largely as a form of last-resort protection. It is, however, a potentially valuable alternative as banks increase their interest in insurance risks. Although it may have disadvantages in relation to the overall financial strategy of the company, obtaining standby credit may be appropriate in some cases.

Basics of a feasibility study

Assuming that alternative risk-financing methods to the captive have been discarded, the feasibility study then needs to look closely at the captive option. The basics of the study will include the following:

1. Analysis of the existing insurance programme.
2. Spread of country operations.
3. Service needs including fronting.
4. Premium volume and spread of risk.
5. Cash flow.
6. Overall captive exposure.

Analysis of the existing insurance programme
The study will need to examine in detail the existing insurance programme of the company, including the price being paid and the cover obtained both currently and over the previous five to ten years. In developing the statistical data it will be necessary for the premium cost to be updated in relation to current values and any adjustments to be made if coverage has increased or decreased over the period of time.

Secondly, a detailed loss history of the company should be obtained, preferably over a ten-year period if property risks are involved and over five years if liability risks are involved. Once again, this loss history needs to be updated historically, and details of loss frequency and size of claim must be analysed in some depth. It will also be necessary to include in the calculations any major alterations to the risk that have occurred over the period of time studied. These changing factors could include the following:

(a) Acquisitions of other companies.
(b) New premises or sale of old premises.
(c) Changes in loss prevention.

Analysis of actual claims should investigate whether premises that have been involved in losses have been protected and whether changes in management could have affected the general attitude towards loss activity. Included in the analysis of the insurance programme and coverage should be details of the services provided by the insurers as part of the premium, whether it will be necessary for these services to be maintained in the future and what the cost would be of replacing them in the current circumstances.

The analysis of cover should include details of the levels of self-insurance that have been retained within the company over the period for which information is available. These self-insurance levels will need to be updated on a historical value basis and applied back over the loss history, so that bands of losses occurring within certain levels of exposure can be developed. This will help to make decisions at a later stage on levels of retention and the impact that they would have made, updated to current values, if a captive had been formed. These self-insurance levels, particularly if they take the form of deductibles, will also need to be related to the discounts that have been given by the insurers over the period and the level of credit that might be available in the market at current prices.

The international needs of the company and its style of operation must be considered. The number of countries of operation will have an influence on the choice of insurers to provide fronting and reinsurance facilities. The potential problems locally will also have some impact on levels of self-insurance decisions, on whether the captive can operate on an admitted or non-admitted basis and whether it will be practical for all countries within the multinational operation to be included in the captive programme.

Lastly, in analysing the insurance programme account will need to be taken of current insurance market conditions and, in particular, whether the current rates reflect an insurance market at the bottom of a rate cycle, whether the existing premium levels are reasonable considering market conditions and whether there are any inhibitions in the programme that would prevent implementation of the captive. In the latter connection, the two main areas of investigation will need to be whether long-term agreements, which can continue for up to ten years in some European countries, exist and whether the parent company has any debenture stock arrangements with insurance companies on its properties that could prohibit the inclusion of such premises in the captive programme or influence market co-operation.

Country spread
If the company is multinational and wishes the captive to become involved in risks throughout the world, it will be necessary to obtain details of the countries involved and the insurance position in each of them. Consideration will need to be given to the legislative position in each country, including any restraints on reinsurance, how much reinsurance it will be possible for individual countries to cede to the captive and whether there are any restraints regarding reserves being withheld or delays in premium payments. Table 2.5 shows an example of the position in countries where multinationals commonly operate and some of the financial restraints that may exist. If the captive programme involves a fronting requirement, it will also be necessary to see whether there are any restrictions on the percentage of business held within the local country, and whether there are any mechanisms available to improve the amount of insurance premium that can be passed to the captive.

Other country factors will include any insurance company legislation regarding premium levels, tariff rating restraints, restrictions on credits for a deductible and the extent of policy coverage available. In some countries there will be situations in which it is compulsory to pay premium taxes of one sort or another. Taxes are sometimes imposed on premiums in order to provide a level of catastrophe coverage; in other countries, such as Australia, a tax is imposed upon property premiums to pay for fire brigade services. These factors will

Table 2.5 Summary of the position in various countries that can affect captive programmes

Country	Non-admitted allowed	Max. outwards reinsurance cessions	Reinsurance excise tax	Reserve withholding requirement	Premium tax	Other local taxes	Delay in overseas remittances of over 30 days
Argentina	no	nil	nil	nil	10.5% + VAT 18–24%	0.2% to 2.5%	no
Australia	yes	100%	3.6%	—	*stamp duty 0–25%	*fire levy 0–64%	no
Austria	yes*	100%	nil	40%	11%	8%	no
Belgium	no	nil	nil	35%	up to 27%	—	no
Brazil	no	nil	n/a	n/a	4%	*	n/a
Canada	yes*	100%	10%	40%	3% to 12%	—	no
Chile	yes*	100%	2%	nil	18%	—	yes
Columbia	no	90%	3%	40%	14%	—	yes
Cyprus	no	100%	nil	—	2%	stamp duty C£0.5	no
Denmark	yes	100%	nil	40%	12%	—	no
Finland	yes*	100%	nil	—	22%	3%	no
France	no	100%	nil	40% 105% loss reserve	7% to 35%	18% catastrophe cover	no
West Germany	yes	100%	nil	no	15%	8%	no
Greece	no	95%	2%	yes	12.4%	20%	yes
Hong Kong	yes	100%	nil	—	nil	3%	no
India	no	nil	n/a	n/a	5%	stamp duty max. RS5000	n/a
Indonesia	no	25%*	—	40%	max. Rp 0.20% on SI	—	no
Ireland	no	100%	nil	75%	2%	nil	no
Italy	no	100%	nil	35%	up to 21.25%	2%	no
Ivory Coast	no	95%	—	yes	33%	—	yes
Japan	no	100%	nil	yes	>yen 200 per policy	—	no
Jordan	no	100%	nil	40%	nil	—	—
Kenya	yes	70%	—	yes	variable	—	yes

*variations exist.

57

Table 2.5 Summary of the position in various countries that can affect captive programmes (cont'd)

Country	Non-admitted allowed	Max. outwards reinsurance cessions	Reinsurance excise tax	Reserve withholding requirement	Premium tax	Other local taxes	Delay in overseas remittances of over 30 days
Korea (S)	no	–	–	40%	won 30 per policy	20%	yes
Luxembourg	no	100%	–	–	4%	4%	no
Malaysia	no	70%*	–	40%	R2 per policy stamp duty	–	–
Mexico	no	100%	nil	38%	10% VAT	–	yes
Netherlands	yes	100%	nil	80%*	7%	–	–
New Zealand	yes	100%	5%	–	–	22.8% fire services and catastrophe	–
Norway	yes*	100%	nil	33.3%	nil	nil	no
Pakistan	no	70%	–	–	–	stamp duty >PRS 5,000	yes
Peru	no	variable	2.5%	n/a	18%	–	yes
Phillipines	no	90%	–	40%	6%	2%	yes
Portugal	no	80%	–	–	5%	22%	yes
Singapore	yes	variable*	–	40%	–	S$1 per policy	no
South Africa	no	100%	–	35%	10% VAT	max. R100 per policy	no
Spain	no	100%	–	33.3% 100% loss reserves	5%	max. 20% fire service and consortio	no
Switzerland	no	100%	nil	50%	5%	S Frs 0.05% fire services	no
Taiwan	yes	90%	1%	100% loss reserve	5%	0.3–0.5%	no
Thailand	no	85%	–	42.5%	3.3%	0.4% stamp duty	no
Turkey	no	65%	–	not for fac. r/i. 33% for rest	30%	100%	yes
United Kingdom	yes	100%	nil	varies*	2.5%	nil	no
United States	yes	100%	1–4%	100% loss reserve 40% premium	up to 3.5%	–	no
Venezuela	no	99%	3%		4.25%	–	yes

*variations exist.

We acknowledge the assistance of the Zurich Insurance Group in compiling the South American elements of this chart.

be important to the captive since any taxes paid locally will have the effect of diminishing the premium available. In some cases the application of a premium tax to a coverage that currently does not exist can negate the overall financial objective of the programme.

Servicing needs

Apart from the technical service needs, such as fire engineering and claims handling, that may be required for insurance programmes, fronting facilities may also be needed, particularly if international operations are involved. In addition, it must be determined whether the insurance companies that currently handle the programme or that will become involved have the capability to provide the necessary levels of competence.

Volume of premium and spread of risk

The study will analyse the relationship between the volume of premium which is available for each class of risk, the overall exposure, on both individual and aggregate bases, and the risk within the portfolio. These factors bear a direct relationship to the cost of reinsurance and to the final risk exposure of the captive. In general terms the potential captive owner will be looking at risks which are profitable to the captive from the point of view of either cash flow or underwriting profitability due to low claims history. However, in both of these cases historical information may not show the true position and there could be potential difficulties if unexpected claims occurred. In attempting to optimise the reinsurance cover it will be necessary to show that the loss frequency and the loss potential are low and that the premium available to the reinsurer will be adequate to protect him against serious exposure. The loss control capability and track record of the company may also be influential in these discussions.

For the captive itself, it will be necessary to make sure that the amount of risk it retains is sensible in view of the premium that is available after reinsurance costs are deducted. Taking past loss performance and expected future performance into account, the captive should not be seriously exposed. Where the captive protects itself additionally by the purchase of 'stop loss' insurance, related to the captive's annual exposure, it must be demonstrated to the reinsurers that the loss frequency is low and that the possibility of reaching the 'stop loss' level is remote. Otherwise, the cost of this protection will be too high, in relation to the amount of premium retained, to make the captive venture worth while.

The feasibility study will need to concentrate on these points in an attempt to demonstrate the best possible position while ensuring that the data available is reliable and that the information given to reinsurers and considered by the company when it looks at its own exposure is accurate and realistic.

Cash flow
One important aspect of the captive approach is the possibility of developing substantial investment income from premiums paid to the insurance subsidiary. As mentioned previously, investment income possibilities vary from one class of risk to another, with more opportunities available for long-tail business, if one is comparing the difference between premiums paid to a direct insurer and those paid to a captive. However, cash flow calculations need to take into account claims payments and also the possibility of negative cash flow in the event of claims payments exceeding the premium that is retained by the captive.

The timing of premium payments, whether to direct insurers, the captive insurance company or the reinsurer, needs to be considered, since this can vary considerably. Receipts of premium payments vary from country to country and in some situations the time delay can be very considerable. For short-tail business, where investment income is less important, this could reduce the benefits totally.

Sophisticated investment strategies are now available for captives from international banks and they can add considerably to the financial return on a captive. In this context at least one major American bank has looked at the effect of mixing different classes of risk in order to optimise investment performance. This study has produced interesting results which point to more consideration being given to the investment relationship between different classes of risk than has tended to be the case in the past. Certainly, the investment potential and the positive and negative cash flow advantages of a captive should be an integral part of the mathematical models on captive performance projections and an important consideration of the feasibility study.

Overall captive exposure
Finally, an integrated captive insurance programme involving a number of classes of risk needs to take account of the overall exposure to the financial resources of the insurance company. Examples of this include taking into account the combined effect of retaining losses within property damage and consequential loss policies, where one single event could involve a retention to the captive under both programmes, and retention of liability coverage, where a major fire could involve losses under fire, consequential loss and liability policies. For unrelated events there is still the possibility that the captive could have a bad

year when a number of events involving a serious impact on each class of risk retained in the captive could add up to a major exposure.

While it is technically possible to provide adequate protection across the whole of the captive, it is often difficult to buy this in the market-place unless the reinsurance market is very soft. Even if the possibilities exist, the cost is likely to be high. It is often more economic to be more conservative towards individual loss retentions or to work on combined retentions where classes of risk are closely linked, such as fire and consequential loss, rather than to look on the classes on a strictly individual basis.

Captive Considerations for Different Classes of Insurance

Fire and business interruption

The general requirement for data has already been considered so far as the overall needs of a captive feasibility study are concerned. There will, however, be additional requirements for different classes of insurance, in fire and business interruption it will be necessary to obtain a detailed claims history over, if possible, the last ten years, and to update this to take into account major changes in the business and economic environments. Among the factors for which the claims history needs to be adjusted are the impact of inflation on premiums and claims costs, and the growth of the company, in relation to both its own inherent development and any major acquisitions that have been made, over the period of time under consideration. It is also likely that, over such a period of time, risks will have changed considerably. With property exposures, it is likely that the volume of factories or locations has increased as business has expanded, and that the risk spread, in terms of size of exposure, has altered substantially. Another factor is improvement of locations from a loss control point of view, particularly where losses have occurred in the past. Many companies have introduced sophisticated loss prevention systems over the last decade, including many to a highly protected risk standard. Losses which occurred in premises which are now protected must be considered in attempting to update the historical claims history to reflect current factors. A change in the type of business in which the company is involved may also be important, particularly if this has meant any high-risk exposures becoming obsolete.

Loss frequency over the period of time is important from a number of aspects. First, the loss frequency will have an impact on the claims experience and in particular it will be of interest to the reinsurers if they are asked to consider providing any form of aggregate or stop loss protection. In addition, loss frequency bears a direct relationship to loss control capability and can give a good indication of whether the company's claims history is low due to luck or because of management competence.

For example, there is a direct relationship between the number of small claims that occur and the probability of a major catastrophe occurring. If a company has had a very large number of low cost claims in relation to its business but a major loss has not occurred, it may well be that the loss ratio which is produced is unrealistic in relation to the potential. Conversely, the company with the single major loss but low loss frequency may have had the one unexpected major loss owing to factors outside its control, whereas its inherent loss control approach is excellent and makes the prospect of a good future loss history more likely.

Loss frequency statistics can be produced in combination with charts which show the impact of deductibles on the loss history over a period of time. It is obviously important that, in calculating the impact of variable deductibles or retention levels on past experience, these are updated historically to current values. Table 2.6 shows the development of a five-year claims experience for a property risk and shows how the claims which have occurred have been separated into four categories of self-retention level. Once these data are available it is possible to apply the information to various alternatives of self-retention by the captive and to see, based on past experience, what impact it would have made on the captive fortunes. With this information it is possible to balance the retention level of the captive with the likely cost, and to demonstrate to reinsurers the likely effect of the retention level on their own programme.

Table 2.6 Five years' claims experience: property damage
(updated by inflation index)

	£0 to £50,000	£50,001 to £100,000	£100,001 to £250,000	£250,000 +
1981	100,000	25,000	nil	nil
1982	120,000	100,000	200,000	nil
1983	70,000	nil	nil	nil
1984	200,000	200,000	250,000	500,000
1985	60,000	75,000	nil	nil
	550,000	400,000	450,000	500,000
		950,000		
		1,400,000		
		1,900,000		

The other major factor, so far as property business for captives is concerned, is the calculation of the estimated maximum loss. The estimated maximum loss (EML) has two main purposes. For the direct insurer or the captive, it enables him to decide on the reinsurance that he needs to protect himself. For the reinsurer, it enables him to have some idea of the risk that he is taking. In order to determine exactly what the EML means in this context, a definition is necessary. The following definition is used by the Reinsurance Offices Association and is a good basis on which to operate.

It is important that the EML is conservative and takes account of the following factors:

size, height, shape of area exposed;
construction of roof, walls and floors;
combustible linings: walls, roofs, ceilings and partitions;
fire load: nature of load, distribution, combustibility of content;
use of location and separation: hazardous processes and substances;
susceptibility of contents to smoke, heat and water;
explosion from any source;
hazards from glass or corrosive materials;
concentration of any values in small areas;
management and housekeeping capability.

It is important in order to establish an estimated maximum loss figure to ignore the following:

horizontal separations;
fire-resisting doors;
absence of normal source of ignition;
fire detection, prevention, extinguishing arrangements in sprinklers, fire brigade, etc.

EMLs need to be calculated for each of the locations to be insured, except where these are very low in relation to the overall property values being covered. Having analysed the maximum loss that could occur in any one of the locations being insured, the reinsurer will take this figure into account when deciding on the cost of his protection. It follows that if the estimated loss figure is high in relation to the premium available, the premium required by the reinsurer for the catastrophe loss will leave little premium for the captive to deal with the losses within its own retention level. This is the essence of the spread of risk that is necessary if the captive programme is to be optimised.

If the reinsurance cost and the EML size are a problem it may be possible for the company to separate out a major exposure and keep this risk in the conventional market, while insuring the remainder of properties in the captive. In order to get some idea of this problem it may be useful to develop a chart or graph of the exposures at risk and their individual EML figures. An example of an analysis of a property portfolio by exposure and graph is shown in Table 2.7 and Figure 2.2. These show that if you eliminate from the captive programme the top four exposures, the highest EML would be substantially lower, and it could be possible to optimise the reinsurance cost and probably make the benefits to the captive much more reasonable for the remaining risks. This approach may be important for a company with a very significant number of small risks and one or two major risks. It is certainly worth while obtaining variable reinsurance costings depending on whether the whole or only part of the overall portfolio is included in the captive programme.

Another area of reinsurance presentation which may be valuable is in respect of business interruption exposure, where it will be helpful to persuade reinsurers that loss control activity in this area reduces the overall exposure. It should be remembered that the EML figure will be combined with the property and the business interruption exposure so that anything that can be done within the company to

Table 2.7 Analysis of property portfolio

Range of exposures (US$ million)	No. of exposures	Cumulative no. of exposures	Cumulative % of total no. of exposures
0.0– 0.999	318	318	79.5
1.0– 1.999	11	329	82.2
2.0– 2.999	8	337	84.2
3.0– 3.999	8	345	86.2
4.0– 4.999	4	349	87.2
5.0– 9.999	11	360	90.0
10.0– 14.999	6	366	91.5
15.0– 19.999	6	372	93.0
20.0– 24.999	4	376	94.0
25.0– 29.999	2	378	94.5
30.0– 34.999	3	381	95.2
35.0– 39.999	3	384	96.0
40.0– 49.999	4	388	97.0
50.0– 59.999	2	390	97.5
60.0– 69.999	2	392	98.0
70.0– 79.999	4	396	99.0
80.0– 89.999	1	397	99.2
90.0– 99.999	1	398	99.5
100.0–109.999	0	398	99.5
110.0–119.999	1	399	99.7
120.0–129.999	0	399	99.7
130.0–139.999	1	400	100.0

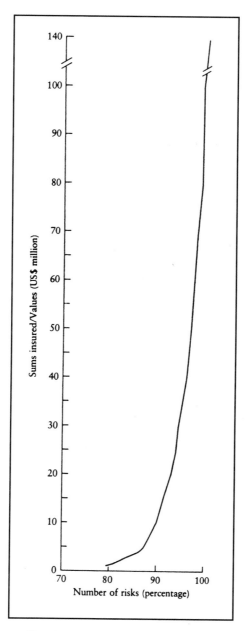

Figure 2.2 Portfolio profile of 400 risks ranging from US$0 to US$140 million

minimise loss expectancy will be beneficial in terms of reinsurance cost. The most effective way of measuring and improving business interruption risk is to carry out a contingency planning study, which will look at the major bottleneck exposures of the operation and consider measures that can be taken to reduce the likelihood of loss or reduce the duration of loss should the event occur. Such an investigation would not be related solely to the individual location, but would also look at interdependencies between other companies and locations within the operation, and at reliance upon customers, suppliers and other external factors, such as strikes, government legislation, shortage of raw materials, transport difficulties and so on. Contingency planning is a valuable risk management technique that can not only reduce insurance costs, because of the likelihood of being able to introduce measures that reduce the indemnity period under business interruption insurance, but also improve overall performance of production processes.

Finally, account will need to be taken of the cash needs of the captive in respect of each class of risk. So far as fire and business interruption is concerned, it is likely that the time of settlement of claims will be on a short-term, low-cost basis for small claims and a longer-term, instalment basis for major losses. For example, small losses will probably have to be paid immediately. A major loss, involving the rebuilding of a site for example, will need to be repaid over a period of, say, two years but on an instalment basis with, perhaps, half of the payment being made after twelve months have elapsed. The time of claims settlement is a factor that must be considered in relation to the investment policy of the captive and its need for capitalisation and reserves.

Liability

The compilation of historical claims data on liability insurance is similar to that for the fire and business interruption in that data needs to be updated to take account of inflation and historical values. However, in addition to this information, it is very useful to have details of individual claims settlements and the time of settlement in each case. This enables calculations to be made of the effect of investment income on the time-lag between occurrence and payment, and also gives some pointers to the types of claims with which the company is involved. Frequency, once again, will be a key factor with liability claims since it points to the type of claims activity and the propensity for catastrophic losses. Where products liability is concerned, this can be an important factor, but it is obviously necessary to take into account the type of business in which the company is involved and the exposure that could materialise in the worst possible situation.

Other factors that are peculiar to liability insurance include the need to take account of legal changes that have occurred over the duration of the claims information and also any legal changes that can be predicted for the future. We have, of course, seen dramatic developments in liability, particularly in products liability, over recent years, where claims costs have escalated and the approach of judges to claims has changed out of all character compared with attitudes in the past.

In addition to legal changes it is also sensible to look in detail at the way in which the company's business has changed, and in particular whether it has acquired any companies which could have a serious impact on loss exposure in the future. There have been a number of examples of companies which have taken over new companies and have inherited serious liability problems that were not a feature of their previous business and that they did not envisage when the acquisition was made. Alterations in the social environment increasing the propensity to claim, hostility towards multinationals and the development of consumer associations are all having an impact on claims frequency and costs and must be included when evaluating the historical information and deciding whether or not it makes sense for a captive to become involved in this area.

One of the main reasons for use of a captive to insure liability exposure is the cash flow advantage. The investment benefits from liability insurance have been demonstrated by the figures shown in Table 2.2. When looking at a particular liability portfolio to decide what cash flow benefits are likely to accrue, it will be necessary to examine the timing of claims settlements, both historically in relation to the real claims experience and in the future in relation to the risks that are being retained, and also to look at the volume of claims settlements in relation to individual risks. Table 2.8 shows a simple method of looking back over historical information to show what impact investment income would have had on the financial performance of a captive. This example looks at cash flow on the basis of 10 per cent investment income which is reduced (for calculation purposes) to 5 per cent on the assumption that claims are paid on average half way through the year. It can be seen from this example that, although the overall claims to premium loss ratio is over 100 per cent, once the investment income is added over the five-year period, a surplus accrues to the captive. This may not be a desirable basis on which to consider captive formation for this particular risk, but it does demonstrate the influence of investment income on premium retention of the captive while claims settlement is delayed. This type of charting can also demonstrate the differences when retaining different types of liability risk within the captive. Clearly, the low-level risk retention will involve a continual outgoing in the form of claims payment, whereas the

Table 2.8 Cash flow calculations (all figures are £s)

	Year 1	Year 2	Year 3	Year 4	Year 5
Initial premium	500,000	225,000	167,500	112,100	91,310
Expenses/Reinsurance	200,000	25,000	25,000	10,000	10,000
	300,000	200,000	142,000	102,100	81,310
Claims paid	100,000	50,000	42,000	20,000	50,000
Retained premiums at year end	200,000	150,000	100,000	82,100	31,310
(a) Investment income 10% on retained premiums	20,000	15,000	10,000	8,210	3,130
(b) 5% on losses assuming claims paid proportionally throughout year	5,000	2,500	2,100	1,000	2,500
Total fund	225,000	167,500	112,100	91,310	36,940

Summary	*Premium*
	500,000
Expenses/Reinsurance	270,500
	229,500
Claims	262,000
	(32,500)
Investment income	69,440
Surplus	36,940

higher-level retention may involve a major loss but could involve substantial investment income even if the claim occurred early in the life of the captive.

The reinsurance needs of the captive considering liability insurance retention will depend very much on where the captive participates in its liability programme. The key aspects in this area are the following:

1. Volatility of the reinsurance.
2. Exposure of the captive.
3. Security of the reinsurers.

Reinsurance tends to be experience-rated so that, if experience deteriorates, the reinsurance cost is likely to escalate considerably and make the premium retention of the captive much lower than originally envisaged. As with other classes, it will be necessary to consider carefully the type of risks that are being retained and to try to ensure that the captive selects those which have the lowest likelihood of producing a poor experience. This must then be balanced with the premium that is available to make the profit potential significant.

The exposure for the captive with liability insurance could be very considerable. Claims awards are escalating and it is important that the reinsurance protection recognises this and ensures that the captive is not dangerously exposed in the light of legal, economic and social changes. Inflation and reserving policies will have their own serious effects on captive performance and, while it may be possible in the short term to protect the captive against exposure, inflation might have the effect of moving claims into the area of the reinsurer with the consequent effect on their pricing. Reserving needs to be prudent and related to the changes mentioned. Advice from knowledgeable claims specialists is essential in this area if the captive is to ensure that adequate funds are available when the claims finally need to be settled.

The potential time-lag on claims settlements means that the necessity for the captive to have secure reinsurers, who are still going to be in existence when the claim is settled in perhaps ten years' time, is of paramount importance. There is often a temptation when the reinsurance market is soft to buy coverage at low rates, but the necessity to take into account the financial stability of the reinsurers who are quoting such rates is crucial.

Claims services
If the captive is to participate in liability risks of a low-level nature or for insurances where there is a compulsory requirement to ensure from the ground up, it will be necessary to purchase claims services and to obtain co-operation from the insurance market in the form of fronting and claims servicing facilities. If the captive is not in this position and decides to operate claims handling itself, it must be aware of the potential conflict of interest, if it is dealing with claims from its employees or from its customers or suppliers. The view is often taken that use of a fronting insurer or of a claims servicing facility does help to act as a buffer between the company and its plaintiff. This reduces the conflict of interests and the potential harm that a direct relationship on claims settlement could have. The cost of these services and their competence are further factors for which allowance must be made when costing the desirability of liability captive participation.

Legislative restraints
As already mentioned, many liability risks are compulsory insurance requirements in many countries. Examples of this are workmen's compensation and motor third party insurance. It will be necessary in these cases to have co-operation of an insurer issuing the policy domestically and providing a range of services. The insurer providing guarantee cover, often up to unlimited levels, will concern himself about

the financial viability of the captive, particularly if it is to participate in any high-level exposures.

Where the captive is involved with international liability pro- grammes, considerations of non-admitted status will be important, and the effect of exchange regulations in both the captive domicile and the country of operation will need to be taken into account. If umbrella policies are involved, where there is a difference between the policy issued locally and the global coverage designed to top up any inadequacy in the local limits, these considerations may be of considerable significance to the validity of the whole programme. Where the global programme is constituted properly using international insurer networks, it should be possible to overcome these difficulties and enable the captive to participate in the worldwide programme without penalty.

Outside the United States it is often difficult to justify the use of the captive for liability insurance to any significant extent because the premiums involved are often small in relation to the amount of protection that is provided. The participation is usually of interest for low levels of risk retention where claims frequency is comparatively low or for participation in any upper layer of the coverage if the premium available is fairly high. Where the insurance market for products liability is difficult owing to high rates or capacity problems, there is often a strong case for the captive to participate as a funding mechanism against events of remote probability. It is for these reasons that outside the United States captives are less involved in liability, whereas within the United States, owing to the size of liability awards and the difficulties within the insurance market liability risks are often funded successfully within the captive.

Marine and aviation

These two classes of risk have similar characteristics in that the exposures for hull coverage are often very high in relation to the premium that is payable. One of the characteristics of the marine market has been the development of mutual and P & I (Protection and Indemnity) clubs which, in many respects, represent the origins of the group captive that is now developing in the non-marine area. The problems of marine and aviation insurance are essentially size of risk and spread. Many of these problems have been resolved by companies grouping together in order to ensure that they have enough premium available so that the residual amount in their joint captive is adequate to deal with the expected loss potential. There is often a major accu- mulation problem in both classes at airports or docks which needs to be recognised. The cash flow advantages follow those already described for property and liability insurance on non-marine exposures.

As far as cargo risk is concerned, the main requirement is for claims handling facilities which need to be costed and are an important part of the premium charged by insurers for this class of business. Loss control is difficult in both areas since packaging losses, theft and damage are usually outside the control of the owners and often large geographical distances and differing attitudes to loss prevention arise. As with the other classes, the importance of evaluating and updating historical loss data is important. This is particularly true of marine hull claims, where there is often a very substantial time delay between the occurrence and the actual settlement after repair. The potential for using captives to optimise risk-financing programmes for shipowners and airlines is considerable and many exist throughout the world. The principles for evaluating such companies for captive formation are basically the same as for those discussed for property and liability. However, the portfolio for such operations is narrower and the justification for more association or grouping plans to increase spread and improve reinsurance buying power is much more significant.

Employee Benefits

There has been growing interest, over recent years, in the use of captives to provide employee benefit facilities. In many individual countries there are restrictions on the use of a captive for this purpose and there can often be a conflict of interest in providing these facilities via a captive. It is therefore necessary to ensure that such potential conflicts involving the use of the captive are resolved and agreed by management in conjunction with their employees. Areas where the captive can particularly play a role are the healthcare benefits provided to employees and the international pooling of employee benefits for multinational companies.

Many providers of healthcare insurance will agree to reinsure a large amount of risk to a captive providing, as part of the reinsurance cession, excess of loss and aggregate protection to limit the level of claims to a fixed amount. These reinsurance facilities are usually linked to the provision of local services which usually include managed care facilities, which help to control losses. Such a facility can be structured to meet the aspirations of employees and also control the cost of the benefit provided by the employer.

Substantial multinational companies often have a wide range and mixture of pension, life insurance and employee benefit structures in the various countries in which they operate. It is possible to put these together under the umbrella of a multinational pooling arrangement and insurance companies providing these services are often happy to involve a captive as a reinsurer (with the appropriate protections for the captive) or by paying the profit commission earned on the worldwide facility, to the captive entity.

One of the disadvantages of using a captive to provide cover for pensions is that, apart from any conflict of interest concerns (which can be difficult to overcome given that pension trustees may not be enthusiastic about the involvement of an insurance company owned by a benefit provider) it is often possible to fund for pensions internally without significant tax advantages. Funding and pension plans are usually under very close government scrutiny or control and, as a consequence, the benefits of using a captive to any significant extent (possibly apart from the pure life insurance element) may not be worthwhile. However, employee benefit development is under active consideration in the United States, where the use of a captive is under debate and we may see future growth in this area. Certainly so far as general employee benefits are concerned, it is a new opportunity area that many captives are contemplating and the use of captives for healthcare, multinational pooling of employee benefits will definitely increase.

Contingent risk

In principle, a captive can insure any contingent risk, providing the necessary funding mechanism for companies that wish to cover the commercial risk that could seriously affect the fortunes of the company. The funding mechanism has obvious attractions for companies wishing to protect themselves against such risks as strikes, product recall, extortion and patent suits. The problem of using the captive for this purpose revolves mainly around the difficulty of acceptance by taxation authorities that the premium paid should be tax deductible. In principle it will be necessary to establish an acceptable basis of premium rating. This may be difficult if there is no loss history and if such risks are not insurable in the conventional market.

A comparatively recent exception to this problem is the use of captives for credit insurance where it is now possible for a captive to participate at a level above its normal bad debt position, with catastrophe reinsurance being provided in excess of the parent company's self-insurance level and the captive's retention. However, for the other areas it could be difficult or impossible to obtain any reinsurance protection for risks which are not commonly insured in the direct market or where the reinsurance market is unfamiliar or reluctant to participate.

Once again, the lack of statistical base could be a difficulty in persuading reinsurers to take on such risks and, in particular, to decide what price should be charged. If, however, it is possible to develop some sort of actuarial basis for the risk undertaken and to issue a policy wording which relates to this and the risk exposed, the possibilities do exist to use a captive for these purposes.

Type of Captive necessary

Having decided that in one particular class or a number of classes of insurance a captive is feasible, the company will then need to decide what type of captive would suit the purpose. Types of captives have already been discussed and, essentially, the choice will be between domestic and offshore, direct or reinsurance, pure or mutual. In making this decision it will be necessary to consider the following:

1. The costs of establishing and managing different types of captive.
2. The convenience to the parent company in locating the captive domestically or offshore.
3. The tax implications of the decision in relation to the parent company's domicile and the attractions of the captive locations.

The necessity for fronting services to provide policy issue and services will be an important factor in deciding whether the captive should be direct or reinsurance. The insurance legislation in the country of domicile will be a factor in deciding the location, as will the attitude of the government towards exchange control and premium deductibility.

Group and Association Captives

The establishment of special mutuals and group captives goes way back to the origins of the captive movement with many of the major insurers of today having their origins in groups of individuals or companies coming together to overcome the difficulties of insurance market conditions. Perhaps some of the most effective and well-known mutuals are the marine P & I clubs established both onshore and offshore in the early part of the twentieth century and whose formula and structure still has relevance to the needs of today. Indeed, many of the mutuals established within the United Kingdom in very recent years have been based on the principles of P & I clubs and in many cases managed by the P & I club managers who have specialised for so long in maintaining integrity and profitability in group captive arrangements.

In more recent times group and association captives have been formed in large numbers by American corporations and individuals such as doctors who have found adequate insurance difficult to obtain during hard and difficult market conditions. Many of these groups were established in the Cayman Islands during the various crises which have affected particularly specialist liability areas such as professional indemnity and medical malpractice, and most have been highly successful in achieving the aims of their sponsors to provide continuity and cover and to maintain this at acceptable cost. Although there have been some casualties on the way these have been largely due to inadequate capitalisation, poor loss control or lack of commitment among the membership to the overriding objectives.

The major issues which need to be addressed when looking at the feasibility of establishing a group, association or mutual structure are the criteria for formation, the most effective structure and the major pitfalls which must be avoided if the arrangement is to have a sustainable future.

Criteria for formation

Under this heading there are six factors which are critical for the survival of any captive which moves from single parent ownership into a wider field. These are:

1. To ensure that the membership has a common interest and the same objective in wishing to establish a group structure.
2. To ensure that the membership has a willingness and an understanding that they will have to share risks and that their own position may be influenced by the management and loss control of others, including possibly their competitors.
3. To ensure that the structure does not involve conflicts of interest, particularly in relation to confidentiality, effects of competition between the parties and possible areas of cross-litigation.
4. An understanding that the development of a successful structure will require a long-term commitment from each of the participating bodies.
5. A requirement that each of the members has a quality approach to risk management and wishes to participate in the group for the correct reasons and understands that loss control will be the foundation on which success of any group captive will be built.
6. That there is an understanding of the different categories of members and that there needs to be a demonstration of equality.

In connection with the last point there are often difficulties where there is too much disparity between the size of individual members and where the very large member in terms of premium volume or turn-over may seek to dominate the others or resent decisions made by smaller companies which override the large members' contribution in premium and other terms. Another obvious but often more contentious area of inequality is the disparity between claims experience, and it is clearly much more difficult to put together a structure where the participants have a wide range of good experience and bad experience as there will be a tendency in these cases for the companies with poor experience to enter such a structure to resolve their own premium problems whereas, of course, those with good experience will resent providing subsidies to others and will expect the premium structure to be more precise in reflecting differing levels of losses and premium allocations.

Structure

The group captive in whatever form is essentially a mechanism for funding and will initially need to be capitalised. There are many ways of capitalising a group captive and the first stage is to determine the initial and long-term requirements. Many groups have opted for the mutual concept in order to establish the company at relatively low capital levels in its early years but are prepared to provide additional finance if the loss experience deteriorates and there is a financial need to provide for supplementary calls, or to enable the company to write greater levels of business becomes a necessary development.

While capital may, in many jurisdictions, need to be provided by cash injection, alternatives in the form of loans provided to the members or letters of credit, are often available and help to overcome some of the difficulties of establishing group captives where large numbers of members are required to contribute capital and where there is often reluctance to do so or where to many of the individual members the likely return is not as great as would be available to them if they retained the funds in their own operations.

One of the key decisions will be the structure, and in particular whether to establish the company as a mutual or a company limited by shares. There is in addition in the United States the option of also establishing a risk retention group or a purchasing group under the new laws introduced in many of the US states to provide facilities which can help groups of companies to overcome some of the difficulties of insurance market conditions and develop their own group structures on a legal basis which is easy to establish and has relatively little regulatory inhibitions.

There are various pros and cons as to whether or not to establish a mutual or a company limited by guarantee or a company limited by shares. The structure of the company should enable the participating corporations of individuals to achieve their joint objectives by providing cover with individual premium rating and an appropriate sharing of any losses. The long-term aim is to provide an economic method of protecting each and all of them, hopefully avoiding price volatility and the lack of continuity which characterises the conventional liability market particularly in specialist areas such as professional indemnity and medical malpractice. In many cases it is not the objective to build up substantial capital and surplus or to repatriate profits by the payment of dividends, and in this situation a mutual may well be the right structure. If, however, there is a desire to build up surplus or to return profits to individual members the company limited by shares might well be the more attractive vehicle. Whatever is decided the approach chosen should reflect the structure of the insurance system chosen.

In the case of mutuals, and particularly the professional indemnity P & I clubs established in recent years, there are a number of advantages which recommend this approach, particularly where the objectives are long-term and there is a desire and understanding among the participating companies to develop a relationship which will spread over many insurance cycles and not encourage individual members to move in and out of the group facility depending on annual insurance costs.

There are a number of reasons why mutuals might be an attraction, including the following:

1. They are particularly well regarded by insurance regulatory authorities, and provided they are managed by a credible organisation are likely to be treated with greater tolerance than a company limited by shares. This means that the mutual may well have greater flexibility in its operations including reserving, rating and investment policy.
2. This favoured regulatory position which often applies in the onshore and developed insurance markets as well as the offshore locations also means that there could well be a lower initial financial commitment from the participating members, as the typical mutual has a minimum guarantee fund which is lower than the capitalisation requirements for companies limited by shares.
3. The simplicity of the mutual concept and particularly the P & I club structure is advantageous in the event of any new members participating or existing members leaving as the computations of purchasing and selling shares and determining their price can be complex, time-consuming and contentious.

Other factors which attract people to mutuals and offer some of the essence of the most effective group approach are the tried and tested method of calculating advanced call income and individual allocation to each member which has successfully overcome the main disadvantage of group insurance arrangements, namely disagreement over pricing and suspicion that some members might be subsidising their competitors.

The call system is an attractive concept as it enables a proportion of the premium, which would normally be paid in full under a conventional insurance policy, to be held in each company with further payments only made if they are necessary as a result of unexpectedly heavy claims. Any successful mutual or group captive will have as its aim the objectives of greater stability of membership which many association and group captive facilities have found il difficult to sustain over a long period of time.

Another important issue in any structural arrangement is the criteria for allowing people to join the group captive. These include capitalisation and loss experience, and in some cases group captives require individual members to have a certain level of turn-over, shareholders funds and profitability in their parent companies as a minimum basis for participation.

Often linked to these joining criteria are penalties for members who decide that they wish to leave the structure and help to avoid companies participating in the structure when conventional insurance rates are high and leaving when they are cheap or being responsible for large claims on the group and then leaving immediately afterwards without making any contribution towards the losses that they have imposed on their fellow members.

One of the most important elements of any group captive is the way in which the underwriting and claims are controlled. It is important that there is a degree of independence in both of these areas, otherwise there will always be potential difficulties with members if they feel that other members are making decisions on their behalf. Many structures have established underwriting or claims committees to make decisions but these often fail or antagonise individual members and is probably much better to have an arrangement where a totally independent management company is responsible for both these areas and is in a position where they cannot be accused of any bias and in particular have no axe to grind if there is a necessity to penalise individual members by charging higher premiums or taking a particularly strong line on any claims that have been reported.

There are often benefits with group captives in the taxation area. The tax legislation which has been introduced in the United States and other parts of the world often separates the tax position for group and association captives from that which applies for pure or single owned captives. This is because of a general view that if an insurance company is owned by a large number of individual members there is actual risk transfer and real insurance and that as a consequence the premiums paid by individual members should be fully deductible, and in addition the application of a tax charge on the individual shareholder in the group captive will often not apply in the same way that it would if the individual member established his own insurance subsidiary.

Other areas that need to be addressed include the policy wording and agreement between members on what type of coverage is to be provided, the management of the company and whether this should be developed from within the structure or whether an independent management operation should handle the affairs of the company, and also the structure of the board and how the individual members will be represented on the board and how these appointments will be determined, whether they should be on a revolving basis where each owner of the company gets an opportunity to be appointed or whether the appointment is determined solely on a simple election where the intention is to appoint those considered to be most capable to carry out such a task.

Pitfalls

There are probably five main pitfalls that need to be overcome if the structure is to have any long-term success.

The first is that there must be long-term commitment from each of the members. No mutual or group captive will succeed if there is volatility in membership or if the commitment and objectives do not have a large amount of common ground.

Secondly, a structure will not succeed either initially or in the long term if individual members have continuing or very bad loss experience.

Thirdly, in some industry captives there is the potential for a massive exposure due to an accumulation of claims in a single event. Accumulation exposures need to be addressed and where these cannot be overcome appropriate clash reinsurance cover purchased to limit the exposure of the captive or the mutual to the minimum possible within the various financial constraints.

Fourthly, group operations are often expensive, and although theoretically one would expect expenses to drop as a wide range of companies join one facility, this is sometimes not the case due to the high levels of management costs charged by many of the group and association captive managers. Costs should be examined carefully and a specific arrangement developed with the managers to ensure that this is not going to cause difficulties with individual members as the group captive progresses.

Finally, a common pitfall is the financial position of the individual members. Many group captives have disintegrated because individual members have gone into bankruptcy, which has created major problems with the other members and damaged the integrity of the group captive itself. It is very important that every effort is made to ensure that the individual companies which join a group or mutual structure do have financial strength and a reasonable track record and future and that financial security of the individual shareholders and their captive, if the captives are participating in the group structure, are monitored on a regular basis and action taken if it is discovered that individual members might be running into financial trouble which could affect the group captive either financially or from an image standpoint.

Any structure will need to be governed by rules or by-laws and these will need to include the following:

1. Arrangements for entry and withdrawal from the structure.
2. The period of insurance.
3. Procedures for obtaining additional premiums or additional capital front members.
4. Principles on which the creation and the use of technical insurance reserves will be based.
5. Risk covered, conditions and exceptions.
6. General conditions applying in respect to claims handling, discretion given to managers for ex gratia payments, etc.
7. Arrangements agreed in relation to the cancellation of cover.
8. Criteria for investment management.
9. Arbitration or other procedures in the event of dispute between members.

Group, association, industry captives and mutuals can be an extremely effective way of handling risks, but they are much more difficult to develop and manage than the single parent captive where the decision-making is very much easier and there is no need to distort objectives because of the influence of other parties. It is of the essence that such structures are not put together as a panic measure to overcome difficult insurance market conditions but reflect a long-term commitment of the individual members to resolve common problems and to acknowledge that they will be entering into an arrangement which requires them to share in the risks of others and be prepared to compromise in the interest of the long-term future of the facility.

Making the Decision

The decision regarding whether to form a captive and which class of risk should be put into it needs to be related to the original objectives of the company. These objectives and the decision-making process can be summarised by the following questions and comments:

1. What are the financial benefits to the company, taking account of the savings, both short- and long-term, in insurance premium, and what impact does the improved cash flow and investment income have on these financial benefits? These benefits need to be compared with the existing insurance market position and how that market is likely to develop in the future.
2. What impact will the captive have on loss control motivation in the company, and what implication does this have for companies with an international structure?
3. Will the captive improve the protection from insurance coverage available to the company?
4. Does the captive improve the company's overall risk-financing strategy? In this context account should be taken of any problems of local implementation throughout the world, opportunities to optimise the funding mechanism, taxation and the implementation of an overall risk retention programme.

Positive answers to these questions when related to original objectives will probably point the company in the direction of establishing a captive insurance company. If they have not already done so during the feasibility study stage, they will need to carry out survey work, obtain reinsurance quotations and develop mathematical models to confirm that the primary results of the study are correct.

Major factors in determining that the strategic feasibility decision is justified will include the following:

1. The detailed risk survey work will reveal the standard of loss control that exists through the company. It will indicate what costs are involved if loss prevention needs to be improved and how long it will take for such improvements to take place. This timing may have an effect on the captive establishment or, in

individual cases, on the decision as to whether all locations should be included or whether there should be some segmentation, so that only those with good loss prevention are included at the initial stage. The surveys will also define the consequential loss exposure of the company and help to optimise the quotations from the reinsurance market.

2. Reinsurance quotations related to various levels of retention by the captive and the available premium for the captive's exposure will enable the final decisions on the basis for the captive's programme to be made.

3. Mathematical models, dummy accounts and cash flow projections related to different loss positions will demonstrate the viability of the captive both on an historical claims basis and also in a worst possible situation should loss experience deteriorate or major catastrophic losses occur. This will enable the company to realise the worst financial implications of the decision to form a captive and ensure that the capitalisation of the captive is at the correct level. It may even lead the company to amend the reinsurance basis to ensure that a more prudent basis for the captive is developed.

These constitute the major financial aspects of the captive decision. Other factors that will need to be considered in the feasibility study include the following:

1. What is the most suitable location of the captive, taking into account the most important factors such as convenience, government attitude and taxation?

2. What is the cost of managing the captive and how should it be managed? Should the company manage the captive itself or use outside services?

3. If the captive requires outside services in the form of engineering or claims facilities, how much are these going to cost and what capability is available both in the country of origin and in other countries of the world in which the parent operates?

4. What will the attitude of the insurance market be to the company's decision to form a captive and how can this be best managed? It is particularly important in this connection to ensure that fronting facilities will be available and that these have been organised before the market generally is aware of the company's decision.

5. What are the taxation implications of the decision in relation to both the captive location that is being considered and the attitude of the country's domestic revenue authorities?

6. Will the fronting companies require parental guarantees or letters of credit, are these acceptable to the company's management and what form will they take?

7. Are there any international problems in the form of insurance legislative difficulties, exchange control or political problems that need to be taken into account? The company may also need to consider the attitude of its local management, whether all countries can be included in the captive and what the problems are in relation to implementation and imposition of a centralised risk-financing strategy.

8. What political considerations need to be taken into account both domestically and elsewhere in the world if a multinational is involved? In some cases, delicate relationships with foreign governments may mean that insurance premiums should be kept in the country rather than ceded away from that country to an offshore location.

9. In relation to the risks that the captive will be retaining and its overall exposure, what are the needs for capitalisation and what are the attitudes of the company to solvency margin? In the first year or two of operation it would probably be prudent to maintain a solvency margin of 50 per cent even though it would be acceptable under most insurance legislation to have a solvency margin of 20 per cent or lower.

10. Are there any exchange control restrictions that need to be taken into account in relation to capitalising the captive both from the company's domicile and the location which is being chosen?

11. Are there any relationships with insurance companies in the form of trust deeds or with government which would have an impact on the amount of business that the captive could retain or the decision as to whether the captive should be located domestically or offshore?

In addition to these factors a feasibility study should include a timetable which recognises potential delays in formation of a captive including market agreements with the insurance industry, expiry dates of existing policies and long-term agreements. Also, if there is going to be a need to improve loss control activity, how long is this likely to take and what impact is the delay going to have on the captive's premium volume?

If the company anticipates difficulties with the insurance market, a plan should exist on the strategy to handle this problem, and the study should also consider the implications for the company if the captive strategy goes wrong and it is necessary to close it down and revert to the conventional market.

Finally, if the company regards the establishment of a captive as a profit centre activity, there should be a rough plan for future development so that as the company develops the overall objectives for such diversification are known and the captive strategy is related to these.

The typical feasibility study will include a whole range of charts showing the effect of reinsurance costs, management costs, fronting fees and set-up costs on the captive's performance. A simple example of how a captive might be developed in its first year of operation is shown in Table 2.9. This example demonstrates a best and worst position without investment income being quantified. It also shows the effect on the capitalisation and solvency margin and the need for prudence in the first year of operation. A mathematical model using this approach would develop the concept over a period of, say, five years and introduce variable loss situations between the best and the worst positions, taking into account in some detail the investment income that would accrue over the period.

Table 2.9 Example of the development of a captive in its first year of operation

(a) Premium to fronting insurer	£1,000,000
(b) Insurer's retention 10%	100,000
(c) Premium to captive	900,000
Fronting fees 10%	90,000
	810,000
Reinsurance cost net of commission	500,000
	310,000
Management fees	30,000
	£280,000

Loss exposure £100,000 per loss
              £300,000 stop loss
Year 1
Best position surplus £280,000 plus investment income.
Worst position deficit £20,000 plus loss of investment income on capital used to pay claims.
Capital at 50% solvency would be £155,000, which would reduce to £135,000.

Feasibility studies usually include spreadsheets showing the development of the captive over a five year period taking into account variations in loss experience, reinsurance costs and the development of investment income. Tables 2.10 and 2.11 show profit and loss accounts and balance sheets for a captive over a five year period. The claims experience in the first example includes a claim which reaches the level of the reinsurance protection and in the second there is good loss experience and as a result the captive's performance is dramatically improved.

Summary

The main objective of the feasibility study is to calculate the trade-off between establishing a captive insurance company and remaining in the direct insurance market on the existing or an improved basis. The captive's contribution to this objective will be achieved primarily by reducing costs, as a result of gaining access to the reinsurance market or using the captive as a mechanism to retain much more risk within the company's own resources. The two components of these factors will be the improvement in cost that the captive offers, in relation to both past experience and expected future trends, and the company's capability to maintain its loss record at current or improved levels. The two factors go hand in hand and, as a combination, there is no doubt that the captive can improve significantly on the cost that the insurance industry is likely to require from a major company to protect its exposures.

Table 2.10 Examples of financial projections used in feasibility studies – Example 1

(a) CRITERIA		
Proposed capitalisation	:	100,000
Rate of local tax	:	0%
Gross premium income	:	450,000
Reinsurance	:	55%
Inflation factors for:	:	
gross premium	:	17%
reinsurance premium	:	17%
claims	:	see below
expenses	:	10%
Investment income rate	:	10%
Formation costs (year one only)	:	0
Management costs	:	4,000
Brokerage	:	15.0%
Fronting insurer's retention	:	10.0%
Fronting fee	:	7.5%
	:	
	:	
Statutory reserve	:	0%
Dividend	:	0%
Payment delay factor:	:	
premium	:	3 months
reinsurance premiums	:	3 months
claims	:	6 months
expenses	:	Quarterly
Claims		
year 1	:	50,000
year 2	:	100,000
year 3	:	80,000
year 4	:	200,000
year 5	:	75,000
Total	:	505,000

Table 2.10 (cont'd)

(b) REVENUE ACCOUNT

	1992/3	1993/4	1994/5	1995/6	1996/7
Gross fire and cons. loss premiums	450,000	526,500	616,005	720,726	843,249
Brokerage	67,500	78,975	92,401	108,109	126,487
Retention by fronting insurer	38,250	44,752	52,360	61,262	71,676
Fronting fee on 90%	25,819	30,208	35,343	41,352	48,381
Premium to captive	318,431	372,565	435,901	510,004	596,704
Reinsurance	175,137	204,911	239,745	280,502	328,187
Net premium to captive	143,294	167,654	196,155	229,502	268,517
Claims within £100,000 each loss retention and £400,000 stop loss	(50,000)	(100,000)	(80,000)	(200,000)	(75,000)
Management costs	(4,000)	(4,400)	(4,840)	(5,324)	(5,856)
Underwriting profit/loss	89,294	63,254	111,315	24,178	187,661

(c) PROFIT AND LOSS ACCOUNT

	1992/3	1993/4	1994/5	1995/6	1996/7
Transfer from/(to) insurance account	89,294	63,254	111,315	24,178	187,661
Investment income	18,047	28,088	40,338	51,980	68,745
Profit/(loss) before taxation	107,341	91,342	151,653	76,158	256,406
Taxation	0	0	0	0	0
Profit/(loss) after taxation	107,341	91,342	151,653	76,158	256,406
Statutory reserve	0	0	0	0	0
Profit	107,341	91,342	151,653	76,158	256,406
Dividends paid and proposed	0	0	0	0	0
Retained profit/(loss)	107,341	91,342	151,653	76,158	256,406

BALANCE SHEET

	1992/3	1993/4	1994/5	1995/6	1996/7
ASSETS					
Cash/Investments	207,341	298,683	450,337	526,494	782,900
LIABILITIES					
Capital	100,000	100,000	100,000	100,000	100,000
Claims reserves	0	0	0	0	0
Statutory reserves	0	0	0	0	0
Retained earnings	107,341	198,683	350,337	426,494	682,900
	207,341	298,683	450,337	526,494	782,900

Table 2.11 Examples of financial projections used in feasibility studies – Example 2

(a) CRITERIA

Proposed capitalisation	:	100,000
Rate of local tax	:	0%
Gross premium income	:	450,000
Reinsurance	:	55%
Inflation factors for:	:	
gross premium	:	17%
reinsurance premium	:	17%
claims	:	see below
expenses	:	10%
Investment income rate	:	10%
Formation costs (year one only)	:	0
Management costs	:	4,000
Brokerage	:	15.0%
Fronting insurer's retention	:	10.0%
Fronting fee	:	7.5%
	:	
	:	
Statutory reserve	:	0%
Dividend	:	0%
Payment delay factor:	:	
premium	:	3 months
reinsurance premiums	:	3 months
claims	:	6 months
expenses	:	Quarterly
Claims		
year 1	:	200,000
year 2	:	50,000
year 3	:	150,000
year 4	:	50,000
year 5	:	55,000
Total	:	505,000

(b) REVENUE ACCOUNT

	1992/3	1993/4	1994/5	1995/6	1996/7
Gross fire and cons. loss premiums	450,000	526,500	616,005	720,726	843,249
Brokerage	67,500	78,975	92,401	108,109	126,487
Retention by fronting insurer	38,250	44,752	52,360	61,262	71,676
Fronting fee on 90%	25,819	30,208	35,343	41,352	48,381
Premium to captive	318,431	372,565	435,901	510,004	596,704
Reinsurance	175,137	204,911	239,745	280,502	328,187
Net premium to captive	143,294	167,654	196,155	229,502	268,517
Claims within £100,000 each loss retention and £400,000 stop loss	(200,000)	(50,000)	(150,000)	(50,000)	(55,000)
Management costs	(4,000)	(4,400)	(4,840)	(5,324)	(5,856)
Underwriting profit/loss	(60,706)	113,254	41,315	174,178	207,661

Table 2.11 (cont'd)

(c) PROFIT AND LOSS ACCOUNT

	1992/3	1993/4	1994/5	1995/6	1996/7
Transfer from/(to) insurance account	−60,706	113,254	41,315	174,178	207,661
Investment income	10,547	14,838	24,763	38,848	62,800
Profit/(loss) before taxation	−50,159	128,092	66,078	213,025	270,460
Taxation	0	0	0	0	0
Profit/(loss) after taxation	−50,159	128,092	66,078	213,025	270,460
Statutory reserve	0	0	0	0	0
Profit	−50,159	128,092	66,078	213,025	270,460
Dividends paid and proposed	0	0	0	0	0
Retained profit/(loss)	−50,159	128,092	66,078	213,025	270,460

BALANCE SHEET

	1992/3	1993/4	1994/5	1995/6	1996/7
ASSETS					
Cash/Investments	49,841	177,933	244,012	457,037	727,497
LIABILITIES					
Capital	100,000	100,000	100,000	100,000	100,000
Claims reserves	0	0	0	0	0
Statutory reserves	0	0	0	0	0
Retained earnings	−50,159	77,933	144,012	357,037	627,497
	49,841	177,933	244,012	457,037	727,497

ANNEX 2.1 : CASE STUDY

PROGRAMME FEATURES AND BENEFITS

- Net underwriting profit generated under the programme would be returned to the participant
- The investment income earned on funds held in an Insurance Profit Centre programme is also returned
- Both the underwriting profit and investment income should accumulate tax-deferred until received by the participant
- The loss experience of each individual Insurance Profit Centre programme determines its underwriting profit
- Contractual relationships are established between the parties, resulting in a level of security which may not be found in other approaches
- Proven insurance and reinsurance expertise is behind the programme
- Programme design is flexible and easily implemented

Each Insurance Profit Centre participant receives a quarterly policy underwriting summary, including an income statement and balance sheet, documenting their programme. Mutual Indemnity Ltd publishes an independently audited annual report summarising their results of operation as well.

Since its introduction in 1980, the Insurance Profit Centre has become the industry's leader, with programmes being developed for over 200 clients.

How the Insurance Profit Centre works

1. The purchase of insurance

An insured wishing to structure an Insurance Profit Centre programme would typically obtain a policy of insurance from a selected insurance carrier. The insurance carrier would fix the premium, issue the policy, handle all claims and provide other desired administrative services.

2. The ceding of funds to Mutual Indemnity Ltd

Mutual Indemnity Ltd would enter into a reinsurance agreement with the insurance carrier and reinsure a portion of the premium which represents the insured's retention, as illustrated below. All funds ceded to Mutual Indemnity Ltd and held under the reinsurance agreement would be secured with a form of collateral acceptable to the policy-issuing carrier.

3. Share ownership in Mutual Indemnity Ltd

Upon entering the Insurance Profit Centre programme, the insured (or its designate) would normally be required to purchase non-voting redeemable preferred shares of stock in Mutual Indemnity Ltd. They are purchased only once and may be paid for with cash or a letter of credit. The net investment income earned on all such funds and amounts subscribed would be returned as a dividend to the designated preferred shareholder. Funds held are invested with a view towards maximising investment returns to preferred shareholders while maintaining the required liquidity and protection of principal. The underwriting profit generated under the programme would be returned based upon the policy form chosen by the insured, i.e. from the insurance carrier under a dividend or retrospectively-rated policy form, or as a preferred share dividend from Mutual Indemnity Ltd under a guaranteed cost policy form.

4. Fee structure

Fees charged will depend on the specific Insurance Profit Centre programme ultimately adopted and will be formulated and agreed upon before the programme is implemented.

Mutual Indemnity Ltd utilises three contractual agreements when structuring an Insurance Profit Centre programme:

The insurance policy
Issued directly to the insured by a selected insurance carrier.

The reinsurance agreement
Between the policy-issuing carrier and Mutual Indemnity Ltd transferring funds (the insured's retention) to the Insurance Profit Centre.

The shareholder agreement
Between Mutual Indemnity Ltd and the insured (or its designate) contractually undertaking the payment of the underwriting profit and net investment income from the insured's insurance policy.

Note: It is intended that the Insurance Profit Centre programme would be structured in such a way as to enable the underwriting profit and investment income to accumulate on a tax-deferred basis until returned to the preferred shareholder. However, potential participants will, of course, need to consider this area in detail in conjunction with their own professional advisers in the context of individual programmes to be entered into Potential participants should also be aware fiscal rules or their interpretation may change.

The value of the preference shares acquired in Mutual Indemnity Ltd is directly related to the favourable or unfavourable loss experience of the individual participant and the investment programme directed by Mutual

Indemnity Ltd. The value of such shares may, therefore, increase or decrease and the investors may receive either more or less than the amount originally invested.

The Shareholder Agreement negotiated between the investor and Mutual Indemnity Ltd contractually binds the Company to redeem the preferred shares on a specified redemption date at a price agreed upon by the parties bound by the Shareholders Agreement. However, there is no recognised market for the shares and, accordingly, it may be difficult for a participant to sell the shares should it wish to do so.

Mutual Indemnity Ltd will provide each preference share participant with a quarterly unaudited financial statement, including a balance sheet, income statement and underwriting summary. Annually, an audited statement of Mutual Indemnity Ltd will be provided to each investor. However, as there is no recognised market for the shares in Mutual Indemnity Ltd, it may be difficult for an investor to obtain information about their value, or to the extent of the risks to which they are exposed, from independent sources. The shares in Mutual Indemnity Ltd will be acquired as part of the Insurance Profit Centre programme and, accordingly, will not be suitable as a medium- or short-term investment.

CHAPTER 3

REINSURANCE, FRONTING AND UNDERWRITING OF CAPTIVE INSURANCE COMPANIES

The Captive Interface with the Reinsurance Market

Captives can be structured in a number of ways but at some stage they need to deal with the reinsurance market in order to protect their exposure and allow greater capacity to be provided to their owners. Typically the captive operates either as a direct or a reinsurance company as shown in figure 3.1.

Companies considering the establishment of captive insurance companies recognise that one of the major advantages of this is access to the reinsurance market. Unlike in the direct insurance market, reinsurers, who in many senses can be regarded as the wholesale market of the insurance industry, are able to operate on comparatively low expense ratios. For this reason the captive can obtain better value for money in return for the premium it pays than the company buying a policy direct from the insurance market. The low expense ratio of the reinsurer reflects the fact that reinsurers do not deal directly with the public, provide very few services compared with direct insurers and often operate on a net basis so far as commissions are concerned.

This chapter is concerned with the reinsurance element of captive structures but it should never be forgotten that the original basis on which the captive operates is a key consideration in how the reinsurance arrangements are put in place and particularly how the documentation is written, issued and will operate.

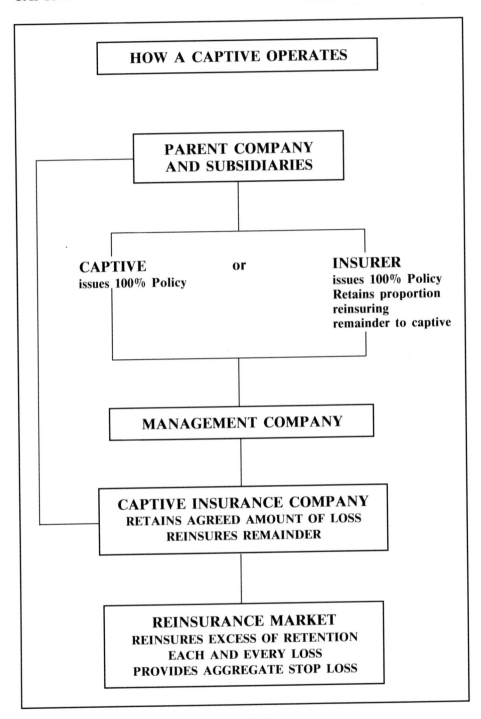

Figure 3.1

The flow of risk where the captive issues cover to its parent on a direct basis is as follows: —

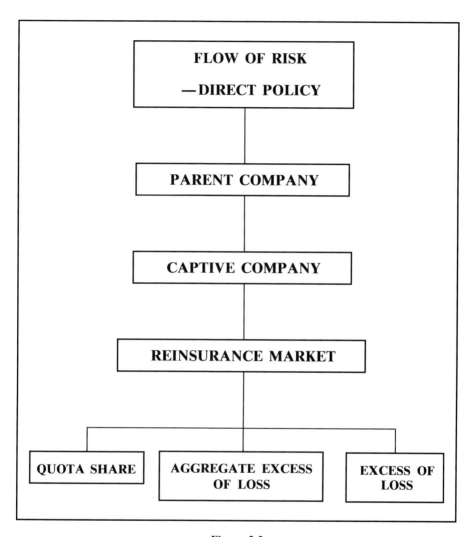

Figure 3.2

The reinsurance market is highly professional since reinsurers deal only with insurance companies or reinsurance brokers. It therefore requires skill and knowledge to do business with them. In addition, the market is more sophisticated than the direct market because of the flexibility that reinsurers offer the buyer, there being a whole variety of alternative methods of protecting his account.

Where the captive is operating as a reinsurer of an unrelated insurer issuing polices to the parent, the flow of risk is as follows:

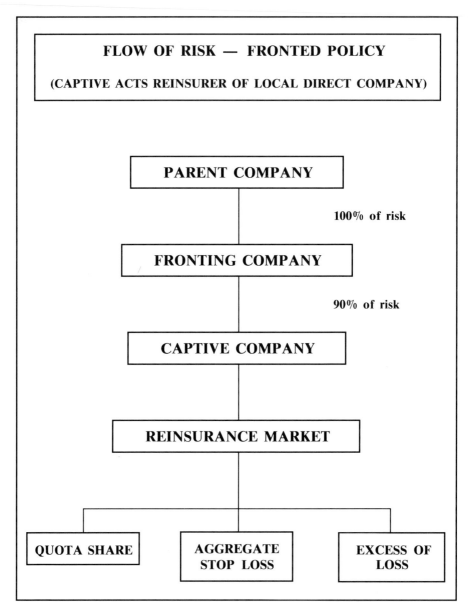

Figure 3.3

The following are some of the methods available from reinsurers:

1. Quota share reinsurance

Quota share is a form of treaty reinsurance where the reinsurer accepts a share of the overall risk on a proportionate basis. Table 3.1 and Figure 3.4 show how quota share reinsurance operates, including the

Table 3.1 Quota share reinsurance

Cedant's retention £50,000
100% gross capacity required £500,000
90% quota share treaty would operate as follows:

Premium

100% OGEPI	£1,000,000
10% retention	£100,000
	£900,000
30% ceding commission	£270,00
Net income to reinsurer	£630,000

(being 63% of OGEPI)

Claims

Loss	Cedant's share	Reinsurer's share	
£ 10,000	£ 1,000	£ 9,000	being 90% of
£ 50,000	£ 5,000	£ 45,000	all losses
£400,000	£40,000	£360,000	

(OGEPI: original gross estimated premium income)

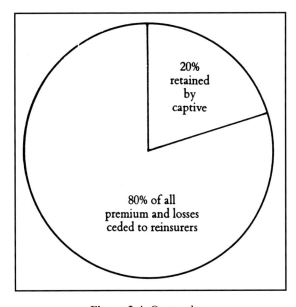

Figure 3.4 Quota share

effect of claims on the various reinsurance arrangements made. The premium paid for this transaction is usually discounted to the insurer offering the reinsurance, by allowing a commission or overrider which recognises the front-end costs of the primary insurer.

2. Surplus or excess line reinsurance

As an alternative to a quota share reinsurance, surplus reinsurance enables the insurer to keep within his own operations a selected amount of each risk, and the reinsurer automatically accepts a multiple of the risk up to an agreed level. For example, if the surplus treaty is four lines, the reinsurer would accept four times the retention by the insurer. In this way the insurer can retain up to the level that he desires, taking account of the quality of the risk, and then automatically receive reinsurance protection up to a multiple of that level. Surplus reinsurance has an advantage over quota share in that, because of this ability to select, the insurer can retain within his own book of business the more attractive business. With quota share reinsurance he has automatically to cede a percentage of each risk regardless of its quality. Table 3.2 shows the effect of a typical surplus line reinsurance programme.

Table 3.2 Surplus line reinsurance

Cedant's retention £250,000
100% gross capacity required £2.75m
Balance of £250,000 placed facultatively
Therefore ten-line treaty would operate as follows:

Gross Capacity Required	£2,750,000	
Captive retention	£250,000	
Being 10 lines of £250,000	£2,500,000	

Original Sum Insurance	Captive's Retention	Reinsurers Share	Percentage
£250,000	£250,000	Nil	Nil
£500,000	£250,000	£250,000	50.0%
£1,000,000	£250,000	£750,000	75.0%
£2,750,000	£250,000	£2,500,000	90.9%
£3,000,000	£250,000	£2,500,000	83.3%

Claims

Claims are settled on the percentage basis the captive's retention bears to the reinsurance share

> i.e. Claims for 50,000 on sum insured of £1,000,000
> Captive pays 25% = £12,500
> Reinsurer pays 75% = £37,500
> £50,000

3. *Excess loss reinsurance*

Both quota share and surplus reinsurance involve a certain amount of complexity from an administrative point of view and largely as a result of this, a new type of reinsurance called excess loss reinsurance was introduced. With excess loss reinsurance the reinsurer agrees to accept all claims costs, from a single event, above an agreed amount and up to an agreed limit. As an example, an excess loss reinsurance may provide protection for £50,000 for each and every loss in excess of £10,000 each and every loss, the £10,000 being retained by the primary insurer.

Premiums for excess loss reinsurance are usually calculated as a percentage of the original net premium and adjustable so that complicated calculations are not required as they are often with surplus reinsurance.

Excess loss treaties can be split into working and non-working structures. The working treaty is designed to deal with claims that the insurer and reinsurer expect to occur with the premiums fixed to this expected level. Non-working treaties are established to protect the insurer from catastrophic exposure, where a potential loss is not expected or where such a claim would occur only on a very irregular basis. Table 3.3 and Figure 3.5 explain the workings of an excess of loss reinsurance programme showing the effect of the treaty arrangement on various loss levels.

4. *Stop loss reinsurance*

Stop loss reinsurance enables an insurer to protect itself above a predetermined limit if the loss history is far worse than originally expected and it is particularly relevant to captive insurers. Whereas with excess loss reinsurance the insurer could be involved in an accumulation of individual loss payments on an each and every loss basis, the stop loss reinsurance protects the insurer if this multiple of individual losses exceeds a particular figure. Stop loss reinsurance is essentially protecting the insurer against a frequency problem in relation to claims in respect of his retained account. There are a number of ways of organising stop loss reinsurance with the protection being related either to the original net premium or to an agreed loss level. As an example, an insurer may have an excess of loss treaty where the reinsurer pays claims on an each loss basis above £50,000 and supports this by a stop loss reinsurance which will come into existence if the total of each loss, under the £50,000, retained by the insurer exceeds £200,000. Tables 3.4, 3.5, and 3.6 show the method of working of three different types of stop loss reinsurance including those based on a premium concept, a fixed annual aggregate limit and the most attractive form of stop loss protection for captives which has no upper limit to it.

97

Table 3.3 Excess of loss insurance

Cedant's retention £100.000
100% gross capacity required £1m
Excess loss treaty £900,000 X/S of £100,000 would operate as follows:

Loss	Cedant's share	Reinsurer's share
£ 50,000	£ 50,000	nil
£ 100,000	£100,000	nil
£ 400,000	£100,000	£300,000
£ 900,000	£100,000	£800,000
£1,200,000	£300,000	£900,000

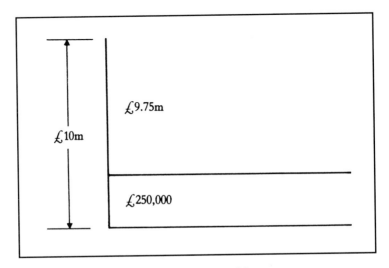

Figure 3.5 Excess of loss

STOP LOSS PROTECTION EXAMPLES

Table 3.4 Stop loss reinsurance: % of premium basis

Cedant's retention 70%
Protection required 90% of aggregate losses up to 110% of EPI

Premium	Loss ratio	Cedant's share	Reinsurer's share
£4m	80%	£2,800,000 +£ 40,000 ———— £2,840,000	£360,000 (being 90% of 10% of £4m)

This protection can also be expressed as
90% of 40% of GPI (max. £1.44m)
in X/S of
70% of EPI (min. £2.8m)

EPI: estimated premium income; GPI: gross premium income)

Table 3.5 Stop loss reinsurance: aggregate excess of loss basis

---

Cedant's retention £100.000 each and every claim
Limit: £1m each claim and in the aggregate per annum
in X/S of
£250,000 each claim and in the aggregate per annum
Therefore captive stands $2\frac{1}{2}$ total losses and thereafter is protected up to the next
10 total before becoming exposed again.

Table 3.6 Stop loss reinsurance: unlimited stop loss

Cedant's retention £100,000 each and every claim
Limit: £100,000 each and every claim
in X/S of
£300,000 each claim and in all
Therefore captive's maximum exposure never exceeds 3 total losses.

The cost of stop loss reinsurance will clearly depend on the loss frequency in the past and it will usually be expensive in relation to the captive's retained premium. However, it does give the captive insurer the opportunity to protect himself, sometimes on a fail-safe basis, in the early years of development. As the account of the captive grows the stop loss protection can be pushed up to much higher levels and eventually done away with as the account becomes profitable and adequate reserves develop.

For normal direct insurance companies the reinsurance programme will include a whole range of different types of reinsurance related to different needs and classes. For the captive insurer there will also be a variation, but in general terms excess loss reinsurance with some form of stop loss reinsurance for new captives will be the normal approach.

For the captive dealing with the reinsurance market it should be remembered that particular technical skills are required in order to retain the best terms and to ensure that the protection developed for the captive is adequate from the points of view of both continuity and security. Although most companies use a reinsurance broker in this context, it is important that the buyer understands the way in which the reinsurance market works and is involved in detail in the submission to the reinsurance market when negotiations take place. It is extremely important that the submission is accurate, particularly in relation to loss history, loss exposure and policy coverage, since reinsurers are likely to be less sympathetic than direct insurers to the payment of *ex gratia* claims.

The broker can assist with the security aspects of the reinsurance placing because he has knowledge of the market and makes regular examinations of insurer solvency. When selecting the broker the company should be looking for a firm which has this market knowledge and understanding, has experience of placing reinsurance plans for captives and has an account which enables it to use 'muscle' in the market.

A reinsurance presentation for a property risk should include the following data:

1. Loss history, indicating variations in coverage particularly in relation to deductibles applicable over the period.
2. A full list of the locations to be insured and their up-to-date values, split between buildings and contents.
3. Risk survey reports or a summary showing the risk situation and the estimated maximum loss both on an individual basis for property damage and consequential loss and on a combined basis to demonstrate the maximum exposure.
4. Details of the business of the company, its countries of operation and its approach to risk management and loss control.
5. Full details of the primary policies.
6. Details of the basis on which the reinsurance is to be placed, showing the primary or fronting insurer's retention, the amount to be retained by the captive and the amount to be ceded to the reinsurer, including a statement of any upper limits required in each case.

Although reinsurance tactics are dealt with a little later in this chapter, it is important to consider the factors that will need to be considered when planning a captive reinsurance programme. In summary these should include the following points:

- Cost
  - Level
  - Stability

- Capacity
  - Availability
  - Extent of Cover
  - Stability

- Security
  - Continuity
  - Ability to pay quickly

◆ Captive Risk Profile
  • Very high exposure
  • Relatively low spread of risk

◆ Tactics
  • Spread of risk
  • Control loss experience
  • Protect reinsurers
  • Recognise the sophistication
  • Understand reinsurers

◆ Payments
  • In to the captive
  • Out from the captive

◆ Security
  • Role of broker
  • Role of the fronting insurer

◆ Spread of Reinsurer
  • Gross lines
  • Net lines
  • Retrocessional arrangements

◆ Reinsurance Agreements and Clauses
  • Simultaneous payment clause
  • Cut through clause
  • Follow the fortunes clause
  • "Pay as Paid" clause
  • Claims control clause

There is no doubt that a professional and helpful submission will improve the possibility of obtaining good terms from the reinsurance market and it is well worth spending time on the preparation. The submission can also act as a record of information given to the reinsurers during the course of negotiations.

One other important fact in relation to reinsurance placings is to recognise that the market can be extremely volatile because of the experience rating approach that is taken in the reinsurance market. For the captive, continuity of cover is all important factor and the original submission and the development of good relationships with the reinsurer will be a great help in this connection. The volatility is two-sided and a good relationship and good underwriting results for the reinsurer will mean that reductions in reinsurance costs can be realised on an annual basis until an optimum level is reached.

For the company embarking on a captive for the first time the reinsurance market will be less inclined to offer low rates than it would for a company which has an established record. It is important that the new captive recognises this but, in deciding on where its reinsurance should be placed, it should aim to improve its reinsurance expenditure over a period of years, maintaining relationships and ensuring that the best reinsurance markets are used.

The captive insurance company needs reinsurance to enable it to limit the risks that it is retaining within its operations to predetermined levels and to ensure that the premium available to it to deal with these risk levels is acceptable. It is usually the case that a combination of reinsurance solutions integrated into a fairly sophisticated programme will prove to be the best arrangement. It is recommended that various alternatives are considered when the original programme is being planned.

Reinsurance tactics

Most captives underwriting their own risks have an asymmetric portfolio compared with an ordinary direct insurer. Due to this tendency towards a very high overall exposure and a comparatively low spread of risk, the reinsurance aim is to reduce the spread of risk, in respect of both an individual exposure and an annual aggregate exposure, to an acceptable level in relation to the captive's retention and to remove to the reinsurance market as much of the risk as it can in relation to the premium that it can keep. The reinsurance plan needs to reflect and understand this aim; but there are other factors which need to be taken into account in both placing the reinsurance and ensuring the continuity of relationship with the reinsurance market.

In more specific terms the specific exposure to the captive needs to be examined to take account of the following three possibilities: —

- the exposure of the captive to any one risk
- the exposure of the captive to any one occurrence
- the exposure of the captive in the aggregate during a financial year

and the exposure limit, that is finally determined, needs to be related to the capital and shareholders funds of the captive insurer.

Given that most captives will write a range of risks it will usually be necessary to examine the reinsurance programmes and quotations obtained for each class of business and consider whether it is necessary to obtain reinsurance protection in excess of any one risk and/or any occurrence and also the aggregate exposure developed in relation to the anticipated net retained premium income of the captive. Once the net retained amounts per class of business have been determined, it will then be possible to examine how a single event might affect more than one class of insurance and if there is the possibility of an accumulation of losses arising from such a single event, consideration should be given to purchasing 'clash' reinsurance cover.

One of the important tactics that should be employed in placing reinsurance is to reduce the captive's dependence on any single re-insurer or any particular part of the reinsurance market. In the same way as it makes sense for the captive to spread its own risk as far as possible, it also makes sense for it to spread its risk in relation to the reinsurers.

Loss control will be crucial if the reinsurance price in the future is to be limited or improved compared with the original premium levels. Apart from limiting the risks to the captive itself in respect of its retained losses, it is important that the captive recognises the need to protect the reinsurers so that the company's image with the market is good and progressive reductions in premiums can be realised. In some cases, where a risk in the captive is of an undesirable nature, it may make sense to separate out the reinsurance placing for this particular risk by the use of facultative reinsurance rather than risking the overall reinsurance placing of the captive.

When placing the reinsurance it is necessary to understand the way in which reinsurers think and operate and to try to fit the captive's particular reinsurance programme to a reinsurer who has similar needs and experience, so that the best form of business relationship can be developed. This approach will help to ensure the continuity of the relationship, which is most important in this type of insurance venture.

In line with the market stability tactic, the security of the re-insurance company used is clearly of crucial importance. With many classes of risk, and liability in particular, the claims payment required from the reinsurer will not be made for many years ahead and it is essential, so far as the captive is concerned, that the markets used are secure and solvent and that they will be in existence to pay the claims when the time comes for settlement to be made.

Tables 3.7 and 3.8 show two examples of simple reinsurance plans for captives. In Table 3.7 the use of quota share insurance on a captive programme with a very wide spread of risk and a low overall estimated maximum loss is demonstrated. The protection includes a

Table 3.7 Example of a captive insurance plan (A)

	£
140 units. Estimated maximum loss (EML) £6m.	
Insured by captive.	Premium £900,000
Cede to reinsurer 20% quota share	180,000
Less 12.5% commission	22,500
	157,500
Captive retains £4.8m exposure	742,500
protected by:	
1st layer £800,000 X/S of £200,000	322,000
2nd layer £4m X/S of £1m	80,000
Stop loss £1m X/S of £1m	27,000
	429,000
Available premium	313,500
to fund:	
£200,000 per loss up to £1m in aggregate	
Losses over £2m in aggregate per annum	

Table 3.8 Example of a captive insurance plan (B)

	£
20 factories. Estimated maximum loss (EML) £35m.	
Fully insured by ABC Insurance.	Premium £1,200,000
90% reinsurance to captive	1,080,000
Less 7.5% fronting fee	81,000
	999,000
Therefore exposure to captive £31.5m	
1st layer £4.75m X/S of £250,000	442,000
2nd layer £26.5m X/S of £5m	161,000
Stop loss X/S of 600,000	62,000
	665,000
Available premium	334,000
to fund:	
£250,000 per loss up to £600,000 in aggregate	
Single loss over £31.5m if EML is incorrect	

combination of quota share, excess loss and stop loss and enables the captive to have available a premium of 50 per cent in excess of an individual loss exposure but with a fairly large exposure in event of an accumulation in a single year.

Table 3.8 is an example of a fairly typical start-up reinsurance programme for a captive underwriting property risk, using a fronting insurer to retain the first 10 per cent of the programme. There is a combination in this example of excess loss and stop loss reinsurance and a fairly attractive trade-off between the available premium and the loss retention of the captive.

Although in these examples it could be argued that there is a fair amount of risk taking, it should be remembered that both are on the basis of the first year of operation. If they are projected to cover the first three years and the loss history is good, the accumulation of reserves will transform the position so far as the captive's retention and available premium position are concerned. It should also reduce the cost of the reinsurance programme.

Table 3.9 gives an example of a captive reinsurance programme for liability insurance where the primary company and the reinsurance company are the same. The important feature of this example is that a substantial income related to the programme will involve investment income earned on the premiums pending final claims settlement, a feature of liability insurance described in the previous chapter.

The use of the primary insurer also to provide reinsurance protection is a valuable concept as it concentrates the decisions over reinsurance security, avoiding for the captive any difficulties if reinsurance collection is difficult in the long term and also giving control to the primary company, which as an exposed primary insurer will obviously be concerned about the reinsurance facilities of the captive, on which it will need to rely when the time comes for claims to be paid.

Table 3.9 Example of a captive reinsurance programme for liability insurance

	$20m limit
Premium to fronting insurer	$500,000
Fronting fee 10%	$50,000
Taxes, etc.	25,000
Brokerage	50,000
ONP to captive	$375,000
Reinsurance	
$19.9m X/S of $100,000 e.&e.1.	200,000
and $300,000 aggregate	£175,000

(e.&e.1: each and every loss)

In his book *Reinsurance in Practice* R. J. Kiln summarised as follows the four main types of reinsurance discussed in this chapter in a way that clearly explains their role:

1. *Quota share* — fixed proportion of all risks.
2. *Surplus treaty* — automatic protection for all risks over a certain size.
3. *Excess of loss* — protects against unfortunate disaster.
4. *Stop loss* — protects against unfortunate aggregation of losses during a certain period of time.

Indication of Viability

The cost and effectiveness of the reinsurance programme will drive the decision as to whether or not a captive will be an effective contributor to the risk financing strategy of its owner. The elements of this decision will probably encompass the following elements:

1. A combination of the captive net retained premium and the investment income generated on premiums and shareholders funds.
2. The likely captive expenses including:
   - projected losses
   - management costs
   - claims handling costs
   - reinsurance costs
3. The projected profit or loss of the captive

A simple costing indication is show in figure 3.14.

Minimum paid up capital	£250,000
100% of original gross premium	£1,150,000
Captive reinsurers 90% of risk	£1,035,000
Fronting/claims handling	(£30,000)
	£1,005,000
Reinsurance	
Excess of £100,000 each and every loss and £500,000 in the annual aggregate	(329,750)
Net retained premium	**£675,250**

Figure 3.6 Proposed captive costing indication

Estimated annual claims = £460,000

Made up of: —
- 3 property losses (a) £150,000
  (b) £190,000
  (c) £120,000

In this scenario the captive will pay claims of £300,000 after reinsurance recoveries as follows: —

Net annual premium received by captive	£675,250
Net claims	(£300,000)
Estimated annual profit	£375,250

The structure of a reinsurance programme for a captive is complicated and may well involve a mixture of the reinsurances discussed. There are other complications of placing reinsurance which are discussed in the next part of this chapter.

Other reinsurance complications

Reinsurance can be a difficult business to understand and it is continually changing its approach to solving the problems of insurers. The following are some of the other tactical problems that a captive may encounter in its reinsurance relationship.

The effect of inflation means that the limits and covers agreed between the captive and its reinsurer will change dramatically even within a few years. If there is no alteration to the levels of retention or cession, the reinsurers will become more at risk than originally envisaged and could become involved in regular claims payments. As a solution to this some reinsurance treaties now include a form of indexing to compensate for any inflationary effect, but at any rate it is important for the captive to review its own position at the end of each year to ensure that its original objectives in reflecting the captive owners' retention capability are continually updated.

For the multinational company, premiums will be received via the fronting insurers on a direct basis in a whole range of currencies. In addition, premium remittances vary from country to country so that the accounting needs of the captive can be complicated and need to be well managed.

For the captive using a combination of excess loss and stop loss protection, the coverage obtained from the reinsurer may be directly related to the agreed estimated maximum loss (EML). Two problems can arise if the EML is not calculated accurately: the captive could be in the position of under-insurance in relation to its overall reinsurance protection or the reinsurer could become involved in claims for which the premium available is far less than originally anticipated. Competence in carrying out the original surveys and establishing the EML is of paramount importance to the protection of the captive's operation.

Completion of reinsurance accounts takes much longer than it does for the direct insurer since several years may elapse before the final settlement of an individual account is made and the business closed.

Reinsurers will include in their treaty agreements a provision that they may examine the books of the captive in order to ensure that they can be protected against any volatility in the business handled by the captive insurer. Prudent reinsurers are concerned about the financial position of a captive and the people handling its management. They will wish to be assured that the captive is properly capitalised to finance its exposure and may in some eases require a parental guarantee that, in the event of default, the captive owner will support the captive financially and meet any obligations.

The typical captive will have need for reinsurance agreements which will be on a quota share basis in respect of the cession between the fronting insurer and the captive and on an excess of loss basis in respect of the reinsurance agreement between the captive and its reinsurers. Examples of these two types of reinsurance agreement are given in the case study at the end of the chapter, kindly provided by the General Accident, Corporate Risks Division. These cover most of the key elements of such agreements and particular attention is drawn to the simultaneous payments clause which is a common feature of such agreements and helps to protect the reinsurer against the inability of the captive to pay claims already committed by the fronting insurer.

Reinsurance differs from direct insurance in that premium payments will often be on a quarterly or half-yearly basis and it is expected that these agreed payment times are adhered to. This requirement to pay reinsurance on a regular basis will also emphasise the importance of ensuring that the premiums paid originally are passed to the captive as quickly as possible, so that the obligations to the reinsurers can be met and the captive is not short of funds. This may be a complicated problem if international operations are involved. For example, premiums may be delayed by currency restrictions, it may be necessary to hold reserves locally to comply with legislation and there may be other problems which delay passing money quickly to the captive. Premium payments vary considerably throughout the world and it is important that the implications of the delays are discussed in some detail with fronting insurers before the programme is developed. It is possible in some situations to obtain a guarantee from the fronting insurers that they will pass premiums to the captive within a pre-agreed time span and that, in the event of their failing to do this, due to their own administrative problems, they will guarantee the payment and accrue any interest lost to the captive's fund. This type of approach will apply only to countries where there are no governmental difficulties on exchange control and where there should be no reason why premiums should not be received by the captive within, say thirty days.

The handling of reinsurance, both from a negotiating point of view and on an ongoing basis from accounting and management viewpoints, is complicated. For the captive going into the business for the first time difficulties can be encountered and problems must be understood. The strength of the reinsurance programme is crucial and is probably the most important part of the captive's operation: it can enhance or destroy the original objectives.

Reinsurance security

Companies moving from a conventional direct market placement to the use of a captive to gain access to the reinsurance market need to be appraised of the implications of this move from the point of view of insurer security.

Whereas a conventional direct placement with a nationally recognised insurance company normally produces insurance security of unquestionable and certainly quantifiable stature, the development of a captive insurance company either writing business on a direct basis or utilising the services of a fronting company brings into play the importance of the captive's own reinsurance arrangements from a security standpoint. Whereas previously there will be an automatic expectation of reasonable and quick claims settlement, the introduction of the captive into the process and a reinsurance placement which may be separate from the arrangements made with the primary insurer produce a position where such reliance on security may not be clear-cut.

The structure of the programme and the quality of the captive's reinsurers both from the point of view of financial stability and attitude towards claims payments is of paramount importance. It is therefore essential that the owner of the captive is confident that unquestionable reinsurance security is obtained and that the best possible advice is obtained in determining the quality of the reinsurers used. The normal captive operation will involve a fronting company that will be issuing policies in the various countries where the risks are located and will have a legal obligation to meet any claims occurring under the primary policy. That company will wish to ensure that it is able to recover claims paid from the captive and the captive will clearly need to ensure that its own reinsurers are in a position to pay the claims that the captive is liable to reimburse the primary insurer at the time of settlement. The factors to be examined in this context are the security of the captive's own reinsurance programme and the reinsurance agreements between the fronting company and the captive and between the captive and its reinsurers.

It is becoming quite common for fronting companies to require a financial guarantee or to be protected by a cut-through clause to the reinsurers so that if the claim does occur they are able to obtain payment regardless of the status of the captive and also to gain access direct to the reinsurers for reimbursement. These parental guarantees have unfortunate disadvantages from a tax standpoint as they are often regarded by tax authorities throughout the world as recognition that the captive is not a separate entity and is merely part of a structure devised to find a tax-efficient means of conventional self-insurance. Parental guarantees should therefore be avoided, but the solutions to them usually involve other restrictions which are normally built into the reinsurance agreement between the primary company and the captive. These clauses often include the cut-through clause of the type we have mentioned but also a simultaneous payments clause which requires the captive to pay the claim to the fronting company at the same time as the fronting company pays the claim to the insured, in this case the owner of the captive. These clauses are acceptable provided that at the same time the captive is in a position to pay the claim having recovered its own reinsurers. The key is therefore the reinsurance programme of the captive and the quality of the reinsurers on this reinsurance schedule.

Owners of captives should recognise the crucial importance of reinsurance security and seek to obtain from their fronting company and the reinsurance brokers all available assistance in evaluating the placement made on their behalf. In addition to obtaining the advice of these two parties who have an important role and an obligation to the captive in ensuring that the reinsurance programme is of the required standard, the owners should also make their own judgements, and particularly should question the security of any reinsurers of which they do not have any knowledge or which they feel might not be of the highest quality. In making such security evaluations it is possible to obtain information on the financial stability of the various companies, from the brokers and the primary insurers, but it is also advisable to make a judgement where there is any doubt about the company by examining its financial statements and obtaining any market information that may be available.

As an aid to making these decisions, Insurance Solvency International produced a summary of the basis on which it produces its own analysis of insurance solvency by examining the performance of various companies and in particular comparing performance over a period of time. The tests used include eight key ratios or percentages which provide bench-marks for developing an impression of the insurer's and reinsurer's financial status. The tests are as follows:

Test 1 — Net premium/Shareholders' funds
This test reflects the standard market practice of considering the relationship between shareholders' funds and net premiums written. The standards vary according to different premium volumes and do not recognise books of business. The ratios indicated show a maximum ratio of net premiums to shareholders' funds highlighting six size categories which are regarded as the normal high point in most circumstances.

Net premium written	Shareholders' funds
£25m or over	not more than 3.3 times
£10m to £25m	not more than 3 times
£5m to £10m	not more than 2.8 times
£2.5m to £5m	not more than 2.5 times
£1m to £2.5m	not more than 2.2 times
Up to £1m	not more than 2 times

Test 2 — Actual/Required shareholders' funds
This test covers the relationship between shareholders' funds and any statutory minimum solvency margin required by the regulatory authority of the country concerned. This, for instance, is an amount calculated in the United Kingdom according to EEC standards by one or two formulae (one relating to gross premiums and one to claims incurred), by which assets must exceed liabilities. The ISI standard is that the shareholders' fund should be at least twice as large as the minimum required solvency margin.

Test 3 — Change in net premium
This test indicates whether the increase or decrease in net premium is more than 20 per cent. Any excessive growth (or indeed decline) in net premium should be noted.

Test 4 — Reinsurance ceded
This indicates whether more than 50 per cent of gross premiums are reinsured. It is felt very important to look at the position if a company reinsures substantially. In the absence of any statutory requirement that

the reinsurance arrangements should be disclosed, the test does not attempt to comment on the quality of the company's reinsurance protection or the shape of the programme and level of retentions, except where such details have been provided by the company.

Test 5 — Underwriting loss/Investment income

This test indicates whether the two-year average of underwriting losses exceeds 25 per cent of the two-year average of investment income. It is calculated on the two most recent published years. The ratio shown is calculated on the data for the current and prior years; if the prior year is lacking, the ratio is calculated based only on the current year. Thus a series of three ratios may contain one single year ratio and two based on averages. The test is designed to highlight in a proportionate way poor underwriting results, but by using a two-year average it does not overstress a single bad year. The trend is the key aspect. A very high proportion of companies do not meet the standards in present conditions.

Test 6 — Technical reserves/Shareholders' funds

If technical reserves are more than 350 per cent of shareholders' funds it is considered that this would expose the shareholders' funds in the event of a significant underestimation of reserves.

Test 7 — Technical reserves/Marketable assets

This test indicates if technical reserves are more than 105 per cent of readily marketable assets (defined as being bonds, etc., equities and cash combined).

Test 8 — Pre-tax profits/Net premium

This test is an indicator to which no standard ratio can be applied. It is the pre-tax profit of the company as whole expressed as a percentage of net written premium. This is considered to be a valuable method of international comparison and a useful guide to profitability overall and to its trend.

Where the reinsurance programme is placed on the basis that a small number of reinsurers are taking substantial retentions, it is worth examining the retrocession arrangements of these reinsurers to ensure that their retention is protected by the security of the reinsurance arrangements that they are making themselves in respect of their own retention strategy. Reinsurers writing large gross lines in this way should be willing to provide details of the internal excess of loss retrocession arrangement that they have made on behalf of the risk they are reinsuring for the captive, and investigation of this nature will only help to develop an understanding of the way that the reinsurance market operates; and the security that is in existence for the captive itself on the business that it is taking from either its own direct insurer, or on a direct basis if it is operating as a non-admitted insurer.

International Problems and Fronting

In most countries of the world it will be difficult for the captive insurance company to operate on a direct basis. This problem is exacerbated if the captive owner is a multinational operating in a variety of countries. The best solution to this problem is the use of a fronting insurer who is licensed in the particular country of operation and who can therefore issue policies and provide local services on a legal basis.

The role of the fronting insurer in the captive context is to provide these services in exchange for a fronting fee or overrider on the premium which he passes to the captive as reinsurance. For example, the fronting insurer will issue a local policy for 100 per cent of the risk, retain 10 per cent of the risk for his own benefit and then pass the remaining 90 per cent to the captive as reinsurance. The fronting fee would be charged on the 90 per cent proportion of the risk and might vary between 3 and 15 per cent depending on the services required within the fronting facility. The fronting insurance company can be involved in a considerable amount of work, and it is important that the fronting commission reflects this and that the company chosen has the right level of capability and credibility in the country in which the facility is required. It is now relatively easy to obtain fronting facilities in most countries and the multinational will attempt to ensure that these services are provided on a co-ordinated basis, hopefully through one insurer and certainly through no more than two or three.

As already mentioned, the complexities of legislation, the with-holding of reserves and currency problems vary throughout the world and can be extremely difficult to handle without local assistance. The international insurance company will have considerable knowledge of these problems and may also, in some countries, be able to pass more premium to the captive within a shorter time than a small, local insurer who has less international flexibility in its operations. The fronting insurer will be interested in providing the facility only if the premium volume is reasonably substantial and in some countries the multinational may find that the premium volume does not justify involving the captive in the programme. Here again, the use of an international insurer who is being given the opportunity to handle all of the group's operations will be more likely to bring fruitful results than the use of a splintered, myriad type of international programme.

The fronting services which may need to be obtained from the fronting insurer include the issue of policies and other essential documents, the handling and settlement of claims in the country of policy issue and local accounting. The fronting insurer may also be involved in providing engineering or loss control services either as part of the fronting fee or charged separately and paid for directly by the captive.

The only alternative for the multinational company with a captive to the use of fronting, is to become 'admitted' in each of the countries of operation. Where the country involved allows 'non-admitted' insurers the problem does not, of course, exist but such countries are few and far between. It will generally not be practical for the company to consider becoming admitted because of the cost of complying with the necessary legislation, or the possible need to place deposits or to have a physical presence in the country so that policies and other documents can be issued. For this reason, the multinational will usually establish a reinsurance captive using fronting services provided by local insurers and will probably find this more economical, despite the cost of fronting fees, than trying to set up its own network of international subsidiaries.

Underwriting

The captive will need to calculate the premium that it requires for the risks that it is underwriting. It will probably need to allocate this premium between different companies in its group, each country, and, different divisions or units of operations. In principle, the premium that it charges will need to cover the following:

1. The average cost of the claims anticipated.
2. The amount required to develop catastrophe reserves and to pay reinsurance premiums.
3. The cost of marketing or acquisition of business.
4. Expenses of administration.
5. Brokerage or commission for business introductions or administration.
6. Profit.

Compared with the normal insurance company, the captive can show advantages that are due to the following factors:

1. The captive's owner should be able to demonstrate better loss control than the market average with a resulting effect on claims cost.
2. There should be no requirement to allocate marketing or acquisition costs since by definition the business that the captive is handling is only derived from its parent.
3. Since the captive does not need to have a sizeable management or clerical operation, the costs of administering its operation should be lower on a percentage basis than the direct insurer.
4. The captive may not pay any brokerage or commission for business introduction or handling and may, indeed, be in a position of actually receiving commissions from reinsurers for reinsurance cessions to them.
5. The captive can use the premiums that it receives for investment income purposes.

In deciding how to develop its premium structure, the captive has the choice of a number of alternative methods. First, however, it is probably worth while to consider the main systems used in the normal insurance market for rating purposes.

The first system is the class rating system where the insurer collects statistics over a large group of risks — for example, all factories in a particular industry and in a particular country — and then calculates a premium which is the average of the loss history of each of the components of the group. For the captive it is likely that the reasons for establishment have been to beat this system because the captive owner's risks are better than the average of the group in which he has been placed by the insurance market.

Second is the experience rating system where the premium charged is directly related to the claims experience of the risk. This method is often used for liability or motor insurance where a large part of the exposure is high frequency, low cost claims which can be calculated on a reasonable basis to a predetermined figure and where the insurer can develop a premium which reflects the potential claims cost plus expenses and profit.

Thirdly, there is the psychological rating system, used where statistical data are not available and where the risk is new or of an unknown nature. In these cases the premium will be related directly to the underwriter's own subjective assessment of the risk which he is being offered. Naturally, the charge in these cases will vary from one underwriter to another depending on his attitude to and philosophy concerning the risks presented to him and his own risk-taking approach.

There are four main alternatives that the captive can use in its approach to premium rating:

1. The captive can use market rates established by the conventional market. If the captive is a better risk than the average market risk, this will mean that with the same premium cost the captive will be profitable and the profits resulting from this can be accumulated offshore.

2. The captive could use the normal market rates less a discount which reflects the improved experience that the company has compared with the market overall. By using this method it is possible for the profit from using the captive to be returned, either completely or in part, to the individual company divisions or units in the form of reduced premium expenditure. This method will give local management a strong incentive to use the captive because its pricing structure is better than that of the normal market and may help considerably to integrate an international programme in those multinationals where the local management is autonomous.

3. The captive can use a structure based on the cost of its reinsurance plus a loaded premium for the risk that it is retaining. This pricing structure approach will reflect directly the reinsurance cost and where the risk is improved there will automatically be significant reductions in the premium expenditure or increases in the profitability of the captive.

4. The captive can evolve its own rating system. This may be a dangerous method if a significant factor in the make-up of the premium is overlooked and the premium is therefore inadequate. It may also create a situation where the captive is grossly selected against and the loss experience deteriorates compared with the expected position.

In addition to the above the captive may also be under pressure to produce a rating system which reflects the loss experience of the various operating companies of the parent. The use of a captive to produce equitable rating between operating companies in order to reflect loss experience and risk management capability can produce valuable results provided it is not carried to extremes. A balance needs to be achieved between the 'carrot-and-the-stick' approach and the cost of developing sophisticated pricing methods which make up more time and costs in analysis, computer time and justification than the net result of the apportionment in reducing losses.

CASE STUDY – STANDARD REINSURANCE AGREEMENT WORDING

REINSURANCE AGREEMENT

between

Insurer

and

(hereinafter referred to as the 'Reinsurer') of the other part

ARTICLE 1

SCOPE

Subject to the terms and conditions as set forth herein, this Agreement applies to policies of insurance as detailed below issued by the 'Corporation' to Name of Insured

Details of policies included in the Reinsurance Agreement

ARTICLE 2

REINSURANCE CESSION (PRO-RATA)

The 'Corporation' will cede to the 'Reinsurer' _____ percent (____ %) of insurances detailed in Article 1 less any local policy retention by or on behalf of the 'Corporation' and/or compulsory local reinsurances.

The 'Corporation' reserves the right to effect Excess of Loss Reinsurances in respect of the amount retained for its own account and it is understood and agreed that recoveries under such reinsurances shall inure to the sole benefit of the 'Corporation'.

ARTICLE 3

TERM

This Agreement shall take effect from _____ at 00.01 am standard time and shall continue in full force and effect until terminated by either party giving 90 (ninety) days notice of termination in writing, to take effect at _____ of any year.

In the absence of mutual agreement to the contrary, the 'Reinsurer' shall, upon termination of this Agreement, continue to be liable for its proper share of the risks ceded prior to the date of termination. The 'Reinsurer's' liability shall continue until the natural expiry or renewal date of the policy but in no event exceeding a further twelve months plus odd time after termination of the Agreement except for losses which may have occurred during the effective period for which the 'Reinsurer' has received and accepted premiums.

At the end of ____ months after inception of each underwriting year, the 'Reinsurer's' liability in respect of each year of reinsurance shall be terminated by payment to the Corporation of an amount to be agreed at that time.

ARTICLE 4

ORIGINAL CONDITIONS

The 'Reinsurer' shall be subject to the same terms, conditions and waivers and to the same modifications, alterations and cancellations as agreed by the 'Corporation' under the original insurances.

ARTICLE 5

LOSS SETTLEMENT

The 'Reinsurer' agrees to pay on demand to the 'Corporation' its share as defined in Article 2 of all settlements, compromises (including *ex-gratia* payments) made by the 'Corporation', and to contribute its share of any gross loss reserve which may have to be set up by the law of any country.

The 'Corporation' may at its discretion commence, continue, defend, compromise, settle or withdraw from actions, suits and proceedings and generally do all such things relating to any claim or loss which in its judgement may be expedient and the 'Reinsurer' shall pay its due share of expenses connected therewith.

The 'Reinsurer' shall share in proportion to its participation in all amounts which may be recovered by the 'Corporation' in respect of any loss or claim, other than as defined in Article 2.

ARTICLE 6

PREMIUM CLAUSE

The 'Corporation' shall pay to the 'Reinsurer' the original gross premiums which it receives on the original insurances less:

1. Original commission.
2. Local policy retentions or compulsory reinsurances.
3. Commissions as specified in Article 8.

ARTICLE 7

CLAIMS FUNDS AND ACCOUNTS

Notwithstanding the obligation to pay on demand under Article 5 the 'Reinsurer' shall provide the 'Corporation' with a fund of £_____ from which claim payments under this agreement may be made. The fund will be topped up monthly by the 'Reinsurer' as hereinafter provided.

After initial gross premium transaction specified in Article 6, subsequent accounts of all claims paid will be presented monthly within 15 days from the end of each calendar month and settled within a further 5 days to maintain the claims fund at the level prescribed.

In the event that the Corporation certifies that the claims payments to be made in any month will exceed £_____ the 'Reinsurer' shall forthwith increase the said fund for the duration of that month only, to an amount sufficient to cover the 'Corporation's' payments as aforesaid, and appropriate adjustments will be made on the next monthly account.

ARTICLE 8

COMMISSIONS

The 'Reinsurer' agrees to allow the 'Corporation' a Ceding Commission payable in respect of each underwriting year or a proportionate part of such amount in respect of any part of an underwriting year.

ARTICLE 9

FOLLOW THE FORTUNES

The 'Reinsurer' shall in all cases follow the fortunes of the 'Corporation' and no errors or accidental omissions on the part of the 'Corporation' shall relieve the 'Reinsurer' of liability in respect of claims hereunder provided that such errors and/or omissions are rectified as soon after discovery as possible.

ARTICLE 10

CONFIDENTIAL AGREEMENT

This Agreement is recognised by both parties as strictly confidential. Neither party shall at any time during the currency, or thereafter, of this Agreement make any use, directly or indirectly, of information afforded hereunder to the detriment of the other party.

ARTICLE 11

MODIFICATION

Any mutually agreed modification to this Agreement (whether by addendum or correspondence) shall be binding on both parties and shall be added as a part of this Agreement.

ARTICLE 12

TERMINATION

Should at any time either party:

(a) lose the whole or any part of its capital, or

(b) go into liquidation or have a receiver appointed, or

(c) be acquired or suffer a transfer of its capital stock to another company or corporation, or

(d) fail to carry out its financial obligations under this Agreement within thirty days of receipt of a notice in writing specifying the failure,

the other party shall have the right to terminate this Agreement forthwith by giving notice of its intention as soon as practicable in writing by registered or recorded delivery letter, telex, cable or telefacsimile.

If any Law or Regulation becomes operative in the country in which either of the parties to this Agreement is domiciled or in any country to which this Agreement applies which renders illegal the arrangements hereby made, this Agreement shall terminate immediately in respect of the business to which such Law or Regulation applies.

ARTICLE 13

REINSURER'S INSOLVENCY CLAUSE

The 'Reinsurer' hereby agrees that if the 'Reinsurer' is at any time placed in the hands of a receiver, assignee or trustee for the purpose of liquidation on account of insolvency, notice shall be given to the 'Corporation' of said happening. In such event the 'Reinsurer' hereby irrevocably assigns unto the 'Corporation' all the benefit and interest in or under its retrocession treaties so tar as they relate to liabilities assumed by the 'Reinsurer' under this reinsurance Agreement with the 'Corporation' together with the right so far as may be necessary to demand performance or sue for and enforce the same in the name of the 'Reinsurer', to hold the same unto the 'Corporation' absolutely.

ARTICLE 14

ARBITRATION

Any dispute or difference arising between the 'Corporation' and the 'Reinsurer' shall be referred to the decision of two Arbitrators one to be appointed in writing by each of the parties. Before entering upon the reference the Arbitrators shall appoint in writing an Umpire who shall act only in the event of disagreement between the Arbitrators. If either party refuse or neglect to nominate an Arbitrator within thirty days after being required to do so or should the two Arbitrators fail to appoint an Umpire within thirty days any appointment so failing to be made shall be left to the choice of the Secretary General for the time being of the Association of British Insurers.

The Arbitrators and Umpire shall be active or retired officials of Insurance Companies or Underwriting Syndicates carrying on a similar type of insurance or reinsurance business to that covered hereunder. The seat of arbitration shall be in London, England unless otherwise agreed.

Each party shall submit its case in writing to the Arbitrators within one month of the constitution of the artibration tribunal which shall give its award in writing at the earliest convenient date.

The Arbitrators and Umpire may abstain from following the strict rules of law and shall be entitled to settle the dispute or difference referred to them according to an honourable rather than a strictly legal interpretation of the provisions of this Agreement.

The costs of the Reference and the Award and of the parties shall be in the discretion of the Arbitrators and/or Umpire who may direct to and by whom and in what manner those costs or any part thereof shall be paid.

The obtaining of an Award in accordance with this Article shall be a condition precedent to any right of action in respect of any difference falling within the scope of this Agreement.

executed in duplicate and signed

in

This   day of   19

FOR AND ON BEHALF OF THE INSURER

and in

This   day of   19

FOR AND ON BEHALF OF

Annex 3.1

VARIATIONS TO
REINSURANCE AGREEMENT WORDING

ARTICLE 2A

REINSURANCE CESSION (FIRST LOSS)
The 'Corporation' cedes to the 'Reinsurer' and the 'Reinsurer' accepts from the 'Corporation' insurances detailed in Article 1 and the 'Reinsurer's' liability shall be limited to

    (a) the first £＿＿＿＿ in respect of any one claim under each and every Section of the said insurance and in the annual aggregate for the period of insurance in respect of any Section where an annual aggregate limit applies, and

    (b) £＿＿＿＿ million in the annual aggregate for the period of insurance.

The 'Corporation' reserves the right to effect Excess of Loss Reinsurances in respect of the amount retained for its own account and it is understood and agreed that recoveries under such reinsurances shall inure to the sole benefit of the 'Corporation'.

ARTICLE 2B

USE WHEN REINSURERS LIMITS OF LIABILITY TO BE SHOWN FOR CROSS CLASSES

REINSURANCE CESSION
The 'Corporation' will cede to the 'Reinsurer'＿＿＿＿＿＿ percent (＿＿＿＿ %) of insurances detailed in Article 1 less any local policy retention by or on behalf of the 'Corporation' and/or compulsory local reinsurances and the Reinsurer's liability shall be limited to:

    (a) Policy No＿＿＿＿＿ – Motor Fleet – £＿＿＿＿ each and every loss for accidental Damage losses – £＿＿＿＿ each and every loss for Theft losses. £＿＿＿＿ each and every loss for all other losses.

    (b) Policy No＿＿＿＿＿ – Property Damage/Business Interruption – £＿＿＿＿ each and every loss.

    (c) Policy No＿＿＿＿＿ – Employers Liability – £＿＿＿＿ each and every loss.

    (d) Policy No＿＿＿＿＿ – Contractors All Risks – £＿＿＿＿ each and every loss resulting from defect in design as detailed in the policy. £＿＿＿＿ each and every loss in respect of Tools, Personal Effects and other belongings of Employees. £＿＿＿＿ each and every loss in respect of all other losses.

(e) Policy No _____ – Group Personal Accident and Travel – £ _____ each and every loss for Personal Accident losses and £ _____ each and every loss for Travel losses.

(f) Policy No _____ – Fidelity Guarantee – £ _____ each and every loss.

The 'Reinsurers' Liability is further restricted to £ _____ annual aggregate for the period of insurance across all classes.

The 'Corporation' reserves the right to effect Excess of Loss Reinsurances in respect of the amount retained for its own account and it is understood and agreed that recoveries under such reinsurances shall inure to the sole benefit of the 'Corporation'.

ARTICLE 3A

ADD TO STANDARD ARTICLE 3 TO GIVE RUN-OFF OPTION
or by the purchase of a suitable run-off retrocession agreement which is acceptable to the 'Corporation'.

ARTICLE 3B

ADD TO STANDARD ARTICLE 3 TO GIVE REINSURER'S CONTINUED LIABILITY OPTION
In the event that the amount referred to above cannot be mutually agreed at the time specified, the 'Reinsurer's' liability will continue for a further 12 months at which time the termination of liability will be renegotiated.

ARTICLE 5A

ADDITIONAL CLAIMS SERVICE OPTION
LOSS SETTLEMENT
The 'Corporation' shall keep the 'Reinsurer' informed of developments on all claims and shall submit a quarterly claims bordereau.

ARTICLE 5B

CREATES SIMULTANEOUS PAYMENTS CLAUSE
Change 'on demand' in first line to 'simultaneously'.

ARTICLE 6A

LIMITS TIME CORPORATION MAY RETAIN REINSURERS
PREMIUM TO _____ WORKING DAYS PREMIUM CLAUSE
Initial gross reinsurance premium shall be payable to the 'Reinsurer' within _____ working days of receipt by the 'Corporation' of the gross premium due under the original insurance.

Annex 3.1

ARTICLE 6B

INCLUDES RETENTION OF PREMIUM BY CORPORATION FOR EXCESS OF LOSS AND AGGREGATE COVER. LIMITS RETENTION BY CORPORATION TO _____ WORKING DAYS
PREMIUM CLAUSE
The 'Corporation' shall pay to the 'Reinsurer' the original gross premiums which it receives on the original insurances less:

1. Original commission.
2. Local policy retentions or compulsory reinsurances.
3. Agreed premium for the amount of the original policy limits in excess of £ _____ each and every loss and £ _____ in the aggregate for the period _____ to _____ .
4. Commissions as specified in Article _____ .

The reinsurance premium shall be payable to the 'Reinsurer' within _____ working days of receipt by the 'Corporation' of the gross premium due under the original insurances. This is defined as the 'initial premium transaction'.

ARTICLE 8A

SPECIFIES MINIMUM CEDING COMMISSION
COMMISSIONS
The 'Reinsurer' agrees to allow the 'Corporation' a minimum Ceding Commission of £ _____ on the original gross premiums paid to the 'Reinsurer' as defined in Article 6, payable in respect of each underwriting year.

ARTICLE 14A

VARIATION TO ARBITRATION CLAUSE MAKING AGREEMENT STRICTLY SUBJECT TO ENGLISH LAW.
REPLACES PARA 4 IN STANDARD.
The arbitration shall be carried out under the ICC rules of Arbitration and be subject to English law.

Note that when using any of the variations to the Standard Reinsurance Agreement care should be taken that cross-references to Article numbers or paragraphs in other Articles of the Agreement remain correct.

A number of service providers to captives have developed special reinsurance pools which are dedicated to providing reinsurance facilities for captive insurance clients.

There are a number of special reinsurance pooling facilities which can be accessed by captive insurance companies. Amongst the most well known and effective are those developed by Alexander Howden Group – the reinsurance brokers, – covering a range of possibilities including property treaty facilities, global liability capacity and a 'cross-class' and aggregate and stop loss reinsurance programme. In addition there are risk financing and finite risk products which provide a number of alternative possibilities depending on the particular requirements of the captive client. A brief summary of these facilities follows:

Synopsis of Captive property facility offered by Alexander Howden

Type: All risks Property and Consequential Loss business including Boiler and Machinery and Inland Transportation.

Terms and Conditions: Separate declarations for each insured which are negotiated individually with commissions and premiums based on insured's own portfolio and loss record.

Main Benefits: Access to stable leading professional reinsurance market; beneficial cash flow conditions: profit sharing opportunities: quoting and binding is agreed by the two leading reinsurers only, so fast response time is ensured.

Reinsurance Commission: The reinsurance panel are prepared to include ceding commission in most programmes with the provision of such commission being subject to the performance of the individual reinsured. Typically ceding commissions go up to 25% with profit commission starting at 5% with the potential to increase above this level.

Underwriting Criteria: The reinsurers subscribing to this facility are looking to form long-term relationships with our client Captives which are committed to the Captive philosophy of risk retention, coupled with risk management and loss prevention, and it will be necessary to demonstrate these commitments prior to final acceptance.

Captive Liability Facility:

Alexander Howden also have a liability facility with the following basic structure:

The facility offers a complete global liability package for Public/General, Products, Employers and Motor/Automobile Liability for any business or service company, anywhere in the world.

CAPTIVE INSURANCE COMPANIES

Type: Public Liability, Products Liability, Employers Liability, Motor Liability.

Form: Occurrence of Claims Made – wording to be based on wording used by Captive and where applicable its Front.

Limits: US$25,000,000 or local currency equivalent.

Attachment Point: Minimum attachment point of £500,000 with lower attachment points and aggregate stops negotiable.

Territorial scope: Worldwide (including USA/Canadian domiciled operations).

Security: First class professional reinsurance capacity.

Conditions: Seepage, pollution and contamination clause for Worldwide operations, excluding USA/Canada, to be on a sudden and accidental basis: Named Peril, seepage, pollution and contamination buyback endorsement available for USA/Canadian operations. Workers Compensation Act will be excluded where there is a USA exposure, although negotiable on an excess basis. Long term agreements are negotiable. Fronting arrangements are available.

Underwriting Panel:

- Swiss Reinsurance Company
- Zurich Insurance Company
- American Reinsurance Company
- General Reinsurance Company

Cross Class Specific and Aggregate Stop Loss Reinsurance Programme:

Whilst captives can forecast annual total expected loss figures and obtain stop loss protection for specific individual lines of cover, they have not always been able to find one product which will efficiently protect their balance sheet from an unpredicted deterioration in claims frequency and/or severity across all lines of the exposure retained.

One such mechanism, in which there has been much interest from captive insureds in recent years, is a portfolio or 'cross-class' aggregate stop loss programme. Until fairly recently, however, there have not been many markets prepared to participate in such programmes as underwriters have been loath to offer one policy for a base of widely differing coverages.

Times have now changed and Howden have completed a number of cross-class aggregate stop loss programmes for captives. These programmes can include a range of coverages (amongst others):

- Products/General/Automobile/Employers Liability
- Property Damage/Business Interruption
- Group Healthcare
- Contractors All Risks

The cross-class aggregate protection would typically be called into force after erosion of a pre-agreed captive net retention and would only attach excess of original (operating company) deductibles. The cover can also be arranged on a specific and aggregate basis, where the reinsurers would provide each and every coverage on a 'first loss' basis as well as aggregate stop loss cover – all within the same reinsurance policy.

Underwriters will normally require a substantial amount of information to be able to consider such programmes including:

- Full original policy wordings
- Full exposure information
- Captive and parent company financial reports
- Claims past 10 years
- Details on who administers, adjusts and actuarially reviews the captive's claims

The underwriters who now participate in this type of innovative programme are the specialist captive and professional reinsurance markets seeking to establish long term relationships with captive insurance companies.

Alternative Risk Financing/Finite Risk Products

The professional reinsurance markets are offering a wide variety of alternative products to captive reinsurance companies that are not available in the traditional insurance market.

The products available are very flexible and usually designed around the particular needs of each captive. Coverages will vary from straightforward funding arrangements to non-conventional protections, all depending on the individual particular requirements.

CAPTIVE INSURANCE COMPANIES

Coverages include but are not limited to:

- Prospective aggregate insurance/reinsurance
- Retrospective aggregate insurance/reinsurance
- Loss portfolio transfer
- Chronological loss stabilisation programmes
- Total Corporate Risk Protection

Advantages to captives/corporations purchasing these products are:

- Multi-year protection
- Balance sheet management
- Extending the range of risks that can be covered
- Funding for uninsurable classes
- Coverage and management of long tail exposures
- Smoothing the effect of large losses on the company/captive's results
- Management of the overall exposures of captives

The security offered for these products is from reinsurers with an established reputation and financial strength.

CHAPTER 4

LOCATION OF A CAPTIVE

Location Factors

At the start of the consideration of establishing a captive one of the key decisions will be where the company should be located. The comparison between a captive in the country of the owner's domicile and offshore will be considered later, but the main criteria that need to be taken into account in deciding the location apply to both of these alternatives.

First will be the operating convenience of the location in relation to the parent company. The factors that need to be taken into account in this decision are the geographical location and how this would affect the management of the captive, from the point of view of both cost of management time in travelling to the location and its convenience in relation to time changes, bearing in mind that in some parts of the world it would be difficult to contact the insurance company during the parent's business hours, for example to increase cover, because it would not be open for business. Other factors in this context will include the cost of travel and the level and sophistication of communications, such as travel, telephone, telex and other services.

Another key factor in the decision will be the legislation that exists in the location for the formation of insurance companies. The company will probably be looking for a situation where it is relatively easy to form an insurance company and where the requirements for returns of a financial nature, insurance statistics and detailed paperwork are limited. Methods of application to form the company and time this is likely to take may also be an important factor in some countries. It is mainly the complexity of the insurance legislation that exists in most developed countries that has persuaded owners of captives to move to offshore locations, where the controls are less rigid and establishment is much more rapid than it would be in most industrialised countries.

The next factor that needs to be taken into account is taxation. The taxation aspects of captive insurance companies can be complex and fall into two main categories. First, the company will need to be concerned about the potential for the premiums paid to their captive to be tax deductible. The location that they choose in this respect may have some influence on the attitude of their government to allow such deductibility. Second, the taxation rate in the location chosen for the captive will be relevant in relation to the ability to build up reserves quickly and expand the base of the captive so that it can retain more of its own risk and expand its operations as a profit centre. Although the avoidance of tax on the profits of the captive is only of a deferral nature, since they will usually be subject to tax when the surplus is returned to the company in domicile, the ability to delay this tax payment and to operate in an environment which is either tax free or has minimal taxation is of great advantage to the captive company.

Another major location factor is the cost and capability of the companies that offer management services. Cost and capability should be looked at together and it should certainly not be the policy to minimise cost at the expense of overall service. Captive management is of great importance to the company and it is vital that it should be competent, both in the eyes of the company itself and in relation to the image presented to the insurance industry who will be interested in the people chosen to run the company's insurance subsidiary.

Last is the difficult question of the political stability of the location that has been chosen. Where offshore locations are chosen there is always a degree of political risk since they are usually environments where governments are less stable than they would be in the country of the parent's domicile. There is a continual debate about the respective political stability in captive locations such as Bermuda, the Bahamas, the Cayman Islands, Gibraltar, Hong Kong, Vanuatu and so on. It would not be possible or wise to give in this book any specific advice or to comment on the existing political situations since the position is of a changing nature. It should be said, however, that political stability should be a factor in the consideration of location. At the very least some form of contingency plan should be considered, whatever the location chosen, to ensure that the company is aware of the possible risk of sequestration of funds and that it would be able to cope with such a problem and, as a last resort, move the captive operations to a more friendly environment if the need arose.

Considerations When Investigating a Potential Location

When analysing the various locations throughout the world there are a whole range of factors that need to be taken into account before a final decision is made. The following questionnaire is designed to cover a broad range of captive operations and some of the points will not apply in individual situations. However, it is intended to help companies develop a profile of the individual location, so that they can have a greater understanding of the environment and its sophistication in offering facilities to insurance companies.

1. First, what types of company can be formed in the location?
   (a) Resident and fully licensed locally.
   (b) Non-resident and exempt corporations.
   (c) Reinsurance companies.
   (d) Direct writing companies.
2. What is the procedure for obtaining permission for company formation?
   (a) Who decides within the government authority?
   (b) Who influences them — for example, the insurance market?
   (c) What are the chances of success? Have captives been formed previously and on what basis?
   (d) What is the likely time-scale for consent from the authorities? This consent period can vary from one week in some locations to one year in the more sophisticated insurance environments.
   (e) What are the detailed formalities of procedure to establish a company?
3. What are the criteria for official consideration?
   (a) Are the authorities concerned with the ownership of the captive?
   (b) Are the authorities concerned about what type of business the captive is to handle — for example, do they accept pure captives writing the company's own business or do they limit captives to particular lines of business or allow captives to operate on a mixed basis including own business and outside activities?
   (c) What are the minimum requirements for capitalisation and solvency levels?
   (d) Does the consideration take into account the companies that will be managing the captive? Does it have to meet

131

certain levels of capability in relation to the insurance expertise or locally known personnel?

4. Which laws or practices govern the operations of insurance companies?

(a) Are there any minimum solvency requirements and are these linked to any restrictions on admissibility of assets?

(b) What is the degree of supervision over the establishment of the captive in the first place and its ongoing operation?

(c) What is the nature of the official returns required by the authorities, how complex are these returns and what is the position of confidentiality?

(d) Are there any limitations on the growth of the insurance company? Is it able to write business throughout the world or is it restricted to a particular country of operation?

(e) Are there any restrictions on risk acceptance in relation to both size of exposure and type of risk? There are some locations where there is restriction on certain liability risks or where insurance companies can operate only in respect of conventional insurable risk and not in respect of contingent funding.

(f) Are there any restrictions on policy wordings that can be used from the point of view of legal restrictions or insurance market restrictions?

(g) Does the local requirement involve the necessity for the parent company to provide any form of financial guarantee to the authorities, the fronting insurers or the reinsurers?

(h) Is there a difference of approach by the authorities to resident and non-resident companies?

5. What is the tax position?

(a) Is tax payable within the location and, if it is, is there a separation between the tax payable on investment income and/or underwriting profits?

(b) Which of the reserves that the company needs to establish are allowable as tax deductions and, as far as technical reserves are concerned, what allowances are there for claims which are incurred but not reported?

(c) Is there any difference in tax treatment between the various types of captive (for example, pure or mutual) or the nationality of the owners (for example, double tax agreements, special situations such as The Netherlands and the Netherlands Antilles)?

(d) Does the authority require any tax or registration fee on formation of the captive?

(e) Is there an annual corporation tax or something similar which needs to be paid?

6. Other financial matters.
   (a) Are there any requirements as to the nominated currency of the paid-up capital, reserves or other liquid funds?
   (b) Are there any exchange control problems for companies dealing internationally which may have an impact on the ability to receive premiums or pay claims?
   (c) Are there any restrictions on the use of the fund developed by the captive insurance company and what is the position with regard to loans being made by the captive to its parent?
7. Services.
   (a) Does an established financial system with lawyers and accountants who understand international insurance business and especially captive insurance companies exist in the location?
   (b) What is the position in the location with regard to available management services and from whom are they available?
   (c) Are there any restrictions on company title?
   (d) What is the position on the location of the staffing of existing management companies and what methods are used by them?

Offshore Versus Domestic

There is no doubt that the tax haven or the captive location which has low tax and easy insurance legislation is much more attractive to the company contemplating captive establishment than the domestic alternative. However, problems do exist with offshore locations that need to be recognised. It is important that, so far as control is concerned, the captive managed offshore is seen to be at arm's length from the parent company. This may produce problems of increased cost and lack of convenience compared with the domestic company. In addition, the offshore location may involve communication problems such as travel expenses, the amount of management time spent attending board meetings, lack of efficient communication services, for example telephones and telex, and language difficulties. Also, there may be an element of political instability in the location which needs to be taken into account and many tax havens produce hostility from the parent government in the form of taxation restrictions, exchange control restraints and general animosity which may not be acceptable to the captive owner.

The domestic captive is a valid alternative for the company that is restricted by its parent government or does not envisage any tax advantages from being offshore. Its value lies in its credibility in the light of the host government and from the viewpoint of convenience, control and management. For many countries, and particularly those which for political reasons cannot go offshore, the domestic captive is of great value and should not be discounted when considering a location.

Alternative Offshore Locations

Although theoretically captive insurance companies can be formed in most areas of the world, there are a number of locations offshore which have developed a particular interest in captive insurance companies and which are used to a significant extent. The most popular of these is Bermuda, closely followed by the Cayman Islands. These two island locations are used primarily by United States corporations owing to their close proximity to North America and the common language.

In Europe the United Kingdom has primarily used Guernsey, owing to the historic restrictions on exchange control, but in more recent years other locations such as the Isle of Man, Luxembourg and Gibraltar have become available to most companies. Since the withdrawal of the exchange control rules in 1979, UK companies have begun to establish once again in Bermuda and, of course, the other locations will also be available to them.

In Europe the preference for a particular location varies depending on the country and its relationship with various often dependent territories. For example, Netherlands based countries have made considerable use of Netherlands Antilles, with which it has special relationships so far as tax is concerned, but there are a number of Dutch companies located in Guernsey and Bermuda. There has been a tendency for Swedish companies to locate in Luxembourg and Dublin and for French and Belgium companies to use Luxembourg because of the familiar legal system and language. From a more general perspective, there are a wide range of locations that continue to be used and many others are arriving on the scene. These include Aaland, British Columbia, Jersey, Labuan, Malta, Nauru, Singapore, Turks & Caicos, British Virgin Islands, US Virgin Islands, Vanuatu and a number of onshore locations including Denmark, Sweden and Switzerland.

Table 4.1 shows each of the popular captive locations and comments on their positions, their main status as locations from communications, service, tax and control viewpoints and briefly outlines the current legislative position in each.

Table 4.1 Captive location analysis

	Aaland	**Bahamas**	**Barbados**
Geography	Scandinavia	Between Florida and Haiti	Caribbean
Language	Finnish/Swedish/English	English	English
Currency	FIM	B$, parity US$	B$
Communications **Access** **Post/Telex**	Fair Good	Good Good	Fair/Good Good
Bank Services	Fair	Good	Good
Legal System	Finnish	British	British
Applicable Legislation	Finnish Insurance Law 1979	a. Insurance Act 1969 and the non-resident insurer (exemption) regulations 1979; or b. The External Insurance Act 1983	Offshore Banking Act 1979 − 26 1980 − 23 International Business Co Act 1965 − amended 1977 and 1979 Exempt Ins. Act 1983
Supervisory Jurisdiction	Aaland Government Finnish Insurance Regulator	Minister of Finance Registrar of Insurance Companies	Minister of Finance and Insurance Supervisor
Limits on Investment		None for non-resident companies	None except auditors to indicate whether liquidity or assets sufficient to meet liabilities
Local Office Restrictions		Principal office in Bahamas and principal representation	Registered office and one local director required, licensed manager
Financial Reporting	Annual Report	Both Acts − Audited Financial Statement. 1983 Act − Auditors, Managers & Directors confirmatory certificates	Annual Returns to Minister of Finance
Registration & Incorporation		Incorp − a. initial $1000 b. annual $1000 c. stamp duty: $60 for first $5000 of authorised capital plus $3 for each additional $1000 Registration − initial $1000	Stamp duty and incorporation fees Application fee US$250 Licence fee US$2,500
Capitalisation	Minimum FIM 6 million	1983 Life: $200,000 General: $100,000	US$125,000. Some exemptions for "Shelf" companies LOC's can substitute capital
Reserves & Solvency		If premium less than $7,000,000, 20% of premium to $7m. $1.4m plus 10% of premium over $7m if premium over $7m	20% solvency ratio
Taxation	17% local tax plus	Initial tax $1000 Annual fee $2,500 No income or premium taxes	US$2,500 annual fee No income/withholding tax

Table 4.1 Captive location analysis (cont'd)

	Bermuda	British Columbia	Cayman Islands
Geography	Off East Coast USA		Caribbean/Miami/ Jamaica
Language	English	English	English
Currency	B$ parity US$	C$	C$
Communications **Access** **Post/Telex**	Good Good	Good Good	Fair Good
Bank Services	Good	Good	Good
Legal System	British	Canadian	British
Applicable Legislation	Insurance Act 1978 Companies Act 1981 effective from 1st July 1983	Insurance (Captive Company) Act 1978	The Insurance Law 1979 (Law 24 of 1979) Companies Law 1969
Supervisory Jurisdictions	Registrar of Companies Insurance Advisory Committee	Supervisor of Financial Institutions	Superintendent of Insurance
Limits on Investment	75% of general insurance liabilities must be "admissible assets"	None	None for exempt companies
Local Office Restrictions	Registered office, two resident directors required and principal representative	Local Office	Registered Office
Financial Reporting	Annual audited Financial Report. Solvency certificate must be reviewed by auditors	Annual	Class B — written confirmation on annual accounts
Registration & Incorporation	Annual Government fee $1,680 to $25,000 Initial reinsurance licence fee $2,205. Annual insurance licence fee $1,100	Initial C$500 Renewal Fee C$2500	US$1050
Capitalisation	General business $120,000 Long term business $250,000 Both classes $370,000	Min C$200,000	Restricted Class B (pure captive) — none. Unrestricted Class B General Business net worth US$120,000 Combined net worth US$360,000
Reserves & Solvency	Minimum solvency margin 5 to 1	As necessary to support business plan. Min. C$100,000 reserves	Superintendent works on 5:1 ratio premium to capital and 1 to 10 retained risk to capital
Taxation	Annual fees range from $1,600 to $8,000	No Federal Excise Tax	Total $5,000 annual

Table 4.1 Captive location analysis (cont'd)

	Colorado	Cyprus	Delaware
Geography	Mid-West USA	Mediterranean	USA
Language	English	Greek/Turkish	English
Currency	US$	C£	US$

Communications
    Access
    Post/Telex
	Good
	Good
		Fair
		Good
			Good
			Good

Bank Services	Good	Good	Good
Legal System	USA	British	USA
Applicable Legislation	Colorado Captive Insurance Company Act 1972 Revised 1973 Revised 1987 Revised 1989 Revised 1994	Exempted from Insurance Companies Law 1967 to 1976	Title 18 Chapter 69 Amended 1988
Supervisory Jurisdictions	Division of Insurance Department of Regulatory Agencies	Superintendent of Insurance	Department of Insurance
Limits on Investment	As for commercial insurers	None	Limit of 10% any person for Association captives
Local Office Restrictions	Principal office in Colorado	Registered Office	Delaware Office
Financial Reporting	Annual convention statement	Annual Accounts	Annual Accounts
Registration & Incorporation	Feasibility Study $500 licence fee $200 application fee	C£50 minimum to C£150 maximum plus £0.25% of nominal capital	Incorporation $40 Charter fee $500 Annual fee $450 Renewal fee $300 Examination fee $200
Capitalisation	Flexible format Letters of Credit permitted Minimum $500,000	C£10,000	Pure captive $250,000 Association captive $750,000 Industrial Insured $500,000
Reserves & Solvency	As for Commercial Insurers	None — solvency	Premium to surplus ratio 3–1 for P & C companies
Taxation	Minimum premium tax $5,000 General rates are: Direct Written Premiums: Rate First $25 million 0.50% Next $50 million 0.25% Thereafter 0.10% Reinsurance Premiums Assumed First $20 million 0.25% Thereafter 0.10%	4.25% on profits	1% premium tax on Delaware risks

Table 4.1 Captive location analysis (cont'd)

	Denmark	**Dublin**	**Georgia**
Geography	Scandinavia	Capital of Ireland	USA
Language	Danish	English	English
Currency	Danish Kroner	Irish Punt	US$
Communications **Access** **Post/Telex**	Good Good	Good Good	Good Good
Bank Services	Good	Good	Good
Legal System	Danish	Irish	USA
Applicable Legislation	Insurance Business Act 1984	Insurance Act 1983 Memorandum 1988	Georgia Insurance Company Act 1988
Supervisory Jurisdiction	Insurance Supervision Service	Department of Industry & Commerce for direct captives. I.D.A. for R/I captives	Commissioner of Insurance
Limits on Investment	None	None	None for pure captives or industrial insureds
Local Office Restrictions	Local office required	Office in F.S.C.	Local office
Financial Reporting	Annual. However quarterly for first 3 years of operation	Annual	Annual
Registration & Incorporation	4% of share capital + DKK 2,700	Need to obtain Certificate from Industrial Development Authority of Ireland (IDA) I£2,000 application fee I£142 registration fee 1% of capital	$400 annual fee $1000 renewal fee
Capitalisation	Minimum capital ECU3,000,000 (DKR 2,350,000) but ECU400,000 if writing liability, credit or guarantee insurance	Direct IR£500,000 Reinsurance as agreed	Pure $500,000 Association $500,000 Ind. Ins $500,000
Reserves & Solvency	EEC rules i.e. max of a. 18% of net premium for preceding year up to ECU 10m Thereafter 16% b. 26% of net losses based on average over last 3 years up to ECU 7m Thereafter 23%	EEC Rules	At Commissioners discretion
Taxation	Good opportunities for pre tax reserving, though subject to Supervisor, and taxation approved on a case by case basis	10% for International Financial services operative to year 2005	Exemption for non-Georgia based risks 2.5% municipal tax 1% on some investments

Table 4.1 Captive location analysis (cont'd)

	Gibraltar	Guernsey	Hawaii
Geography	Spanish peninsular	Off North Coast France	Pacific
Language	English	English	English
Currency	Gib.£	£	US$
Communications **Access** **Post/Telex**	Good Good	Good Good	Fair Good
Bank Services	Good	Good	Good
Legal System	British	British	USA
Applicable Legislation	Assurance Companies Ordinance, 1954 Insurance Companies Ordinance 1987	The Insurance Business (Guernsey) Law 1986, operative January 1987	Captive Insurance Law 1987 Amended 1988
Supervisory Jurisdictions	Commissioner for Insurance, Insurance Supervisor and Insurance Advisory Committee	Superintendent of Insurance Guernsey Financial Services Commission	Department of Commerce and Consumer Affairs
Limits on Investment	Admissible asset requirement	75% "approved" assets	Approval by Insurance Commissioner
Local Office Restrictions	Registered Office and authorised insurance manager	Registered Office and approved management	Office in Hawaii Local manager
Financial Reporting	Annual accounts (confidential)	Annual accounts required (confidential)	Annual reporting
Registration & Incorporation	.05% duty on authorised capital (initial). No continuing duty Registration £1,000	Application fee £1300 Annual fee £1300 Filing fee £100 Registration fee £25. Document Duty 0.05% of authorised capital. (Minimum £25, Maximum £5,000)	Application fee: $1000 Licencee fee: $300 Renewal fee: $300
Capitalisation	No minimum prescribed but for EU direct companies: General: ECU 160,000 Property: ECU 80,000	Minimum £100,000	As required by Insurance Commissioner. Minimum: Pure: $250,000 Assn: $750.000
Reserves & Solvency	EU basis but separate rules for captives/ reinsurers	18% of net premium to £5m plus 16% of net in excess of £5m	Set for each company
Taxation	Exempt co.'s £225. No tax on investment or trading income	— Negotiated between Nil and 30% of profit — Exempt (Nil but fee of £500) — Sliding on investment income (up to 20%) — 20% profit	Pure captives: .25% of premiums Assoc: 1% of premiums if premium taxes not paid elsewhere

Table 4.1 Captive location analysis (cont'd)

	Hong Kong	Illinois	Isle of Man
Geography	South East of China	USA	North West Coast of England
Language	English/Cantonese	English	English
Currency	HK$	US$	£
Communications Access Post/Telex	Good Good	Good Good	Good Good
Bank Services	Good	Good	Good
Legal System	British	USA	British
Applicable Legislation	Insurance Companies Ordinance No. 6	Insurance Code	Isle of Man Insurance Act 1986.
Supervisory Jurisdiction	Inland Revenue Commissioner	Department of Insurance	Financial Board
Limits on Investment	None	None for pure captives	Admissible asset requirement
Local Office Restrictions	Registered Office	Administration Office	Registered Office
Financial Reporting	Annual Accounts	Annual	Annual Accounts
Registration & Incorporation	HK$300 + 4% of capital	$3,500 application fee	Registration fee £1,000 and annual business fee of £2,500 Duty of 1% on authorised capital
Capitalisation	HK$5 million	$2 million 80% by LOC	£50,000 minimum for pure captives or group or association captives. Non distributable reserve requirement where net retention exposure per loss exceeds 25% of net worth
Reserves & Solvency	None — solvency	Individual net risks must not exceed 10% of capital/surplus	£50,000 plus 10% of net premiums up to £2m and 5% of rest
Taxation	Corporate 16.5% Nil if offshore business	6.5% on net Illinois income + extra 2% if principal office elsewhere	Exemption allows for a tax rate between nil and 20%

Table 4.1 Captive location analysis (cont'd)

	Jersey	Labuan	Luxembourg
Geography	Channel Island	Malaysia	Europe
Language	English	Malay/English	French
Currency	£	M$	Franc

Communications
  Access
  Post/Telex
	Fair
	Good
		Fair
		Good
			Good
			Good

Bank Services	Good	Fair	Good
Legal System	British	Malaysian	Luxembourg
Applicable Legislation	Insurance Business (Jersey) Law 1983	Offshore Insurance Act 1990	1984 Legislation Tax Directive Nov. 1985 1991 Legislation Text
Supervisory Jurisdictions	Financial Services Department	Bank Negara Malaysia	Minister of Finance Insurance Commissioner
Limits on Investment	None	None	None, but investment policy needs approval by Insurance Commissioner and certain assets must be held locally
Local Office Restrictions	Registered local office	Registered local office	Local manager with staff based in Luxembourg
Financial Reporting	Annual audited accounts	Annual audited accounts	Annual — audited by approved auditor
Registration & Incorporation	Registration fee: £1000 — general business £5000 — long term business Incorporation fee: minimum £50, maximum £2,500	Annual fee M$10,000	Incorporation Lux Frc 50,000 & 1% tax on capital Annual fee Lux Frc 100,000
Capitalisation	Minimum capital £100,000	M$1 million for a captive	Minimum capital Lux Frc 50m
Reserves & Solvency	Set for each company Solvency Max 20% of net premium	20% of net premium income Captive M$1 million	Non-life 10% of net premium with minimum Lux Frc 50m Life 2% of net technical provision with minimum Lux Frc 50m
Taxation	20% but option to pay 2% on investment and inil if the company is tax exempt	Tax 5% on net audited profits with an option of M$20,000	40% income tax, deferral possible by using catastrophe reserve

Table 4.1 Captive location analysis (cont'd)

	Malta	Nauru	Netherlands Antilles
Geography	Mediterranean	Central Pacific	Off Venezuelan Coast
Language	English & Italian	English/Nauruan	Dutch/English
Currency	£m	A$	NAG
Communications **Access** **Post/Telex**	Good Good	Poor Poor	Good Good
Bank Services	Good	Fair	Good
Legal System	English (Commercial)	British	Dutch
Applicable Legislation	International Business Activities Act 1988	Insurance Act 1974 Nauruan Corp. Act 1972 Insurance Amendment Act 1974 Insurance Amendment 1978 Insurance (Application for Licence) Regs. 1974	Insurance Supervision Act (Public Sheet 1990 no. 77)
Supervisory Jurisdictions	Malta International Business Authority	Registered Corporations Minister of Finance Registrar of Banks	The Central Bank of the Netherlands Antilles
Limits on Investment	None	None	None
Local Office Restrictions	Registered local office	Registered Office	1 resident director
Financial Reporting	Annual	Audited Balance Sheets etc.	Annual Accounts
Registration & Incorporation	Registration £M1,000 for captives	Initial annual registration fee A$250	Related to amount of authorised capital, approximately US$3,000
Capitalisation	Min. US$250,000	No minimum Usual A$4,000	US$500,000 authorised 20% paid up
Reserves & Solvency	Awaited probably 15%	None — solvency	Non-life business 10% of the net premium with a minimum of US$167,600 Life business 4% of the net technical provisions with a minimum of US$223,500
Taxation	5% of income	Approx. A$85 charge No tax	3% of first US$55,900 profit with a minimum of 6% thereover. Non-treaty business is 2.4% profit tax (Maximum US$55,900)

Table 4.1 Captive location analysis (cont'd)

	Puerto Rico	**Singapore**	**Sweden**
Geography	Caribbean (US-link)	S.E. Asia	Europe
Language	Spanish/English	Mandarin/English	Swedish
Currency	$	S$	SKR

Communications
  Access
  Post/Telex
	Good
	Good
		Good
		Good
			Good
			Good

Bank Services	Good	Good	Good
Legal System	USA	—	Swedish/European Union
Applicable Legislation	International Banking Centre Regulatory Act 1989	Insurance Act (Chapter 193) of 1967	Insurance Law 1982 with amendments
Supervisory Jurisdictions	Commissioner of Financial Institutions Commissioner of Insurance of Puerto Rico	Monetary Authority of Singapore (MAS) Insurance Commissioner	Insurance Inspection
Limits on Investment	$300,000 must be physically located in Puerto Rico or acceptable financial guarantees to the Commissioner	Encouraged to use Singapore based fund management services	EU rules
Local Office Restrictions	Registered principal local office Minimum 6 full time employees 1st year: (40% Puerto Rican residents) 2nd year: (60% Puerto Rican residents) 3rd Year: (80% Puerto Rican residents) 4th year: (100% Puerto Rican residents)	Registered Office	Local Office requirement
Financial Reporting	Annual audited accounts	Annual Accounts	EU Rules
Registration & Incorporation	Application fee $1,000	Annual fee S$5,000	None
Capitalisation	$5m ($250,000 fully paid up)	$1m minimum	EU rules, but must be minimum ten times per risk retention and five times per event retention
Reserves & Solvency	Must possess $300,000 unencumbered assets	Surplus of assets over liabilities of $S1m	EU rules, but safety reserve allowances include:— Industrial insurance —50% net premium plus 15% loss reserves Reinsurance —150% net premium plus 45% loss reserve
Taxation	Annual fee $5,000	10% on profit from non-Singapore business, 33% on Singapore business — refer formula	30% but non-insurance reserve allowances can reduce this

CAPTIVE INSURANCE COMPANIES

Table 4.1 Captive location analysis (cont'd)

	Switzerland	Tennessee	Turks & Caicos
Geography	Europe	Central East USA	Caribbean
Language	Swiss	English	English
Currency	CHF	US$	US$
Communications **Access** **Post/Telex**	Good Good	Good Good	Poor Fair
Bank Services	Good	Good	Fair
Legal System	Swiss	USA	—
Applicable Legislation	Federal Insurance Supervisory Act 1979	Tennessee Captive Insurance Companies Act 1978 — Amended 1987	Insurance Ordinance 1989 Insurance Regulation 1990
Supervisory Jurisdictions	Insurance Commissioner	Tennessee Dept. of Commerce and of Insurance	Financial Secretary
Limits on Investment	None	Requirements for other Tennessee Companies	None
Local Office Restrictions	Local office requirements	Office required	Resident Insurance Manager Local designated office
Financial Reporting	Annual for reinsurance captives	Annual Conventional Statement	Audited Annual Report
Registration & Incorporation	Stamp duty of 2% on capital and organisational fund	$100 Initial $100 Annual plus 10% tax $500 Review fee	General Insurance $3,200 Credit Life $700
Capitalisation	Minimum 20 of net premium or CHF 1 million plus CHF200,000 organisational fund to be deposited	$750,000 for wholly owned captive £1m for Association captive Letter of Credit permitted	$100,000 General $200,000 Life as a guideline
Reserves & Solvency	Case by case treatment. Special consideration for captives including special technical reserves	Individual risks must not exceed 10% of capital and surplus	General only: 20% of premium upto $5,000,000 10% of premium + $100,000 over $5,000,000 Long term only: $180,000
Taxation	Net tax, federal, canton and communal, estimated to vary between 4% and 12.4% of profit on non-Swiss based risks. Full tax charge on profit on Swiss based risks.	Tennessee premium tax 1% on direct premiums. Exemption from mandatory pools and guarantee funds subject to US income tax. Minimum $5,000 for pure captives and mutuals $10,000 for association	General $2,230 annual fee Credit Life $250

144

Table 4.1 Captive location analysis (cont'd)

	US Virgin Islands	**Vanuatu**	**Vermont**
Geography	Between Dominican Rep. & Puerto Rico	Pacific — North of Australia	East USA
Language	English	English/French	English
Currency	US$	V.Fr	US$
Communications Access Post/Telex	Fair Fair	Poor Fair	Good Good
Bank Services	Fair	Fair	Good
Legal System	USA	French/British	USA
Applicable Legislation	Virgin Islands International Insurers Act 1993 plus amendment	Legislation 1971 Insurance Regulation 1973	Special Insurance Act 1981 Amendment 1988, 1989 and 1991
Supervisory Jurisdictions	Director, Division of Banking & Insurance, Office of the Lieutenant Governor	The Resident Commissioner	Department of Banking & Insurance
Limits on Investment	None for pure and industrial captives Some valuation restrictions for association captives	—	No-exempt for Association Captives
Local Office Restrictions	Locally kept records Authorised local manager One local board meeting per year	None	Principal place of business in the State
Financial Reporting	Annual report 3 year examination of solvency can be extended to 5 years	Limited	Annual audited statement
Registration & Incorporation	$1,000 application fee $400 incorporation fee $1,000 franchise tax $6,000 insurance license fee	Registration $1,000 for exempted companies	Registration $1,700 Annually $300
Capitalisation	Single parent US$50,000 Industrial US$75,000 Association US100,000	No requirement	Pure $250,000 Industrial insured $500,000 Association $750,000
Reserves & Solvency	Surplus: — Single parent US$70,000 Industrial US$125,000 Association US$220,000 Mut. Indust. US$200,000 Mutual Assoc. US$320,000	None	Solvency — surplus of $150,000 to $350,000 depending on category. Actuarial opinion on reserves required
Taxation	No local taxes USA F.E.T. applies unless. para. 953 (d) election is made	Stamp duty No income tax or corporate tax Annual fee $1,000	**Direct R/I** $1−20m .7% .25% $20−40m .5% .2% $40−60m .3% .15% Over $60m .1% .1% (on gross premium written)

CAPTIVE INSURANCE COMPANIES

Bermuda

Bermuda has been a very popular location for captive insurance companies for many years and is used by over 900 US corporations. In 1979 and 1980 the island first introduced regulations for insurance companies to ensure a degree of control over solvency and the type of business being underwritten. Broad details of the insurance law and regulations are given in the appendices, but an outline of a number of the important characteristics of Bermuda captive legislation is given below.

First, new companies wishing to set up insurance subsidiaries on the island are screened by a committee which examines their insurance plan and the type of business that they intend to underwrite.

Annual returns need to be submitted to the Registrar of Companies and they are reviewed by him as a form of monitoring their performance.

All insurance companies must now be registered and make an annual registration fee payment. They are also required to meet certain asset and liability requirements including a 75 per cent liquidity test related to laid-own criteria of asset admissibility.

In the last year or so Bermuda has re-examined its insurance law and capitalisation levels depend on the type of business a Bermuda based insurance company is going to underwrite. For captives, the position is largely unchanged and reflects the 1978 Insurance Act which requires a minimum share capital requirement of US$120,000 for companies writing normal business and a capital requirement related to net premium written. This has the effect of requiring a solvency margin of 20 per cent where the premium income is lower than $6 million and a solvency margin of 10 per cent for premiums in excess of this level. In addition, the authorities require the insurance company to be properly managed by recognised local companies and for the company to appoint auditors approved by the Registrar, who submit annually an audit certificate with the insurance company's accounts.

There are some exemptions to the new regulations in respect of pure captives and also for P & I clubs which have always been dealt with under separate legislation. In addition, there are extra requirements for companies who intend to handle long-term product liability or medical malpractice business.

Recent amendments to regulations in Bermuda include changes to the annual fees for exempted companies which were previously on a fixed basis and have now been changed to reflect the capital of each company. These new fees range from US$1,600 for companies with a capital of less than US$120,000 up to US$8,000 for companies with a capital in excess of US$12 million.

In addition to these changes the Bermuda authorities have made some changes to the solvency margin requirement of which the basic proposal requires insurers to maintain capital and surplus of at least 10 per cent of loss reserves. In addition to this change other alterations include the following:

1. Companies discounting their loss reserves and who would not otherwise have been able to meet the solvency margin now have to have their discounting practice reviewed and certified by an actuary.
2. The principle representative and directors of the captive now have to declare annually that the company has complied with the conditions of the Bermuda operating licence.
3. Directors are now responsible for explaining what corrective action has been taken in cases where the captive has failed to comply with the solvency and liquidity ratios.
4. Insurers that write property and casualty insurance are now required to segregate related and unrelated gross premiums in their annual returns and in addition have to reveal details of any stop loss reinsurance indicating the maximum annual aggregate net losses retained under each class of business.

Other than the annual fees, there are no tax requirements in Bermuda.

Bermuda naturally includes all of the major international captive management companies and boasts the largest number of captives and premium volume.

Figures produced at the end of 1994 indicate that the Bermuda insurance market overall encompasses gross premiums of over US$19 billion, and capital and surplus of US$30 billion.

Barbados

Barbados has been a successful Caribbean domicile with particular attractions for Canadian owned captive insurers. The legislation is controlled by the Exempt Insurance Act 1989 but there have been a number of alterations over the years including important changes at the end of 1995 (which bring it into line, so far as admissible assets are concerned, with Bermuda and other locations) and changes to the tax law designed to maintain the fiscal advantages that Barbados offers to Canadian companies.

The insurance sector is controlled by the Supervisor of Insurance on behalf of the Minister of Finance and the general basis is a requirement to provide a minimum capital of US$125,000, and maintain solvency margins at a level of 20% reducing to 10% for income in excess of US$5 million. Financial reporting requires annual audited statutory returns and for long term business the need for actuarial certificates. Tax exemption applies for the first fifteen years and there are few restrictions from an investment or exchange control standpoint.

As with other jurisdictions, there are annual costs in the form of licence fees and formation costs which incorporate government fees and an audit fee. Letters of Credit are allowed for capital purposes and shelf companies are permitted — these do not require capital until they intend to commence business. More detailed information on the Barbados regulatory environment is included in the appendices.

Cayman Islands

The Cayman Islands have grown rapidly as a captive location since 1978, mainly as a result of the restrictions imposed by Bermuda on a number of medical malpractice captives which were submitted to the Bermudan authorities. The Cayman Islands accepted a number of these captives and this initiated their important growth. At roughly the same time as Bermuda, the Cayman Islands introduced their own new insurance law and subsequently appointed an insurance supervisor to oversee the introduction of the regulations. The law is similar in many respects to that in Bermuda with a requirement for the captive insurance company to have a net worth of US$120,000 for general business, with net worth being defined as the excess of assets over liabilities.

There is a requirement for the business that the captive is writing to be disclosed to the authorities and for the records to be kept on the Islands. It is also necessary for companies to have an annual audit carried out and have a certificate available, although this is not yet required automatically by the authorities to be deposited with them.

The insurance regulations require captives to maintain as an initial step a net premium-to-surplus ratio of no higher than 3:1. Once the company has been established the ratio can be reduced to 5:1. Like Bermuda there is an annual licence and registration fees must be paid on initial registration and also on an annual basis. There is in addition a requirement that each captive must have a manager on the Islands and the captive manager or an auditor must provide a certificate of compliance that indicates that the captive has adhered to the business plan. Captive managers pay an annual licence fee, which is around US$10,000.

There are currently in the region of 350 insurance licences issued in the Cayman Islands and the Island is well supported by the major international captive managers.

Bahamas

The Bahamas introduced insurance legislation in 1969, which resulted in a number of captive insurance companies already established there moving to Bermuda. The main problem with the 1969 legislation was the imposition of a small tax coupled with an indication that controls would become more onerous. In 1979 new legislation was introduced which eliminated the taxation and also repudiated the original requirement to publish financial statements. It is still necessary to deposit financial statements with the Registrar of Companies but these are no longer public knowledge.

The Bahamas have a Registrar of Companies who monitors the performance of captives, which are required, as in Bermuda and the Cayman Islands, to register and file audited returns on an annual basis. The financial requirements for general business are capitalisation of $140,000 with a variation depending on the premium income to the captive. There is also an initial registration fee and an annual fee, both of which are minimal and relate to premium income.

The Bahamas now has a full-time insurance supervisor whose task it is to review the overall insurance legislation and accelerate the growth of captives. The insurance adviser reports to the Registrar of Insurance Companies, with the Registrar having responsibility for the general review of insurance business in the Bahamas including examination of the various insurance companies under licence. Insurance legislation in the Bahamas is regulated primarily by the 1969 Insurance Act and the External Insurance Act 1983 which are expected to be reviewed and probably integrated in the near future. The following gives some outline of the way in which the insurance laws operate and the approach that the Bahamian authorities take towards licensing their insurance companies.

The authorities are engaged in a review of the overall insurance legislation but this is not yet completed. Details of the basic approach currently in operation providing amendments to the 1969 legislation are included in Appendix II. In addition, details of the External Insurance Act 1983 are included, but in order to summarise the approach which was outlined in February 1986 the following gives an indication of the attitudes being taken by the authorities.

Although the two insurance laws lay down a statutory minimum net worth figure and net premium to capital and surplus ratios, applicants need to be realistic in their determination of a suitable financial base of operation. In view of this the registrar of companies would not normally expect to see any application with less than $250,000 initial capital and in any event the proposed amount is expected to be more than adequate to support the proposed volume of business. Likewise, working ratios should be established in the light of current market thinking and practice. A net premium to capital and surplus ratio of 1:1 but not wider than 3:1 is considered to be a good starting-point.

Initial capitalisation, certainly in relation to the statutory minimum, should be by way of cash. Letters of credit are not likely to be acceptable unless they represent amounts over and above working capital level. There is no legal requirement for capital funds to be held locally, but most companies do use the extensive local banking and ship system. In that regard companies which are planning to act as direct insurers may be required to put their deposits either locally or in the state where business is being transacted in order to provide the necessary level of comfort.

The ongoing reporting requirements are at present minimal but their importance should not be overstated. Basically, the requirements are that each company should continue to carry on its business in the manner described in the business plan. Audited financial statements should be filed annually, within six months of the close of the financial year. In addition the companies registered under the 1983 Act are required to fill in a statutory statement indicating compliance with terms of registration.

In addition to the above, new companies are required to complete detailed application forms and the registrar will wish to be satisfied before making any positive recommendations that certain basic areas are to his satisfaction. The main areas which the registrar will examine are as follows:

1. The identity of all key parties involved (sponsors, shareholders, directors, officers and managers).

2. The fitness of key parties to engage in the proposed operation.
3. The business ethics involved.
4. The feasibility of the planned business.
5. The security of any outward reinsurance.

In addition the Act requires insurers to use the services of a registered underwriting manager. To obtain a licence the underwriting manager has to demonstrate that he is able to deliver the service expected by his clients and also demonstrate a reasonable level of underwriting and insurance expertise. The manager will also need to have a local office, employ Bahamian staff and have at least one prospective client.

British Virgin Islands

Although the BVI has been around, as an offshore insurance sector, for many years, its development has increased in the last few years following the introduction of a new Insurance Act in 1994. Details of the Act are included in the appendices but generally speaking it follows many other jurisdictions in the sense that the minimum capital requirements are US$100,000 for general business, it is necessary for the insurer to maintain a principal office in BVI and have an insurance manager who is resident in that territory. The managers are required to hold a certificate of authority and obliged to report to the Insurance Supervisory Authority (which is the responsibility of the Commissioner of Insurance who reports to the Minister of Finance) if the insurance company, they are looking after, is getting into difficulties or is failing to meet certain other criteria.

There is a reasonable amount of flexibility with regard to investments and also the usual Government fees.

United States of America and Canada — domestic locations

For US companies there is the opportunity to establish captive insurance companies within the United States on a preferential basis. Colorado and Tennessee were the original states to introduce specific legislation in 1973 and 1978 respectively. Both of these states introduced lower local taxes in order to attract captive insurance companies and also gave some exemptions from mandatory pools and guarantee funds that would normally be subject to US income tax. In addition there were restrictions on the types of insurance that could be written, including limitations in Tennessee so far as personal lines were concerned and restrictions on reinsurance for certain liability coverage. In Colorado the original legislation did not allow business to be written by a captive which was generally available in the conventional insurance market.

The major change in the development of domestic US captives came about when the state of Vermont introduced special insurance legislation in 1981 which swept away the previous restrictions imposed by the two original states and allowed captives to be formed for the first time in an environment which provided a competitive alternative to many of the offshore locations, such as Bermuda and the Cayman Islands, used by US corporations.

Since the development of Vermont, which has been spectacularly successful, many other states have introduced special captive legislation in order to attract this sector of the insurance market. The position at the present time in the main states providing such facilities is dealt with in the following sections.

Vermont
Details of how to form a captive insurance company in Vermont, and the regulations, are included in the appendices and also in the location chart, but broadly speaking captive insurance companies in Vermont are governed by a specific chapter in the Public Act which denotes a special Insurer Act designed to provide an attractive statutory framework for captive insurance companies. Unlike the other jurisdictions the 1981 Act introduced a number of special features which were not available elsewhere. These include the following:

- No proof of insurance unavailability needed.
- Single parent, association and group captives permitted.
- Lower capitalisation requirements.
- All commercial lines acceptable other than workers compensation which may only be written on a reinsurance basis.
- No approval of rates or forms.
- No minimum premiums required.
- No investment restrictions other than for association captives.
- Simplified annual reporting.
- No participation in pools or guarantee associations.

At the end of 1995 the number of captives in Vermont exceeded 300 with further growth during the first half year of 1996. In addition to captives Vermont includes a number of risk retention groups.

Regulations have been amended since the original legislation in 1981 with an important change taking place when the local tax on premiums was amended to a sliding-scale basis ranging from 0.7

per cent for premiums up to $20 million to 0.1 per cent where the premium volume exceeds $60 million. In many respects Vermont has developed as an alternative domicile to Bermuda for US-owned captives and the observers believe this will continue as the move towards more onshore development grows.

Colorado

Although Colorado was the first onshore captive location it has not grown significantly in recent years, having at the present time twenty-four licensed captives, which is virtually the same figure as over the previous five years. The original 1972 Captive Insurance Company Act has been amended over the years with an authorisation in 1987 of risk retention groups and various technical revisions during 1989. The most recent amendments include allowing single parent captives to make loans to their parent companies above the minimum capital requirements of $300,000 and surplus requirements of $200,000. As with Vermont, single parent captives are exempt from filing policy forms and rates (although association captives still have to do so) and there are no investment restrictions for single parent captives or industrial insurance captives, which are defined as a collection of entities in which each member has a full-time risk manager, a minimum of twenty-five full-time employees and a minimum aggregate annual insurance premium for all risks of $25,000. In addition captives can now be formed by operations other than stock corporations, thereby allowing captive formations by associations of individual professional practitioners or groups, corporations or partnerships as it is now possible to obtain from the insurance commissioner an extension on the required filing date for annual reports, moving this date from 1 March to 1 July each year.

Details of the capitalisation for Colorado and the local taxes are included in the location charts

Tennessee

Tennessee has around fifteen captives and the major change in recent years has been the introduction of the 1987 law which allows risk retention groups to operate for the first time. In addition Tennessee has specific rules for so-called industrial insureds which include, somewhat unlike some other jurisdictions, groups where the participating companies are in different industries. This change was expected to increase the number of captives in this category, but so far this growth has not taken place.

Hawaii

At the end of 1995 there were twenty captives licensed in Hawaii, a number of which are subsidiaries of Honolulu-based companies.

CAPTIVE INSURANCE COMPANIES

The Hawaii captive law became effective in July 1987 with changes in 1988 designed to introduce greater flexibility into the regulations. Requirements for Hawaiian captives include the following:

- Maintaining a principle place of business in the state.
- Appointment of a local resident agent to represent the captive.
- A non-refundable premium of $1,000 for a licence application followed by an annual registration fee of $300.
- At least one directors' meeting to be held in Hawaii every year.

Illinois
Insurance regulations in Illinois were changed on 1st September 1989 to allow captives to reinsure workers compensation insurance underwritten by fronting insurers and allow owners of captives to post required capital and surplus through subordinated debt and to liberalise the use of letters of credit. There are just ten captives domiciled in Illinois and these have been established since the original captive statute was passed in 1987. The state has comparatively high capitalisation requirements of US$2 million, but captives are exempt from premium taxes but subject to a tax rate for Illinois risks of 7.3 per cent which it is anticipated will drop to 6.5 per cent from the middle of 1991.

Illinois captives are at the present time almost entirely limited to association and industrial insured captives.

Georgia
The special captive statute in Georgia came into effect in 1988 and allows the formation of single and group captives with conditions similar to the other states trying to entice captives.

Minimum capitalisation is $500,000 and there is a requirement to maintain a principle business office in Georgia. Premium taxes up to 5 per cent are the same as those charged in respect of conventional insurance companies.

One negative feature is that each policy form has to carry a notice advising policy holders that the captive is not subject to all of the Georgia state insurance regulations and captives are not able to write personal lines, life, health or accident insurance.

Delaware
Delaware is home to two very large nuclear industry captives who were previously located in Bermuda and who between them write premiums in excess of $250 million.

Changes in the Delaware law made in 1989 amended the tax position for captives by introducing a sliding scale arrangement similar to that which exists in Vermont. These changes were introduced to try to attract more captives, but so far this has not been successful, with only four captives (including the two nuclear captives already mentioned) licensed as at April 1990.

Virginia

Virginia has no captives although it has a special law which was introduced in 1980. Licensing requirements are very similar to those in place for conventional insurers, with the exception that captives in Virginia can use letters of credit, rather than cash, to satisfy capital and surplus requirements.

British Columbia

British Columbia is the only province in Canada which has made an attempt to encourage onshore captives and has been successful to the extent that at the end of 1995 twelve captives were licensed in the province.

Captives are governed by the Insurance (Captive Company) Act which came into force in 1987, and the main advantages of British Columbia are the tax-related advantages which allow companies to reduce their liability to federal excise tax which would automatically be payable in respect of premiums paid to an offshore insurance subsidiary.

In addition to this advantage minimum capitalisation is relatively low at $200,000 and there is an annual registration fee of $2,500 and an application fee of $500. In addition to permitting single parent and association captives to be formed, the captive law also allows so-called sophisticated insureds, which are captives owned by unrelated groups which have a sufficient base of premium income and insurance expertise. Details of the law and the regulatory requirements are included in the appendices.

Guernsey

When Guernsey originally entered the captive scene it permitted two forms of companies for the writing of insurance. The first was the Corporation Tax Captive, which was an exempt company managed away from the island, not allowed to use the word insurance in its title and required to pay a nominal annual payment to the Authorities. The second company was the full captive insurance company, which was permitted to have the word insurance in its title and was taxed on its investment income and dealing profits but not on its underwriting profits. In 1986 formal insurance legislation was introduced into Guernsey and this phased out the corporation tax company by not allowing new corporation tax companies to be formed. All insurance companies in Guernsey are now subject to the Insurance Law which operates on the following basis: —

1. Anyone who carries on, or holds himself as carrying on, insurance business must register as as insurer in respect of long-term business or general business or both.
2. An insurer is deemed to be holding himself as carrying on insurance business if he occupies premises in Guernsey or has his name in a directory or has a letterhead that gives a Guernsey contact address or invites a person in Guernsey to enter into an insurance contract or is otherwise seen to be carrying on insurance business in Guernsey.
3. Lists will be published annually of all registered insurers including their principal place of business. Lists of authorised 'insurance managers' will also be published. A comparison of the two lists will therefore show the managers of each company. The list will state any restriction applicable to insurers or managers.
4. A registered insurer must appoint a general representative who is either:
   (a) an executive director or employee who is ordinarily resident in Guernsey and who is approved by the Advisory and Finance Committee as a fit and proper person to act; or
   (b) an authorised insurance manager; who shall act generally for the insurer, accept service of any document and be responsible for making returns, depositing accounts and furnishing all other information required of the Insurer.
5. Insurance managers must apply for authorisation to act as such in Guernsey and the Committee will need to be satisfied that they are fit and proper persons and have sufficient special knowledge and practical experience of insurance business so to act.
6. Registered insurers must maintain a margin of solvency of not less than:
   (a) for general business, 18 per cent of the first £5 million of net premium income plus 16 per cent of the excess;
   (b) for long-term business $2\frac{1}{2}$ per cent of the value of the long-term subject to a minimum of £50,000.
   Net premium income is defined as gross premium income during the last preceding financial year (or the estimated maximum gross premium income in the first year of operation for new

applications) reduced by rebates, refunds and reinsurance commissions payable by the insurer and the gross amount of reinsurance ceded.

7. 75 per cent of assets required to maintain the solvency margin must be approved assets (general business) and 25 per cent must be approved assets for long-term business.

8. Reinsurance ceded to an associated person shall not be taken into account for solvency margin purposes and amounts receivable or balanced due from an associated person shall not be taken as approved assets unless the Committee consent in any particular case.

9. A minimum paid-up capital of £100,000 must be maintained or its equivalent (on registration) in any other currency. This may be waived in lieu of an irrevocable letter of credit provided by a Guernsey-registered bank, although it is anticipated there would have to be some very cogent reasons for this waiver to be exercised.

10. All registered insurers will be required to submit audited annual accounts within four months of the close of the financial year.

11. Registered insurance managers must declare annually all insurers for which they have acted on a continuing basis, whether as a manager or by providing any insurance advice, consultancy, administrative or secretarial service, whether or not that insurer is a Guernsey-registered insurer. Further, any other person who provides such services on a continuing basis to unregistered insurers must also declare the fact and the nature of the services together with such other information as the Committee may request about the insurer. The objective, of course, is to avoid Guernsey's reputation being besmirched by someone on the island getting involved with an insurance operation which is not subject to the same controls as would apply in Guernsey. This may be an onerous requirement but is accepted as a necessary one.

Guernsey has around 250 captives with a premium income of well over £1 billion. It continues to grow and has developed a wider geographical spread of captive owners than many of the other European domiciles which, generally speaking, attract captives from a limited number of territories.

The most significant change in Guernsey, in recent years, has been revisions to the taxation position which allows captives to determine their tax position under three different basis of computation. The three options allow complete flexibility and in summary are as follows:

OPTION 1 NO TAX	Exempt company fee £500

OPTION 2 MINIMAL TAX	Tax only on investment income of shareholders' funds on sliding scale as follows:

	Shareholders' Investment Income	Rate of Tax	Tax Payable
	up to £250,000	20%	£50,000
	next £250,000	1%	£2,500
	next £500,000	0.5%	£2,500
	next £2	0.3%	£6,000
	million	0.1%	£1,000
	excess		per million

OPTION 3 FULL TAX	20% on net profits. Payment can be postponed until claims are paid or profit is taken

Jersey

Although Jersey in fact introduced its insurance legislation before Guernsey's legislation arrived on the statute book, the approach is very similar and the taxation system in practice is identical. Like Guernsey there is a requirement for a minimum capitalisation of £100,000 and control over ownership of the company, management arrangements, type of business being written and the application of a solvency margin ranging from 15 own to 10 per cent depending on the net premium income.

However, unlike Guernsey the insurance law in Jersey used only to permit the writing of insurance business covering the following areas: —

1. Contracts of insurance of the risks of the insurance company's holding company and any company associated with it.
2. Contracts of insurance of risks of more than such number of companies as may be prescribed holding between them all of the issued shares of the company holding the permit and in the company associated with any of them; the maximum number in any one of these groups will be fifteen.
3. Contracts of reinsurance of risks already insured by an insurance company.

However, this situation was changed in 1996 to allow captives to operate in any format and, in addition, Jersey has indicated its determination to have a bigger role in the offshore insurance sector by employees in 1996 insurance supervisor with both a regulatory and marketing responsibility. Because of the dominance of Guernsey, the growth of captives has been limited and this has been influenced by the fact that most of the captive management facilities in the Channel Islands are based in Guernsey which has, of course, been in the captive business for many more years than its neighbour.

Isle of Man

As an island in the scheduled territories interested in the development of financial services, the Isle of Man introduced captive insurance legislation in 1978. This legislation was similar to the then draft law in Guernsey and attracted little growth. However, in October 1981 the Isle of Man authorities introduced new insurance legislation which removed the 20 per cent tax which previously applied to the investment income earned on captives. This development generated considerable interest in the island and as a means of encouraging expansion the authorities have subsequently appointed an insurance supervisor with the task of developing business and also of rewriting the insurance legislation. In September 1986 this legislation became law, and a broad outline of the law and the controls is included in the appendices.

The Isle of Man has been one of the most successful European captive locations in recent years, with the captives in early 1996 reaching a total of 150, most of which are owned by UK companies. These include the majority of the very large UK public corporations which were privatised during the late 1980s and early 1990s and provide a substantial asset base which probably makes the Isle of Man the largest European location so far as captive assets are concerned.

In a speech the Insurance Supervisor in the Isle of Man summarised his approach to captives operated and listed a number of factors that would normally be taken into account when an application is made. These are interesting and give an insight into an Insurance Supervisor's approach. They included the following comments:

1. Captives writing only the risks of the parent or associated companies or members of a common industry or association can apply for a restricted licence. This would allow them to write any class of business subject to a satisfactory business plan.
2. For a restricted licence to write general business only, solvency margin requirements are £50,000 plus 10 per cent for the first £2 million of net premium written and 5 per cent of any amount

in excess of £2 million. Clearly, the higher the premium volume the lower the solvency requirement. In the case of long-term business the solvency margin is increased by £100,000.

3. As to share capital, the minimum requirement is £50,000 paid up in cash in any Isle of Man bank. However, every applicant is required to present a business plan which demonstrates there will be adequate resources to support the business proposed. This invariably means the requirement is in excess of the determined minimum. This minimum can be met by any admissible asset including, in most cases, an irrevocable letter of credit or guarantee by an approved bank.

4. Where a captive insurer writes unrelated business, then the solvency and capital requirements would be that of a general insurer but where it is writing only reinsurance business then it needs only satisfy the capital and solvency requirements of a reinsurer, which is rather modestly set at £100,000. The rationale for this solvency level is simply that supervision of professional reinsurers is perhaps more for the security department of ceding companies and the reinsurance brokers. It is they who have the resources and inside track. In practice, a fronting company may require a much larger capital base, and if it doesn't, I likely will.

5. Business plans must be discussed with nominated auditors and it is a prerequisite of authorisation that the auditor confirms that the plan has been properly prepared in accordance with the assumption stated. It must stack up. The auditor must have professional indemnity insurance of not less than £10 million and should preferably be resident on the Island.

6. I shall need to consider the claims experience. A more favourable claims experience than what I might normally expect might place me on the defensive. I may have to be persuaded as to the expected course of events and this may result in a requirement for supporting justification.

7. There is the matter of IBNRs for long tail business, except that this is sometimes a difficult matter, but be assured I shall seek to require demonstration that these reserves are realistic. Where the net retention any one loss gives exposure ratio greater than 25 per cent of net worth then the regulations require a non-distributable statutory reserve as part of the shareholders' funds. When the exposure ratio is brought to a prudent level (circa 15 per cent) then it may be released and this will then permit an increase in the profits allowable for distribution.

8. The reinsurance programme must be acceptable. For this reason I may scrutinise the security behind any reinsurance portfolio.

9. Copy insurance records and books of account must be kept on the Island and must be available for inspection at any time.

10. The ownership and ultimate beneficial interest in the ownership of the company must be fully disclosed. Ownership by discretionary trust is not acceptable.
11. Management can be exercised solely by the directors, provided they are judged to be competent for the business to be undertaken. Alternatively management may in conjunction with an insurance manager resident on the Island and registered under the Insurance Act. Normally two resident Manx directors are required. I will not have any brass plate operation — even if the management company has a proper establishment elsewhere.
12. All those in control, directors, CEOs and managers of a company have to satisfy me that they are fit and proper persons to hold their respective positions in the company.

It can be seen from these comments that in the Isle of Man, as in the other jurisdictions, it is necessary to look at the way the insurance supervisor approaches captives outside of the bare bones of the insurance legislation and regulations. Much store is put by the quality of the captive parent, the capability of the chosen insurance manager and the professionalism and credibility of the business plan.

Gibraltar

In many respects Gibraltar is seen as a new and potentially important captive location. Although, there have been captive insurance companies in Gibraltar since the 1960's it has struggled to develop a position and has been slow in developing the appropriate insurance legislation and marketing its advantages to potential captive owners. However, a number of important changes have taken place in the last year, with the introduction, into Gibraltar law, of the Second and Third European Union non-life insurance directives which will enable Gibraltar insurers to underwrite risks anywhere within the European Union without the need to establish a base or obtain a separate licence in each territory. This is an advantage that is shared only, at present, by companies established in Dublin and is therefore of benefit to those companies that wish to avoid fronting arrangements for their European risks. In addition, Gibraltar has a flexible tax regime which provides the opportunity to avoid tax completely or adopt a variable tax rate of between 2% and 35%.

Gibraltar is trying to organise itself so that it is competitive in the whole range of captive regulations and has made changes to encompass the following:

- discretionary capping of stamp duty on capital at a figure of £5,000

- the permission of hybrid capital
- redomiciliation law allowing existing captives, based in jurisdictions that have reciprocal legislation, to relocate to Gibraltar

Gibraltar seems well placed to develop as a tax exempt captive location within the European Union insurance environment. There are still concerns about its relationship with Spain and how this might impact political stability but the U.K. Government appears to have committed itself to supporting Gibraltar in its endeavours to establish as an offshore insurance centre. Whether or not it is successful will depend on Gibraltar's own ability to market its services and provide the sort of response rate and infra structure necessary to gain acknowledgement as a credible offshore centre.

Luxembourg

In 1984 Luxembourg made a decision to enter the world of offshore reinsurance by exacting special legislation primarily designed to attract pure captives.

The basic rules of Luxembourg are as follows:

1. All reinsurance enterprises must have a licence issued by the Ministry of Finance before commencing their activities.
2. In order to obtain a licence the enterprise must adopt the form of a limited company having a fully paid-up share capital of at least Luxembourg F50 million. The company will be subject on a continuing basis to an annual subscription tax of 0.2 per cent of the share capital.
3. The share capital may be less than Luxembourg F50 million. If the company is a reinsurance company limiting its activity to reinsuring risks from industrial and/or commercial enterprises who are members of the same group of companies (the equivalent of a captive) the capital will be Luxembourg F6 million.
4. There are a number of other requirements built into the legislation:
   (a) reinsurance companies must hold as their own funds, in addition to the basic capital and excluding technical reserves, an amount equal to at least 10 per cent of their annual premium income net of reinsurance ceded;
   (b) this rate is reduced to 7 per cent for reinsurance companies which exclude from the insurances that they are providing risk for civil liberty in respect of third party claims;
   (c) this 7 per cent is reduced to 5 per cent for those reinsurance companies who limit their activity to writing risks

of commercial and/or industrial enterprises which are members of the same group that provide the majority shareholders of the reinsurance company (in other words, a captive). This means that the captive writing, for example, casualty business could have a net premium income of US$2.25 million and a share capital of US$225,000.

5. The Minister must agree the company's Articles of Incorporation, the identity of directors and managers and the identity of the shareholders.

6. The company must appoint an external auditor from a list of agreed auditors kept by the insurance commission.

7. An annual licence fee of Luxembourg F100,000 on application and Luxembourg F50,000 each year thereafter has to be paid.

8. All reinsurance companies must have a manager resident in Luxembourg with acceptable professional qualifications and the experience necessary to exercise the function correctly. This manager must be licensed by the Ministry.

In addition to this broad legislation the taxation position in Luxembourg is of interest; in particular, the ability to establish substantial reserves, thereby avoiding corporation tax for a considerable time. These specific reserving requirements were introduced in late 1985 and are of particular importance to captives as the establishment of what is in effect an equalisation reserve reduces the profit and thereby the tax due to the Luxembourg authorities or probably to the tax authorities of the country of the parent. The basic rules for the establishment of the equalisation reserves are as follows:

1. The amount of the reserve on an annual basis may not exceed an amount such that the trading result for the period, taking into account taxes due, is neither a loss or a profit that is too small to cover losses brought forward from earlier periods.

2. The total amount of the reserve may not exceed a ceding which is equal to a multiple of the average amount of premiums due for the last period and the tour preceding periods net of cancellations and rebates and after deduction of reinsurance cessions

The multiple to be used is a function of the rank of the risk in the classifications of risks established by the insurance commission. For the calculation of the reserve, the multiple to apply to the average amount may not exceed:

(a) 12.5 times the amount for Class 1 risk;
(b) 15 times the amount of Class 2 risk;

(c) 17.5 times the amount for Class 3 risk;

(d) 20 times the amount for Class 4 risk.

For explanatory purposes the Class 1 risk is likely to be the low value/high frequency exposure such as household insurance whereas the Class 4 risk is likely to be liability exposure or the high value property risk.

Luxembourg has been particularly successful in attracting captive insurance companies owned by Swedish multinational companies who probably account for the majority of the Luxembourg-based captives. At the beginning of 1997 Luxembourg had attracted over 200 captives writing in the region of US$2 billion in gross premiums.

The disadvantage of Luxembourg has always been the inability to establish a direct insurance company, a facility which is now available within the European Community in Dublin, but Luxembourg continues to prosper and in more recent times has attracted a number of captives from France, Belgium and, more recently, Japan.

Cyprus

Cyprus has specific insurance legislation for captive insurance companies with a very low tax requirement on profits and a minimum capitalisation of Cyprus £10,000. The infrastructure on the island is good so far as financial and communication facilities are concerned and the number of captive management companies is increasing. The island has been of particular interest to companies operating in the Middle East because of its geographical convenience and the attractiveness of the legislation, and also to Australian companies because of the double tax treaty arrangements and the fact that until recently Cyprus, like Singapore, did not require offshore captives to obtain approval from the Australian Federal Reserve Bank.

Netherlands Antilles

The Netherlands Antilles is a location of particular interest to captives owned by Dutch parents because of the relationship that exists between the two countries. There are a number of captives and management companies on the islands and the financial infrastructure is good. There is minimal taxation and a minimum capital requirement of Dutch Guilders 200,000, of which 20 per cent has to be paid up.

The Antilles has been working on revisions to its insurance law over the last few years and has a new draft law which is still awaiting approval from the Antilles government. In addition to the insurance law, changes have been made in the tax structure, which means that captives and reinsurance companies have the option of being taxed at the 2.4 per cent rate on their profits with the taxation limited to an amount based on a fixed profit figure of NAf100,000. In addition to this fixed tax rate there is now a fixed fee of NAf3,000 making a potential maximum annual charge of NAf5,400, which is roughly equivalent to US$3,000. These new changes can be used by captives whose parents are domiciled in the country with which the Netherlands Antilles do not have a tax treaty but those in treaty countries will probably prefer to operate on the full tax basis in order to gain the treaty advantages, particularly in relation to dividend payments.

Panama

Panama originally introduced legislation, in 1976, to try to make it a particularly attractive location for reinsurance companies. Minimum capitalisation was US$150,000 with annual registration and incorporation taxes of a fairly minimal nature. Where the underwriting profits on reinsurance arise from foreign risk there is no taxation. Annual filing of audited accounts is required and there is overall control under the authority of the Registrar of Companies.

In an attempt to encourage the formation of captive insurance companies, Panama introduced an Insurance Act in 1996 which involves minimum capital requirements of US$150,000, the licencing of insurance managers (including the necessity for managers to place a surety bond of US$100,000) and corporation and annual fees of around U$3,200.

There is a great deal of interest in the development of captives in South America and it must be assumed that Panama has decided to introduce a more pro-active approach to attracting captives because of this important development. More details of the Panama approach to captive regulation are included in the appendices.

Hong Kong

Hong Kong does not differentiate between captive insurance companies and others. It has an exceptionally good financial business infrastructure and there should be no tax penalty for captive insurance companies writing non-Hong Kong business. The insurance regulations require a high capitalisation of Hong Kong $5 million with a minimal registration fee. The regulatory authorities are under the control of the Inland Revenue Commissioner and there Is a requirement to report annual accounts.

CAPTIVE INSURANCE COMPANIES

Switzerland

Nordic Mutual, the captive management company, has been developing the concept of captive location within Zurich with some success. Some of the advantages associated with Switzerland include agreement from the Zurich tax authorities that special reserving requirements for captives can be established, the attraction of low tax on profit (the range is between 3.63% and 9.8%) and a separate tax on capital involving a fixed rate of 0.0825% of taxable equity.

In addition, Switzerland has numerous double tax agreements and tax rates, payable in Switzerland, on dividends ranging between 0% to 32.%. As a consequence, the treaty withholding tax rates on dividends are at present:

0% for Denmark, Luxembourg, Netherlands and Sweden
5% for Austria, Egypt, Finland, France, Germany, Greece, Malaysia, Norway, UK, Poland and USA
10% for Belgium, China, Hungary, Indonesia, Ireland, Japan, Korea, Portugal, Singapore, Spain, Sri Lanka and Trinidad

In addition, it is possible to reduce the local taxes for foreign owned captives, which do not operate in the Swiss market. Nordic Mutual indicate that they, in one instance, obtained a tax deduction for reinsurance for captives of 85%, i.e. only 15% of the profit was taxable to the local community.

More details of the attractions of Zurich Switzerland as a captive location are included in the appendices

Vanuatu

These islands, previously called the New Hebrides, located in the Pacific north of Australia, have been used by companies to set up exempt captives. Legislation was introduced in 1973. There are no requirements for either capitalisation or reporting of accounts, and there is no taxation. There is a registration fee and an annual tax fee, both of which are nominal. Vanuatu became independent in 1980, following its joint control by the French and UK authorities.

Singapore

Singapore is interested in encouraging large, reputable and financially sound multinationals to set up 'pure' captives in Singapore. Particular attention will be paid to the business track record and reputation of the parent company or group in the admission policy. Captives have to be registered under the Companies Act (Cap 185) and the Insurance Act (Cap 193). Taxation in Singapore is governed by the Singapore Income Tax Act (Cap 141). For pure captives whose business is offshore, control is liberal compared with commercial insurers. Such captives would not be required to set up a Singapore insurance fund for their insurance operations and would not be subject to the Insurance Act requirements on insurance funds. They would also be able to enjoy a concessionary tax rate of 10 per cent on profits from offshore business.

The major financial requirements for captives involve a minimum paid-up capital of S$1 million combined with a solvency margin that involves a surplus of assets over liabilities of S$1 million. Annual fees are S$5,000 and although there are no investment restrictions captives are encouraged to utilise fund management services available in Singapore where they find it advantageous to do so.

One of the key factors of the Singapore situation is the preferential corporate tax rate for captives which involves a concessionary rate of 10 per cent on profits from offshore business. The calculation of concessionary tax rate is complicated; full details of the income tax act related to captives are included in the appendices and include details of the formula used to calculate the net tax charge.

Ireland — Financial Services Centre, Dublin

The Financial Services Centre in Dublin has been established as the result of an initiative by the European Community in conjunction with the Industrial Development Authority of Ireland. Linked to the development of the Financial Services Centre is the introduction of special attractions for captive reinsurance companies and the ability for direct insurance companies to be formed which can, as a result, write direct business into other European Community countries. Although captive reinsurance companies are not subject to regulatory control they must file annual audited returns and are expected to produce business plans.

Direct insurance companies are required to establish with a minimum paid-up capital of I£500,000 and maintain solvency margins in line with those laid down by the European Community legislation. They must also be incorporated and resident in Ireland and employ qualified staff or alternatively use the services of an established captive insurance management operation.

One of the key factors of the Financial Services success has been the introduction of a special 10 per cent tax rate for captive insurance companies, which is guaranteed to operate until the year 2005 and is expected to be extended for a further period to the year 2010. This low tax rate only applies to companies operating from within the International Financial Services Centre and is aimed at encouraging companies to establish in the centre and more particularly to employ local staff.

Malta

The Malta International Business Activities Act 1988 combined with the Insurance Business Act of 1981 enables captive insurance companies to be formed with preferential establishment requirements and regulations and a special low tax rate. Once again details of the legislation are included in the appendices but in broad terms insurance companies are required to establish with a minimum capitalisation of US$250,000 and are not subject to outwards reinsurance restrictions, investment restrictions, dividend payments and admissible asset requirements which apply to ordinary insurance companies. In addition captive insurance companies are subject to annual fees of LM1,000 and a special tax rate of 5 per cent.

Turks and Caicos

The Turks and Caicos have been used for many years and have a major position so far as credit life captives are concerned. In recent years they have attempted to regulate their position by the introduction of new insurance legislation, culminating in the Insurance Ordinance of 1989, which combined with the Insurance Regulations 1990 came into force in February in 1991).

The new insurance legislation is designed to bring the Turks and Caicos islands into line with licensing and control regimes applicable in major captive jurisdictions such as the Cayman Islands and Bermuda. The new Ordinance Regulations are flexible and the Financial Secretary, who is advised by the Superintendent of Insurance, has authority to waive requirements or grant exemptions wherever appropriate. Guidelines have been informally issued by the Superintendent of Insurance and the principle features are as follows:

1. Licences will be issued, initially, against submission of a detailed business plan showing, inter alia, a five-year projection, anticipated risk exposure, annual asset base, anticipated premium income, expected claims ratios, etc.
2. Thereafter, approved offices must be appointed and in the majority of cases a qualified actuary to provide valuation

reports. Audited profit and loss statements and balance sheets will have to be submitted.

3. The minimum capitalisation requirement for companies engaged in reinsurance life or general insurance business is likely to be of the order of US$100,000 but will be determined according to the size of the company, risk exposure and the type of business written.

4. The annual licence fee will be US$2,000.

5. Considerable exemption from the requirements of the Ordinance will be possible for companies engaged solely in reinsurance of risks covered by a single named insurer — this will not, however, include exemption from the licence requirement but may involve a reduced or even a nil fee.

Australia

The introduction of the Australian Accruals Tax Legislation and the opportunity seen by the Australian Insurance Commissioner to persuade many Australian-owned Singapore captives to move onshore has resulted in the Commissioner introducing special regulations for captive insurance companies under the 1973 Insurance Act. In the submission made by the Australian Insurance Commissioner the rationale for the establishment of captives and justification for special legislation is outlined. In the preamble the Insurance Commissioner argues that captive insurance can be viewed as a closed shop arrangement where a separate company (the captive), within a group of related companies, is specifically set up to perform the function of insurer to that group. The Commission concludes that as a result there are no members of the general public directly or indirectly contracted as policy holders.

On the basis of this argument the Commission takes the view that there is justification for special regulations and supervision for captives and that while captives should remain supervised under the Insurance Act the potential for loss by the public is indirect and significantly less than in normal circumstances, and that in these situations special provisions are justified. In particular it has not been attractive to establish captives in Australia because of restrictions on outwards reinsurance. Although the Insurance Commissioner intends to maintain the minimum paid-up capital requirement of A$2 million and a solvency level of A$2 million or 20 per cent of premium income or 15% of outstanding claims in Australia, whichever is the greater, important changes have been made to the reinsurance requirements. The guidelines have been significantly relaxed for captives and the following is a summary:

169

CAPTIVE INSURANCE COMPANIES

1. Premium cessions

In general, a captive will be allowed to cede up to a maximum of 90 per cent of gross premium income to reinsurers and all of this reinsurance can be placed with offshore reinsurers, that is, companies which are not resident and not authorised in Australia. This is a significant relaxation of the guidelines for commercial insurers which allows a maximum cession of only 60 per cent of gross premium income with no more than 50 per cent of gross premium income ceded to offshore reinsurers The requirement for 10 per cent of gross premium income to be retained by a captive assumes reasonable involvement in the business underwritten.

2. Spread of reinsurers

Contracts of reinsurance with shares taken up by insurers and reinsurers not authorised under the Act will be reviewed on a case-by-case basis, although a reasonable spread will generally be required. In this respect it is unlikely that shares in excess of 20 per cent will be accepted.

3. Risk retentions

Differing capital requirements will apply depending on the types of risk (e.g. single loss or multi-loss from one event catastrophe) retained by the captive, a level at which participation is taken (e.g. does the captive pay all losses or does a policy excess apply?), and the basis of underwriting (e.g. is an annual limit on losses in force). A summary of the more common situations is as follows:

- Single loss retention with no policy excess — generally a captive will be expected to maintain a ratio of retained risk to net tangible assets of no greater than 10 per cent.
- Single loss retention with policy excess applied — the size of the policy excess will determine whether the captive is exposed potentially to a large number of claims or only those which occur once or possibly a few times in any one period. For a retention involving a large number of claims in a year, the above 10 per cent guideline is applied. However, for a retention where it is likely that only one claim will occur over a number of years, a captive will be required to maintain assets equivalent to the net retention in addition to statutory solvency margin. For example, if the captive has a statutory solvency margin of A$1 million and a retention of A$750,000, net tangible assets of A$1.75 million will be necessary for authorisation.
- Single loss retention subject to an annual limit in aggregate — this basis of underwriting will need to be discussed in detail with the Commission prior to authorisation, but provided net premium income plus investment return on these premium

monies will cover the annual limit on losses, no retention to net tangible asset limitation will be imposed.
• Multi-loss from one event (catastrophe) retention — the captive will be required to maintain assets equivalent to the net retention in addition to the statutory solvency margin.

In relation to surplus assets, that is, those assets required to meet retention requirements in addition to the statutory solvency margin, the Commission may be prepared to recognise investments with or in related bodies.

Although each proposal for establishment of a captive insurance company in Australia will be assessed on its merits it is clear that the authorities have decided to try to encourage onshore establishment of captives and have gone a long way to revise the existing rules in order to encourage such decisions.

Other locations

New locations are continually developing, and among those which have been trying to attract offshore captives in recent times are Denmark, Cook Islands, Liechtenstein, Madeira, Western Samoa, Åland Islands, Antigua, Uruguay, US Virgin Islands, Seychelles, Mauritius and Labuan.

It does, however, remain important to select a location very carefully and to make sure among other things that there is an infra-structure which can provide the necessary financial and insurance management expertise that is necessary for the successful operation of a captive, and also to make sure that the location is properly regulated, well supervised and will be recognised as such by the insurance and reinsurance market as well as the parent company and other interested parties.

Summary and Future Developments

The captive scene so far as locations are concerned is always changing. New legislation is introduced, and new locations make an effort to establish themselves on a regular basis. The information given is correct at the time of writing but should be double-checked to ensure that it is still applicable when any captive location decision is being made. Particulars of current legislation are usually freely available from the local authorities or banks.

The growth of insurance legislation in many of these captive locations is an indication that the authorities are concerned about the way in which the insurance companies operating in their country are being controlled. In most reputable and substantial locations there is now usually a requirement of minimum capitalisation and a related relationship between the capital requirement and the business being written. Methods of testing solvency margins differ but are usually linked to a specific solvency requirement based on the ratio between capital-free reserves and net premium written. Alternatively, there may be an individual examination of the capital proposed and the types of business that the captive is considering undertaking.

In addition, there is a growing requirement to examine the assets of the company to ensure that there is a reasonable amount of liquidity to deal with claims arising from particular types of business that are being handled by the company. Where the company is involved in outside business there are sometimes more onerous requirements in order to protect innocent third parties.

The submission of annually audited accounts which are reviewed by local government authorities is now becoming common and it is usually necessary for these accounts to be prepared by qualified and acknowledged accountants. Another development is that the authorities require that the companies managing the captive are competently run and staffed by people with expertise in the areas of insurance and financial management.

Finally, there is usually some method of screening new companies to ensure that the motives are acceptable to the authorities and that the operation submitted will be well run and have a good chance of surviving.

The potential owner of a captive should welcome these developments and should be more inclined to set up his company in an environment where sensible legislation exists. Although it would be undesirable for legislation requirements to become too onerous and begin to mirror legislation applicable in the major industrial countries, a limited amount of legislation and control of any abuse must be welcomed. Any deterioration in the image of the location could have a harmful effect on those people who are running their operation prudently and responsibly.

Although for some people the introduction of legislation may eliminate one of the advantages of going offshore, it is a development that will enable the captive scene to continue to grow and become an important and credible part of the International insurance market.

CHAPTER 5

MANAGING A CAPTIVE

Captive Management Requirements

The basic requirements of a captive from the management viewpoint can be separated into the following nine categories:

1. Legal.
2. Documentation.
3. Accounting.
4. Taxation.
5. Underwriting.
6. Claims handling.
7. Investment.
8. Administration.
9. Loss control.

Each of these aspects will now be considered in more detail.

Legal

The captive will need to have legal advice on both an initial and a continuing basis. The lawyers chosen will need to be conversant with the requirements for company formation, including the regulations under the local laws, and also link these to the normal requirements of the company for whom the captive is being established.

The company will need to be aware of the detailed local procedure for insurance company formation and the detailed requirements so far as directors, company name, authorised capital, names of officers and so on are concerned. Account will also need to be taken of the local legislative controls and for these to be monitored on a regular basis to take account of any specific changes. Included in this area will be operating returns to the authorities, and compliance with procedures laid down on submission, including adherence to time requirements. In addition, it is important to remember the potential overseas legal problems that the captive can be involved in so far as international programme, exchange control and claims settlements are concerned.

Although many companies would be able to handle the majority of these matters within their own company or with their domestic legal adviser, it is often advisable to involve local lawyers who are more involved with the day-to-day needs and have the necessary connections with the authorities. As an example of the documentation that needs to be completed when a company is established, the list below is a summary of the data required by the authorities in Bermuda from companies wishing to incorporate an insurance company or appoint overseas directors, and the information required for a submission to the Bermuda Registrar of Companies.

The information needed by Bermuda lawyers to incorporate an insurance company is as follows:

1. Name of company.
2. Objectives, including the insurance classes to be underwritten.
3. Name, occupation, nationality of each shareholder showing percentage share and additional details if the shareholder is a public company.
4. Authorised capital, including value of each share.
5. Paid-up capital.
6. Number, name, address and nationality of each director including any alternates.
7. Names of officers of the company.
8. Registered office of the company in Bermuda
9. Names and addresses of auditors.
10. Financial year.
11. Bermuda bank to be used and signatories.
12. Banks outside Bermuda and signatories.
13. List of foreign bank references.
14. Specify if tax exemption to year 2006 is required.

In addition to this cheek-list for submission to the company's lawyers, the following information is required from overseas directors:

1. Name.
2. Age.
3. Nationality.
4. Residential address.
5. Business address.
6. Previous occupation.
7. Current and previous directorships.
8. Professional qualifications.
9. Details of companies in which the proposer has over one-third of voting power.
10. Percentage of capital of the captive that the applicant will own.
11. Specify whether the applicant will be employed by the captive insurance company.
12. Details of any criminal convictions anywhere in the world.
13. Details of any previous bankruptcy or association with a liquidated company

The overseas director must answer these questions in detail and support his application with bankers' references, character references and references supporting his business experience and professional qualifications.

The submission to the Registrar of Companies to form an insurance company will be reviewed by the Insurers' Registration Sub-committee and the following is the format of the document that will need to be submitted:

1. Name of proposed Bermuda company.
2. Name(s) of owners and/or stockholders.
3. Hospital/firms to be insured.
4. Special risk involved (e.g. hospital malpractice, products liability, etc.).
5. Other perils (e.g. workmen's compensation) to be covered. Is additional general insurance business from other sources to be written? If so, on a direct or indirect basis?
6. Stock or mutual company (delete where applicable).
7. Proposed capital (authorised paid-up) and proposed surplus.
8. Would the company be a direct insurer or a reinsurer (if the latter, state fronting company)?
9. Expected net annual premium income.
10a. Maximum retained risk by Bermuda company (per loss and annual aggregate). (If more than one class, break down 9 and 10 by main classes.)
10b. A five-year projection (balance sheets and revenue accounts for the proposed Bermuda company).

11. Bermuda manager.
12. Bermuda lawyer.

This application form needs to be supported by seven copies and submitted to the office of the Registrar of Companies.

In addition to this application, there is a requirement for appendices supporting each submission, depending on the type of business involved. For example, there is detailed information required if the captive is to cover medical malpractice or products liability insurance. For all other classes it is necessary to support the application by details of the claims experience, the rating programme being utilised and the reinsurance programme for the captive.

Documentation

As a fully constituted insurance company, the captive will have to provide evidence of the cover that it is providing in the form of policies or certificates and will need to comply with legal requirements and contractual or other requirements related to the documents involved. In addition to the legal necessity for policies or certificates, these documents will also help to justify the tax deductibility of the premium to the captive and help to satisfy the operating company's needs.

It is important that these documents are real, are to a good general insurance standard and are issued in a proper manner.

Accounting

There will be a considerable accounting requirement and it needs to be recognised that insurance accounting requires specialist skill as it is very different from other forms of accounting. This area will be discussed later in the book, but it is important to remember the necessity to separate premium funds, to categorise unearned premiums and unpaid claims and to have a careful and credible reserving policy. Accounting services may be provided by a chosen company or local accountants and will need to be supported in most locations by a firm of qualified and accepted auditors, who may also be required to issue a certificate confirming that the captive's accounts are correct.

Taxation

Taxation as a part of the accounting process is also important. In a number of locations there is a separation of tax treatment depending on whether investment income or underwriting income is involved. So far as reserving is concerned, this provides considerable scope for tax minimisation, which should be utilised to the full within the limitations of the appropriate legislation. It is also important that the accountants have an understanding of the impact that premium taxes can have on the amount of premium likely to be received by the captive and their impact on the funds that are available.

Again, it is generally sensible for a company to use accountants who have considerable knowledge and understanding of insurance accounting as there are many differences from conventional company accounting.

Underwriting

As discussed in Chapter 3, the captive will need to have an underwriting policy using one of the alternatives which was considered. Naturally, if it is to go beyond its own business, it will require underwriting skills to ensure that the underwriting strategy is implemented successfully, and this once again can be a consideration in deciding which management alternative to operate.

Claims handling

The captive will be involved in the payment of claims. It will therefore need to have a method of making these payments, dealing with the mechanics of claims assessing and considering whether the claim should be paid. Methods of dealing with claims involve the captive paying and handling the claim on a direct basis, utilising the expertise of loss adjusters, lawyers or claims settling agents, each of which could be suitable in different cases. Complications can arise in claims handling due to currency problems, in-group or customer conflict of interest and the attitude of the reinsurers to the claims payment and method of handling.

It is important at the outset to determine the claims objective of the captive and to ensure that the method agreed with the management company meets these aims.

Investment

An important consideration for the captive management decision is the investment policy. The captive will have a range of funds which can be used to accrue investment and it is important that advice is sought on the best means of optimising this investment policy and also to ensure that the captive is able to pay claims and does not have its funds tied up in long-term deposits if short-term payments are necessary. Investment strategy and advice will involve the development of cash flow forecasts, consideration of variability in these forecasts and the short-term financial needs in relation to the type of business being underwritten.

It is important that the investment strategy meets the captive criteria in relation to solvency and location requirements, but it should also be related, where possible, to the parent's overall financial strategy and objectives.

Administration

The administration of the captive involving an office of operation, staff, telephone, telex and local directors will be important, particularly as it will be needed in most cases to satisfy themselves that the people providing the administration service are capable, have a good track record and are recognised in the particular market. The administrators will need to have the capability to carry out the following:

1. Issue policy documents.
2. Settle claims or instruct assessors of claims handling agents.
3. Keep financial statements and accounts.
4. Issue statutory returns required.
5. Set up and organise ordinary and other meetings that will be necessary to manage the company.

Loss control

The future of the captive will depend on maintenance of its loss control programme, and it will need to concern itself with the re-sources available to it to maintain or improve the business that it is underwriting. These resources will include its own personnel or the personnel of the parent company, the insurance company (often the company providing the fronting facility), a broker and other persons such as consultants and engineers.

It is important that the loss control activity is related to the overall strategy of the captive and that this is also reflected in some of those areas previously discussed, such as underwriting and rating strategy, reinsurance tactics and motivation of local management.

Selecting the Managers

The exhaustive list of captive management needs will vary from company to company but most captives will require most of the services covered above. In captive locations, management companies or facilities exist which can provide most or all of these services. The needs of the particular captive will depend on the type of captive that is being established and its location.

In Chapter 1 the three types of captive — paper, small-scale and full-scale — were discussed and for each of these there are two main alternatives.

The first alternative is to manage the company 'in house', either using an existing organisation within the company or setting up a new and separate organisation. Depending on the location chosen it is very important that great care is taken over this decision as it may result in severe penalties if the captive is managed by the parent company on a direct basis when the domestic legislation forbids such activity. It is usually the case that the residence of a company for tax purposes is related to the location of the management. If this situation exists, it is crucial that the management of the captive should be seen to be separate from the country of residence of the parent company, that the parent should not issue any directives to the captive and that board meetings of the captive should be held away from the country of the parent. Even where a separate management company is used, it is important that this company is resident in the location of the captive. Any management agreements must take into account these delicate matters.

The other alternative is the appointment of an outside manager. Companies offering management services fall into the following categories:

1. Independent captive management companies.
2. Underwriting agents, including existing insurance.
3. Management companies owned by brokers.
4. Others, including lawyers, banks and accountants.

In considering the choice of manager, it is important first to ensure that the management company has the knowledge and technical capability to provide you with the services that you need. This capability should certainly include a knowledge of managing insurance companies, and in understanding of reinsurance and, particularly, the needs of captives. In order to discover whether this knowledge exists it is useful to find out what experience the management company has of running captives, how many captives they run and the methods that they use to manage captives.

179

Associated with this experience, it is important that the management company selected has a good reputation in the location and is not regarded hostilely by the local legislators. If the management company is also dealing with the insurance market, perhaps by placing reinsurance, the philosophy of the management company should link with the parent company both in its attitude towards techniques of negotiation and also in its leverage and negotiating strengths in extracting the best and most reasonable arrangements. The management company should also be cost-effective and it is advisable to ensure that the method of remuneration is on a fee basis rather than related to premium turn-over.

Bearing in mind the considerable responsibilities that the managers have in administering the captive insurance company, it is important to ensure that the managers have adequate errors and omissions insurance so that in the event of any errors on their part insurance protection is in place to protect the owners of the captive for any losses that occur. This is particularly important if the manager is deeply involved in reinsurance placement and through error may give reinsurers an opportunity to avoid payment of claims which would otherwise be accepted by the captive or its fronting company.

Finally, check all claims that are made by the management company in its proposals to you and, once appointed, monitor their performance on a regular basis, seek information on developments in the market, talk to other managers and other companies who are operating in the location and, most importantly, play a role in the management of the company and how developments are changing in the world of captives.

The appointment of a manager for the captive is a crucial decision; you are entitled to answers from those proposing to be manager and you should consider their claims and the alternatives available to you before making the final appointment. Although it will take time and effort to do a good job in managing the captive, it is one of the most important parts of the process and such time will be justified in the long term.

Captive Set-up and Operating Costs

The set-up costs for a typical captive will involve the following expenses:

1. Paid-up capitalisaltion.
2. Registration fee.

3. Stamp duty on capitalisation.
4. Application fee.
5. Advertising of captive in compliance with regulations.
6. Initial legal fees.
7. Annual legal fees.
8. Directors' fees.
9. Management fee.
10. Annual audit fee.

The registration tee, legal costs, directors' fees, management fees and audit fees will be a recurring cost.

Table 5.1 shows an example of set-up and operating costs for a captive insurance company in Bermuda. These costs, particularly the

Table 5.1 Start-up and annual operating costs for a Bermuda-based captive insurance company

	Estimated incorporation and first-year operational costs (US$)	Future annual operating costs (US$)
Minimum paid-in capital (for transacting general insurance business i.e. excluding life)	120,000	—
*Registration/Government fees (also payable annually)	4,200	4,200
*Stamp duty on capital ($\frac{1}{4}$ of 1% of authorised capital)	300	—
Application fee	150	—
Advertising of captive name	105	—
Legal fees	7,300	3,300
*Annual management fees	25,000 +	25,000 +
*Annual audit fees	7,000 +	7,000 +
Other incorporation costs	500	
	$164,555	$39,500

*These costs are dependent on the size of the company, in terms of both paid-in capital and number of transactions. The above numbers would apply to a small-medium size captive capitalised at $120,000. Government/Registration fees have the following scale.

Authorised capital $	Annual business fee $
120,000	3,200
120,001 – 1,200,000	4,800
1,200,001 – 12,000,000	6,400
12,000,001 +	8,000

August 1990

management, audit and legal costs, will vary depending on he size of the captive but for a typical captive the initial set-up costs including the minimum capitalisation cost will be in the region of $180,000 and annual operating costs will be in the region of $100,000.

Management Agreements

Management agreements in relation to the captive are a crucial area and, for reasons mentioned previously, it is important that they are constituted in a proper legal way otherwise problems could arise regarding the tax deductibility of premiums paid to the insurance subsidiary.

Essentially, management agreements need to contain a number of principle agreements which lay down the responsibility of the managers and the areas where the managers operate within agreed board decisions. A typical agreement would include the following points:

1. The official appointment of the manager.
2. Acceptance that the appointed managers can:
   (a) accept writs on behalf of the captive;
   (b) employ sub-agents to collect premiums;
   (c) pay or settle claims;
   (d) control underwriting;
   (e) issue policies, certificates, endorsements, etc.;
   (f) maintain bank accounts;

With the authority of the board the agreement should also lay down that managers should:

1. Render statements of premium and claims of an agreed timetable.
2. Render final accounts on an annual basis.
3. Submit the appropriate documents to the authorities in compliance with the requirements laid down.

In addition the agreement should lay down the position in the following areas:

1. The overall investment policy of the captive.
2. The policy on funding for claims and the methods used for reserving on outstanding cases.
3. The position on errors and omissions of the managers; the position should the managers or the captive or owner become insolvent are taken over by another company or decide to close down the captive operation.

The management agreement also needs to stipulate the basis for the remuneration of the managers and their reinsurance authority.

Annexes 5.1, 5.2 and 5.3 at the end of this chapter show sample management agreements. Annex 5.1 is a management agreement for a Colorado captive, Annex 5.2 is a more general management agreement based on a Bermuda management company and Annex 5.3 is a management agreement developed by a UK insurance company and can be utilised in any of the normal captive locations.

So far as particular management activities are concerned, the investment policy of the captive would normally be as directed by the parent, but the management company should be able to give advice about potential cash flow needs and investments necessary to ensure adequate liquidity.

If the captive intends to accept business from outside companies, the responsibilities of the managers will increase and the ability of them to obtain good outside reinsurance and to underwrite a selection of risks on a profitable basis will be an important factor in their selection.

Finally, it is important when the management agreement is developed that the extent of the managers' discretion and authority is defined precisely and that this is related to guidelines laid down by the hoard of the captive insurance company.

Constitution of the Captive Board

It is usually advisable for the board of the captive to be composed of a majority of directors domiciled locally. In a typical situation the captive could be composed of two directors from the parent company, supplemented by three local directors. It is important that at least one of the local directors should have insurance experience and certainly in some locations there will be a legislative requirement for this to be the position. It is normal for provisions to be made for the sanction of decisions made by the captive in the location either by the approval of the resident board members or through proxies, appointed from the parent company, acting on behalf of the board members. As an alternative to this, decisions can be ratified by resolutions circulated to all directors of the company.

The captive should be an operation which is entirely separate from the parent company, as any infringement of this principle might mean that the premiums paid to the captive are not regarded as genuine premiums for taxation purposes.

ANNEX 5.1

CAPTIVE INSURANCE COMPANY MANAGEMENT AGREEMENT
(COLORADO)

THIS AGREEMENT, made and entered into this first day of _____ , 19 __ between _____ MANAGEMENT CO., a Division of _____ , a Maryland corporation (hereinafter referred to as _____), and _____ a Colorado corporation (hereinafter referred to as 'INSURANCE COMPANY').

WITNESSETH:

WHEREAS, _____ is a company engaged in managing and administering insurance companies; and

WHEREAS, INSURANCE COMPANY desires to employ _____ to perform certain management and administration services in connection with the operation of the INSURANCE COMPANY established pursuant to Title 10, Article 6, Colorado Revised Statues, 1973 (Captive Insurance Company Act), and _____ is willing to perform such services subject to the terms and conditions hereinafter setforth;

NOW THEREFORE, in consideration of the premises and the mutual covenants and conditions herein contained, the parties hereto agree as follows:

1 _____ hereby agrees to use its best efforts to arrange for:
(a) All underwriting functions in connection with risks submitted to the INSURANCE COMPANY including such matters as the preparation and issuance of insurance contracts (policies); establishment, filing and approval of rates; and compliance with the rules, regulations and requirements of the Department of Insurance, State of Colorado, respecting 'Captive Insurance Companies'.
(b) Preparation, auditing and otherwise processing, as necessary, of all insurance documentation to be issued by the INSURANCE COMPANY, such as policies, reinsurance contracts, binders and endorsements.
(c) Preparation of all experience statistics required by the INSURANCE COMPANY.
(d) Preparation of insurance statements required by the Department of Insurance, State of Colorado, or INSURANCE COMPANY.
(e) Establishment and maintenance of complete insurance accounting service, encompassing the establishment of all necessary reserves such as those for unearned premiums, loss reserves and reserves for expenses,

and any other accounting records, statements, or reports as required by the Department of Insurance, State of Colorado, or INSURANCE COMPANY.

(f) Preparation of all tax statements and returns required of the INSURANCE COMPANY with respect to premiums and all other taxes or statements required by the Department of Insurance, State of Colorado, EXCEPT those relating to the investments of the INSURANCE COMPANY.

(g) Preparation of a quarterly profit and loss statement with respect to all aspects of the INSURANCE COMPANY operations, EXCEPT as respects investments.

(h) Periodical advice, at such intervals and with such frequency as the INSURANCE COMPANY may specify, as to the amount of reserves and other funds available for investment from time to time by the INSURANCE COMPANY.

(i) Maintenance of a home office and principal place of business in Denver, Colorado, during the term of this Agreement, and to further provide an officer who is a resident of the State of Colorado, of and to the INSURANCE COMPANY, such officer to be bonded at the expense of the INSURANCE COMPANY as may be required by direction or regulation of the Department of Insurance of the State of Colorado.

(j) Securing and maintaining in force reinsurance with financially responsible reinsurers for all risks insured excess of the amount of coverage retained for the account of the INSURANCE COMPANY.

(k) _____ agrees to indemnify and hold INSURANCE COMPANY harmless of and from loss arising out of the dishonest acts or negligence of _____ employees and officers during the terms of this Agreement.

2 INSURANCE COMPANY hereby agrees:

(a) TO pay _____ a management fee of _____ in addition to the amounts set forth in (c) hereof.

(b) To promptly comply with any request for instructions or information which _____ or the Department of Insurance of the State of Colorado may make in order to efficiently perform the management duties under this Agreement.

(c) To promptly pay _____ invoices for INSURANCE COMPANY management services as required under this Agreement, in addition to administrative expenses such as necessary telephone, traveling, filing fees and costs, supplies, documents, books, records and files which are the property of the INSURANCE COMPANY, and underwriting services where necessary or requested to the proper operation of a captive insurance company.

(d) To appoint, as required by the Department of Insurance, State of Colorado, an officer to serve on behalf of the INSURANCE

COMPANY and to give such officer adequate authority to comply with all statutory requirements and the regulations of the Department of Insurance, State of Colorado, on behalf of the INSURANCE COMPANY.

3 _____ and the INSURANCE COMPANY mutually covenant and agree:

(a) That this Agreement shall become effective as of the date hereof and shall remain in full force and effect thereafter until terminated by either _____ or the INSURANCE COMPANY upon giving at least thirty (30) days advance written notice to the other party and to the Insurance Commissioner of Colorado.

(b) That termination of this Agreement shall not relieve either party of liability for the performance of obligations required during the effective period of this Agreement which have not been performed up to the time of its termination.

IN WITNESS WHEREOF, the parties have caused this Agreement to be executed by their officers or agents thereunto duly authorized as of the day and year first above written.

MANAGEMENT COMPANY

ATTEST:

By _____
PRESIDENT

_____
SECRETARY

_____ COMPANY

ATTEST:

By _____
VICE PRESIDENT

_____
SECRETARY

ANNEX 5.2

MANAGEMENT AGENCY AGREEMENT effective this _____ day of _____ , 19 __ , by and between AMERICAN INTERNATIONAL COMPANY LTD (hereinafter referred to as 'AICO'), a Company organized and operating under the laws of Bermuda with its principal and sole office located in the American International Building, Richmond Road, Pembroke Parish, Bermuda, and _____ (hereinafter referred to as the 'Company'), a Company organized and operating under the laws of _____ , located at _____ .

WITNESSETH:

WHEREAS, the Company is desirous of receiving certain management insurance services to be conducted by a professional insurance manager; and

WHEREAS, AICO is authorized under its Articles of Incorporation to render insurance management services from Bermuda to Companies incorporated within and without Bermuda;

NOW, THEREFORE, in consideration of the mutual promises hereinafter set forth, the Parties hereby agree as follows:

FIRST: Subject to the overriding authority of the Board of Directors and Company's principal representative, AICO is appointed to represent the Company in Bermuda with authority:

1 to do all things necessary or incidental to the conduct of the insurance or reinsurance business which the Company now is or hereby may be by its charter authorized to transact; and
2 to invest and reinvest the funds of such Company within the guidelines as approved by the Board of Directors of the Company and attached hereto as Exhibit A;
3 to maintain books and records with respect to the business hereunder and render annual accounts and other schedules in such form and detail as the Company may reasonably require.

SECOND: AICO hereby accepts such appointment and agrees faithfully to perform the duties thereof to the best of its skill and judgment and to obey promptly such instructions as it may receive from the Company.

THIRD: In full compensation for the services required of AICO under this Agreement the Company shall pay AICO the annual fee of

_____ ($ _____) Dollars
payable quarterly.

The said fee for the next succeeding year shall be subject to review on each anniversary date after the effective date of this agreement. Such fee shall not include commissions payable to AICO or any other affiliates or subsidiaries of the American International Group with respect to the business written by or on behalf of the Company. The Company shall, in addition, reimburse AICO for out-of-pocket expenses such as telex, long distance telephone and similar charges resulting from and necessary for the proper operations of the functions and services performed hereunder.

FOURTH: Without derogation from the authority hereinabove conferred upon AICO, such authority shall include the collection and payment of premiums and return premiums on insurance and reinsurance, the adjustment, compromise and payment of losses and expenses in accordance with the directions of the Company; the entry into reinsurance arrangements by treaty or otherwise for such part of any risk as the Company may direct; the recovery of losses and expenses from reinsurers; and the payment of any fees imposed by the Bermuda Government.

FIFTH: AICO agrees to arrange and assist in audits of the Company when requested by the Company and to prepare the books and records of the Company in accordance with Bermuda statutory accounting requirements.

SIXTH: AICO agrees to treat any information received with respect to or on behalf of the Company in conducting this Contract, including all financial books and records maintained on behalf of the Company, as the confidential property of the Company. AICO shall only release such books and records to any party (other than Directors, Officers or Auditors of the Company) when so instructed in writing by two (2) Directors of the Company. Employees of AICO may from time to time serve as Officers of the Company to perform the functions described above upon the request and appointment of the Company. No appointment of an employee of AICO to serve as an Officer(s) of the Company shall be binding upon the employee of AICO without the written consent of such employee.

SEVENTH: When an employee or employees of AICO are appointed Officers of the Company, the Company shall inform such Officers of any Contracts binding the Company as executed by other Officers of the Company and effective on the date of the execution of this Contract. The Company shall thereafter undertake to notify AICO of any insurance or reinsurance contracts which Officers who are not employees of AICO may enter prior to their execution. The Company agrees to indemnify any employees of AICO

Annex 5.2

for any of their acts performed on behalf of the Company in their capacity as officers for the Company except in the case of gross negligence. The Company shall provide Directors' and Officers' liability coverage for such AICO employees who may act in such capacity for the Company.

EIGHTH: This Agreement may be amended from time to time by an exchange between the Parties hereto of letters which shall be considered of the same effect as formal addenda to this Agreement. The functions of AICO as Managing Agents may be further limited (but not broadened) without AICO's consent by written instruction sent to the offices of AICO from time to time by the Company.

NINTH: The appointment of AICO hereunder is unlimited in its duration and may be terminated at any time by either party giving to the other, in writing, three months' notice of termination. Such termination should be delivered to the offices of AICO or of the Company at the address designated herein. Violation of any provision of this contract may cause termination thereof by either party without providing the prior notice referred to above.

IN WITNESS WHEREOF, the Parties hereto have caused this Agreement to be executed in duplicate at the Parish of Pembroke Bermuda by their respective officers thereunto duly authorized.

AMERICAN INTERNATIONAL COMPANY, LTD

Attest:

_____   By _____
              (Title)   (Title)

                                     (COMPANY)
Attest:
_____   By _____
              (Title)   (Title)

189

MANAGEMENT AGREEMENT

1 PREAMBLE

THIS AGREEMENT is made the _____ day of _____ , 19 ___
between [the Management Company] (hereinafter called _____
_____), and [the Captive] (hereinafter called [Captive]), both being
companies duly organised and existing under and by virtue of the laws of
_____ [the Location].

WITNESS THAT:

WHEREAS, [the Captive] is a Company formed to underwrite various
classes of insurance and reinsurance, and

WHEREAS, [the Management Company] is engaged in similar business
in [the Location] and elsewhere in the world and also the Provision of
Management and Administrative Services; and

WHEREAS, [the Captive] is desirous of obtaining Managerial and Administrative Services and General Assistance from [the Management Company]
as more particularly described hereafter and [the Management Company] is
willing to furnish such services and assistance to [the Captive] on the terms
and conditions set forth herein;

NOW, THEREFORE, in consideration of the premises and mutual
promises contained herein and intending to be legally bound hereby, the Parties
mutually agree as follows:

2 AUTHORISATION AND UNDERTAKINGS

(a) [The Captive] hereby authorises and directs [the Management Company]
to provide it with management services and assistance subject to the
terms and conditions hereof, and [the Management Company] agrees to
provide [the Captive] with said services and assistance as [the Captive]
may from time to time require in respect of the furtherance of its
business as insurer and reinsurer. Such services and assistance shall
include but not be limited to the specific items hereinafter set out.

(b) UNDERWRITING AND REINSURANCE
(i) Vetting of and advising on underwriting and acceptance of individual
risks and treaties, overall rating and premium calculation on all
such business; provided however that [the Management Company]
shall have first obtained the written approval of [the Captive] to

underwrite those classes of insurance business within the restrictions set forth by [the Captive] and for which approval has been secured.

(ii) Issuance, countersignature and endorsement of insurance and reinsurance contracts in those classes for which approval has been secured.

(iii) Cancellation of insurance and reinsurance contracts as well as the issuance of notices of cancellation in accordance with contract terms.

(iv) Vetting of and advising on securing such facultative or treaty reinsurance contracts as may be required and subject to [the Captive]'s prior approval.

(v) Acceptance and payment of or rejection of claims and defence costs arising out of contract of insurance and reinsurance.

(vi) Submission to [the Captive] of a written report at least once annually regarding premium composition and growth trends, loss development and trends, underwriting expense, investment income and operating income.

(c) FINANCIAL AND CLERICAL SERVICES

Provision of all financial and clerical services required by [the Captive] in pursuance of the operations to which this agreement relates, including but not limited to the following:

(i) *Documentation* – Preparation, auditing and otherwise processing, as necessary, of all insurance documentation to be issued by [the Captive], including policies, reinsurance contracts, cover notes and endorsements.

(ii) *Statistics* – Preparation of all experience statistics required by [the Captive].

(iii) *Accounting of Receipts and Payments*

– Premium billing, recording of premiums received and rendering of receipts for premiums paid to [the Captive] in accordance with the terms and conditions of contracts and insurance and reinsurance issued. To which end [the Management Company] undertake to use due diligence in its efforts to collect all such premiums and shall have full authority to take whatever action is necessary to collect premiums, including cancellation of policies.

– Premium payment on proper notice for premiums due under all facultative and treaty reinsurance ceded.

– The opening and maintaining of any bank accounts in [the Location] in the name of [the Captive] which [the Management Company] may deem advisable or necessary and to make deposits therein and disbursements therefrom. Collect, receive and deposit money from Insureds or otherwise, and endorse all cheques or other commercial orders payable to [the Captive] and deposit such cheques or commercial orders in such bank accounts. [The Management

Company] is specifically authorised and empowered to conduct such transactions and [the Management Company] agrees to execute all documents necessary to accomplish such purpose.

(iv) *Records* – Maintenance in a manner and form prescribed or approved by [the Captive] true and complete records and books of account of all business conducted under and pursuant to this agreement and, at all reasonable times, make available for examination and inspection to a duly authorised representative of [the Captive] all such books, records and accounts.

(v) *Preparation of a profit and loss statement* with respect to all aspects of [the Captive] operations prepared in accordance with generally accepted accounting principles as adopted in [the Location].

(vi) *Financial advice* – provision of advice on Solvency and Liquidity requirements, Loss Reserving, Capitalisation, Net Worth requirements and Dividend Policy.

(d) STATUTORY RETURNS, ETC.

(i) Establishment and Maintenance of liaison with all relevant Regulatory or Government Authorities, specifically the Superintendent of Insurance with a view to maintaining in force all necessary licences or other Statutory instruments for conducting of [the Captive]'s business and in all respects acting as principal representatives in [the Location] with authorisation to accept service of process and documents on behalf of [the Captive] in [the Location].

(ii) Preparation of statutory insurance statements as required by any Government authority responsible for monitoring the activities of insurance companies in [the Location].

(iii) Establishment and Maintenance of all accounting services, including the establishment of all necessary reserves such as those for unearned premiums, loss reserves and reserves for expenses and records, statements or reports as may be requited by [the Location] insurance authorities.

(iv) [The Management Company] shall maintain in being such Registered and Principal Offices and such staff for [the Captive] as may be required by any law governing the operation of such a company in [the Location] and as may be considered by mutual agreement to be beneficial to the efficient operation of [the Captive].

(e) TAX RETURNS

Preparation of all tax statements and returns as may be required of [the Captive] by revenue or taxation authorities in [the Location] and providing [the Captive] with such advices on taxation as it may require.

(f) INVESTMENTS

Provision of advice to [the Captive] as to the amount of reserves and other funds available for investment from time to time by [the Captive] and implementation of the investment instructions of [the Captive] investment representative or adviser.

(g) MANAGEMENT REPORTS

Preparation and rendering of reports to [the Captive] quarterly or such other period as may from time to time be mutually agreed, between [the Management Company] and [the Captive] after the end of each period on such basis and covering all such matters as may from time to time be mutually agreed between [the captive] and [the Management Company].

(h) SECRETARIAL

[The Management Company] shall provide an Officer to act as Company Secretary as ratified by the Board of Directors of [the Captive] who will perform all necessary secretarial functions including but not limited to:

(i) The issuing of Notices, Agendas and Draft Resolutions for any General Meeting called in accordance with and as required by the Articles of Association of [the Captive].

(ii) The issuing of Notices, Agendas and Draft Resolutions for any meeting of the Board of Directors of [the Captive] called in accordance with and as required by the Articles of Association of [the Captive].

(iii) The taking, preparation and distributing of minutes in respect of and at all board meetings.

3 FEE

– [The Captive] shall on or before the 1st day of January each year during the currency of this agreement pay to [the Management Company] a sum representing [Amount] as consideration for the services and assistance given by [the Management Company] pursuant to the terms hereof.

– The terms of this section shall apply for a period of one year from the commencement of the Agreement at which time it shall be the subject of renegotiation by the parties concerned.

– The Fee determined in accordance with the terms set down in this Section shall be payable by [the Captive] to [the Management Company] independently of and unaffected by any expense chargeable to and payable by either party as determined hereunder by the provision of Section 4 of this Agreement.

4 EXPENSES

(a) *Expenses to be paid by [the Management Company]*. The following items of expenses shall be chargeable against and paid by [the Management Company].

(i) *Offices:* [The Management Company] shall provide and pay the costs of occupancy of all offices which it occupies and also the furniture, fixtures, business machines and equipment required in such offices.

(ii) *Employees' Salaries and Other Fees*: [The Management Company] shall pay all salaries of its personnel rendering services under this agreement, and all fees, charges and expenses of any person, firm or corporation retained by [the Management Company] to assist it in performing its obligations hereunder unless such person, firm or corporation is retained in connection with any item specified in (b) below.

(b) *Expenses to be paid by* [*the Captive*]. The following items of expense shall be chargeable against and paid by [the Captive].

[The Captive] shall pay for all Audits by independent auditors, printed policies, endorsement forms, stationery, books, invoices and similar items necessary to its insurance business, together with all Governmental costs, charges and taxes, as well as, all legal, survey and adjustment costs, charges and expenses relative to the processing, handling and adjustment of claims, losses and coverages authorised and/or written by [the Captive]. [The Management Company] is authorised to pay all such costs and expenses, as well as, all taxes, duties and levies, and any other expenses attributable to [the Captive].

It is hereby agreed between the parties chat all expenses, costs and any and all other fees paid by [the Management Company] on behalf of [the Captive] in any currency other than [Currency], shall be converted to [Currency] at the conversion rate in effect at the date such expenses, costs or fees were paid by [the Management Company] so that all exchange, gain or loss incident thereto shall be incurred by or inured to the benefit of [the Captive].

(c) *Signing Authority bank accounts*. Unless otherwise agreed in writing by the directors, two directors together shall sign for disbursements from any of [the Captive]'s bank accounts.

5 EFFECTIVE DATE

This Agreement shall take effect from incorporation notwithstanding the date hereof.

6 TERMINATION

This Agreement may be terminated by mutual consent at any time. Or, in the absence of such mutual consent either party may terminate by giving to the other not less than six months' written notice of its intention. Termination of this agreement shall not relieve either party of liability for the performance of obligations imposed upon said party during the effective period of the agreement which have not been performed at the time of its termination.

7 ARBITRATION

All disputes arising in connection with this agreement shall be referred to a single arbitrator to be agreed upon by the parties or if they cannot agree upon a single arbitrator to the decision of two arbitrators one to be appointed in writing by each of the parties or in the case the two arbitrators cannot agree to the decision of an umpire to be appointed by the two arbitrators. Arbitration to take place at London in accordance with the procedures then pertaining in the London Court of Arbitration and under English law.

8 REPORTING AND APPROVAL

In carrying out its functions in terms of this agreement [the Management Company] shall report to the Board of [the Captive] and be subject to the instructions issued by the said Board from time to time, provided that the said instructions are not in conflict with the rules of the Company and the laws of [the Location]. The Parties record that the directors of [the Captive] are not resident in [the Location] and where [the Management Company] is required to give [the Captive] notice of any matter of copy of such notice shall be directed to the Directors per telex to [Telex Number], [Address].

Any instructions by [the Captive] to [the Management Company] shall be in the form of a formal Board Resolution or a written or telex instruction by two Directors.

9 INDEMNITY

[The Captive] hereby undertakes to sufficiently indemnify and to keep effectively indemnified [the Management Company] against any liability, loss or damage wheresoever and howsoever incurred by [the Management Company] in any way relating to or arising out of any of the information, advice, services or assistance provided pursuant to the agreement and against all actions suits proceedings claims demands costs and expenses whatsoever which may be taken or made against [the Management Company] or incurred or become payable by [the Management Company] in respect thereof provided always that such liability, loss or damage so incurred shall not be due to any default by [the Management Company] in carrying out the terms of this Agreement.

10 GOVERNING LAW

This Agreement shall be governed by the laws of [the Location].

THE COMMON SEAL OF [the Management Company] WAS HEREUNTO AFFIXED AS AUTHORISED BY THE DIRECTORS.

_____   _____

DIRECTOR   DIRECTOR

THE COMMON SEAL OF [the Captive] WAS HEREUNTO AFFIXED AS AUTHORISED BY THE DIRECTORS

_____   _____

DIRECTOR   DIRECTOR

CHAPTER 6

ACCOUNTING, TAXATION AND INVESTMENT NEEDS

Accounting Aspects

In most countries where captives are located no distinction is made between captives and normal insurance companies. However, many countries do draw a distinction between exempt companies trading offshore and those trading domestically, examples of these being Bermuda and Cyprus. It is therefore important that the accounting systems and records of the captive follow closely those used by direct insurance companies and that the particular requirements of insurance company accounting are taken into account.

Capitalisation

The first important financial decision that will need to be made by the captive is the level of capitalisation. There will automatically be a requirement within the jurisdiction in which the captive is located to comply with certain levels of capitalisation and solvency. In addition to this the company owning the captive will need to decide the level at which the capitalisation should be set in order to run the business properly and to protect the captive in the event of any dangerous loss situation. In the early years of operation it is recommended that the solvency margin, which is the percentage of capital-free reserves over the net premiums retained by the captive, be kept at a comparatively high level: it may be prudent to establish this at 50 per cent. In the first year of operation free reserves will not be available, but as the captive develops these reserves are carried forward from the profit and

197

loss account and other capital reserves will enable the solvency margin to be boosted and the captive to improve its capability to retain risk. While in most parts of the world solvency margin is usually expressed as a percentage, in the United States it is sometimes expressed as a ratio so that, for example, a 40 per cent solvency margin would equal a ratio of 1 to 2.5.

Another development has been the requirement in some jurisdictions that in its early years of operation the captive should have shareholders funds and net retained premium income which is at least equal to its total aggregate exposure. The reason for this is to ensure that the captive insurance company is able to pay for any claims that might occur within its retention level and not, as a result, be reliant on its parent company for capital injections should the worst loss scenario develop in the first years of operation. This clearly requires the captive to purchase unlimited aggregate stop loss reinsurance, otherwise it would not be possible to adhere to the regulatory requirements and this may be difficult in hard market conditions. As the captive grows the requirement to meet the combined and cumulative aggregate exposures will diminish and eventually it will be possible for the captive to be treated as any other insurance company with the solvency margin requirements based on its annual exposure or net premium income related to its capital, retained earnings and other free reserves.

A similar view towards capitalisation has been taken by a number of taxation authorities who argue that a captive which is not able to meet its claims obligations is not a genuine insurance company and that as a consequence any premiums paid to it should not be regarded as deductible to its parent as such premiums are not insurance transactions but more properly capital contributions. It therefore remains the best advice to ensure that the insurance company is capitalised at suitable levels and that attempts to structure the company with an inadequate capital based should be resisted.

It should also be borne in mind that in some locations it is necessary for the capital to be held in particular currencies, although in most of these situations there is freedom for premiums and reserves to be held in other suitable currencies, including those from which the premiums originated.

Accounting requirements

One of the main requirements will be the development of an underwriting or profit and loss account that will show the gross premiums received by the captive less losses and recoveries allocated, provisions for outstanding losses brought forward from previous years and carried forward, reinsurance premiums and claims allocated, allocation of expenses and possibly interest.

Because of the problems of insurance which involves the potential claims payment over a period of time beyond that of the annual account, it is very difficult to determine the underwriting result at the end of a single year. Various accounting methods may therefore be used to develop underwriting results.

Some insurance companies and Lloyd's use a three-year method of accounting so that the transfer to and from the account at the end of each third year reflects the annual review of liability. This fund method includes all outstanding liabilities from each year opened and closed. The Lloyd's system is slightly different in that three open years are kept and at the end of the third year reinsurance on the reserve outstanding is charged as claims. This is necessary within the Lloyd's system since there is the requirement to determine the liability on a year-by-year basis because of the variation in syndicate membership.

The development of annual funds as all alternative to the three-year method means that at the end of each year it will be necessary to deduct reserves for premiums that have been unearned, and also for any outstanding claims, if a net trading profit is to be produced. For any ongoing business the unearned premium and outstanding claims need to be brought into the premium fund.

The distinction between annual revenue accounting and fund accounting is an important one and has a number of implications particularly so far as deferral of taxation, preferred location and regulatory issues are concerned. In a paper presented at a workshop organised by Risk & Insurance Research Group Limited and subsequently published by RIRG in one of their newsletters, Christopher Talavera, a partner of Coopers & Lybrand in the Isle of Man, examined the pros and cons of revenue verses fund accounting and it is worthwhile sharing this excellent paper with the reader.

Captive Strategies for the Next Decade: Annual Revenue Accounting Versus Fund Accounting — Christopher Talavera, Partner Coopers & Lybrand, Isle of Man

Legal & Regulatory Framework

When discussing the pros and cons of various forms of accounting for a captive or indeed any company, we should start with the legal

and regulatory requirements for those accounts as these set the overall parameters within which we must remain.

Companies Acts

When companies prepare their annual financial statements, they must comply with a substantial number of accounting principles, rules and regulations. All companies' financial statements must comply with the accounting provisions of their country of domicile's Companies Acts as to their form and content. Most European and Caribbean offshore captive domiciles' company law broadly follows that of the UK, as they have common origins. Whilst the general principles are similar the detailed requirements are usually less onerous. However, for the purposes of this article it is only the general principles that we are concerned with. As I am most familiar with the Isle of Man's legislation and because I believe its company law is representative of offshore domiciles I shall use its legislation as an example. The three key points relating to companies accounts are:

Isle of Man Companies Act 1983 — Key Points (paraphrased)

Section 1   "Every company shall keep accounting records that show and explain the company's transactions and enable it to disclose within a reasonable time and with reasonable accuracy the company's financial position at any time".

Section 2   "Once a year the company must present audited accounts to its shareholders consisting of a profit and loss account and a balance sheet".

Section 3   "The company's accounts so presented must show a "true and fair view" of its profit or loss for the year and of its state of affairs at the year end".

The business of an insurance company is very specialised, and because of this any country with a developed insurance industry will have a second layer of company legislation which will amend the disclosure requirements for insurance company accounts to have regard for their specialised nature. For example, in the Isle of Man's case this legislation is contained in the Insurance Act 1986. The main issues regarding accounts in this legislation, which again are typical of most developed captive domiciles, are: —

Isle of Man Insurance Act and Regulations 1986 Accounting Issues — Key Points (paraphrased)

Section 11   "Accounting records must be kept on the Island and shall include all policy and claims records".

Section 12   "As well as a profit and loss account and balance sheet, the annual accounts must also contain a general business revenue account and/or general business fund account as appropriate".

Regulation 6   "Undisclosed reserves may be included in General Business Insurance Provisions and funds".

Regulations 7–10   "Allows specialised format of accounts which, in general terms, allows less disclosure of detail and valuation methods".

Regulation 11   "Requires additional information with form of supplementary returns to be made to the Regulatory Authority".

EC Insurance Accounts Directive

Insurance accounting throughout countries within the EC differs significantly at present, partly as a result of the various purposes for which insurers prepare sets of accounts (reporting to shareholders, regulators and tax authorities) and partly as a result of the historical development of insurance accounting practices. Thus, in some countries one set of accounts satisfies the needs of shareholders, regulators and tax authorities, while in other countries separate sets of accounts are prepared for each.

Because of these varying uses, there are different views as to the appropriate information to include in insurers accounts; and while some of these variations will be eliminated by the directive, some will remain. The rigidity of the required formats, together with agreed definitions of balance sheet and profit and loss account items will do much, so far as the presentation and information is concerned, to harmonise practices.

This EC directive will not be directly applicable in most captive domiciles, for example it will not apply in the Isle of Man, Guernsey or of course in the Caribbean locations. However, it will apply to places such as Luxembourg and Dublin. Having said this, it is likely that its requirements will, in time, be followed by all European captive domiciles because it will become and will form part of, "best practice" and the vast majority of captive parents in these locations will be required to follow EC directives at group level.

The directive is an important part of the European Commission's plans to open up the community insurance market by removing differences in practice. The directive will help remove these differences; captives looking to write business throughout Europe should look to follow it.

Accounting Policies and Standards

There is no insurance accounting standard in the UK that deals specifically with the financial accounting and reporting requirements of insurance companies. However, the requirement that a captive's accounts show a true and fair view means that a captive still has to comply with Statements of Standard Accounting Practice (SSAP) generally to the extent that specific insurance legislation does not provide exemptions. Consequently captive insurances companies may, without contravening any requirements of SSAPs, take advantage of certain exemptions that relate to disclosure. In practice, SSAP 6, "Extraordinary items and prior year adjustments", is probably the accounting standard where these exemptions are most usually invoked.

The absence of a specific accounting standard on insurance business has generally led to a wide divergence of accounting practices amongst insurance companies both domestically and in offshore captive locations. The Association of British Insurers (ABI) issued a Statement of Recommended Practice (SORP) on Accounting for Insurance Business in May 1990. The primary aim of the ABI SORP is to narrow the areas of difference and variety in the accounting treatments of matters unique to insurance business. The AIB SORP, which is intended to supplement accounting standards, sets out recommended accounting practice in respect of both general and long-term insurance business.

As I have mentioned already the overriding objective for any set of accounts is that they show a trust and fair view of the company's results and state of affairs. General Accounting Standards and the ABI SORP lay down detailed rules and guidance to achieve this key objective. These rules are all based upon four fundamental accounting concepts, that must be followed to achieve this, they are going concern, consistency, prudence and accruals.

It is when we start to consider these fundamental concepts that we must realise insurance companies must have the ability to use different approaches in their accounts when dealing the very different types of insurance business they write. These have developed into the different accounting bases we refer to as annual revenue or fund accounting: —

The Different Accounting Bases

General insurance business may be accounted for on an "annual", "deferred annual" or "funded" basis. Each of these bases, together with an indication of the circumstance under which they may be appropriate is outlined below: —

The Annual Basis of Accounting

The ABI SORP recommends that the annual basis of accounting should be used where the underwriting result can be determined with reasonable certainty at the end of each accounting periods for business written in that period. This will be the situation for classes of business where premiums and claims are reported to the insurance company relatively quickly, such as direct property and casualty insurance.

Under the annual basis of accounting, claims, net of reinsurance recoveries, incurred in the financial year are charged against the premiums ceded, earned in the financial year. The principal features of the annual basis are that:

- All premiums should be accounted for in the year in which they incept and the accounts should include an estimate of premiums in respect of risks incepting in the period, which have not yet been recorded in the accounting records.

- Premium income should be recognised in the accounts over the period of risk. At the end of an accounting period provision should be made for unearned premiums, representing the unexpired portion of policies in issue with periods of cover extending into the following accounting period.

- Unearned premiums are usually computed on the daily pro rata (365ths) basis or the monthly pro rata (12ths) basis and should be computed gross of commissions and other acquisition expenses.

- Deferred acquisition expenses should be calculated as accurately as possible and should not be carried forward without limitation. Both the basis of calculation and the amount of the deferred acquisition expenses carried forward should be disclosed.

    Provision should be made for "unexpired risks", in addition to unearned premiums, where the latter are likely to be sufficient to meet future losses arising on business in force at the balance sheet date. Investment income on provisions may be taken into account in calculating the unexpired risk provision.

- When estimating the cost of incurred claims, provision is made for outstanding claims including incurred, but not reported (IBNR). The provision for outstanding claims is based on the best estimate of the ultimate cost of settlement and includes provision for expenses, such as legal fees directly attributable to individual claims. Provision should also be made for the overhead expenses of the insurance company that will be incurred after the balance sheet date in settling outstanding claims.

The Deferred Annual Basis of Accounting

For some classes of direct and reinsurance business, such as proportional treaties, it is not possible to obtain the information necessary to determine the results at the end of the financial period in which the business incepted. However, where the information becomes available during the following financial period, the "deferred annual" basis of accounting may be appropriate. The ABI SORP recommends the use of the deferred annual basis in these circumstances. Under this basis:

- All items in the revenue account are reported one accounting period in arrears, but otherwise this basis is the same as the annual basis of accounting. The revenue account for the current financial period includes all items relating to the previous accounting period (known as the "closed year"). The transactions for the current financial period (known as the "open year") are deferred and included in the revenue account of the next accounting period.

- Alternatively the transactions for the open year may be recorded in the current financial year and carried forward in the balance sheet as a fund.

If the information available for the open year indicates that a loss is likely to arise then a provision for the deficiency should be made.

The Funded Basis of Accounting

For classes of business for which long delays are experienced in the notification of premiums and settlement of claims (such as marine, aviation and transport business, certain types of liability business and non-proportional treaty reinsurance) the funded basis of accounting is normally adopted. The most common examples of fund accounting in captives relate to liability business.

Under the funded basis of accounting, premiums are related back to an "underwriting" year. Claims are allocated to the same underwriting year as the related premium irrespective of the date of occurrence of the event giving risk to the claim. Underwriting transactions are included in the fund account in the financial year in which they are notified and it is unusual for estimates to be made of written but unreported premiums.

The "three year" basis is the usual form of the funded basis of accounting, although longer periods are sometimes used. On this basis, in respect of each underwriting year a "fund" is created consisting of the balance of premiums received, less the related commission, expenses and claims paid. A separate fund is usually established for each class of business, although more than one class may be grouped together if these classes are managed together. This does not tend to arise in the captives. At the end of an underwriting year and at the end of the following financial year the balance on the fund is carried forward in the balance sheet and no underwriting profits are released (that is, the underwriting year is left "open"), when two years have elapsed since the end of the underwriting year, the year is "closed" and the underwriting profit is determined by calculating the balance of the "fund" that needs to be carried forward to settle the remaining liabilities of that underwriting year. Expenses should be accounted for in the accounting period on an incurred basis and allocated to the appropriate underwriting year.

The fund carried forward in the respect of each open underwriting year must be sufficient to cover the estimated ultimate liabilities, including claims not yet reported, which have to be settled from that fund. Any premiums for the underwriting year not yet reported, which have to be settled from that fund. Any premiums for the underrating year not yet recorded can be taken into account in determining the fund required. If the fund appears likely to be insufficient, provision must be made to cover the deficiency. Transfers from one fund to another to cover deficiencies, the cost of which will otherwise be met by means of a charge to the profit and loss account (known as "cross-funding"), are not permitted although transfers between classes of business within the same fund and underwriting year may be made.

The underwriting result for the accounting period will, therefore, comprise the results for the year that has just been closed, adjustments to estimates used in arriving at the results of previously closed years and provisions for anticipated deficiencies and adjustments to provisions previously established for the open years. At the balance sheet date, the fund will comprise the outstanding liabilities of the closed years, the net income less outgoings (that is claims and expenses) for each open year and any provisions for anticipated deficiencies for the open years.

The Factors Determining Which Basis to Follow

Quality of Data

A captive insurance company, like any other, should account for all its business annually if it is possible. Also, it should be able to do this to a reasonable degree of accuracy and within a reasonably short period from the year end.

To achieve this it is important that historical claims data is completely and accurately recorded both for the purposes of computing provisions for known outstanding claims and to provide the necessary statistical data for the projection of total claims liabilities, including IBNRs. The usefulness of historical data for projection purposes depends not only on the accuracy of the individual components of the data, but on the way in which the data is accumulated.

Since the different projection methodologies will be used in different circumstances it is not practicable to define "adequate data" in absolute terms, but there are a large number of issues to be addressed in the review or design of data.

It is worth emphasising that use can only be made of historical data as a basis for projecting the future if sufficient information is available to interpret the data and developments within it. Adequate data must by implication therefore include an understanding of changes in business written, in reinsurance and in processing methods or business practices.

Inadequacies in the quality of data or the ability to interpret it may lead a company to fund account due to increased uncertainty within a reasonable time after the period end. This is an unsatisfactory situation and all efforts should be made to avoid this.

Timing

If there is a significant delay in the reporting of the occurrence of insured events to the captive that cannot be avoided, then it is unlikely that it will be able to account annually for that business and it will probably use the fund basis. There is no hard and fast rule regarding what is a significant delay. I would suggest that anything over a year's delay would cause problems. However, the better the historical data and with it the ability to use statistical projection techniques, the longer this period may become before there is a problem. A typical example of a line of business being written in captives where delays in reporting occur is Employers' Liability.

Even if the reporting of an event is fairly rapid there may still be delays in determining whether a liability actually exists or not. An example of this type of business products liability. The occurrence of an incident may be reported quickly but it may take a number of years of technical enquiry and then legal argument to decide if there was a fault with the product that caused the incident. Delays of this nature will also tend to lead to fund accounting.

Lastly, an event may be reported quickly and liability agreed but the agreement of quantum may take a considerable time. A good example of where this type of problem arises is with litigation where legal costs are covered.

Spread of Risk

As well as timing delays and quality of data another issue to consider is the captive's spread of risk as this, or the lack of it, is often a problem. Exactly the same business may be accounted for differently in different companies if one company has a spread of risk in that area and the other does not.

Examples of Practical Applications

Having looked at the bases available and then the factors that need to be considered when determining which to follow, we now look at some practical applications.

From the range of possible classes usually written by captives I have selected four types that, in my experience, I consider to be good examples to demonstrate the different issues which will determine the accounting base to follow. These are:

— **Property Damage**
— **Motor**
— **Product Liability**
— **Employer's Liability—Industrial Injury**

Examples:

Property Damage

Details of Business   UK locations only PD/BI. Cover maximum,/ Retention £250,000 each and every, £750,000 in the annual aggregate. Cover written on an occurrence basis.

Historic Data	Good, short reporting period
Reserving Technique	Review of known cases—no IBNR due to short reporting period
Accounting Basis	Annual revenue basis
Comments	No special features

Motor

Details of Business	UK located vehicles, quite large fleet, mostly heavy vehicles. £75,000 any one loss, £250,000 in the annual aggregate. Cover written on an occurrence basis.
Historic Data	Good, reporting can be a little slow, but consistent. Provision made for IBNR's
Reserving Techniques	Known case reviews and IBNRs statistical extrapolation techniques (chain ladders) used for IBNR element.
Annual Accounting	Annual revenue accounting
Other Comments	No special features

Public/Product Liability	Worldwide public/product liability. Cover is arranged on a notification basis.
Details of Business	Maximum retentions are £2,000,000 each and every and £5,000,000 in the annual aggregate. The insured is a UK based manufacturer with significant exports including to the US. Annual premium £1,300,000
Historic Data	Very good with effective systems for picking up potential future claims
Reserving Techniques	Review of known cases
Accounting Basis	Three year general business fund
Comments	Open years closed by reinsuring further development

Employers' Liability — Industrial Deafness

Details of Business	Retrospective industrial deafness, exposure covers injuries incurred gong back up to 25 years from fixed recent date. No overall aggregate or each and every exposure limit. But experience shows individual claim s average £2,000 and fall within the range £1,000–£3,000. Potential claimants estimated to be in the region of 20,000. Similar features re current exposure but considerably smaller number of potential claimants.
Historic Data	Good in recent years, but not so good for over fifteen years ago and before.
Reserving Techniques	Retrospective cover, actuarially defined long term fund. No split into underwriting years, i.e. one fund similar to life business. Overall assumptions and trends reviewed annually but full actuarial review carri ed out probably only every three years. Current cover statistical extrapolation techniques.
Accounting Basis	Retrospective long term fund
Comments	Retrospective cover more akin to life business than general need for actuarial involvement. Reserves, i.e. the fund, are discounted because of long period funds held and very sensitive to investment returns. Retrospective cover separated from current exposure

Regulatory and Taxation Considerations

In my experience regulators have a fairly relaxed attitude as to the accounting basis to be followed. This is, I suppose, due to the initial assumption that companies will account normally.

There is then a move to fund accounting when problems are experienced in being able to reserve with accuracy within a reasonable time scale from the year end. It does not tend to happen the other way around, i.e. companies that should account on a fund basis do not in my experience look to move to an annual basis.

209

As the fund basis is more prudent a regulator will tend to be quite happy because his main concerns are capital adequacy and solvency. Fund accounting will usually improve the company's standing in these areas because it tends to delay the recognition of profit. Regulators will on balance prefer this more prudent approach.

Taxation

I would suggest taxmen tend to have the opposite view and will be cautious about an accounting basis that tends to defer profit recognition, suspecting that it is being used for the wrong reasons.

The main tax area that is brought into play when considering fund accounting as opposed to annual revenue accounting for UK owned captives is compliance with UK CFC legislation. There are two main strategies that such captives will tend to follow to minimise UK tax. The most common is having the captive follow an acceptable distribution policy and the second is paying tax, in the captive domicile, of at least 75% of what would have been due under UK corporation tax rules. The second route is still rare but will, I believe become more common.

Taking the acceptable distribution policy route first. A company which finds it needs to account on a fund basis may run into problems because if there are no profits, which is likely in the early years of a fund, the company cannot pursue an acceptable distribution policy as there are no profits to distribute. However, after completing a tax computation chargeable profits might arise, so theoretically a UK tax charge may follow.

Having said this, if the company can demonstrate its accounting and the reserving policies are appropriate and reasonable and have not been manipulated to reduce the amount available for distribution then no charge should arise, as I believe the Revenue will not seek a direction in these circumstances. The point being made here is, if the fund approach is being followed, make sure it is justified; if it is not, you could have a tax problem.

A similar point needs to be made regarding the 75% of UK tax route. If this is followed, chargeable profits are calculated using UK Corporation Tax computational rules. If the accounting basis produces over-prudent reserves, i.e. again by creating a fund that is not justified, the figures will be reworked and chargeable profits may be created.

[This article was written before the changes announced by the U.K. Government in 1995. However, the principles remain the same and, in many respects, **Mr. Talavera anticipated the approach that was adopted.]**

One other tax issue that I find cropping up when a company is considering following a fund accounting basis is the question of a proper transfer of risk.

The point here can be that the company is set up with inadequate capital, the risk being predominately financed by way of premium. Because of this there is a tendency to be over prudent when reserving because of the lack of capital should the reserving be understated. To cover this a company may consider fund accounting to avoid transferring any premium to profits for three years. This prevents it from paying any dividends and the capital base is built up. It is an appropriate reason for fund accounting, the proper course being to capitalise properly in the first place.

Not to do so may bring into question the allow ability of the premiums paid as there my not have been a proper transfer of risk in the first place.

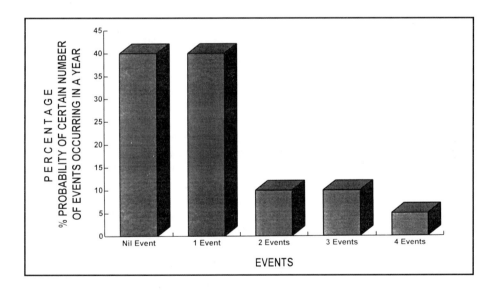

- **Product liability — high value/low volume**
- **Exposure limited by reinsurance**
- **Reporting delays one to two years, with possible further delays in agreement of liability and quantum**
- **Good quality historic data**

Company "A"—One insured
      —Aggregate limit £2 million
      —E&E limit £2 million   **FUND ACCOUNT**
      —Premiums £1.6 million

Company "B"—Ten insureds
      —Aggregate limit £2 million   **ANNUAL REVENUE**
      —E&E limit £200K   **ACCOUNT**
      —Premium £1.6 million

Other requirements of the accounts will be to separate the operation into different classes of business and to apply different approaches to reserving for outstanding claims. These outstanding claims can be separated into two areas: first, those claims which have been reported and on which it is possible to produce some estimate of what the outcome is likely to be; and, second, the much more difficult area of the incurred but not reported (IBNR) claims where, if the class of business being underwritten is of a long-term nature, it will be very difficult to apportion a reserve figure, particularly if the type of business is of a volatile nature, such as products liability, or where the captive has no historical basis on which to calculate its IBNR figures. Once data on a historical basis have been developed, the application of IBNR becomes more simple, but in the early years it is difficult to decide what the prudent approach should be other than to release no profits until some sort of IBNR pattern is established.

Reserves for insurance companies fall into two main areas: free reserves and technical reserves. Free reserves are unrelated to specific obligations of the insurance company and are generally formed from taxed or capital sources, because of this they are considered as belonging to the shareholders. Technical reserves are related to specific obligations, usually the payment of outstanding claims or premium that has not yet been earned. These reserves are not available to shareholders and are subject to taxation only if they are found to be unnecessary and released into the profit and loss accounts. Other reserves that might be found in insurance company balance sheets could include currency reserves to deal with fluctuations between annual variations, investment reserves reflecting the profit or loss of a difference between cost price and book value, tax equalisation reflecting the difference between tax estimated and tax actually assessed and reserves for catastrophic exposure.

Insurance company accounts may be kept for a variety of reasons. First, to comply with the law, where the format will generally be laid down and will probably require separation into different classes of business, with details of the run-off calculation and the reinsurance programme. Second, there are published accounts where the classes of business are likely to be integrated, so that, for example, fire and accident will be treated as one class and marine and aviation treated as another class. The third set of accounts may be management accounts which would be used by the captive and its owners for detailed supervision of the underwriting programme, cost control, cash flow, etc. There is considerable variation in published accounts and convention and the captive needs to choose the best method in relation to its parent company's approach to accounting and the need to monitor the operation.

Tables 6.1–6.4 are examples of profit and loss accounts, underwriting accounts and balance sheets that might be the basis for a captive insurance company operation. Table 6.5 shows the development of an account in relation to premium and claims, separated into quarters and developed until the account is completely run off.

Other accounting factors that need to be taken into consideration include commissions payable or received from reinsurers, expenses of the company, and fluctuations which can be split into the following areas:

1. Stock market value, property value, inflation factors.
2. Currency, effect of economic activity and volume of business.
3. Effect on rating levels of capacity and competition and variable taxation between various countries and various years of operation.

In addition, account needs to be taken of the calculation of unearned premium and delays in payment, especially in respect of any treaty relationships. Claims, assessment, the size of the claim, the length and the shape of the claim in both volume and duration need to be considered and it is also necessary to take account of the reinsurance programme, the existing capacity and future rating characteristics as well as the security.

Requirements for legislative return

The need for differing forms of account will depend on legislation requirements. A typical example of the legislative requirements for a one-year revenue account is shown in Table 6.6. These accounts should be developed for each class of business and individual totals should be produced.

For the revenue account developed on a three-year basis the information required is likely to be as shown in Table 6.7. Figures

Table 6.1

SPASMODIC INSURANCE LIMITED
Profit and Loss Account

INCOME
    Transfer to/from premium funds
    Interest

EXPENSES
    Directors' fees
    Management
    Audit fee

Profit before tax
    Income tax
            Retained profit
            P & L B/F

Supporting
schedules   Dividend
for each
fund   P & L B/F

Table 6.2

SPASMODIC INSURANCE LIMITED
Underwriting Account

Account at ....   all figures in £ sterling

Risk	Prems.	Paid claims	Settled ratio	Outstanding claims	Incurred ratio
94_____					
94 Total					
95_____					
95 Total					
96_____					
96 Total					

This table prepared
  (A) Gross
  (B) Net of reinsurance

Table 6.3

SPASMODIC INSURANCE LIMITED
Balance sheet at ....

Capital employed
  Share capital
    Authorised
    issued
  Reserves
  Retained profit
  Future taxation

Employment of capital
  Current assets
    Debtors
    Government securities
    Bank balances
  Current liabilities
    Creditors
    Income tax
  Net current assets
    Ins. fund   1994 Account
             1995 Account
             NET

Table 6.4

SPASMODIC INSURANCE LIMITED
Underwriting account at ....

1995 Account	At 31.3.96	Quarter	At 30.6.96
Premium (class or policy)			
Reinsurance			
Premium *less* reinsurance			
Claims paid			
Claims total			
Underwriting fund			
(Ditto each year)			

215

Table 6.5

SPASMODIC INSURANCE LIMITED			
£ thousand	1994 PCLR	1995 PCLR	1996 PCLR
1Q			
2Q			
3Q			
4Q			
5Q			Columns
6Q			for all →
7Q			open years
8Q			
9Q			
10Q			
11Q			
12Q			
13Q			Different tables
14Q			for
15Q			Gross account
16Q			and
		Continue	Net account
17Q		until run-off	(After reinsurance)
18Q		↓	
19Q			

Table 6.6 Example of the legislative requirements for a one-year revenue account

Income	Expenditure
Unearned premiums brought forward	Claims (net of salvage, reinsurance and other recoveries)
Unexpired risk brought forward	
Claims outstanding brought forward	Commission (net of commission on business ceded)
Claims equalisation brought forward	
Fund brought forward	Taxation
Premiums (net of refunds, rebate and premiums for reinsurance ceded)	Other expenditure (particulars to be specified)
Interest, dividends and rent (before tax)	Unearned premiums carried forward
Other income (particulars to be specified)	Unexpired risks carried forward
Transfer from profit and loss account	Claims outstanding carried forward
	Claims equalisation carried forward
	Fund carried forward
	Transfer to profit and loss account
Total	Total

Table 6.7 Example of the legislative requirements for a three-year revenue account

Income	Expenditure
Profit brought forward	Claims (net of salvage, reinsurance and
Premiums (net of refunds, rebates and	other recoveries) for each class of
premium reinsurance ceded) for each	Insurance
class of business	Commission (net of commission business
Interest, dividends and rent (before tax)	ceded)
Other income (particulars to be specified)	Expenses of management
Transfer from profit and loss account	Taxation
	Other expenditure (particulars to be
	specified)
	Fund carried forward
	Transfer to profit and loss account
Total	Total

on the three-year revenue account are required for each year of the underwriting account.

Claims frequency analysis

There may also be a requirement to provide detailed information of claims, separated by each class and each risk group. This type of analysis would include information of the exposure during the year of account, in respect of both contracts which commenced during the previous year and contracts commencing during the current year of account.

In addition there would be a requirement to indicate the exposure carried forward to the financial year following the year of account, in respect of contracts commencing during the year of account.

A detailed analysis should be made of the number of claims, separated into categories: claims related to early years but first notified during the year of account, closed in earlier years but reopened, originating during the current year of account and notified before the closure of records, an estimated number of claims originating during the year but not notified before closure of the record, and the estimated total number of claims attributable to the current year of account.

Similar information may be required in respect of claims settlements, also separated according to class, risk group and underwriting year. This settlement information will include the year, the number of claims closed, the number of claims outstanding, the amount of payments made in the year both in settlement and on account, the aggregate payments made to the end of the year, the claims outstanding at the end of the year and the total claims paid and outstanding. Tables 6.6 and 6.7 give some assistance in developing this formation which, even if it is not required by the legislative authorities, will be very useful in managing the captive and examining any positive or negative trends in its performance.

In developing an accounting policy for the captives the main decision will be whether the account should be prepared on a one- or three-year basis. In addition will be the requirements of the local legislation for financial statements and audited returns, and finally the need of the captive itself to have financial information or to monitor its performance. There is a range of variations available but the essential factors are that advice should be sought from accountants who specialise in insurance accounting and that the management company chosen has the capability to produce the required information in the form requested and ar the time required both by the parent company and the local authorities.

Taxation

The taxation benefits for the captive in relation to the ability to have tax deductibility of premiums and to build up reserves for the purpose of smoothing major losses were discussed earlier. The taxation implications separate into the two following areas:

1. Tax considerations for the parent, including tax deductibility of premiums, positions on contingent funding.
2. Tax considerations for the captive, including the system for developing premium funds and reserves, separation of investment and underwriting income and account of premium taxes which may be applicable in different parts of the world.
3. Tax considerations which deal with the problem of the extent to which a captive would be able to withstand an attack by taxation authorities charging that it is actually managed and controlled in the same country as its parent and thereby liable to full corporate tax on the whole of its income.

Tax considerations for the parent

The tax considerations for the parent are of considerable importance since any denial of the tax deductibility of premiums to the captive may negate the original purpose for its establishment.

In the United States two tax rulings by the Internal Revenue Service (IRS) dating back to the late 1970s have formed the basis for assessing the tax authority's attitude to captives and premium deductibility. The 'economic family' theory was born of the first of these two rulings; subsequently it has been a question merely of looking to see how the IRS has developed this theory.

With the economic family theory, a deduction may be denied a parent company for premiums paid to a captive if the captive is found to be a member of the parent's economic family. There is no real risk transfer in such transactions and therefore no real insurance for which premium deductions may be claimed, the theory holds. In Revenue Ruling 77–316 the IRS denied premium deductibility to the single owner of a captive that insured only its parent's risks.

The three situations cited in the IRS ruling were as follows:

1. A direct transfer of premiums by a US parent company to a newly organised, wholly-owned foreign insurance subsidiary of the parent in respect of contracts entered into for fire and other casualty insurance.
2. The payment of insurance premiums by the domestic corporation but in this case to an independent and unrelated domestic insurance company. However, a contractual arrangement exists under which the independent insurer agrees to immediately transfer 95 per cent of the risks under a reinsurance agreement with the US parents' wholly-owned foreign insurance subsidiary.
3. Insurance premiums paid directly to the foreign captive which in turn, again under a contractual agreement, transfer 90 per cent of the risk through reinsurance plans to an unrelated domestic insurance company.

In another ruling, 78–338, the IRS allowed a deduction for premiums paid to a hypothetical captive with thirty-one owners, all of which insured risks in the captive.

In pursuing its economic family theory as a test for deductibility, the Government has prevailed in three cases that did not involve 'unrelated' business: Carnation Company, Stearns-Roger Corporation and Beech Aircraft Corporation. Following these cases, some captive owners concluded that a sufficient amount of unrelated business — non-parent or affiliate business — should ensure premium deductibility. The Mobil case proved that they were wrong to do so but the Humana Inc case questioned the whole basis of their 'economic family' argument.

The Carnation case
In August 1971, Carnation Company incorporated a wholly-owned Bermuda subsidiary, Three Flowers, to insure and reinsure multiple-line

risks only of Carnation and its other subsidiaries. Carnation capitalised Three Flowers in early September 1971 by purchasing 120,000 shares of common stock at its par value of $1 per share.

On 22 September 1971, Carnation purchased a three-year blanket insurance policy from an unrelated insurance company, American Home, which reinsured 90 per cent of the risks under this policy with Three Flowers. Prior to the consummation of the reinsurance contract, American Home expressed concern about Three Flowers' ability to cover Carnation's losses and requested Carnation to deliver either a letter of credit or a guarantee of Three Flowers' performance. Carnation refused these requests but agreed to capitalise Three Flowers up to $3 million upon demand (by purchasing an additional 288,000 shares of common stock at $10 per share) to provide American Home with added assurance of Three Flowers' solvency. American Home then ceded 90 per cent of the risks under Carnation's policy on a quota share basis to Three Flowers for 90 per cent of the premium paid by Carnation less a ceding commission and reimbursement for premium taxes.

In the tax year in question — 1972 — Carnation paid American Home an annual insurance premium of $1,950,000 and American Home paid Three Flowers $1,775,000 under the reinsurance agreement. In the Tax Court, the Government and Carnation stipulated these amounts to be the product of arm's-length negotiations. For the 1972 year, Carnation deducted the entire $1,950,000 premium paid to American Home; acknowledged that Three Flowers was a controlled foreign corporation and reported $1,647,216 as a deemed distribution of Three Flowers' income derived from the insurance of US risks; and computed its foreign tax credit limitation by treating the $1,647,216 as income from foreign sources. The Government denied Carnation's deduction of $1,755,000, an amount equal to the premiums ceded to Three Flowers; recharacterised the $1,755,000 as a contribution to capital thereby reducing the amount of Three Flowers' subpart F income reportable by Carnation; and accordingly redetermined Carnation's foreign tax credit limitation. The Tax Court concluded that there was not shifting of risk from Carnation as the risks reinsured by American Home with Three Flowers lacked an essential element of insurance.

The Court of Appeal's opinion affirmed the Tax Court's determinations that the insurance agreement between American Home and Three Flowers, and the reinsurance agreement between American Home and Three Flowers and the capitalisation agreement between Carnation and Three Flowers, were interdependent and that, considered together, 'these agreements neutralised the risk to the extent American Home reinsured with Three Flowers'.

Trends foreseen at the time of the Carnation decision were these:

1. Increasing the volume of third-party (outside) business.
2. Participation in pooling arrangements with fellow captives.
3. Formation of association or industry captives.
4. Diversifying captive ownership and structure.

The Stearns-Roger case

Then came the Stearns-Roger case. The worldwide manufacturer of mining, petroleum and power generating plants lost the battle with the IRS in the United States over the deductibility of premiums paid to its Colorado captive between 1974 and 1978 — because the insured risks never left the parent company's 'economic family'. Thus ruled a US District Court judge in Denver to make the first captive case decision since Carnation with a ruling specifically on tax deductibility.

The decision seemed to reinforce Revenue Ruling 77–316. In the United States, if you were insuring only the risks of the parent, according to this decision it was not insurance. The implication was that US captives should take up unrelated risks, though this was recognised as not a watertight situation because the revenue still had to rule on the deductibility of third-party premiums.

The Beech Aircraft case

Then, in 1984, came the Beech Aircraft decision. A US court ruled that Beech Aircraft Corporation could not claim tax deductions for premiums paid to its Bermuda-based captive insurance company, Travel Air Insurance Company. The verdict prevented the corporation from deducting from its 1973 tax liability about $1.7 million in premiums it paid to Travel Air. The court upheld the view that the transaction between the two companies did not move risk outside the economic family and was therefore only a 'paper transfer'. If there had been no losses incurred by the captive, the court argued, 'the deduction of purported insurance premiums could become a tax loophole for the parent company'. Conversely, when a loss did occur this would be met by Beech in so far as its net worth would be reduced accordingly just as though it had paid the loss itself.

The Mobil case

Then came the most important case: Mobil. The US Department of Justice took the position that the amount of unrelated premium, insured or reinsured by an affiliated insurer or reinsurer, was irrelevant for the purposes of determining whether premium paid to such a company by the parent or other affiliates was tax deductible. It followed that under such an approach premiums paid by affiliates would not be considered deductible even if the amount of unrelated business were substantial. What would it mean for group-owned captives?

It also said that transactions between related companies did not constitute insurance for tax purposes and the Government described captives as 'profit maximisation centres'. In addition it said that their use by Mobil was 'an incredible tax avoidance mechanism'.

Mobil was challenged over tax deductions for at least $35 million in premiums paid to its four overseas captives by some thirty-five subsidiaries during the tax years 1961–9. The four Mobil captives were General Overseas Insurance Company Limited (GOIC) of the Bahamas, Bluefield Insurance Limited of Bermuda, Bishopsgate Insurance Company Limited of the United Kingdom and Westchester Insurance Company Limited of Cape Town, South Africa. Mobil paid the disputed taxes but filed suit in the Claims Court for a refund. Mobil contended that its captives were separate corporate entities operating at arm's length from the parent corporation; therefore Mobil was justified in taking deductions for premiums paid to them. Mobil's general line was that the captives were formed for valid business reasons and not for the purpose of avoiding or evading Federal Income Taxes.

The Government's post-trial brief stated that 'there is absolutely no insurance theory that supports the conclusion that the presence of unrelated insureds converts the relationship among affiliates into insurance'. Anticipating the rebuttal that tax payers and their attorneys have been led to the conclusion that the underwriting of unrelated insurance business by the captive is important to establishing the bona fide status of the captive for tax purposes by private letter rulings from the Internal Revenue Service and a published internal IRS memorandum, the Government said: 'any informal opinion of the Internal Revenue Service to the contrary is clearly incorrect'. Quite a shock to the captive community.

Mobil's payments to its captives were essentially self-insurance, the Government said, since the company retained risk. 'Whether the taxpayer retains its exposure merely by a formal accrual on its books and records or engages in an elaborate device through the use of unrelated corporations and wholly-owned insurance affiliates, where risk has in reality been retained, insurance does not exist as a matter of Federal Tax Law. And that is precisely the situation in this case.'

The point of insurance, the Government argued, was to relieve companies of financial uncertainty; therefore, how can risks placed in a company it owns relieve a business of its financial uncertainty?

The Government further stated that the captive insurance company owner 'has not parted with the premium, nor the financial consequences of the risk; the true insured has parted with both'.

'The quintessential difference between a captive insurance transaction and an insurance transaction is that the person who owns the insurer does not shift its uncertainty to another, he still retains the full uncertainty he had before the affiliate issued a formal contract of insurance.' Mobil was bereft of insurance either as a matter of economic reality or as a matter of insurance theory, the Government argued.

Mobil, of course, took a contrary view. It cited the first IRS ruling against tax deductions for premiums paid to the captive, Revenue Ruling 77–316, in support of its argument that because the losses of the few are paid out of the premiums of the many, a parent company will be regarded as having shifted its risk outside the economic family when it obtains insurance from an insurance subsidiary which insures risks of other parties. Ruling 77–316 states that 'the sharing and distribution of the insurance risk by all the parties insured is essential to the concept of true insurance'. Mobil's captive, Bishopsgate, for instance, derived between 50 and 90 per cent of its annual net premium income from the insurance of unrelated parties from 1964 to 1968. Bluefield and GOIC wrote and reinsured a substantial amount of insurance for the benefit of parties other than Mobil and its subsidiaries, Mobil's brief claimed. Mobil saw the Government's case as dependent upon Ruling 77–316, and consequently attacked this vehemently as wrong, inconsistent and fundamentally opposed to the 'separate corporate entities' doctrine espoused by the US Supreme Court. Ruling 77–316 holds that the risk of loss cannot be shifted from one member of an economic family to another member of the family. But Mobil said that this contradicts the separate corporate entity doctrine and therefore conflicts with decisions of the Supreme Court and the basic corporate pattern of the Internal Revenue Code.

The argument was that corporations exist to limit the liability of their stockholders, and corporations can reduce their risk by incorporating and thereby limiting their exposure to loss to the amount invested in that corporation. And if a corporation can shift the risk of a casualty loss to its subsidiary, as is commonly done, the error in the reasoning in Revenue Ruling 77–316 is fundamental, said Mobil.

In the end, US owners of captive insurance companies were dealt a severe blow by the decision of Claims Court Judge James F. Merow on 1 August 1985 to deny Mobil Oil Corporation's claim for a refund of its $35 million in taxes, paid for payments to offshore captives between 1961 and 1969. These taxes were the price Mobil had to pay when the Internal Revenue Service disallowed deductions for premiums paid during those years to Mobil's four offshore captives: General Overseas Insurance Company Limited (GOIC) of the Bahamas, Bluefield Insurance Limited of Bermuda, Bishopsgate Insurance Company Limited of the United Kingdom and Westchester Insurance Company Limited of Cape Town, South Africa.

Judge Merow's ruling cited the *Carnation Company* v. *Commissioner* case; hence, it was based on the time-worn argument that risk cannot be transferred by a so-called premium payment made to a wholly-owned subsidiary. In such circumstances the transaction does not constitute insurance for tax purposes and the amounts paid are not premiums. The ruling therefore did not directly address that other area of interest about which captive owners were still waiting for court guidance — the extent to which the writing of non-group risks will influence the tax treatment of premiums paid to a captive for related company risks.

Risk was not shifted, Judge Merow said, because: 'Any losses suffered by the insurance affiliate would be reflected on Mobil's financial statements. Conversely, any profits realised by the affiliates benefited Mobil.'

Other points made by the judge were these:

1. Insurance with a wholly-owned captive is effectively the same as setting up a self-insurance reserve account because any loss will be reflected in the parent company balance sheet and profit and loss account.
2. Mobil's argument that the Government's position conflicted with the legal doctrine of separate corporate entities was wrong because disallowing insurance premiums paid to captive insurance companies does not totally disregard the separate nature of corporate entities; it is an example of reclassification of a transaction.

Fair or not, sensible or nor, the decision went against Mobil. The rationale of risk-financing via captives had to be reworked. Indeed, in anticipation of a continuing hard-nosed approach from the authorities, insurance buyers had been working for some time on revamping their risk-financing approaches.

The Clougherty case
In the case *Clougherty Packing Company* v. *Commissioner*, filed 20 May 1985, it was held that the petitioner failed to shift 92 per cent of

its risk of loss; therefore, 92 per cent of its premiums paid to Fremont, an unrelated insurance carrier and reinsured to Lombardy, the wholly-owned captive insurance company, was not deductible as an ordinary and necessary business expense for insurance. Lombardy was incorporated under the laws of Colorado on 24 November 1976, pursuant to the Colorado Captive Insurance Company Act. The management concluded that a captive insurance arrangement would reduce the cost of its liabilities for workers' compensation coverage in the following ways:

1. Increasing investment income above the amount received on the securities deposited with the State Treasurer of California.
2. Eliminating the underwriting costs paid to outside insurance carriers.
3. Receiving favourable Federal tax treatment for the captive insurance company subsidiary, which treatment is available to all insurance companies.

Lombardy was capitalised for $1 million.

The petitioner and Fremont Indemnity Company (an unrelated insurer licensed to write workers' compensation insurance in California, hereinafter referred to as 'Fremont') negotiated for a captive insurance programme for petitioner. Fremont offered, in writing, to provide a captive reinsurance programme for petitioner, the pertinent terms of which were as follows:

1. The cost to be 5 per cent of the annual earned premium plus premium taxes, bureau fees and non-incidental costs.
2. The 'Clougherty Captive Company' (as Fremont identified it in its offer) would assume the first $100,000 of any risk being furnished by Fremont.
3. All funds were to be remitted to 'Clougherty's captive' monthly, based on remittance by petitioner to Fremont less costs and deficiencies in collateral.

In essence, Fremont would be assuming the risk up to $100,000 but would reinsure that risk with Lombardy. 'The turnaround time on money, both from Fremont to Lombardy and from Lombardy to Fremont, will be no more than five days.'

On 30 December 1977, the Colorado Division of Insurance issued to Lombardy a certificate of authority to conduct business as a captive insurance company in the State of Colorado. The officers and directors of Lombardy were also officers or employees of petitioner or

Frank B. Hall Management since the organisation of Lombardy. Lombardy's sole business was the reinsurance of petitioner's workers' compensation coverage. Lombardy had no employees but, instead, conducted its day-to-day business through employees of Hall pursuant to a management agreement between Lombardy and Hall.

During April 1978, petitioner insured its workers' compensation coverage for one year with Fremont, effective 1 January 1978. Lombardy agreed to reinsure the first 5100,000 per occurrence for all of petitioner's risk insured by Fremont. In addition, Fremont agreed to cede (transfer) to Lombardy 92 per cent of the premiums it received from the petitioner. Under the reinsurance agreement Lombardy was required to and did secure a $200,000 irrevocable letter of credit to be held by Fremont as security for unpaid open losses and unearned premiums.

There was no agreement that the petitioner would indemnify Fremont, that it would pay additional capital into Lombardy, or that it would take any steps, direct or indirect, to assure that Lombardy would perform its obligations under its reinsurance agreement with Fremont. The premium paid by petitioner to Fremont was set by the Workers' Compensation Insurance Rating Bureau of the State of California; the rates for reinsurance cessions were negotiated between Fremont and Lombardy but had to be approved by the Insurance Commissioner for the State of Colorado.

The Commissioner, in the statutory notice of deficiency, disallowed that portion of petitioner's deductions for premiums on workers' compensation insurance which represented the 'reinsurance premiums' paid by Fremont to Lombardy. All the judges appeared to reject the economic family theory, but most of them decided that there was no risk transfer involved in the case. The consensus also suggested that the same result would have been reached even if the taxpayer had not wholly owned the subsidiary or there had been some 'unrelated' business.

The Gulf Oil case
Another important case concerned a ruling in November 1987 by the US tax court in respect of the case brought to them by the Gulf Oil Corporation in respect of the denial by the Internal Revenue Service of deductions of premiums paid by Gulf to its Bermuda captive in 1974 and 1975.

As with the Carnation and Mobil decisions the court denied the deductions of the premium making a particular point that most of the captive's business in the two years in question was parent business and that as a result there was none of the risk-shifting required if premiums arc to be treated as deductible insurance payments.

The most interesting factor in the case was that in a footnote the court suggested that if there had been a larger volume of unrelated business this might have allowed the parent company's premiums to be deductible. They even went to the extent of saying that the court believed that if at least 50 per cent of the captive premiums had been unrelated, sufficient risk transfer would have been present to allow a deduction.

The footnote comment was not well received by the Internal Revenue Service, who subsequently stated that it would not follow the Gulf Oil approach 'to the extent that it rejects the economic family concept of Revenue Ruling 77–316 and suggests the presence of third party insureds might under certain circumstances produce requisite risk shifting'. The whole question of whether the writing of outside business in any way effects the tax deductibility of the premiums remains outstanding but may well be resolved over the next years, and most observers are looking to the conclusion of a case involving the IRS and the major US insurer Allstate, which is owned by a non-insurance entity Sears Roebuck, where Allstate writes some of Sears Roebuck insurance business although the amount written, given the size of Allstate, is very small in relation to Allstate's total premium volume.

The Humana Case
The Internal Revenue Service has not had everything its own way, and the most positive ruling for captive insurance company owners arose in July 1989 when the US Court of Appeals for the Sixth Circuit decided in *Humana Inc.* v. *the Commissioner of Internal Revenue* that the premiums paid by a 'brother' corporation to its 'sister' insurance affiliate should be deductible. The Humana position is best summed up in a brief memorandum produced by the New York lawyers Baker and MacKenzie, as follows:

"Humana Inc. ('Humana') established a wholly-owned insurance subsidiary called Healthcare Indemnity Inc. ('Health Care Indemnity') as a Colorado captive insurance company. Health Care Indemnity was adequately capitalised and offered medical malpractice insurance to Humana and Humana's subsidiaries under a standard insurance policy. Thus, the ownership relationship between Humana's subsidiaries (i.e. the insureds) and Health Care Indemnity was a 'brother-sister' relationship.

The court affirmed the holding of the tax court that amounts paid by Humana to Health Care Indemnity, its wholly-owned subsidiary, for the insurance of Humana's own risks were not premiums paid for 'insurance' and hence were not deductible. The court stated that the characteristics of insurance are risk-shifting and risk distribution. In the wholly-owned context, there was no risk-shifting because a loss sustained by the insurance subsidiary would lower the value of its stock, which would then be reflected on the balance sheet of the parent/insured. The assets of the parent bear the economic impact of a loss paid by the insurance subsidiary.

Premiums paid by Humana's subsidiaries, however, were held to be deductible. The court reasoned that a loss incurred by Health Care indemnity with respect to these risks would not be reflected on the balance sheet of the insured/subsidiary since the insured/subsidiary owned no stock in Health Care indemnity. Therefore, the Humana subsidiaries had shifted their risk loss to Health Care Indemnity because the assets of the Humana subsidiaries did not bear the economic impact of a loss paid by a sister insurance company.

In holding for the taxpayer the court responded to the assertion that taxpayers could readily structure the ownership of their insurance affiliates and insured affiliates as brother/sister companies and thus would be allowed a tax deduction which would not be allowed in the parent/subsidiary context:

> Such an argument provides no legal justification for denying the deduction in the brother/sister context. The legal test is whether there has been risk distribution and risk-shifting, not whether Humana Inc, is a common parent or whether its focus on the relationship of the parties per se of the particular structure of the corporation involved. We look to the assets of the insured. If Humana changes its corporate structure and that change involves risk-shifting and risk distribution, and that change is for a legitimate business purpose and is not sham to avoid the payment of taxes, then it is irrelevant whether the changed corporate structure has the side effect of also permitting Humana Inc's affiliates to take advantage of the Internal Revenue Code 162 (A) (1954) and deduct payments to a captive insurance company under the control of the Humana parent as insurance premiums.

The court also discussed the effect of third party unrelated risks on risk-shifting, although this question was not raised by the facts of the case. As mentioned above, the tax court in *Gulf Oil* v. *Commissioner* has indicated that the insurance of unrelated risks enhances risk-shifting with respect to related party risks, and went so far as to suggest that if unrelated party premiums were at least 50 per cent of the total premiums, risk-shifting was present. The

Humana court questioned this conclusion and hinted that the insurance of unrelated risks affected only risk distribution and not risk-shifting.

It is now known that the internal Revenue Service will not petition for a rehearing of the ease to the Sixth Circuit and/or for certiorari to the US Supreme Court. It seems likely that they will wait for a better ease with which to obtain a successful Supreme Court Ruling or alternatively seek a legislative solution to the question of premium deductibility."

The Malone & Hyde Case

Following the Humana case, a further important event occurred when the Six Circuit Court of Appeal decided that premiums paid by Malone & Hyde (a USA corporation) to Malone & Hyde captive insurer were not deductible insurance premiums because the entire transaction was a sham, based on three factors. Firstly, the Court held that Malone & Hyde had lacked a business purpose in forming the captive. Second, the Court noted the captive operated on the "extremely thin" minimum capitalisation regulatory basis and thirdly, the court pointed to the existence of hold harmless agreements executed between Malone & Hyde for the benefit of its captive insurer.

The existence of these three factors, the Court held, distinguished the case from Humana in which the Six Circuit held that insurance premiums paid to a captive insurance subsidiary on behalf of the parents other subsidiary were deductible as ordinary and necessary business expenses because a loss suffered by the captive insurer would not be reflected in the balance sheets of the insured subsidiaries. Because the court held that the Malone & Hyde insurance arrangements were a sham, they indicated there was no need to address the question which was dealt with in Humana of whether the ostensible insurance transaction involved risk shifting and risk distribution.

In a paper which analysed the Court's decision in Malone & Hyde, the lawyers Baker & McKenzie concluded in relation to the three elements that the decision that the tax payer lacked a business purpose in forming the captive was highly suspect given the facts of the case. They commented that the virulence with which the court attacked Malone & Hyde's motives were surprising in as much that the Tax Court in Malone & Hyde have found, and the Six Circuit affirmed, that Malone & Hyde had formed a captive insurance company to be able to obtain "less expensive insurance coverage". There is no support for the Six Circuit conclusion that reducing costs is not a valid business purposes or that a crisis situation must exist before a tax payer can show a valid business purpose.

So far as thin capitalisation is concerned, Baker & McKenzie said:

"There is no doubt the captive insurers incorporated outside the United States prepare the burden of showing that they operate as real insurance companies, a burden that becomes even more difficult to meet if the captive fails to show that it is subject of the same general regulatory framework to which insurance companies are subject in the US. Beginning in the 1980's, Bermuda exerted considerably more regulatory authority on captives than it did in the years of issue (1978–1980). Thus, the impact of the Malone & Hyde decision in this regard, cases involved in more recent years will likely be somewhat reduced."

So far as the final element — the hold harmless agreement — is concerned, Baker & McKenzie say:

"The Six Circuit took a different approach to the issue than did the Tax Court. Under the Tax Court's logic, which it derives from the Human decision, if the effect of a hold harmless agreement or guarantee is to negate the shifting of risk from the insured to the insurer, and insureds are to be viewed on an entity by entity basis, the fact that the parent is providing the hold harmless or guarantee should not eliminate risk shifting with respect of the subsidiary/insureds. Not so, concluded the Six Circuit Court of Appeals. Under the Six Circuit formulation, even though premium deductibility is looked at on an entity by entity basis, a parent hold harmless agreement or guarantee will prove fatal, presumably because it demonstrates the captive is incapable of paying losses on risks allegedly shifted from the insured to the captive. The concepts of under capitalisation and hold harmless should theoretically be related to one another – if the captive is adequately capitalised it should have no need for a hold harmless agreement or guarantee. The Six Circuit, treats these concepts separately and apparently, even if the captive is fully capable of paying its losses, a parent hold harmless agreement or guarantee will render brother-sister premiums non deductible. This conclusion seems odd with the rationale of the Humana decision, which looks at entities on an independent basis."

Other USA tax factors

Other changes to affect captives and their US owners include the following (some of which result from the 1985 Tax Reform Act):

1. A new definition of a controlled foreign company (CFC) that brings more insurers into the classification. Owners of a CFC pay tax on its annual income; if the captive is not by definition a CFC, tax is paid only when income is repatriated.

2. A change in the definition of income generated by CFCs to include as subpart F income all insurances of non US-based risks. This means taxing it in the current year.

3. The precluding of the balancing of low-taxed foreign source income against high-taxed foreign source non-insurance income when working out the foreign tax credit limit.

4. Redefinition of Subpart F income to include all types of captive, bringing association and group captives into the net for the first time.

5. Requirement for insurers, including captives to discount loss reserves.

The United States Internal Revenue Service has not restricted its interest in self-insurance to captive insurance companies. At a Federal Bar Association insurance tax seminar a speaker from the IRS dealt with four other risk-financing and financial reinsurance issues as well as describing the mechanisms indicated the IRS's position. The four issues discussed were retro-active insurance, sale of loss reserves, cash flow plans and rent-a-captives. The following is a summary of the presenter's remarks.

Retro-active insurance

Retro-active insurance arrangements will be closely scrutinized to determine whether they qualify as transactions of insurance for federal tax purposes. Under a retro-active insurance arrangement both the loss event and the amount expected to be paid are known by the parties before the contract is made. Generally the insured pays a premium that equals the present value of future losses. In other words the insured is paying for his own losses. Therefore there is no transfer of an insurance risk.

Sale of loss reserves

Sale of loss reserves or loss portfolio reinsurance is another form of retro-active insurance and is reviewed upon examination. As already indicated under these arrangements there may not be a transfer of an insurance risk but only an investment risk. Opinions in other cases, particularly *Helvering* v. *LeGierse* indicates that an investment risk by itself does not constitute insurance for federal tax purposes.

In a July 1978 Ruling the Internal Revenue Service ruled that

a premium is the consideration paid by a person for insurance protection against a risk uncertain as to occurrence or time of occurrence. In the case, the reserves for incurred but unpaid losses transferred to the reinburser were not intended to protect against a contingent liability but to liquidate already established claims. Thus, the transfer of historical reserves for incurred but unpaid losses does not constitute the shifting or distributing of an insurance risk to the reinsurer.

Although this ruling dealt with whether federal excise tax applied to such a transaction, the point is that these transactions may not qualify as insurance transactions for federal tax purposes.

Cash flow plans

The service has also issued two rulings involving retrospective insurance arrangements, commonly referred to as 'cash flow' plans. The service determined that the total amount of insurance premium bill under the plan was not deductible as a trade or business expense because not all of the amount constitutes insurance premiums.

To the extent that the amount ultimately payable by the insured is based on its actual losses, no risk has been transferred, and therefore no deductible will be allowed. In addition, the amount allowed as a premium deduction will never exceed the minimum premium.

Rent-a-captive

Rent-a-captive usually involves an arrangement whereby an insured obtains the benefit of a captive insurance account without owning the captive. The captive rents its capital, surplus, licence and usually provides administrative services. For this service, the captive receives a fee which may be fixed or computed as a percentage of income.

Although some of these arrangements may qualify as true insurance or reinsurance, many do not. Generally, in a rent-a-captive situation, separate accounts are maintained for each participant. There is no risk sharing. The insured pays for its own losses and therefore there is no risk-shifting. The arrangement is merely an attempt to disguise the transaction as one of insurance with an unrelated third party insurer.

Revenue examiners will be alert for rent-a-captive situations and closely review the transaction to determine whether it qualifies as insurance for federal income tax purposes.

It is clear from these comments that the alternatives to captives often promoted as more effective self-insurance mechanisms are unlikely to be treated any differently, at least by the US Internal Revenue

Service. These issues clearly need to be taken into account when reviewing the captive's position and whether or not to take an aggressive posture from a tax standpoint and how this will affect the longer-term financial position and possibly the viability of the captive.

Tax issues in other parts of the world

Similar attacks on the tax deductibility of insurance premiums have not been very successful in other parts of the world although there are one or two examples of this being attempted, particularly in Canada and The Netherlands. The Canadian case involved a large Canadian company, Consolidated Bathurst, where in 1985 a court decided that the separate corporate identity of the Consolidated Bathurst insurance subsidiary could be disregarded and payments to it were little more than a means of creating their reserve fund, even when insurance cover was not available in the market. This original decision was reversed by the Canadian Federal Court of Appeal in November 1986 and a number of important points of principle were established by that court decision, as follows:

1. The US 'economic family' concept could not be employed outside that country. It amounted to a 'wholesale disregard of separate corporate existence' and was, as such, 'unacceptable'. In other words the fact that the insurance company is in the same group as the insured has no bearing on whether there has been a shifting of risk from insured to insurer.
2. There must nevertheless be a shifting of risk to the captive and risk distribution if premiums are to constitute genuine insurance.
3. A distinction may be made if the parent guarantees the liabilities of the captive to a fronting insurer. In such circumstances, the parent is putting itself in a position where it could be called upon to fund its own claims and the risk-shifting principle is, therefore, undermined.

The presence of such guarantees in the Consolidated Bathurst case, for the captive's early years (1971-4), meant that premium payments were not deductible: however, in 1975 the captive had sufficient funds of its own to meet claims and the parent company guarantees were removed — the requisite shift of risk thus became effective and premiums became deductible for tax purposes.

In the case of The Netherlands the deductibility of premiums paid by a Netherlands company to an offshore captive was confirmed in a case before the Dutch Supreme Court in August 1985. The court held that premiums paid by a Netherlands company to a bona fide captive located in a low tax country was deductible from taxable income.

In the United Kingdom the Inland Revenue have indicated their belief that the UK courts would in general terms follow the decision in the Consolidated Bathurst case by the Canadian Federal Court of Appeal. A speaker from the technical division of the Inland Revenue in 1987 said the following:

> differences emerge when we come to consideration of the 'economic family' argument which has found favour with the American courts in the Stearns-Roger and Mobil cases. In essence this approach relies on the fact the eventual profit or loss of the captive is for the account of the parent company on consolidation and risk has not therefore effectively been transferred from the parent. Revenue Canada attempted to use the same concept in challenging the Consolidated Bathurst, but the Appeal Court Judgement stated that this 'would amount to a wholesale disregard of separate corporate existence regardless of the circumstances in a particular case. I find that to be unacceptable'.

From this decision it would appear that Canadian courts are likely to be more reluctant to pierce or lift the corporate veil than their American counterparts, but it should be noted that Justice Stone appears to have left open the possibility that the corporate structure might still be disregarded in the circumstances of a particular case. The point has not been tested in the United Kingdom, but the Inland Revenue believes that while our courts would show a similar reluctance to accept the blanket application of the economic family concept, there might well be circumstances in which they would be prepared to disregard the corporate structure.

However, the speaker went on to clarify the position of the Inland Revenue and gave the following warning:

> If the UK Revenue does not automatically disallow premiums paid to a captive as a result of a general application of the economic family argument, it should not be assumed that all captive arrangements are free from the challenge that they fail to provide a mechanism for the effective transfer of risk. Simplifying things a little, our legislation provides that expenditure can only be regarded as allowable when it is incurred wholly and exclusively for the purpose of the trade. When we encounter captives which have insufficient resources to provide the level and quality of cover purportedly being offered we take the view the parent must have had some non-business purpose in mind when paying premium since the payment is failing to achieve an effective transfer of risk. Given such a lack of commercial logic we argue that the test

for allowability would not have been passed. Clearly therefore it is because of the terms in which our legislation is couched that we are more concerned than the IRS to test whether a captive has the ability to meet the risks it underwrites.

As captives expand revenue authorities in Europe and other parts of the world show a growing interest in captive operation. This has been demonstrated not only by more aggressive positions being taken on the deductibility of premiums and residency issues but also by the introduction of legislation aimed at taxing offshore companies at the tax rate of their parent or to treat them as though they were actually resident within the same country as the captive's owner. Legislation in this area now exists in the United Kingdom, Australia, New Zealand and Sweden and is also effective in other parts of Europe in the sense that older legislation impacts offshore captive insurance companies.

For example, in the UK, the tax authorities have introduced legislation in respect of offshore companies which impinges on captive development to the extent that profits generated offshore will be taxed at the domestic corporation tax rate.

The UK Finance Act 1984 introduced legislation on 'controlled foreign companies' to bring into the tax net those offshore companies which are mote than 50 per cent owned by UK interests and which are enjoying a rate of tax which is less than half of what they would pay in the United Kingdom. In detail, the main points of the Act are as follows:

1. Controlled foreign companies are companies which are more than 50 per cent owned by UK residents, whether the shareholding is directly or indirectly held.
2. To qualify as a low-tax regime the offshore location's tax must be less than 75% of what the UK corporation tax charge would be.
3. Corporation tax is to be applied to the income of a CFC which is resident overseas in a low-tax regime.
4. Taxable profits of a CFC are attributed on a proportional basis to the UK corporate shareholders.

Up to now companies operating offshore have not been liable to UK tax unless resident or operating here through a branch.

United Kingdom captive insurance company owners have various ways of meeting the new legislation. If they can persuade the Inland Revenue that their CFC is a genuine 'arm's-length' insurance subsidiary and not a vehicle for the diversion of profits from the United Kingdom, they will gain exemption from the legislation There are the following other escape routes:

1. There will be no tax charge for a UK company which has less than a 10 per cent share in the CFC.
2. There is no tax on profits from the CFC of less than £20,000 a year.
3. If the CFC pays at least 50 per cent of its profits, after local taxes, to UK residents, in the form of dividends, no charge will be levied.
4. There will be no tax if you can convince the Inland Revenue that you are engaged in 'exempt activities' — that is, the CFC has a business establishment and effective management in the country of residence and less than 50 per cent of its income comes from 'associated or connected' persons, whether or not located in the United Kingdom.
5. A list of countries that are exempt from the legislation on the grounds that they are not regarded as low-tax regimes has been published. None of the popular captive insurance company locations, such as Bermuda and the Cayman Islands, is on the list.

What the Act meant in terms of future strategy is that captive insurance company owners in the United Kingdom can consider meeting the less-than-ten-per-cent share criterion by entering into group or association captives. But an owner can bypass this problem if he can satisfy the primary motive test by arguing that the captive has been formed for genuine commercial reasons, such as that cover for certain risks was not available, or not available at an economic rate, in the traditional insurance market. Another important motive can be the avoidance of stringent Department of Trade and Industry insurance regulations. At worst, the captive can carry on as before and opt to return half its profits, after local taxes, as a dividend. This is likely to be the most popular alternative.

Not many captive insurance company owners are likely to choose to accept more than half their underwriting premium from unaffiliated sources: they will be deterred by the experience of US companies who tried doing this to avoid falling foul of the US tax authorities.

In 1996 the UK government updated the 1984 CFC legislation by increasing the 50% distribution requirement to 90% and, in addition, the basis upon which the percentage figure is to be applied was changed from a calculation based on the after tax profit of the captive as per the accounts as prepared under the local law of the captive's territory of residence. In future the 90% figure is to be levied on the taxable profits of the captive as computed under UK tax principles. In a paper written for Captive Insurance Company Review, Malcolm Finney, Head of International Tax at London based lawyers Nabarro Nathanson analysed the impact of the new rules in some detail as follows:

A simple example may demonstrate the dramatic impact of the new proposals. A captive in the Isle of Man (subject to a nil tax rate) may show in its annual accounts an after tax profit of 100 units. This 100 units may have been arrived at after reserving say 200 units. Under the pre 28th November 1995 law only 50 units (i.e. 50% of 100 units) needed to be distributed to the UK in the form of dividends.

Under the new proposals the profit of the captive would be recomputed under UK tax principles to arrive at a "notional" UK taxable profit on which the 90% would be levied. On the above figures the UK taxable profit might be as high as 300 units on the basis that the 200 units of reserves would not be allowed on UK tax principles. The dividend distribution would therefore need to be 270 units (i.e. 90% of 300 units) which is a significantly greater dividend repatriation than under the old rules.

Certainly it seems clear that it will be in this area of "reserving" that most arguments are likely to arise. The new Budget proposals regarding equalisation reserving are unfortunately unlikely to be of much help to the typical captive.

The proposals, according to the UK Inland Revenue, merely bring into line offshore controlled foreign trading companies with the law as applied to offshore controlled foreign investment companies. As no doubt many will be aware, the UK Inland Revenue has for some time sought to argue that many captive insurance companies were not in fact trading companies but purely investment companies. This was a line of attack, in my view, that was completely misguided and could only apply in the most exceptional of circumstances. However, this misconceived attack will no longer need to be mounted in view of the new proposals.

The issue is therefore what action, if any, can a UK parent company take with a view to mitigating the impact of the present proposals? It is to be appreciated that the new proposals will apply to accounting periods which began on or after 28th November 1995. Thus, the 90% distribution requirement is now in operation.

There are perhaps four options worthy of consideration but, inevitably, not all will in practice be feasible:

Domicile Not Designated "Low Tax"

In order for a captive insurance company to be caught by the CFC legislation in the first instance it is necessary, inter alia, that tax paid in its jurisdiction of residence should be less than three quarters of the tax which would be paid were the captive to be deemed to be UK resident. Although not strictly correct, in broad terms this would require that the captive be liable to tax in its jurisdiction of residence at a rate of less than 24.75%. As a consequence, if the rate of tax applicable in the captive's residence jurisdiction is in excess of 24.75% the captive will no longer qualify as a CFC. The new proposals would then not apply.

In the past this approach made no sense. However, this will no longer be the case. For example, if the tax rate in the captive's jurisdiction of residence was, say, 27% this would compare to an effective UK tax rate on a 90% distribution of 29.7% (i.e. 90% of 33%). There would thus be a net tax saving by moving the captive to a higher tax jurisdiction and out of the ambit of the UK CFC legislation.

The "Motive" Test

Another option would be to seek to argue that the captive was in a position to satisfy the "motive" test (a let out already contained in CFC legislation). In practice, however, this test has proved virtually impossible to satisfy and there would appear to be no reason why the UK Inland Revenue should change its approach in this regard. Thus satisfaction of the "motive" test seems unlikely.

"Exempt Activities" Test

One of the other let outs contained in the CFC legislation relates to the so-called "exempt activities" test. In the past, for the "pure" captive, this test has not proved capable of satisfaction due to the fact that the majority of the captive's income arises from related parties (i.e. its parent plus fellow subsidiaries). Whether the captive's business could now be somehow diluted to include unrelated third party business may be something worthwhile considering in view of the now penal provisions being introduced. In the past, this approach typically was perhaps not worth pursuing.

Jointly Owned Captives

Perhaps the only other option is the possibility of some form of jointly owned captive where the other major shareholder is itself a non

UK resident company. Unless "control" is with UK residents the CFC legislation does not apply.

It is in fact not really surprising that the CFC law has now been significantly tightened; perhaps what is surprising is that it has taken some ten years or so since the legislation was first introduced in 1984 for the UK Inland Revenue to achieve its no doubt intended goal.

However, even if complete circumnavigation of the new proposals cannot be achieved, as owners of offshore investment companies have discovered, even with a 90% dividend distribution requirement a significant positive cashflow advantage still arises (as a consequence of a deferral of UK tax on any distribution of up to some 39 months)"

The 1996 changes were, in fact, only part of the story. At the same time as announcing the changes, the UK government produced a consultative document aimed at adjusting the CFC rules furthermore and also introducing a "self assessment" regime.

The Chancellor announced the release of a Consultative Document (The Document) entitled The Controlled Foreign Companies Legislation on which representations are sought on or before 29th March 1996. Although The Document relates to all CFCs, the reality is that the proposals will primarily impact on offshore captives.

So, what are the key proposals contained in The Document and what impact, if any, will they have on offshore captives?

The Inland Revenue state that the changes to a "self-assessment" regime for corporation tax purposes will require modification to the operation of the CFCs provisions. The self-assessment regime requires UK companies to determine their own taxable profits and the associated UK corporation tax liability, with such tax then being paid automatically by a specified due date without any direct involvement of the Inland Revenue. Under current practice, the Inland Revenue raise what is referred to as a Notice of Assessment which is an estimate of a company's corporation tax liability. Discussions then ensue with the final liability ultimately being agreed possibly many years later.

At present the CFC legislation is technically only in point when, and if, the Inland Revenue raises an appropriate direction. It is suggested by Inland Revenue that, this will not sit comfortably under the self-assessment procedures and The Document suggests how the CFC legislation will, in future, operate. Although this might therefore suggest that the changes proposed in the document will be perhaps only administrative — this is not in fact the case.

The key proposal contained in The Document is the abolition of the "acceptable distribution" let out. It will be remembered that the acceptable distribution let out is the one which has in the past permitted UK owned offshore captives to remit each year 50% (increased to 90% under the Budget) of their annual profits in the form of dividends. The other 50% remaining offshore UK tax free.

As a consequence of the proposal, it will no longer be feasible to avoid the full impact of the CFC legislation merely by remitting a proportion of the captive's annual profits back to the UK parent company in the form of dividends. The Document requires any UK corporation shareholder in an offshore captive to report each years its pro-rata share of the captive's annual profits (as computed under UK tax principles). By way of example, if a UK parent owns 100% of an offshore captive, say, resident in Bermuda with annual profits of £2m, then, under The Document's proposals, the UK parent company will be required to report the £2m as part of its own profit for UK corporation tax purposes, with the consequence that an immediate 33% corporate tax liability will arise on the £2m. Before The Document, and prior to the recent Budget, the UK parent company would merely have needed to remit £1m in the form of dividends to the UK with the balancing £1 remaining in Bermuda, UK tax free. Post Budget and pre The Document, the dividend repatriation requirement will not be 50% of £2m, but 90% of £2m, i.e. £1.8m, (only £0.2m remaining UK tax free).

Unfortunately this is not all. The Document is even more penal that at first sight appears. Under the acceptable distribution let out the dividend paying (whether 50% or 90% of profits) does not need to be brought back to the UK until 18 months after the relevant captive's year end. With suitable accounting year ends, the resultant UK corporation tax charge on the dividend income may be deferred for up to approximately 3 years after the year in which the dividend was paid. The Document proposals, however, require that the captive's annual profits be brought within the charge to UK corporation tax in the same year, thus removing the above cash flow advantage. It is, however, suggested in The Document that in order to ameliorate the consequent severe impact of The Document's proposal only 80% of the captive's annual profits should be immediately brought within the charge of UK corporation tax on the part of the UK parent company.

To perhaps understand more clearly the impact of the Budget proposal (increase of 50% to 90%) and the proposal contained in The Document, a simple example may be of help.

Summary

	UK Tax Charge	Timing of Tax Payment
Pre-Budget (Nov. 1995)	£330,000	36 months
Post-Budget but Pre The Document	£900,000	36 months
Post The Document	£800,000	9 months

Assume the offshore captive shows taxable profits of £2m as computed under the local law in which the captive is resident. Assume, however that if the captive's profit were to be recomputed under UK tax principles, the figure of taxable profit would in fact be, say, £3m (perhaps as a consequence of £1m of reserves not being deductible for UK tax purposes). In the past, the worst case scenario was that the UK parent company would be exposed to UK corporation tax at 33% on £3m i.e., approximately £1m of tax. This worst case scenario was capable of amelioration by adopting the acceptable distribution let out i.e. remitting as dividend 50% of the captive's annual profits, i.e. 50% of £2m (not £3m), namely £1m producing at 33% a UK tax of £330,000. This latter tax charge itself being postponed for up to 3 years.

Under the Budget proposal, the acceptable distribution let out would require that a dividend distribution of 90% of the UK taxable profits i.e., 905 of £3m, namely £2.7m be remitted producing at 33% a UK corporation tax charge of £900,000. Again, this £900,000 tax charge possibly being paid some three years later.

The Document proposal would require the UK parent company to account for UK corporation tax on 80% of the UK taxable profit, namely, 80% of £3m, producing £2.4m at 33% resulting in an £800,000 UK corporation tax charge. This £800,000 however being payable within nine months.

On a net cash flow analysis, and assuming an internal rate of return of 10%, if The Document proposals were to equate to the most recent Budget changes, The Document percentage of 80% to equate to the 90% Budget figures should be closer to 75%. Thus, the inference on the Inland Revenue's suggestion that an 80% figure compensations for the bringing forward of any UK corporation tax charge is perhaps a little misleading. Indeed by comparison to the pre-Budget position. The Document percentage should be closer to 27%!

It can therefore be seen that the recent proposals are significantly more penal than have applied during the last ten years since 1984.

Unfortunately, there is little light that can be seen through the impending darkness. One "chink", in the author's view — not much more than that — is The Document's proposal that under the self-assessment regime only 20% or greater UK corporate share holders will be caught whereas at present 10% corporate shareholders are caught. However, for the offshore captive which is a wholly-owned subsidiary of a UK parent company, this proposed relaxation will be of no value whatsoever. It may help however, group or association captives.

The Document indicates that all the other current "let outs" contained in the CFC legislation will continue to be available. Thus, the exempt activities let out, the Excluded Country List etc., will all continue to be available to mitigate the adverse impact of the proposals. Again, in the author's view, this will offer little comfort to most captive owners. If, in the past, these let outs have been incapable of satisfaction, then almost certainly this will continue to be the case post introduction of The Document proposals and, therefore, little comfort can be drawn from the comments by the Inland Revenue in The Document in this regard.

What is clear is that not only will captive owners be significantly penalised in tax terms but those captive owners hitherto undiscovered will be in for a significant shock. As indicated above, the CFC legislation needed to be invoked by the UK Inland Revenue. It may be the case that for certain UK parent companies with offshore captives no investigation has occurred to date, with the consequence that the CFC legislation has had no impact. In other words the Inland Revenue may simply not have known of the offshore captive's existence. The Document will put an end to this situation. The self-assessment system will require an automatic disclosure of any shareholding interest of a UK parent company (whether directly or indirectly) in an overseas resident company (e.g. offshore captive) where the interest therein is 20% or greater. The Inland Revenue may therefore for the firm time discover the existence of offshore operations of UK parent companies which hitherto have remain undisclosed. A potential pot of gold for the Inland Revenue.

What Does All This Mean for the UK Owned Offshore Captives?
Perhaps, first and foremost it is to be appreciated that the proposals contained in The Document are, at present, proposals and not yet law. The Document has invited representation by interested parties. Although in the past proposals of UK Inland Revenue have been

withdrawn, in the author's view this is a most unlikely conclusion in the present case. In any event the damage has already been done by the Budget's proposals. The increase in the 50% to 90% and the change in the base to which the percentage is applied are the proposals which have done the damage. Quite frankly, The Document proposals are insignificant in this light. Serious damage loss mitigation will require either that the base to which the 90% or the 80% figure is to be applied should remain as was the case pre-Budget, or alternatively (but of less help), if the base is to change, the 90% or 80% figures should be reduced back to the 50% level.

It has been suggested earlier that one possible option which might be worthy of consideration was to ensure that the offshore captive does not qualify as a CFC. This might well be achieved by ensuring that the tax paid in the captive's country of residence is higher than 75% of equivalent UK corporation tax payment. In such as case, neither that the recent Budget proposals, nor those contained in the Document would be of relevance. Alternatively, if the captive concerned is in a position to underwrite extensive third party business, satisfaction of the "exempt activities" let out may become a possibility and again the recent Budget and The Document proposals would not be in point.

If neither of the above two options are in reality feasible and assuming the Budget proposals and that The Document proposals become law, the long term viability of offshore UK owned captives would seem to be in serious jeopardy. The proposals will in essence cause serious dissipation of a captive's net worth and thus its financial capacity to continue to underwrite serious levels of risk. For the so-called "mature" captive which has to date built up significant retained earnings, the full impact of the proposals may be deferred for some time but ultimately "will bite". for the potential new captive start-up any tax advantages which might have accrued would now appear to have been seriously eroded."

At the beginning of 1990 the Swedish Parliament approved a plan by the Swedish tax authorities to introduce controlled foreign company legislation. The proposals are complex, but in basic terms the legislation will achieve the following. The rules will define a 'foreign company' — if the captive is 'foreign' the tax charges will *not* apply. To be 'foreign' the company has to be located in a country which:

1. Has a tax treaty with Sweden and is covered by the treaty terms.
2. Taxes the company in a similar way to Sweden. This presumably means similar corporate tax levels.

If the company is not 'foreign' it will be taxed in Sweden on its income regardless of whether a distribution is made.

The proposals also indicate that the management and control aspects will be examined, and if a captive is owned (more than 50 per cent) by Swedish residents, it is a 'passive' company and if it is managed and controlled from Sweden a full tax charge will be made. This could impact on captive management companies currently managing offshore insurance companies from Sweden.

There is at the present time a loophole in the proposals which means that interposing a company located in a territory which has a tax treaty with Sweden between the captive and the parent will overcome the new rules. However, it will be important to ensure that the interposed company is a trading company otherwise the problems envisaged will apply.

Australia and New Zealand have also introduced controlled foreign company legislation which is in many respects much more restrictive than that introduced in the United Kingdom and Sweden. In both of these countries the captive will be taxed as though it were resident in Australia and New Zealand if it is located in a country listed by the Australian and New Zealand Tax Authorities. The list produced covers all of the common captive locations plus a number of high tax countries which allow tax concessions for captives, for example Luxembourg, Singapore and the Financial Services Centre in Dublin.

In addition, authorities virtually everywhere would likely attack a captive operation if they felt that the company was not being managed on a proper insurance basis or if there were any question of companies using the insurance process to build up funds offshore by charging premiums unrelated to the exposure, controlling the captive directly rather than on an arm's-length basis, establishing the captive in such a way that no insurance transaction or risk-shifting is involved, or if there were any question of the captive, in fact, retaining risks which it was not able to take owing to lack of resources.

The residency of a captive insurance company for taxation purposes is becoming a major issue in the tax arena. Residency will normally be a key factor in determining the extent to which the captive pays tax on its underwriting profit and investment income and a captive which is regarded as resident for tax purposes in a high tax jurisdiction could be required to pay tax on its total profits. The issue of captive residency was outlined in a paper presented at the Second Luxembourg Captive and Insurance Rendezvous in June 1990 by Brian

Sadler from the United Kingdom Inland Revenue Technical Division. His paper is worth review and the following is an edited version.

The Issue of Captive Residency

The United Kingdom is a jurisdiction where residence is vitally important. A company resident in the United Kingdom is liable to corporation tax on its worldwide profits (not only on those arising in the jurisdiction). So an understanding of the law and practice which determine UK residence is essential for those who wish to use captives.

A company is resident in the United Kingdom if it fulfils either of two criteria. This dual approach has applied since 15 March 1988 when the UK law on company residence was changed in a fundamental way by the introduction of a statutory rule that a company is resident in the United Kingdom if it is incorporated under UK laws.

Before 1988 the residence of companies was decided by principles which had emerged from case law. There was no general guidance in statute law. The classic statement of the case law dates back to 1906, where the House of Lords in *De Beers Consolidated Mines* v. *Howe* (5 TC 198) said:

> A company resides, for the purposes of income tax, where its real business is carried on .... That [is] the true rule; ant the real business is carried on where the central management and control actually abides.

Those words have been said to be as precise and unequivocal as if they were statute law.

The central management and control approach is, broadly, directed at the highest level of control of the business of a company. It is concerned with the top policy decisions about that business and should not be confused with either the control which shareholders are entitled to exercise or the lower level of day-to-day management of the business (even where the latter implements policy decisions taken elsewhere).

It is important to realise that the traditional central management and control rule still applies to companies incorporated outside the UK or which escape the incorporation rule. This is the case with many captives, so the principles which have developed from case law are still as relevant as ever they were.

What is central management and control?

The Inland Revenue view on the case law test for residence is explained in a Statement of Practice issued in January 1990.

In UK company law the persons *entitled* to manage the company's business are normally the directors; the shareholders either individual or collectively in General Meeting are not entitled to interfere with the directors' action (although they can dismiss them if they do not like those actions). The same approach can be seen in the systems of some other jurisdictions, particularly those whose roots can be traced back to the United Kingdom. So central management and control — the top policy decisions of the company — will normally be exercised by the directors and the company will be resident where the board meets. But this will by no means always be the case. Management and control is essentially a question of fact and can be exercised by persons who, in law, are not entitled to exercise it. For example. a dominant shareholder, who is not a director, may actually take the top level management decisions, the directors either standing aside completely or meekly rubber stamping what the *de facto* manager decides.

Moreover, even where the directors do manage and control the company's business it does not inevitably follow that the place where the board meetings are held decides the place of residence. What is done and decided outside board meetings can be more important than formal actions and may lead to a conclusion that the company is resident in a place different to that where board meetings are held.

Management and control does not require a great deal of activity or intervention. Passive oversight may well be sufficient, particularly where the overseers are entitled to intervene if they wish. And the place of central management and control need not be where the main business operations take place. It is possible, for example, that, as a question of fact, a company's business can be managed and controlled by a few directors, or other persons, in Country A when everything else done by the company is in Country B.

The usual Inland Revenue approach is step-by-step. First, what is done by the directors is examined to decide if those directors in fact exercise central management and control. If they do, the Revenue considers where that exercise takes place. If the directors do not exercise central management and control, the Revenue establishes where and by whom it is carried out.

Parents and subsidiaries can pose very difficult problems. A parent can and often does influence the actions of the subsidiary. It would be surprising if it did not. But that immediately raises the issue of the central management and control of the subsidiary's business. Is the parental influence so extensive and dominant that it has taken over the role which normally lies with the subsidiary's directors? The answer must always be a matter of fact. If the parent does no more than a shareholder is entitled to do then that will not cause residence problems for the subsidiary. But if the parent usurps the directors' functions or if the directors simply do as they are told then that will usually mean that the subsidiary has the same residence as its parent. Between these two extreme situations are innumerable gradations, and close examination of the way in which business is actually conducted is required to decide where on the scale a particular case falls.

Where then for captives?

The Revenue's approach to captive insurance companies so far as residence is concerned follows the same general principles which are outlined in the Statement of Practice and the earlier paragraphs. But the Statement also says the following:

> Where ... it appears that a major objective underlying the existence of certain factors is the obtaining of tax benefits from residence or non-residence, the Revenue examines the facts particularly closely in order to see whether there has been an attempt to create the appearance of central management and control in a particular place without the reality.

Many captive insurance companies have been investigated by the Revenue. Many and varied reasons have been put forward as to why these captives have been formed; obtaining tax benefits is rarely at the top of the list and no doubt there are other sound non-fiscal reasons why, say, a UK-based group should want to insure its risks in some jurisdiction which just happens to have a beneficial tax regime. But the Revenue is likely to adopt a sceptical approach to many of the explanations. Captives have, for example, been found to be no more than moneybox operations intended to provide the group with a tax deduction in the United Kingdom and the opportunity to invest its funds tax free. Most jurisdictions accept, in principle, that a non-resident subsidiary should benefit from what the United States calls 'deferral': that overseas profits should not be taxed until they are returned to the parent as dividends. But it is increasingly accepted that deferral can be abused when funds are unreasonably retained abroad or diverted from the home country. The United Kingdom shares these concerns and since 1984 has had specific legislation which deals with the problem of Controlled Foreign Companies (CFCs). But that legislation depends on the overseas company being non-resident in the United Kingdom. It can be seen as a partial remedy to the problem of unjustified deferral because the payment of dividends of a specified level by the CFC can avoid a full charge on the profits and still leave significant amounts overseas.

However, the Revenue have not had it all their own way so far as residency is concerned. In November 1995, the special commissioners handed down their decision in the "*Unigate* v *H.M. Inspector of Taxes*" and held that Unigate Guernsey Limited, a company incorporated in Guernsey and Untelrab Limited, a company incorporated in Jersey, had their central management control in Sark and Bermuda respectively, and both companies were not resident in the UK for UK tax purposes. A fourth company, Porten Insurance Company Limited (the Unigate captive) had also been under attack and lodged an appeal against assessments raised by the Inland Revenue on the basis that the company was UK resident. Four weeks before the hearing, the Inland Revenue indicated they would not, in fact, be proceeding with the assessments against Porten. The case is a fascinating one so far as mind and management issues are concerned and Malcolm Finney concluded that "although the case before the commissioners was not concerned with Unigate's offshore captive specifically, all of the principles discussed are of relevance and importance to any captive insurance company subsidiary of a UK parent company which wishes to retain its residence status outside of the UK."

Perhaps a point of key significance which emerges is that even if the Board of a captive meets and all its decisions are in line with the wishes of its UK parent company, its residence status will not be tainted so long as the Board of a captive can clearly demonstrate that it did meet and did consider the various issues with the decision then following. A willingness to adopt suggestions and advice of its parent company will not thus, per say, taint the captive's resident status. Although the Inland Revenue would in such circumstances in the past, have argued that the decisions of the captive Board were in such circumstances nothing more than those of a "rubber-stamp" it is clear from the commissioners decision that this view will not be supported".

Perhaps even more interesting was the session of the Australian Court, who examined the role of the Coca-Cola Amatil ("Matila") captive in the insurance of its parent. This captive was set up to underwrite the products liability risks of its parent who, at the time, was heavily exposed to products liability risks emanating from its activities as a producer of cigarettes. Perhaps surprisingly the courts found in favour of the captive in a judgement summarised as follows: —

An Australian captive owner, W.D. & H.O. Wills (Australia) Pty Ltd., has won an important victory against the Commissioner of Taxation following appeal in the federal court of Australia New South Wales District. Wills appealed against four decisions by the Commissioner who disallowed deductibility for premiums paid by Wills in the four years 1986 to 1989 to the Singapore insurer, Matila Insurance. During these years Wills was a wholly owned subsidiary of Amatil Ltd, now known as Coca Cola Amatil Ltd, as was Matila Insurance. The premiums involved were substantial — A\$4.2 million in 1986, A\$4.7 million 1987, A\$167,966 in 1988, and A\$3.6 million in 1989 — and the courtroom dispute over their tax deductibility raised issues of interest to captive owners all over the world. Namely:

❑ were the premium outgoings necessarily incurred in gaining or producing assessable income or in producing such income or were they necessarily incurred in carrying on a business for the purpose of gaining or producing such income?

❑ were the premiums really outgoings of capital, or of a capital nature?

❑ even if the captive owner could answer these first two questions satisfactorily, was it nonetheless party to a "scheme" for the dominant purpose of obtaining tax benefit? (This is a bit like the "motive" test which arises under UK Controlled Foreign Company legislation.)

A little of the history of Wills and its parent Amatil, which eventually led to the formation of the Matila captive, is necessary to understand the dispute between Wills, Amatil and the taxation authority, and the reasoning which led the appeal court judge to decide in favour of Amatil.

One of Wills' businesses was that of manufacturing and marketing tobacco products. Until October 1983 Amatil Group had a general and products liability insurance from QBE, which was arranged by the risk and insurance manager Mr Watson. This policy excluded liability consequent on or traceable to cancer arising from consumption of cigarettes or other tobacco products sold by Amatil companies. Then, around October 1983 QBE decided to extend the cancer exclusion to include other diseases attributable to tobacco consumption. Amatil was told that from renewal the policy limit would be \$5 million and the new exclusion would read:

"TOBACCO
Based upon or alleging the contraction, aggravation or exacerbation of carcinoma, arteriosclerosis, heart disease or other disease of the human

body as a result of consumption or use of tobacco products sold, handled or distributed by the Insured."

Mr Watson sought the opinion of Amatil's insurance broker, Reed Stenhouse (NSW) Ltd, as well as information from BAT Industries in the UK (an associated company) concerning its experience with product liability insurance for members of BAT Group. Then, on advice from the broker, QBE was asked for terms to delete the new exclusion, Wills' letter making the point that its major competitors in Australia had no such exclusion nor was it difficult to find exclusion free cover in other countries.

QBE agreed, subject to additional premiums of $20,000 reviewable annually (it had now found a way of reinsuring the risk).

The insurance was renewed in October 1994 but problems developed in placing excess coverage over the $5 million primary layer: in November 1994 American Home cancelled its second excess layer of $15 million and then, in January 1985, withdrew cancellation because reinsurance of the cancer cover had been completed.

Around this time — November 1984 — Amatil's risk manager, Mr Watson, raised the question of a captive in an internal document, making the following points:

❏ Amatil now needed covers more easily obtainable from reinsurers than insurers, but direct access would only be possible through a captive
❏ the high limits sought by Amatil — $500 million for combined property/business interruption — meant that most of the premiums were already being channelled to overseas reinsurers
❏ Amatil's present insurers in Australia were, in the main, overseas controlled
❏ Amatil was therefore considering a captive to help control and place its reinsurances. Offshore was preferable because it was cheaper to establish and operate in Hong Kong.

Mr Watson formally applied for a tax clearance certificate to invest capital in a Hong Kong captive, saying that the motivating factor was to reorganise material damage/consequential loss insurance arrangements but that any class could become a candidate for the captive. The project fell through as Amatil could not agree the Australian Taxation Office's conditions. Then the insurance market hardened and in October 1985 QBE decided it wanted the all-purpose health exclusion back again — the risk was not underwritable in the company's view.

Mr Watson sent a memorandum to his finance director concluding that the hardening market added support to the Group's "established philosophy of self-insuring regular and predictable losses and limiting reliance on insurance to catastrophic type losses."

In May 1986 Sedgwick was appointed as Amatil's consultant, but the problem of health cover remained. Sedgwick suggested that even if an insurer could be found, which was unlikely for Amatil as a new client coming to the market, the premium cost for health risks would be extremely high and the cover would be claims-made only. Converting premium on-line to a rate on turnover for cover of $10 million (the largest limit placeable, and even then only if the underwriter could find reinsurance for most of the risk), Sedgwick suggested that Amatil would need to be thinking of about 5% gross. Why 5% on turnover? Sedgwick knew that Wills's turnover was $1,000 million and believed that an underwriter would look at the risk as a "two to one shot". That is, he or she would want $5 million premium for a £10 million risk, and $5 million was 5% of £1,000 million.

Not surprisingly, the captive idea emerged again. In August 1986 Sedgwick prepared a report for Amatil setting out the objectives and advantages and disadvantages of establishing a captive instead of an internal fund or external insurance. The point was made that a captive would help Amatil "protect the health risk in connection with products liability for which conventional insurance cannot be obtained." The other "usual" advantages/disadvantages were touched upon. One section of the report made suggestions for the initial portfolio of the captive, with policies to be issued on a claims made basis. In particular, in respect of health risks, the products liability and recall section included the paragraph:

"The indemnity provided by this section shall apply to liability and legal costs based upon or alleging the contraction, aggravation or exacerbation of carcinoma, arteriosclerosis, heart disease or other disease of the human body as a result of consumption or use of tobacco products sold, handled or distributed by the Insured anywhere in the world."

The report noted that there had been no tobacco health risk liability losses to date and proposed Singapore as the best captive location. The feasibility plan assumed a gross premium of $5 million a year, a single claim of £3 million in the second year, funds invested at 15% a year, a 25% provision of premiums into reserves each year for IBNRs.

Mr Watson recommended to his finance director that the captive be established as a matter of urgency: to protect Amatil against tobacco suits now that conventional insurance was no longer available or absurdly expensive (i.e. $5 million premium for $10 million cover) and in light of a court case then taking place in Australia against the American Cigarette Company. Amatil decided in favour and sought approval from the Singapore authorities. The captive was incorporated in October 1986 with a paid-up capital of $1.2 million and authorised capital of $8 million; and Sedgwick was appointed manager.

Everything was up and running and the first policy period began 27th October 1986. The products liability cover was £10 million and the premium was close to Sedgwick's original suggestion — i.e. $4.2 million.

The policy provided that Matila would pay to or on behalf of the insured all sums which the insured became legally liable to pay in respect of claims arising, or allegedly arising, out of, or attributed to, the consumption or use of tobacco products manufactured, sold or supplied by the insured. Matila was also to pay all legal costs, charges and expenses incurred in connection with claims in respect of which the insured was entitled to indemnity. Matila did not attempt to reinsure the product liability risks covered by the composite policy, because Segwick advised that reinsurance was not available.

Subsequently (June 1987) Amatil sought quotations from its broker for professional indemnity insurance. It was told that a quote from Matila would be as good a prospect as any because local under-writers were not interested in professional indemnity except as part of the public and products liability policy. Amatil also sought terms for renewing the composite policy with Matila with increased liability limits. Premium rates were unchanged but loadings were required to reduce deductibles or increase limits, which in any event Matila would not increase beyond $12.5 million in the aggregate; however, Matila provided an acceptable quote for professional indemnity.

In July 1988 Sedgwick tried to obtain an alternative "better" quote for Amatil, for the next renewal, than Matila was providing but neither Lloyd's nor the London company market could improve the wording or premium rate. Similar efforts were made, with similar results, in the next renewal period.

So much for the history of events leading to the court dispute ...

The argument between the Commissioner and Wills was divided into two parts: one relating to Section 51(1) of the Income Tax Assessment Act 1936 and the other to Part IVA.

S.51(1) says:

"All losses and outgoings to the extent to which they are incurred in gaining or producing the assessable income, or are necessarily incurred in carrying on a business for the purpose of gaining or producing such income, shall be allowable deductions except to the extent to which they are losses or outgoings of capital, or of a capital, private or domestic nature, or are incurred in relation to the gaining or production of exempt income."

The policy said to underlie Part IVA runs:

"The proposed provisions ... seek to give effect to a policy that such measures ought to strike down blatant, artificial or contrived arrangements, but not cast unnecessary inhibitions on normal commercial transactions by which taxpayers legitimately take advantage of opportunities available for the arrangement of their affairs ...

"In order to confine the scope of the proposed provisions to schemes of the blatant or paper variety, the measures in this Bill are expressed so as to render ineffective a scheme whereby a tax benefit is obtained and an objective examination, having regard to the scheme itself and to its surrounding circumstances and practical results, leads to the conclusion that the scheme was entered into for the sole or dominant purpose of obtaining a tax benefit."

Arguments And Decision On S.51(1)

The Commissioner argued that in order to constitute expenditure necessarily incurred in carrying on a business, the claimed deductions had to be "clearly appropriate or adapted for" the purpose of gaining assessable income, and that the premiums in this case were not appropriate or adapted for this purpose. In order to assess the essential character of the voluntary outgoings, it was necessary to take account of the relationship between Wills and Matila; the fact that the risk was practically uninsurable on the open market; the size of the premiums compared with the limit of liability, and the fact that there was no distribution of risk outside the Amatil group of companies. Taking these factors into account, the Commissioner believed that the contracts of insurance and the premiums paid amounted to an inter-group arrangement for the creation of a capital fund to meet possible future liabilities. The purpose of the exercise was to set up a capital fund which, from a practical and business point of view, was to remain available to Wills to meet any health risk claims that might materialise. The premiums were therefore not outgoings of the kind within S.51(1).

Wills, for their part, submitted that the composite policies issued by Matila to Wills were properly to be regarded as contracts of insurance. There was the requisite element of speculation for both insured and insurer and the size of the premium in relation to risk was no barrier to the policies being so characterised. Similarly, the relationship between Wills and Matila did not prevent the policies being regarded as contracts of insurance. As such, the premiums paid by Wills were incurred in carrying on a business for the purpose of gaining or producing income.

Wills submitted that there was a real and substantial connection between the outgoings and Wills' business. That business consisted of the manufacture and marketing of tobacco products for human consumption. The outgoings were premiums in return for coverage against claims made for disease of the human body arising out of or attributed to the use or consumption of such products.

Wills also contended that the outgoings could not be characterised as of a capital nature. The loss insured against was on the revenue account because any such losses arose directly out of Wills' business operations, and these were the very activities which produced Wills' assessable income.

The judge decided in favour of Wills. In his view, the premiums paid to Matila by Wills in respect of the health risks should be characterised as necessarily incurred in carrying on Wills' business as a manufacturer and distributor of tobacco products. The composite policy was intended to and did provide coverage against major risks arising out of its business operations. This follows from the terms of the policy and the circumstances which gave rise to the perceived need to obtain coverage from a related company. The risks insured against went to the very heart of Wills' business. The absence of available coverage through the open insurance market created a commercial need to develop a strategy for covering those risks. The connection between the premiums and the conduct of Wills' business was, in his opinion, clear.

Whilst it was true that the premiums were very large and were paid to an associated company, and he accepted that there were circumstances in which the disproportionate or excessive nature of expenditure can suggest that the outgoings were not made for the purpose of obtaining assessable income or for the purposes of the business incurring the expenditure, the judge thought the premiums paid in the present case were not disproportionate to the advantage gained by Wills. Namely, coverage within the limits specified by the health risks component of the composite policy. "... the premiums were not unreasonable for the coverage obtained and there were valid commercial reasons for Wills to seek coverage. There were also valid commercial reasons for Amatil to establish a captive insurer to provide that coverage."

The fact that, in the event, Wills made no claims under the health risks component of the composite policy was not to the point. Had Wills made any such claims, it was entitled, assuming the claims to be covered by the policy, to be indemnified by Matila, subject to the terms of the policy. There was nothing in the evidence to suggest that Matila would have been unable to comply with its obligations, if necessary by calling up the balance of unpaid capital. Viewed objectively, the premiums were reasonably capable of being seen as desirable or appropriate from the point of view of Wills' business.

Commenting on the fact that Wills had the option of self insuring rather than insuring with a captive, which would have meant no tax deductibility of premiums, the judge accepted that Wills' reasons were "commercially valid" and made the interesting point:

"Indeed, the choice made (i.e. forming a captive) might have resulted in Wills obtaining a higher assessable income than if no insurance coverage had been obtained. This might have occurred had a number of consumers instituted proceedings against Wills, thereby causing it to claim indemnity under the policy in respect of legal costs and damages."

The question was not what strategies Wills might have adopted to cope with the difficulty in obtaining health risk coverage, but whether the outgoings it in fact incurred were allowable deductions under S.51(1) of the ITA.

On the question of whether the premium payments were tantamount to setting up a capital fund, the judge said:

"The payments made by Wills to Amatil, as the documentation makes clear, were by way of premiums for coverage against health risks created by Wills' business operations. There was nothing to suggest that the documentation was not intended to operate in accordance with its terms. On the contrary, the evidence supports the conclusion that the composite policy, as renewed from time to time, was intended to provide coverage to Wills subject to the policy limits. The risks covered by the policy ... may or may not have materialised. If they did, Wills was entitled to be indemnified in accordance with the terms of the composite policy. The premiums were paid regularly and were subject to reassessment by the insurer and the insured, as is commonly the case with insurance renewals. The premiums were not one-off payments providing a pre-determined benefit to the tax-payer." Accordingly, there was nothing to "compel or even suggest the conclusion that the premiums paid by Wills are to be characterised as capital payments in the nature of an investment, or payments to establish a capital fund to meet future liabilities."

The fact that premiums were paid to a related company was no necessary barrier to them being classified as allowable deductions under S.51(1) or as payments on account of revenue, in the judge's opinion.

Arguments And Decision On IVA

The Commissioner submitted that the scheme had been correctly identified as constituting the arrangements and transactions by which Wills "purportedly" had obtained insurance coverage for its health risk. The tax benefit obtained by Wills was the obtaining of deductions which it would not have received had the scheme not been entered into.

The Commissioner further submitted that the dominant purpose to be attributed to the parties, in entering into or carrying out the scheme, was that of obtaining the tax benefit, adducing these reasons:

(a) The risk was practically uninsurable.
(b) The decision to insure was practically made by Amatil and it obtained the entire commercial advantage of the money being placed in Matila, save for any advantage obtained by Wills under the "policy".
(c) Mr Priest (financial director of Amatil) was a director both of Amatil and Matila and Mr Watson (risk and reinsurance manager of Amatil) was the insurance and risk manager in Amatil for the groups and a director of Matila; two directors of Amatil were also directors of Wills.
(d) If the scheme was not entered into, no deduction would have been available to Wills for the amount of the premiums.
(e) By reason of the scheme being carried out Wills obtained indemnity up to $10 million in respect of tobacco health risks, but if it had set aside a fund itself of the same amount as the premiums and invested that fund, the fund (subject to the effect of taxation on the income it produced) would have been sufficient to reach the amount insured at the earliest time it

was likely to be payable. To the extent that no health risk has ever manifested itself as a claim, the benefit of the payment of the premiums would be enjoyed by Matila itself and indirectly by Amatil, both companies closely related to Wills.

(f) The substance of the scheme involved the creation of Matila of a capital fund substantially by the payments by Wills in the form of "premiums", themselves sufficient or almost sufficient to fund the largest possible claim under the policy when there was no certainty of any such claims arising.

(g) Only a few risks were insured with Matila and in order for it to be viable financially it was necessary for the premiums to be very large.

(h) The scheme was hurriedly entered into just before the end of the fiscal year for Amatil and Wills.

(i) Matila's funds were managed by a group fund manager, Amatil Hong Kong.

(j) Tax in Singapore was payable at 10% on premium income and received a concessional rate of 10% on all income derived by Matila from offshore business.

(k) The health risk of Wills was not reinsured and only Amatil companies were insured by Matila and substantially only for uninsurable risks.

(l) Matila itself had no employees, office space or other separate existence; it was essentially an empty shell."

Wills did not dispute that there was a scheme in place, within the broad definition adopted by Income Tax Act (ITA). Wills disputed, however, that, had the health risk not been insured with Matila, it was reasonable to expect that cover would have been obtained through some other means, such as a captive insurer located elsewhere, even in Australia. It was not reasonable to expect that the only course open to Wills was to create an internal fund to meet possible claims. Even if Wills had adopted that course, Wills suggested it may have been able to claim deductions in account of liabilities incurred but not yet reported (IBNR's), just as insurers are entitled to claim.

Wills further submitted that this was not a scheme entered into or carried out for the dominant purpose of enabling Wills or Amatil to obtain a tax benefit in connection with the scheme.

In substance, the scheme comprised transactions which were genuine and commercial and carried out in a commercial and business-like fashion. The policies were intended to operate in accordance with their form and there was nothing to suggest that the risk was not to be met by Matila. When the matters specified in ... ITA were taken into account the only purpose that could be discerned was the obtaining of insurance cover for health risks created by Wills' products. This was a commercial purpose, directed to Wills' business ends.

The judge acknowledged that the tax benefit was the obtaining of deductions which Wills would not have been able to claim, had the scheme not been entered into or carried out.

He further commented that it was necessary to pay regard to the "manner in which the scheme was entered into or carried out".

The Nature Of A "Scheme" Under IVA

"(a) a taxpayer ... has obtained ... a tax benefit in connection with the scheme; and

(b) having regard to:
  (i) the manner in which the scheme was entered into or carried out;
  (ii) the form and substance of the scheme;
  (iii) the time at which the scheme was entered into and the length of the period during which the scheme was carried out;
  (iv) the result in relation to the operation of this Act that, but for this Part, would be achieved by the scheme;
  (v) any change in the financial position of the relevant taxpayer that has resulted, will result, or may reasonably be expected to result, from the scheme;
  (vi) any change in the financial position of any person who has, or has had, any connection (whether of a business, family or other nature) with the relevant taxpayer, being a change that has resulted, will result or may reasonably be expected to result, from the scheme;
  (vii) any other consequence for the relevant taxpayer, or for any person referred to in subparagraph (vi), of the scheme having been entered into or carried out; and
  (viii) the nature of any connection (whether of a business, family or other nature) between the relevant taxpayer and any person referred to in subparagraph (vi);

it would be concluded that the person, or one of the persons, who entered into or carried out the scheme or any part of the scheme did so for the purpose of enabling the relevant taxpayer to obtain a tax benefit in connection with the scheme or of enabling the relevant taxpayer and another taxpayer or other taxpayers each to obtain a tax benefit in connection with the scheme ...".

Although the idea for a captive insurer originated within Amatil, the detailed proposal for a Singapore captive was formulated by Amatil's recently appointed broker. The proposal identified a number of commercial advantages, from the perspective of the Group, in establishing the captive. Not all of these advantages came to fruition; for example, Matila was unable to gain access to the reinsurance market to offset the whole or a portion of the health risk component of the composite policy, because no reinsurance was available. Nonetheless, the creation and continued operations of the captive insurer were designed to obtain for the Amatil Group the benefits identified by Sedgwick.

There were also clearly identified commercial advantages in the captive being located in Singapore. These included the availability of an appropriate infrastructure and suitable investment opportunities. One further advantage was Singapore's relatively low tax rate, but this was only one of a number specified in the Sedgwick report.

Furthermore, the captive was incorporated and its capital structured in accordance with the requirements of the Singapore authorities. Matila's affairs were clearly conducted in a business-like fashion and in conformity with the law of Singapore.

Matila's insurance business was limited in scope, but restrictions were inherent in the conditions imposed by the Singapore authorities. Moreover, the scope of Matila's activities reflected the nature of the commercial needs of Wills and other companies in the Group.

In the judge's view, having regard to the matters specified in the ITA, the scheme identified by the Commissioner had two principal commercial purposes. First, the scheme enabled Wills to obtain indemnity against health risks that otherwise was not available to it. Secondly, the scheme provided the Amatil Group with a number of commercial advantages. These included more effective risk management and claims handling, better chances of gaining access to the reinsurance market and the opportunity to retain the underwriting profits that might have flowed (and in fact did flow) from a somewhat speculative underwriting venture.

One of the benefits of the scheme, as understood by the participants, was the possible tax advantages. The contemporary documentation referred to the relatively low tax rates in Singapore (although not to any benefit accruing to Wills by reason of the premiums being allowable deductions). But any taxation advantage was incidental to the principal objectives, the judge decided. Specifically, in the judge's view, it could not be concluded that any of the participants entered into the scheme or carried it out for the claimed purpose of enabling Wills to obtain a tax benefit.

This was not only a victory for the taxpayer, it was a total victory: the Commissioner was annihilated.

Since the early 1980s tax authorities have been paying increasing attention to international tax aspects and stepped up efforts to ensure that groups doing business across fiscal frontiers pay the correct amount of tax. This has brought to light a number of overseas subsidiaries operating in ways which cause concern and which, more often than not, have not previously been known. The CFC legislation in the UK has been used where appropriate but, more importantly in the context of this paper, it has sometimes seemed likely that the companies were resident in the United Kingdom. Investigations have been carried out and many substantial negotiated settlements reached. Three broad categories can be seen. Some companies, on enquiry, were accepted as non-resident and left to the CFC legislation. Others have been found to be resident and full tax paid on that basis. In yet others a compromise solution has meant, for example, that the company becomes resident beyond doubt from a certain date but pays up a dividend beforehand so that tax will effectively be paid on all or part of the profits accruing during the disputed period. Captive insurance companies have been part of this population in all three categories.

The Revenue approach in the U.K. has had to be selective. It is not in the business of generally reviewing residence status and, indeed, there is little practical point in examining companies where substantial tax has been paid overseas because relief for that tax would wholly or partly eliminate UK liability if the company were resident. But captives give companies advantages apart from deferral and often operate in offshore locations where the tax burden is light or non-existent. So it is not surprising that a number of these captives have been selected for investigation. And it is safe to assume that that approach will continue and that captives are likely to have their operations generally and perhaps their tax residence in particular subject to scrutiny.

Organising the captive

How, then, should a captive's business be organised if it is to be non-resident in the United Kingdom. In the paper referred to earlier Mr. Sadler said that the Inland Revenue is not in the business of telling companies how to arrange their affairs, but the sort of advice given by outside tax planners usually includes some standard features which are designed to make the captive appear to be non-resident. Typically they would include the following (although to repeat them is not to indicate Revenue endorsement):

1. The company should be incorporated outside the United Kingdom and have its registered office, books and records in the offshore location. Its internal regulations (the equivalent of the Memorandum and Articles of Association) should give the power of management to the directors, require that board meetings be held overseas and stipulate that a quorum can be made up only of directors resident outside the United Kingdom.

2. All 'working' directors should be resident offshore; they should include people who are experienced in insurance matters and able to contribute substantially; and they should be paid a proper commercial level of reward for their work.

3. The appointment of directors who simply make up the numbers and who clearly cannot contribute sensibly to the decisions of the board should be avoided.

4. The use of 'professional' directors (those who are on the boards of scores, perhaps hundreds, of companies) should be kept to a minimum, even where they are qualified.

5. All important decisions should be taken at board meetings and full documentation to support those decisions should be prepared and retained.

6. Correspondence or other contacts with the parent company should not be capable of being read as the imposition of the parent's will. Only advice should flow down and the captive should not seek parental approval of its decisions.

7. Transactions between the captive and associated companies should not be inconsistent with those which could be expected between unconnected concerns.

This is not to say that the parent must have a totally 'hands-off' attitude. It can legitimately do things as shareholder and clearly has a role in the following:

1. The initial creation (incorporation) of the company.
2. Appointing the directors and dealing with changes.
3. Deciding the scope of the business in terms of the internal regulations, for example the objects clause, and instituting changes.
4. Approving dividends and directors' remuneration.
5. Initiating and/or approving changes in, say, the share structure.

This list is not exhaustive and must depend to some extent on the law of the state of incorporation. But some advisers caught up in an investigation do tend to stretch too far the idea of shareholder rights. If a negotiated settlement is desired, that approach will not help matters.

If a Revenue investigation is launched, the inquiry will address the specific context of an insurance company. The sort of decisions which one would expect to find handled by the directors — and not the parent company — are as follows:

1. Decisions regarding the fields of insurance business in which it engages (within those permitted by its internal regulations).
2. Decisions on the acceptance or rejection of proposals for insurance of major financial significance to the company.
3. Decisions on negotiations with any local regulatory body on, say, its capital requirements and its business plan.
4. Decisions on the choice and level of remuneration of, say, the underwriters, loss adjusters, investment managers, management company, auditors and senior staff in these areas:
   (a) where funds should be invested and who should have access to them;
   (b) the extent of any reinsurance;
   (c) the reserving policy.)

The setting up of a captive insurance company involves two discrete stages — planning and implementation. Experience has shown that the planning stage can be masterly and yet the whole edifice will crumble because implementation will not stand up to close scrutiny. At first blush all is well. Board meetings are held outside the United Kingdom; most of the directors are not UK-resident; the minutes of directors' meetings are beautifully written up; a vast quantity of paper appears to underpin the minutes; the UK finance and insurance people appear to give only advice; and the operation appears in truth to be offshore. But then the investigator starts to look below the superficially impressive evidence to the second, third and other tiers of paperwork and other evidence that exists in odd corners of the corporate empire or lies in the hands of third parties. He may visit the offshore location and talk to the local people; he may talk to third parties such as brokers, managers and reinsurers. He may obtain copies of documents from those third parties. He will examine how the system works as distinct from how it was intended to work. A view can then emerge which is totally different from first impressions. The facade is shown to have no substance behind it. Instead the whole operation is seen to be a little play acted out on a script written in the United Kingdom and directed from London.

The UK-based group finance director or insurance manager can be in a difficult position when an offshore operation is set up. The scheme is often his brainchild and he has a particular interest in its success. There is a temptation to oversea its implementation too closely; perhaps, even, for the director to be on the captive's board. On the other hand he will understand that central management and control must in reality be abroad and he should stand back and let the independent board and its directors get on with the job. But that may mean letting people who are otherwise outside the group be in a position to misuse group funds or at least fail to make best use of them. That would cut directly against the job description of the finance director who has responsibility for fund management at group level. It is the process of reconciling these competing interests which can sink the ship.

Once it can be seen that there is some reasonably significant degree of central management and control from the United Kingdom that will be sufficient to establish UK residence. There can, at the same time, take place in the offshore location quite genuine acts of management and control — the law recognises the possibility of such a division — but that does not save the company from being resident in the United Kingdom. A company which has a peripatetic lifestyle can expect particularly close scrutiny. Meetings held every month or so in the various capital cities of Europe in turn may be a means of keeping out of the grasp of any fiscal authority — but it does not seem to be the way to run sensibly a genuinely commercial business.

Mr Sadler's paper not only clearly demonstrates the position taken by the UK Revenue but can be read as an indication of the attitude of taxation authorities in most parts of the world. It is also helpful in the sense that it provides some insight into the issues of residency and how a captive insurance company might be structured to go some way to avoiding the problems that being regarded as resident in the same country as the parent will develop for the captive's owner.

Finally, two general points. First, should the venture prove a failure and decision to terminate the captive's existence be taken, then 'loss treatment' will no doubt be sought by the parent. This will be achieved only if the right structuring decisions were taken at the beginning. But, as an example, in the United Kingdom a loan from the parent to the captive, if proved irrecoverable, would not be available for loss treatment. Only if it had been structured as 'debt on a security' would full loss relief be available.

Second, many captives seek to use some of their money as loans back to the parent. Is this advisable or not? Also, the parent company may decide to issue a guarantee in respect of the captive. Both these measures serve to weaken rather than strengthen the case that the captive is a true independent entity operating on its own in a true commercial sense. In particular, captive owners will be strongly advised against the issue of any parental guarantee.

The tax position for the captive itself will depend very much on the location in which it is situated. Where taxation does apply, this will often be separated between investment and underwriting income, so that the accounting practice will need to take account of this factor. Taxation generally for the captive involves income transferred from and to premium funds, investment income and expenses. The reserving policy of the captive will also affect taxation and account needs to be taken of the treatment of outstanding claims, the development of IBNR, which may not be allowed in some countries, and unearned premiums. Another external factor is the imposition of premium taxes in countries where the primary insurance policies are issued and where these taxes will need to be deducted before premiums are ceded to the captive itself.

With the developing number of captive locations and the greater interest in captives being shown by tax authorities throughout the world, the reserving policy of the captive and the attitude of the regulatory and tax authorities in the area where the captive is established are becoming of increasing importance. For example, a negative feature of the Singapore captive position has been the unwillingness of the Singapore authorities to make any allowance for IBNRs when making the tax computation. Similarly the reserve amounts in the Financial Services Centre in Dublin are very much less generous than those pertaining in Luxembourg (where reserves can be established of up to twenty times annual net premium) and in the Isle of Man, where, until recently, there was a special statutory loss provision of 20 per cent of profit where the captive does not achieve an exposure ratio, on any one contract, greater than 20 per cent of the adjusted net assets shown in the relevant solvency margin calculation.

The logical extension of a combination of restrictive controlled foreign company legislation and differing attitudes towards tax allowances for reserves could mean that in the future it would be more beneficial for a captive to be established in a high tax area where there is substantial allowance for technical, equalisation or safety fund reserves than to maintain the captive in a nil tax regime which is subject to the full weight of CFC legislation, residency problems and all the other difficulties which establishment in a tax haven involves.

One final taxation factor is the position in respect of the funds which have been accumulated in the captive and which are required by the parent company. Although taxation situations vary throughout the world, the general position would be that profits brought back to the parent company would be regarded as income and taxed at the rate of the domicile in which the parent is based. This means that, in essence, the tax advantages of the captive are those of a deferral nature, although the ability to build up reserves offshore without or with little tax penalty and to develop investment income benefit from untaxed reserves makes the captive, from this point of view, still very advantageous.

Investment Basics

For the captive insurance company resources available for investment include the capital, the premium reserves and the premium funds. Utilisation of these available resources can add significantly to the captive's profitability. Care does need to be taken, however, to ensure that the captive remains liquid in relation to its obligations to its policy holders, reinsurers and normal working expenses. The use of cash forecasts which indicate premiums received, pattern of re-insurance premiums out and claims out should enable the captive to develop cash flow forecasts and its investment strategy on the basis of the results.

The development of funds in differing investment opportunities must be related to the pattern of underwriting, the availability of funds for emergencies and the relationships of the investment strategy to the function of the parent company's financial operation. Earlier, the variations of investment opportunity for differing classes of risk were demonstrated and it will he remembered that these were related to the size of claims payments and the time that they were paid after the original premium was received. In addition to these factors the investment approach will need to take account of the premiums received from the captive's operations worldwide, bearing in mind particularly delays from some countries of the world as a result of legislative restraints on external reinsurance premiums or the necessity for reserves to be held for some period of time in the country of origin.

Payments outwards in the form of reinsurance premiums may be on a regular instalment basis and if the relationship between the premiums in and the premiums out is not carefully handled and the difficulties of overseas operations and currencies not taken account of, the captive could find itself in a difficult financial position and have its opportunity for investment severely inhibited.

Tables 6.8 and 6.9 show methods of developing cash flow forecasts, recording investments and measuring liquidity. As banks show more and more interest in assisting captives in their investment policy the traditional approach of giving precedence to liquidity over

Table 6.8 Cash flow forecast

	1.1.96	1st qtr	1.4.96	2nd qtr	1.7.96 ....
INCOME					
Share capital					
Balance					
Net prems.					
Recoverable claims					
(R/I)					
Interest and dividends					
Other					
Total					
EXPENDITURE					
R/I prems.					
Claims payable					
Expenses					
Taxation					
Other					
Total					
Balance C/F					
O/S Claims					

Table 6.9 Method of recording investments and measuring liquidity

(a) RECEIPTS

Balance at ....
   Current Account
   7 day call
   Fixed deposit
   Treasury bills

Premiums ....

Interest received
   7-day
   Fixed deposit
   Matured Treasury bill

Supporting
   schedules   Total
   for detail

Table 6.9 Method of recording investments and measuring liquidity (cont'd)

(b) PAYMENTS

Directors' fees
Reinsurance premiums
Claims paid

Income tax
Balance at ....
   Current
   7-day
   Fixed deposit
   Treasury bills

Supporting
  schedules   Total

(c) SUPPORTING INVESTMENT SCHEDULE

Careful Bank Limited
  Current
  Deposit

International Trust
  Call deposit (6%)
  Fixed deposit
    To .... (6.5%)
    To .... (6.75%)

Treasury bills
  £250,000 due .... (   )
  £500,000 due .... (   )

                  Total

investment return is beginning to be blurred. Banks are developing sophisticated mathematical models which not only attempt to maximise the investment opportunities, based on the portfolio of the captive's business, but can also make a contribution to optimising the mix of classes of risk to ensure that the investment opportunities are taken full account of in the decisions made to decide which types of insurance the captive should most logically participate in. Care obviously needs to be taken by the captive when examining proposals of this nature because of the insurance company's responsibility to its policy holders and reinsurers and its need to comply with legislation on investment policies. In the latter connection there is a move in a number of the captive locations to include asset liquidity tests in their annual returns and this type of approach may inhibit some of the more adventurous investment managers. Although investment income plays a very important part in the development of the captive's resources, it should not be used to the detriment of either the underwriting profit objective or the financial standing of the insurance company.

CHAPTER 7

LOSS CONTROL AND CLAIMS

Loss Control

There is no doubt that the success of the captive will depend on its ability to control the losses which it is retaining within its operation. In addition it will need to ensure protection of its reinsurers, so as to maintain reinsurance expenditure at a level which enables the captive's profits to be maintained and hopefully to improve these profits by progressively reducing the reinsurance cost and enabling the base of the captive to expand and retain even more of its parent's risk as it develops in size.

Loss control services are available from within the parent company, from the insurers, the brokers and other loss control specialists. These sources can all make significant contributions to the success of the captive but will be successful only if the motivation of the management is right and there is a commitment to improvement of loss control in order not only to reduce the current claims cost but to improve the position in the future and increase the captive's profitability. The structure of the captive also makes it a useful vehicle to motivate local management. This is the case particularly if the captive premium structure is designed to reflect good performance by reducing insurance costs or if the overall risk management strategy and financial policy ensure that there is accountability in the event of losses occurring in the form of management and financial penalties for those that do not keep to the required standards.

The original feasibility study will have collated past loss experience but will not be able to anticipate accurately how the future loss experience is to develop. Loss control incentive for the captive and its owner will be meaningfully available because of the improvement that can be realised in reinsurance expenditure if loss history improves. As reinsurance is to a large extent experience rated, any improvement in loss history means that future premiums will also be low. This benefit from loss control activity can be used either to benefit the captive from increased profitability or to reduce premiums to the captive owner and then through him to the individual managements.

In developing a policy for future loss control the key factors are as follows:

1. Allocation of responsibility.
2. Motivation.
3. Training.

Allocation of responsibility

Effective risk management strategies are designed to ensure that each manager of the company realises his own responsibility for the people, property, operations and activities in his area and under his control. It is important that the implementation of the risk management programme ensures that this direct responsibility is in writing and that systems exist to monitor performance and ensure that, by the use of budgetary systems, the financial responsibility is related to the performance of the people concerned.

Motivation

Motivation in loss control areas needs to have three main components. First, top management should show its concern about loss control by its attitude to losses and its commitment to improving the prevention of losses by loss prevention investment policies which reflect how management sees the importance of protecting its operations. Second, management systems should include methods of reward and punishment where local management action results in good or bad performance. Third, in the event of losses occurring there should be effective management reaction to the problem both as an individual incident and also as an example to other management of how problems can arise and the methods that can be used to alleviate them.

Training

Training programmes should be introduced for managers so that they understand the implication of risk-management and have the ability to develop, on a formal basis, a risk-management strategy that enables them to recognise risks and hazards in their area of operation and systems which record such risks and indicate methods than can be used to handle them effectively. Training should also involve assistance on the handling of loss control equipment and a programme for regular practice to ensure that in the event of a potential loss occurring the management and staff have the capability to deal with the preventative measures.

In addition to the recognition and control factors it is important that the parent company management understand the need to review continually and record changes in their business which could affect the loss situation. They must also make sure that such changes are brought to the attention of management, so that any potential lessons can not only be learned in the particular area of activity but also be applied throughout other parts of the company.

In order to assist the management in developing identification of risk, various charts can be used to record risk factors and methods of control. Table 7.1 is a simple example of a risk factor analysis table which is used to develop the question of how the risk arises. The line manager completes the chart in relation to his area of activity, highlighting the processes involved and the hazards which are of concern. This chart can be extended to include possible methods of controlling the risk or can be used to measure the risk potential so that the loss control decisions made bear some trade-off relationship to the risk exposed.

Table 7.1 Sample chart for risk factor analysis

Risk factor analysis		Site:		Date:
Activity	*Equipment involved*	*Operations involved*	*Hazards*	*Comments*

Analysis carried through by: (risk management adviser)
Checked by: (line management)

As an example, in developing answers to the question of how risk arises we can separate the hazard to properties into two areas: first, the passive hazard related to the building, plant, equipment and stock, and, second, the active hazard which would be related to the activity both inside and outside the property, of a normal or abnormal nature, which could give rise to a particular hazard. Other active factors in this example would be individual circumstances and timing. Thus, for example, the analysis would take into account not only the position while, say, a factory is in operation but also while it is closed for three weeks during the summer holidays or when it is left unattended at weekends. A normal activity would take account of the fact that, although there may be a no-smoking restriction on the premises and special smoking areas are designated, there is still the possibility of hazard, particularly related to areas where flammable liquids are stored.

After analysing the hazard factors it will be necessary to consider the question of whether it is possible to control the risks Potential methods of control can be split into three main areas. The first is the design of the location, including the management organisation, the system of processing and the design of the building plant or equipment It should be considered whether these facts can be changed to ensure that the loss potential is reduced The second control area is that of protection, whereby equipment can be protected by various devices and systems, such as contingency planning, introduced to alleviate the loss potential should the loss occur. Finally, risk control involves people, and programmes can be introduced to ensure that people are adequately trained and motivated to look after the company's assets and earnings, and also to make sure that systems exist to monitor the performance of people in the loss control area on an ongoing basis.

The final three concepts of risk control can be explained in more detail by an example related to a potential fire. We can separate the loss control measures into three segments: the pre-event activity, activity during the event and the post-event action.

Looking at the pre-event situation we can introduce separation of the location and reduce the energy by a number of techniques. An example of ignition control could include the use of flameproof equipment, the closure of dangerous processes, the elimination of matches and lighters, a review of operating temperatures and pressures and the introduction of various relieving systems. We can control fire load by reducing the volume stored at any one time, reviewing the materials used in various processes, separating the storage and process areas and limiting storage areas to carefully defined levels.

During the event the activity is to reduce energy and introduce protection. Various means are open to us in this context. The introduction of detection systems, such as smoke and heat detectors and fire alarms, will be of some assistance. In addition, manual and automatic fire-fighting equipment, such as water, sand, foam, extinguishers, hose-reels, sprinklers and deluge, carbon dioxide and halon systems, make a contribution. During the event it is also possible to have goods and equipment removed and to introduce some protection against water and smoke if there is a storage problem. Even at this stage routes for the growth of fire can be controlled by the use of fire doors and roofs and the introduction of differing connecting routes.

If our pre-event and during-event control measures have failed, we can still alleviate loss in the post-event situation by emergency action which protects any further assets exposed to possible damage. In the area of earnings exposure we can have predetermined contingency plans which can be sophisticated and can help to provide alternative means of production. This would enable the company to take steps to restore normal working as quickly as possible.

It is not the purpose of this book to deal with loss control in any considerable detail. However, it would be wrong to underestimate the importance of ensuring that the company that is establishing a captive insurance company recognises that the viability of its operation will depend upon the effectiveness of its loss prevention methods and activities. Effort in this area and, in particular, in introducing risk management programmes will be of considerable benefit in optimising the financial opportunities that the captive offers.

Handling Claims

Depending on the type of captive and particularly its country spread of operation it will be necessary to have a mechanism for handling and settling claims. These services may be provided by the captive management company, the fronting insurer or outside specialists.

It is important to agree at the outset who will investigate claims on behalf of the captive and how the payments will be authorised. Where a fronting insurer is involved, it will normally be convenient for them to deal with the claims investigation and payments. This will also help to prevent any problems in relation to claims payments, if currency control factors are a problem in particular parts of the world.

Another factor to take account of in the handling of claims is unreasonable in-house pressure to settle on an ex gratia basis. It will be

273

understandable if the management of the captive owner feel that their own insurance company should be more generous than the normal market, but it would be dangerous for this posture to be upheld in the actual negotiations. Apart from the dangers that this has in relation to the profitability of a captive, it should be remembered that in many cases other people, including fronting insurers and reinsurers, will be involved in the decision.

Where the programme is supported by a fronting insurer, the captive will have a significant interest in how the claim is handled, since the fronting insurer may be retaining only 10 per cent of the risk whereas the captive will be retaining the remainder before cessions to the insurers. In this case the captive should insist on having a role in both the negotiating and the handling of the settlement. This can be achieved by the introduction into the agreement between the fronting insurer and the captive of a claims co-operation clause. Such a clause could be worded on the following basis:

> It is a condition precedent of liability under this policy that all claims be notified immediately to Captive Insurance Limited, and the Fronting Insurance Limited hereby undertakes in arriving at the settlement of every claim that they will co-operate with Captive Insurance Limited and that no settlement shall be made without their prior approval.

Another requirement that is sometimes encountered is where the fronting company is anxious to ensure that, in the event of the captive becoming insolvent, it still has access to the reinsurers to pay the residue of the claim for which the fronting company may have paid 100 per cent, well in excess of its own retention Such a problem may be resolved by a cut-through clause which could read:

> All claims under this agreement shall be paid by reinsurers direct to Fronting Company Limited and Fronting Company Limited shall have the same rights under this agreement as the company.

Other important aspects of claims handling and settlement involve financing problems for the captive during the time between the payment of claims to the policy holder or fronting company and the collection of those claims settlements from the reinsurers. It is important that, if these claims are of a sizeable nature, claims payments are synchronised so that the captive is not in a difficult financial problem while awaiting settlement from the reinsurers. Similarly, where the captive is operating on a direct basis it may encounter exchange control problems in the payment of premiums from its country of domicile or it may be affected by fluctuations in currency rates.

The use of international insurers to front for a captive does enable some protection from these difficulties as they are often able to provide solutions which would not be open to an insurance company operating on a direct basis and especially to an insurance company operating on a non-admitted basis. Where such potential problems exist the use of fronting facilities is often the only practical solution to what could be a difficult handling problem.

An effective and well-thought-out procedure for the handling and settling of claims is of the utmost importance to the captive. It is also important that the arrangements made include prompt and accurate reporting of incidents, so that at an early stage the captive is aware of its obligations and more importantly can involve both its own personnel and the reinsurers in the decision-making process. The choice of how to handle a claim is somewhat difficult and will depend on the types of business in the captive, but it is likely that the typical captive insurance company will have to make use of external services either from insurers or specialists to ensure that the service given is of a high standard. This will be particularly necessary if the captive's operations involve multinational activities and where it will be impossible for the captive itself to get involved in detailed local investigations.

The cost of claims handling fees must also be taken into account in anticipating the captive's cost. These can be remunerated either within the fronting fee or on an individual fee basis if outside specialists are appointed. Claims services should include recovery and salvage services in order to mitigate the size of the loss once the claim has occurred, and the specialists appointed will need to be skilled in the particular country in which the claim arises so as to get the maximum benefit from a recovery viewpoint.

As a support to the use of outside specialists, some captives use a regular claims audit which is either handled by themselves or used in another external source. The audit examines in detail the capability of the claims handlers, evaluating their performance, the accuracy of their reserving and the extent to which they have obtained subrogation or recoveries in post-loss situations. All of these activities will help to reduce claims cost and improve the profitability of the captive.

Loss control and claims handling are activities that impinge on each other and the lessons that can be learned from the loss can have an impact on future prevention activity. Both of these areas can make a significant contribution to the performance of the captive and to improving the overall efficiency and profitability of the captive parent organisation.

CHAPTER 8

THE FUTURE DEVELOPMENT OF CAPTIVES

This concluding chapter will take a broad look at the future for captives, both reflecting developments in recent years and involving a certain amount of guesswork as to whether these developments will continue and what impact they are likely to have on the insurance markets and the needs of major insurance buyers. The chapter will also include a section on the pros and cons of captives expanding into unrelated business. There are a number of current trends which seem most likely to have a long-term impact. These are as follows:

1. The reaction of the direct insurance market to the growth of captives and the methods that they may utilise in order to retrieve some of the business that has been lost to them over the years, and also ways in which they might seek to co-operate more willingly and successfully with the captive sector.
2. The increasing legislative restraints and requirements in locations used for captive formation, and linked to this the increasing hostility of tax authorities throughout the world towards captives and other offshore companies. These factors combined are likely to have an impact both on captives themselves and where they are established in the future.
3. The problem of how to develop a captive insurance company as its shareholders' funds increase and its role in underwriting the risk of its parent reach saturation point, whereas its financial ability to write more business is significant.

277

4. The development of new risk financing techniques particularly financial reinsurance and its application as a support mechanisms to the captive insurance company.

Market Reactions to the Captive

We have seen previously that the developments of the captive insurance company usually result from the inability of the insurance market to provide what the major insurance buyer feels is necessary for him to optimise his risk-financing programme. The development of captives has seen changes in the attitudes of both insurers and brokers to the concept. Initially there was hostility, but as the insurer and broker have recognised the inevitability of the captive development they have become conciliatory and eventually heavily involved in the captive business.

There has been a response from the market to captives by adaptation of techniques to try to reflect the needs of the buyer and to dissuade him from the captive insurance company step. Although these new solutions have not stopped captive development, they have enabled many companies to improve their insurance programmes and, to some extent, perhaps these developments have stemmed the growth that might otherwise have occurred.

It is, however, inevitable that captives will grow but that this growth will be related to the willingness shown and the innovative skills used by the direct insurance market to this particular challenge. The United States publication *Risk Management Reports* looked at this problem in its January/February 1980 edition following a request from one of its own readers, an insurance company, which asked what insurance companies could do to change their services and try to combat or participate positively in the captive development. The following response is based on the answers that *Risk Management Reports* felt were most relevant:

1. Insurance companies should offer to provide fronting facilities for captives.
2. Insurance companies should write the excess insurance cover for self-insurance programmes and particularly for liability and workers' compensation.
3. They should create a separate major commercial account department which has greater freedom of action and operates as a separate profit centre.
4. They should be prepared to underwrite the whole of the insurance buyer's business and not just selected individual lines.

5. Services offered should be separated from the pure risk-financing need offering technical and other services on a free basis to customers. This would also have the advantage of eliminating premium tax on the services selected by the buyer.
6. Quotations should be on a net of commission basis enabling brokers to be remunerated on a fee basis and once again eliminate premium taxes on the commission portion.
7. The buyer should be given the opportunity to pay his premium direct to the insurer therefore avoiding his premiums being held by intermediaries unnecessarily.
8. Retrospective rating and other innovative underwriting plans should be developed even more to ensure that the buyer gets the maximum investment control over the reserves generated particularly from 'long-tail' business

These conditions were generally accepted as market conditions softened and insurers became hungry for business. However, in tough market conditions the situation can reverse and many of these facilities either no longer available or in limited supply. This is particularly true of fronting facilities, whole account underwriting, and the cost of retrospective rating plans.

However, if we look forward we can anticipate that when the insurance cycle produces a more amenable situation for buyers, these and other ideas are resurrected. It is also interesting that the other items in the response have not only come to fruition but have also survived the hard market conditions and are presumably now with us for the forseeable future. This is particularly true of the separation of technical services from pure insurance financing with the services being paid for on an individual basis. For the buyer it means that he can develop his risk-financing plan using his captive innovatively and then buy the best services available to him as they are required, relating these services to his own needs.

The 1986 capacity crisis, particularly for US excess casualty exposures, resulted in many of the major insurance buyers finding ways and means of solving a problem which the insurance was unable to handle. In the first edition of this book the point was made that the future for the insurance industry as captives develop will be that the amount of risk that they retain at the lower levels of risk will be substantially reduced and may even disappear. At that time it was suggested that the insurance market would continue to be heavily involved in the position of catastrophe protection, presumably at an adequate level of rating. While this latter comment is still correct it was not expected, at the time, that it would be necessary for major buyers to join together to form group insurance companies to provide capacity protection which was not able to be provided by the insurance and reinsurance companies themselves. It therefore seems likely that the development of these facilities will continue through providing capacity at a high level and may be moving into areas other than casualty as they prove to be successful investments. This development points to a loss for all time of substantial premiums which were previously paid to the commercial insurance market. With captives retaining more risks themselves at lower levels and now moving into high excess areas in response to lack of commercial insurance market, the growth of premiums paid for commercial risks seems likely to remain static and even decrease when soft market conditions appear. The future for the insurers will be to provide high-quality technical services which are paid for on an individual fee-related basis rather than as an integral part of the original premium payment. They will obviously have an important risk-taking role but recent developments point to this being rather more subservient that it has been in the past.

These developments will change the role of the brokers. They will continue to be heavily involved in assisting companies in developing feasibility studies, managing captives and placing insurance and reinsurance business but their remuneration is more likely to be related to the work that they do than to be a percentage of the insurance business that they are placing. In addition, they will compete with the insurance industry in the provision of technical and other services for fees. All of this should help to improve the service available to the industrial buyer, giving him much more choice and hopefully higher-quality facilities from which to choose.

We may even see the risk element of the insurance package, previously bought as an integrated product, being available not only from the insurance industry but also from the banking fraternity. Banks in the past have had some involvement in the provision of contingent risk to major companies and also, of course, have an understanding of the insurance company operation and captives in particular through their investment and other services. There are definite signs of the growing interest of the banks in the provision of risk-financing solutions to unacceptable variability in the earnings of companies. The unbundling of the technical and other services offered by insurance companies may accelerate this development.

Indeed the development of the excess casualty facilities such as ACE were developed jointly between American insurance brokers and American banks. Although these sponsors were not participating on a risk basis they are certainly aware of the opportunity for providing new facilities for major reinsurance buyers and gaining experience through being involved either as managers of the company or in providing the important investment services. This development together with the unbundling of the technical and other services offered by insurance companies may accelerate the participation of the financial community in this development.

Legislation in Captive Locations

The earlier part of this book looked briefly at the development of the insurance industry, emphasising that the captive concept was at the origins of many of the major direct insurance companies that exist today. As these companies in their early days grew and started to provide facilities to a wide range of the public, governments found it necessary to introduce legislation in order to protect the policy holders and also the financial institutions whose money was at risk. It is interesting to reflect that the historical growth of insurance company legislation in industrial countries is now being reflected in many of the captive locations that are used throughout the world.

It must be beneficial for adequate insurance legislation to exist to protect the interests of the consumer. Equally, for captive insurance companies reasonable control should be welcomed because it gives creditability to the locations used for captives and prevents abuse by the minority which could harm the overall status of these insurance subsidiaries.

Recent developments in insurance legislation in captive locations reflect a number of key concerns that the relevant authorities have about the way in which insurance companies should be controlled. The basic legislative criteria existing in the major captive locations are as follows:

1. There is usually a requirement for minimum capitalisation of the captive, with a related relationship between the capital requirement and the business being written. Methods of testing this solvency margin differ but are usually related to a specific requirement based on the ratio between capital and free reserves and the net premium written or on an individual examination of the capital proposed and the types of business that the captive is considering taking.
2. There is an increasing requirement to examine the assets of the company to ensure that there is adequate liquidity to deal with any claims that might arise from different types of business being handled.

3. There is normally a requirement that annually audited accounts are submitted and reviewed by the local governing authorities and that these accounts are prepared by qualified and acknowledged accountants.
4. There is control over the companies that manage captives ensuring that these operations are well run and staffed by people who have some expertise in the business of insurance and finaneial management.
5. There is usually a method of screening new companies to ensure that their motives are acceptable and that their insurance plan has a reasonable chance of success. The depth of this investigation will depend very much on the type of business involved, with much more detailed investigation into, for example, medical malpractice or products liability risks than into a company's own property business.

The developments in various locations have been considered earlier and they reflect a cross-fertilisation of ideas between the various supervisory authorities who, while maintaining a competitive position in relation to each other, are anxious not to find themselves out of line so far as control is concerned and thereby attract the more undesirable companies looking for an opportunity to take advantage of lax controls.

The majority of insurance company legislation introduced in the various captive areas has been introduced within the last ten years and it can be seen clearly from this that most of the captive locations recognise the need to control the development of insurance companies in the interests of those that are properly managed, controlled and capitalised. In addition more locations have taken on board the controls and regulations in existence in the more mature areas and have reflected the control elements in their own rules. Although it may seem to some people that these increasing controls reduce some of the advantages of going offshore, it is a development that should be welcomed if the captive scene is to continue growing and become an important and credible part of the International insurance market. It is perhaps ironic that captive developments in the onshore areas such as Australia, Denmark, Luxembourg and Dublin have resulted in insurance commissioners and regulators relaxing the insurance legislation that applies to conventional domestic insurance companies to reflect the particular needs of captives, and this may also result in a level playing field for captives whether or not they decide to establish in the same country as their parent or remain as largely offshore insurance companies.

Expanding into Unrelated Business

There seems little doubt, in my mind, that the role of the traditional offshore captive locations will gradually diminish. This will however take sometime as the growth of new captive formations from countries, where the concept is in its infancy, will continue for at least another couple of decades. However, captive owners who have had their operations for many years will want to enhance the performance of their captive by reducing their reliance on the conventional insurance industry. Many captives been forced to use insurance companies to provide fronting facilities in countries where non-admitted insurance is not possible and the captive is therefore not authorised. This is an unnecessary expense which complicates the collection of premiums, the handling of claims and providing service to local business operations. The optimum solution would be to have a captive which can underwrite direct to the subsidiaries without the involvement of an unrelated insurance company. This is difficult to achieve on a global basis but is possible in certain economic areas. Typical of this possibility and the trend, is the establishment, by a number of USA companies, of captives in the Dublin Financial Services Centre to underwrite business direct into the European Union and thereby avoid the expense of fronting operations in countries such as France, Germany, Italy, Spain and Belgium where non-admitted insurance from locations such as Bermuda, Guernsey and the Isle of Man is not possible. This is another reason why Gibraltar is encouraged in its plans to develop an offshore insurance sector with the full authority to write business direct into the European Union. Another example of the onshore philosophy is the considerable growth of Vermont with well over 300 captives underwriting business into other US states and thereby minimising federal excise taxes and other restrictions that pertain when a captive is writing business from an unrecognised offshore area.

Another fascinating development that I perceive over the coming decade, is the ability to establish a dedicated captive syndicate at Lloyd's. This will enable the captive owner to utilise the Lloyd's franchise to write business direct into over sixty countries throughout the world including the European Union countries, the United States, Australasia, most of the Far East and some parts of South America. Although there are some down sides to the concept of establishing a captive Lloyd's syndicate (primarily commitments to the Central Fund) it will be an attraction to many large multinational companies who want to have greater control over their own destiny, avoid being reliant on an increasingly small number of dominant multinational insurers and work towards developing their risk transfer arrangements so that they are limited to the catastrophe insurance area and deals with the major reinsurance companies.

In this respect I see the major reinsurers encouraging the concept of developing direct links with major corporates in order to engender successful, reciprocal long term arrangements, eliminate the frictional costs associated with primary insurers and retail insurance brokers and match the insurance buyer with the entities that are, in reality, providing them with the catastrophe insurance protection they require.

The captive in its early stage will probably have concentrated its effort on retaining as much of the parent company's risk as appropriate. Once the major benefits of using a captive for self-insurance have been realised many financial members of a company will be looking towards the possible diversification into other areas of insurance, including business unrelated to the parent. Although in the United States this development has been accelerated by the attitude of the Internal Revenue Service, it seems fair to assume that even without IRS interference captives would have moved into unrelated business at some stage in the future.

In reviewing a strategy into unrelated business the first stage is to establish the objectives. These are likely to include one or more of the following:

1. To expand the base of the insurance company beyond its potentially restrictive scope of handling the risks of its parent.
2. To increase the retention ability of the captive and its parent by spreading risk and building up additional surplus which can be used to write higher elements of the parent business.
3. To get an additional return on the capital and surplus of the company built up through profitable captive business rather than to allow this to remain unutilised other than gaining income through investment.
4. To improve the tax position of the parent by developing a volume of unrelated business which for some countries will enable the profits on the total captive operations to be tax free, until dividends are repatriated, accelerating the growth of the surplus through investment income which is not reduced by taxation.
5. A conscious decision to diversify the parent's business into insurance and financial services, using the captive as the springboard for such expansion.

Removing the captive from a position where its original purpose was to improve the risk-financing of the parent to business which involves taking risks over which the parent has no control is likely to highlight differences in the attitudes of those concerned with developing the captive and the rest of management. In an interesting analysis of this problem Mitchell Cole (then of Risk Planning Group) produced the chart shown in Table 8.1 which lists the five key areas where this conflict or difference in approach is likely to arise.

Table 8.1 Differences in attitude

Parent attitudes	Captive attitudes
1 Return on capital must exceed corporate hurdle rate.	Return on capital should relate to the underwriting risk taken.
2 Captive should produce a lower cost of risk.	Underwriting should be profitable.
3 Dividends are a means of returning funds to operating units.	The growth of the surplus is important in order to support underwriting, catastrophe losses, etc.
4 The captive should only indulge in limited commercial underwriting.	Unrelated business is important as part of captive's tax strategy and additional profit.
5 Captive should only assume limited risk exposure.	The risk assumption of the captive should be commensurate with its surplus position.

A review of these issues will enable a useful debate within the company on which a strategy for moving into outside business can be developed, taking account of the real objectives of the parent. In deciding which forms of outside business are likely to prove the most beneficial the choices open are wide-ranging, but many include high-risk areas or require the level of technical expertise not normally available within the company or within its captlve operation.

Captive Pooling Facilities

One of the first reinsurance facilities developed for captives was the established by the International Risk Management organisation, which developed a property pool called Hopewell Insurance which was established primarily to provide capacity for clients of IRM on the basis that a confined reinsurance treaty dealing specifically with captive companies would produce continuity in pricing and reflect the generally-held view that captive reinsurance business is more profitable than general reinsurance business. For the purpose of this chapter the important aspect of the Hopewell arrangements was the ability of the captive members to participate in the treaty itself, thus gaining access to captive reinsurance.

Under the basic treaty arrangements, excess of loss reinsurance above the captive retention was ceded to Hopewell (which is owned by the captive clients). The risks of the captive were pooled within Hopewell and Hopewell itself protected by an excess of loss programme above US$25 million arranged with the international reinsurance market. As part of its cession to the Hopewell pool the captive received a 25 per cent ceding commission and up to 15 per cent profit commission based on its results. From a participation point of view captives become eligible for an initial quarter of 1 per cent share of the basic treaty and are able to participate on a greater basis as their premium contribution and involvement in the Hopewell arrangement increased.

The Hopewell Company had a very successful period of operation but entered into difficulties some years ago as a result of worldwide catastrophe losses and a number of very large incidents that affected the pool's profitability. It was closed down a year or so ago but has been replaced by an alternative mechanism which operates in a similar fashion to the original.

During the products liability crisis of the 1970s a number of pooling facilities for casualty insurance were also developed. The International Risk Management Organisation developed a facility, based in the Cayman Islands, called the R Pool, short for the United Surplus Relief Treaty, which provided a pooling facility for working layer casualty risk. This facility had a maximum limit of US$1 million per occurrence and operated on the basis that the original fronting company ceded risk to United Insurance Company who internally ceded 100 per cent of the exposure to the R Pool, which is in fact a type of fund within the United Insurance Books. Exposures in excess of US$1 million were reinsured in the market-place, and the participants in the R Pool shared in all of the risks in proportion to the original gross premiums ceded by them into the facility. This enabled participants to obtain a share in unrelated exposures as well as producing considerable risk spread beyond the position that would have been achieved if they had retained all of the risk within their own captive operations.

Another facility developed before the United R Pool was the establishment of a company in Bermuda called the Corporate Insurance Company Limited (CIRCL). This company developed two facilities, the most important of which was the first excess casualty programme. This programme provided for umbrella, first layer excess and buffer layer casualty insurance programmes as put together by the various participants. The programme had a minimum underlying retention of US$250,000 and maximum coverage of US$2.5 million per occurrence for the 1985 underwriting year. Rating was based on premiums and conditions set by a recognised leading underwriter and a condition that the lead underwriter must retain at least 10 per cent of each risk. Initially, 75 per cent of the premium was charged with an arrangement that the remaining 25 per cent was paid if losses exceeded the initial premium deposit. Under the reinsurance treaty arranged by CIRCL, CIRCL itself retained 10 per cent of each risk and reinsured 90 per cent to participant captives in proportion to the premium they put into the programme. There was a ceding commission of 4 per cent which was retained by CIRCL for administration. Rather like the R Pool this enabled the pooling of the various participants' casualty exposures with the ability to participate in other participants' risks.

In addition to the structure many of these programmes include long-term commitment In the case of CIRCL there was a five-year commitment period and the participants had to purchase 200,000 shares of stock in CIRCL at book value when joining the arrangement. In addition the capital and surplus of the captive had to be a minimum of US$500,000 and the parent company must have had a net equity of at least US$100 million.

These programmes are examples of outside business involvement linked closely to the captive movement. Another facility developed in 1983 with this objective in mind was the Risk Exchange Association set up by a special Company Act in Bermuda following a study commissioned by 23 companies from the United States and Europe. The objective of the Risk Exchange is to provide a facility for insurance interchange among companies sponsored by industrial and commercial companies — in other words, captives. It provides a means for its members to reinsure risks of diverse classifications of other members on a controlled and efficient basis thereby expanding the profits of their operations and the services for their sponsors. The Exchange developed out of a long-standing interest of many captives in establishing a facility for exchanging risks on an economic basis. The main objectives of the Risk Exchange are as follows:

1. To provide profitable non-related business.
2. To increase capacity in difficult market conditions.
3. To keep transaction costs low.
4. To provide inbuilt underwriting support.

The Exchange is an incorporated association with a board of governors and it has contracts with an insurance management company and an underwriting services company who provide the necessary support for the exchange members. The principle source of business is the risks of members and their parents or affiliated companies, and members are able to participate in two main programmes.

The first programme is the property reinsurance programme which involves the exchange of working layer losses with predictable frequencies using a sliding scale commission plan which attempts to provide reasonable profit reciprocity. Each risk is analysed annually with special rating applied based upon past experience and prospective loss evaluations. Since the loss experience on the participants' policies will fluctuate, profit reciprocity will not occur annually on each programme, but it is felt that results should be close enough to be acceptable due to the spread of risks among the group of reinsuring members and that over a period of time, say three to five years, fairly equitable profit reciprocity will occur.

The second facility is the capacity risk facility where members of the Exchange participate in the reinsurance programmes which would otherwise be placed by the members in the international insurance and reinsurance market. By using the Exchange to reinsure a share of their property, casualty and marine risks members can expand the risk retention of their own captives using the Exchange above the working layer level and up to the level above which excess of loss re-insurance is purchased. As an alternative they can offer a proportional share of their existing excess of loss reinsurance programme to other members.

The Exchange contains a considerable amount of flexibility for its members who can either use the underwriter who works in the Exchange on behalf of the members or make their own underwriting decisions. In addition, members can choose which other members they wish to do business with and which risks they wish to participate in either on an individual basis or on a class basis. In order to ensure control over members' underwriting each member's netline capability is limited to a maximum of 3 per cent of its capital and surplus, and in addition there is a security fund which is financed at the level of three-quarters of 1 per cent of the premium ceded into the Exchange and is held on trust to pay for any losses resulting from the default of any member on the Exchange. In addition, the underwriting services company, is required to accept a participation in each risk for its own account as part of the discipline of ensuring that the underwriting on behalf of the Exchange is prudent.

The Exchange is a non-profit-making body and the administration costs are financed by a levy on the premiums ceded to the facility. At the present time these are 1 per cent for the property reinsurance programme and 3 per cent for the capacity risk programme. The benefits of the Risk Exchange are very much like those which will be the aim of any captive moving into unrelated business and are as follows:

1. To increase the captive's own retention.
2. To reduce the amount of reinsurance ceded to the commercial market.
3. To exchange profitable risks with other companies.
4. To increase the amount of non-related business underwritten.
5. To allow an individual approach to underwriting.
6. To provide experienced underwriting back-up.
7. To expand the risk spread of the captive.
8. To keep administration costs low.

The objectives of the various facilities described all relate to developing a means of business reciprocity between captives. In view of the fact that captive business is controlled business and has a very good track record so far as underwriting profit is concerned, it is clear that this type of reciprocity is one of the safest means of moving away from parent business into new areas. There are, however, other forms of reciprocity available which although not as attractive as the captive reciprocity approach are available to those who wish to consider them. The main reciprocal facilities are the business of insurers and the business produced by insurance brokers.

A number of insurers involved with captive programmes have developed pooling facilities which enable their clients to participate in the risks of captives or in the more profitable sections of their own general reinsurance portfolio. A number of these were established in the 1970s but due to the serious underwriting losses which occurred in 1982 onwards most of these facilities did not provide for the participants the benefits they originally envisaged. Presumably as market conditions improve there will be new opportunities for captives to join such facilities as a means of participating in non-captive reinsurance business.

In addition to specific pools set up for captives there is also the possibility for the captive to become a participant in the reinsurance treaties of an insurance company, particularly where a strong relationship exists with that company as part of the corporation insurance buying structure.

Theoretically, the insurance brokers also have the means of providing opportunities for captives to participate in insurance business by adding captives to their list of markets and particularly including them on reinsurance treaties that they are placing on behalf of their own ceding company clients. The difficulty with broker reciprocity is the conflict between the captive which wants to write profitable business and the broker's objective, which is to some extent to provide the best deal for his client — that is, minimal cost and resulting low and even negative profit-ability for the companies for whom the business is placed. In addition, brokers are already, as part of their natural marketing activity, exercising reciprocity through trading profitable and unprofitable accounts with underwriters. Insurer and broker reciprocity are areas worth considering, but it is important that participation involves preferred, above average business rather than participation generally in the treaties or business placed in the market.

Captives who want to go beyond these sources will be able to participate on a more general basis in reinsurance through developing their own underwriting operation or participating in underwriting agencies. There are considerable dangers in this type of expansion as the expense of developing specialised underwriting expertise is extremely high and the likelihood of being able to attract a top-level underwriter who is able to produce the right results is extremely remote. As an alternative, participation in an agency where a single underwriter is acting on behalf of a number of companies is a possibility, but the experience of underwriting agencies has been poor generally and in these cases the captive owners need to consider such a move very carefully as they are in effect passing to a third party underwriting authority over which they will have little control and in many cases where the main motivation of the underwriter is to obtain a commission on premiums written rather than to be motivated totally by the need to produce an underwriting profit.

Beyond the insurance and reinsurance market sources companies can also look towards their own company and examine the possibility of developing insurance products which can be sold to their customers and also to their suppliers. A number of captives have been formed for the purpose of providing insurance to customers and a number of others who have originally been established to handle parent risks have looked and moved into customer insurance areas. This can be an attractive source of business as it is to a large extent controlled and, in addition, provides the benefit of adding a new service to the basic business of the company and enhancing the relationship between the customer and the provider of the service in a way that can be structured to ensure continuity of relationship due to the perpetual nature of insurance contracts. Similarly, suppliers, particularly those on whom the company is reliant, are another source of business which may provide good opportunities for outside business development.

In Chapter 2 we considered the alternatives of external risk funding and rent-a-captive operation. A captive can move into this business, particularly if it has under-utilised capital and surplus, by providing such facilities for outside companies who wish to take advantage of this risk-financing technique. The advantage that such a facility offers is the development of external business, an additional return on the capital and surplus which is not being utilised for writing risks and the gaining of additional expertise in insurance management and perhaps captive management operations.

A move into this area needs to be carefully structured, particularly in relation to the rent-a-captive management agreements that are developed and the tax and legislative restraints that might impinge on captives operating from some countries. In addition there is likely to be a security risk in the event of the default of the client for whom the rent-a-captive operation has been developed; this needs to be anticipated, minimised and built into the fees charged for the provision of such a facility.

The December 1977 issue of *Captive Insurance Company Reports* summarised some of the basic criteria that captives need to take into account in deciding whether or not to move into outside business and the extent of their potential involvement. These criteria are as follows:

1. *Use of resources*
   A captive with at least US$500,000 to US$750,000 of capital and surplus free could use these resources to underwrite outside business. However, for the casualty primary captive, the likely variation in result will make it difficult to decide how free this surplus is and this problem should be taken into account.
2. *Two-times capital*
   A reinsurance intermediary has suggested that a captive should write outside business which represents two times free capital. If the captive is participating in a pool that contains only a few participants, the risks and premiums it receives may not be a function of its own ability to receive them but a percentage of its participation in the pool. The criterion of use of resources therefore argues in favour of commercial outside reinsurance which can be adapted each year to meet the individual captive's needs.
3. *Timing*
   Captive owners used to annual investment returns in their own business may find it difficult to accept the long-term commitment that outside reinsurance represents. Reinsurance results tend to be variable with durations between up and down

market results, and closing of the underwriting book does not mean in reinsurance that the results for the period at the year end are finally declared. The record of any reinsurance company needs to be examined in relation to the cycle and also to previous cycles if this is possible. The captive entering reinsurance needs to be looking at a three-, five- or seven-year time frame.

4. *Initial steps*

It is usual that captives with experience only in their own direct business are more likely to be interested in pool arrangements with other captives whose managers they know and whose parents and risks they can understand. The first phase of outside captive business development seems to be more towards this closed pool reinsurance than commercial reinsurance.

5. *Intermediate steps*

As an intermediate step it is possible for the captive to obtain commercial reinsurance from large reinsurers who have set up special treaties for this purpose. It should he remembered that in these cases the captive may be able to convince the large reinsurer to provide fronting facilities for the captive's reinsurance business, which will enable the captive to participate in external reinsurance without large amounts of new capital.

6. *Commercial reinsurance*

When the captive has been able to develop its own loss history, experience and extra capital and surplus it can then consider the possible acceptance of commercial reinsurance from primary companies. There are a number of legal and administrative problems to be overcome before this step can be taken, but the importance of the captive's reinsurance underwriter will now take precedence over all the other criteria.

Most captive owners interested in the development into outside business will have to consider most of these questions in the course of the development programme.

More generally, the following concerns need to be addressed if it is decided to pursue a move into unrelated business activity:

1. Any facility examined should be profitable and capable of being controlled.
2. It is important to continue to monitor the activity on a regular basis, reviewing performance and questioning the underwriting philosophy that is being adopted.
3. It should be remembered that in the international reinsurance business there is a considerable time-lag between the date that

the policy is originally written and the time that the premium is received by the captive and also subsequently the development of the final underwriting results.
4. It is important that if external assistance is received the capability of the managers is carefully checked and reviewed regularly.
5. The development into outside business should be understood within the parent organisation with particular emphasis on the down side exposures and any conflict with corporate objectives as described in the early part of this chapter.

It has to be understood that the track record for diversification into unrelated business has not been generally successful. The exceptions have been the use of captives to underwrite customer related insurance including areas such as extended warranty and credit life insurance which stand out as particularly successful diversifications. The reader is urged to be cautious and wary of offers placed before them from the insurance and reinsurance community. A captive insurance company is established primarily as a self-insurance mechanism and its role is primarily to contribute to the risk management objectives of its owner and help to reduce the overall cost of loss. It seems difficult to justify, given this objective, any expansion in the wider insurance industry unless this can be done in a fashion where the risks are under the control of the parent or the captives, e.g. customer business, joint ventures, key suppliers. This is not to say that a captive cannot develop into a fully fledged commercial insurance vehicle. In the introduction it was pointed out that many of today's insurers started out as captives. Perhaps the right answer is that if a corporation feels that there is money to be made in the insurance and reinsurance market, the vehicle that it should use should not be its own insurance subsidiary, dedicated to the parent risk, but an investment in another insurance vehicle that has credibility, a strong financial base and excellent management and underwriting skills.

Making Sure the Captive Remains an Effective Contributor to its Parent's Risk Financing Strategy
A captive insurance company is like any other element of a risk financing programme. It needs to be reviewed and audited on a regular basis and its role vigorously questioned. In particular a captive set up ten years ago may no longer fulfil the purpose for which it was established or may not have adapted adequately to a changing environment. The question needs to be asked regularly "Should the captive continue or should it be closed down?". To respond to this important question, I have revisited a paper on this subject I presented to the Luxembourg Rendezvous in June 1996 when the following comments were made: —

- Captive insurance companies are insurance companies that only insure the risks of their owner. They have been around for decades and, given that there are over 3,000 in the world today, they are undoubtedly a success story. Captives have survived the ups and downs of insurance cycles, the attacks of numerous tax authorities and resistance to them from insurers and insurance brokers but on the other hand, reinsurers have recognised that companies that want to take substantial amounts of risk are likely to be good business and have not resisted the captive's presence in the market.
- Captives are recognised as an effective means of financing risk. They have particular virtue when used to provide a formal means of handling self-insurance within large corporations, which some consider to be the main justification for captives.
- Like any other financing method, the necessity and viability of a captive should be examined by their owners on a regular basis, to make sure that it still contributes and has adapted to change. Yet, many owners rarely review the original strategy of the captive or the role of the captive in the operation of the company. Consequently, many captives appear to have changed very little since their formation.
- If captives are to have a continuing and dynamic role as a weapon in the armoury of the risk manager they should be critically and regularly reviewed. The captive should be constantly updated, to adapt to new ideas, concepts and environments. However there may even be situations where a captive should be shut-down rather than fixed because it no longer serves a useful purpose. Listed below are some situations in which a captive would be of more assistance to a company if it were shut down rather than maintained.

Your Captive Is Not Being Used Effectively

- The benefits of the captive are not being critically examined and consequently the captive may not be achieving the desired overall reduction in the cost of risk when account is taken of: —

  - the neutral impact on the parent, once the captive financials are consolidated with it's owner, means that the purpose of using a captive to insure property losses is questionable
  - the low retained premium in the captive and all of the operating costs involved in maintaining it including management time and the time of parent company executives. It may actually be making little, if any, contribution to the risk financing objectives of its parent

- The captive in effect only operates as a simple deductible funding vehicle, makes no real contribution and merely provides extra premium taxes to governments. It would be more cost effective to simply retain losses in-house and gain the advantages that local deductibles can achieve in motivating greater loss control activity.
- The captive is in the wrong domicile. Low tax areas may have often been chosen as much for the locale which provided an opportunity for finance directors and risk managers to enjoy sunshine, golf and a week away from the office as much as they were for good commercial reasons. This is now unfashionable and probably threatens the job of the risk manager rather than enhances his position as a sophisticated innovator in the risk financing area.
- The captive is not accessing the reinsurance market. For property insurance this is probably the only rational reason for having a captive because of the consolidation impact mentioned above. If the benefit of reinsurance is ignored and the lower costs and innovation of the wholesale insurance market are not enjoyed, the usefulness of the captive is diminished.

Your Have Too Many Captives

There is a fashion for captives in many domiciles, but this trend often has more to do with the risk manager's ego than logic. Having a number of captives may not be in the best interest of the owner. Many times, having more than one captive:

- means more money on management fees, directors, travel, audit fees etc.
- hinders the tax position as it reduces the spread of risk which is needed to persuade tax authorities that the captive is a genuine insurance operation
- wastes capital that can be better employed elsewhere in the business

Your Captive Has Become A Tax Menace!

Many captives were originally set up as a vehicle to avoid or lessen taxes. Indeed, these captives may have gained a company some tax advantages early on. However, the tax environment has changed and the tax authorities may want to review what the captive has been up to. They may want to audit the captive's structure and operations. During such investigations, auditors may go back ten years to review the Board minutes, meeting notes and instructions to the captive from the risk management department and the brokers. Not only can such an exercise be exhaustive, but the finding may prove to be embarrassing to the risk manager if he or she is seen to have exercised too much control over the captive's decision making despite clear advice that management of a captive must be seen to be elsewhere. In addition, tax audits can be expensive.

A tax enquiry usually results in companies asking their tax advisors or accountants to help them. Owners need to weigh up the strength of their tax position early on and determine whether the cost of arguing will be greater than the less complicated alternative of pleading guilty to take avoidance and paying the full tax charge.

For some companies it is better to close down the captive rather than to perpetuate long and complex discussions that may range over many years, waste management time and achieve few benefits to the company.

There is no excuse for putting together a captive that will not pass muster with the tax authorities. There are, however, captive owners who fail to understand the basic principles and still maintain captives that:

- are risk free, in the sense that the premium income exceeds the aggregate exposure to risk
- are inadequately capitalised with the result that the risk manager has to justify insuring with a company that does not have the financial capability to pay claims
- charge premiums that are not commercial, are not established on an arms length basis and do not reflect current insurance market conditions

Compounding potential problems are situations where the captive is clearly not managed and controlled in the place where it is apparently domiciled. The risk manager may direct operations while the captive managers and directors have no say in the overall strategy, underwriting policy and investment strategy. In this case tax authorities may regard the captive as being managed and controlled where the parent is based and not in the captive location, with the result that it is taxed in the country of the parent and not in the captive location. This is a particular problem for non-USA owned captive operations.

The Captive Has No Strategy

A captive should have a definitive strategy and purpose. It should have a business plan like any other subsidiary, but how many captives actually do? In reality it is often simply part of an overall risk financing and insurance buying approach decided at the centre, with the role of the captive considered well after the central strategy has been established.

Many insurers and brokers still dislike captives. They will use any opportunity to diminish the role of the captive by discouraging increased retentions and warning that in a soft insurance market is better to buy conventional insurance. These efforts to maintain the status quo and, most importantly for them, insurance premiums, commissions and fees, does not encourage a captive to develop new business or to expand its retention strategy.

Few captives are subject to a regular audit and even fewer captives are reviewed for such simple things as their retention levels on a regular basis. Indeed it is not uncommon to encounter captives whose retention levels have not changed in ten or more years despite inflation, the financial strength of the parent or changes in the insurance market. Given that many captives were established to lower insurance costs, generating aggressive risk retention strategies and reducing reliance on the insurance market, it is absurd that once established, the strategy of the company never changes and is rarely questioned!

Apart from access to the wholesale reinsurance market, there seems little justification for a captive writing property risks as any profit generated from this type of short tail insurance business ends up being consolidated with the parent. This is particularly true of European captives, which seem to have little appetite for getting involved with liability business (e.g. employers or product liability) which some feel is too risky given the long tail nature of the exposure being taken on.

However, there is in fact more justification for using a captive in the liability area, where the long tail element enables the establishment of technical reserves, IBNR's and contingency reserves. Here, the captive can replicate the advantages that insurance companies enjoy, by establishing reserves on a pre-tax basis.

A Captive Often Hinders Risk Management Objectives

Risk managers with captives spend much time travelling the world, reviewing captive accounts, attending Board meetings and reporting to management. But the time might be better spent on risk management and risk control activity.

In some cases the captive is the pre-eminent part of a risk managers job, but that can reduce the amount of assistance that should be given to the operating subsidiaries. For example, some risk-managers use the profits that captives generate from underwriting to boost the profile and apparent financial performance of their risk management department rather than to pass the financial benefits on to the operating subsidiaries, such as providing premium reductions. Not sharing the benefits of a captive may hinder the competitive performance of the business, create animosity between operating divisions, ignore the importance of controlling risks and defeat the need to target a reduction in the cost of risk. Moreover it does nothing toward distributing benefits to those working hard to manage risk.

Your Captive Is Too Expensive

If your company has decided to continue with a captive, owners still need to question its cost effectiveness. How much management time is spent on it? Is it worthwhile? Are the capital and retained earnings in the captive justifiable or could the owner get a greater return by closing down the captive and investing the funds in the core business of the company.

As difficulties arise with tax authorities, accountants and in-surance brokers (who delight in multi captives that feed their captive management business) and, lastly, consultants who create problems, to create more work and greater fees; why not take a fresh look and ask yourself — is this all really necessary?

The process of shutting down a captive can be complex and there can be many difficulties. For instance, shutting a captive down may create capital gains tax on the profit generated. Difficulties can also arise with running off the liability of long tail insurances or transferring outstanding liabilities, by portfolio transfer, to an unrelated insurer or perhaps back to the parent.

However, risk managers needs too weigh the value of a captive against the time, energy and money that is spent to maintain it. Shutting down an inefficient captive can eliminate those extra ex-penditures and help the risk manager to focus on risk management fundamentals.

This is not to say that captives have no role in the risk financing world. Some do, but the role will change as the risk manager examines the current approach and reviews the options with a critical eye. A captive can play an important role as a negotiating tool with the insurance market and can also serve as a continual reminder to top management of the company's vulnerability to losses and the need to manage and finance risk effectively. In these circumstances it may be decided not to close the captive, but rather to review it to ensure that the captive does not stagnate and continues to contribute effectively to the overall aims of risk management.

If it was not for the accounting profession, we would see much wider use of financial reinsurance and other 'off balance sheet' risk financing mechanisms that do not create consolidation problems, provide long term risk spreading and remove insurance from the calendar year cycle so beloved of insurers and accountants.

These comments should not necessarily be regarded as an argument for closing down a captive. They are designed to act as a check list for those that have the humility and self criticism that results in a regular questioning of all activity and the preparedness to admit that a cherished idea has outlived its time. With an increasing number of alternative risk transfer mechanisms arriving on the scene almost every month, it must be sensible to review these alternatives and decide whether they would improve on the captive concept or whether the captive itself should be adapted to reflect or make use of these new concepts.

The Interface Between Captives, Financial Reinsurance and Other New Concepts

For corporate insurance buyers, financial reinsurance is probably better termed finite risk insurance, as a skilful combination of "off balance sheet" financing with real risk transfer is critical if the structure is to pass muster with tax, accounting and the regulatory authorities.

Finite risk insurance is a relatively new term for a variation of financial insurance aimed at offering to corporate insurance buyers a method of risk financing which combines the "off balance sheet" advantages of conventional insurance with a minimum transfer of insurance premium.

Although financial insurance transactions have increased in popularity and are used extensively by many insurance companies, use has been mainly restricted to the insurance industry to help stabilise earnings by spreading the peaks and troughs of annual losses over a much longer period of time. Whilst the traditional method for laying off exposures has been to use the normal reinsurance market, the financial reinsurance product enables the exposure not to be wholly transferred but deferred and spread over time, thereby minimising the loss of income if the anticipated or potential losses do not arise.

The use of financial insurance and reinsurance for many years by the insurance industry is now being recognised as a possible mechanism for major corporate insurance buyers faced with uninsurable exposures, such as pollution; or where the pricing is high, capacity limited or the relationship between the premium and the cover provided ("the rate on line) seems high; and lastly where, given an efficient mechanism, self insurance might be a more cost effective approach.

As we have seen earlier in the book, many corporate insurance buyers have addressed these insurance problems by establishing their own captive insurance company. However, in most cases the need for higher cover at relatively low premium has created difficulties due to the need for substantial capitalisation, questioning by tax authorities on the deductibility of premiums and the fact that any loss within the captive (if it is consolidated with its parent) may not achieve the main objective of spreading the exposure over a longer time frame and outside of the annual accounting period.

The possibility of purchasing an insurance cover which provides the spreading mechanism, enabling the risk to be handled "off balance sheet" and achieving this at a fraction of the conventional insurance cost (if losses do not occur) is clearly an attraction and has resulted in many companies examining the finite risk insurance concept.

The essential idea of financial insurance is to eliminate volatility in earnings. The products are usually composed of two characteristics;

- an annual and/or period aggregate limit to the policy
- the policies are long term (typically five or ten years) with the total price paid based on a combination of claims payments, instalment premiums and the investment income earned on the "fund" over the policy period

Whilst there are many different types of financial insurance and reinsurance, including time and distance policies, loss portfolio transfers, spread loss programmes and funded excess of loss protection, the relevant form in this context is prospective aggregate cover, which attempts to provide a long term commitment to the insured, pricing stability and guarantee of capacity linked to a close involvement of the insured in the result of a contract.

Whilst the early products concentrated on providing risk financing stabilisation rather than insurance risk transfer, it was soon recognised that contracts which involve little, if any, transfer of risk were unlikely to provide a long term guarantee that the premiums paid would be regarded as a tax deductible expense by the tax authorities. This is a complex area but it essentially turns on two key points which relate to the definition of insurance risk. These issues are that for insurance to exist there should be:

- uncertainty with regard to the amount of a loss — "underwriting risk"
- uncertainty with regard to the timing of a loss payment — "timing risk"

Whether or not there has to be both or only one of these uncertainties for insurance to exist differs from country to country. Problems with definitions do not simply relate to the attitude of tax authorities but the approach of auditors and insurance regulators when considering whether the transactions are insurance or reinsurance. Generally speaking accountants in the USA consider that it is necessary for both the uncertainty due to the risk amount and the timing of the payment to be present, whilst in the United Kingdom accountants are currently prepared to accept timing risk alone. Recent developments in Australia suggest that "material" underwriting risk will be necessary to appease domestic tax and insurance regulatory bodies and there seems little doubt that the combined underwriting and timing risk concept will prevail all over the world in due course.

Ironically the difficulties that have developed as a result of the accountancy professions interest in financial insurance structures and the attitude of the tax authorities has been of benefit to corporate insurance buyers. This is because the increasing number of financial insurance companies has resulted in over capacity, a more competitive market and recognition that to attract business from corporate insurance buyers, the twin issues of tax deductibility and favourable accounting treatment need to be addressed. As a result the major companies in the financial insurance market place are prepared to develop structures which involved a genuine transfer of insurance risk combined with the more traditional financial insurance approach. This produces a so called "blended" programme which should substantially increase the chances of premium payments being allowed as a business expense by the tax authorities and the product itself assuming the necessary characteristics to make it an insurance contract.

The possibility of using financial insurance, finite risk insurance or financial reinsurance behind a captive insurance company is being looked at carefully by many large and well respected companies and there are a number of instances where such arrangements have been put in place with success. The development of this area of risk financing is acknowledged by most of the largest reinsurers in the world who have set up specialist teams to work together with major corporate buyers and their captives to develop tailor made risk financing products.

The contracts have mainly been aimed at combining traditional insurance exposures with a substantial level of risk funding for problem areas such as pollution liability and it is expected that these developments will continue as the issues of tax and accounting are resolved and the financial insurance market offers more than the minimum, if any, risk transfer that was a characteristic of the early financial reinsurance policies.

The use of financial reinsurance behind a captive can transform the captive's ability to provide capacity to its owner. With the problems associated with consolidation, capital requirements and an increasingly hostile tax scene, the potential use of financial reinsurance behind a captive to provide additional capacity or possibly to replace traditional reinsurance involvement is a very attractive option. For confidentiality reasons, it is difficult to give useful examples of how financial reinsurance is being used in conjunction with the captive concept, but generally speaking it is designed to permit the captive to offer substantial levels of protection to its owner and, at the same time, avoid the impact of any substantial loss on the annual performance of the captive or its parent and provide an arrangement which ensures that such a loss is spread over an acceptably long time frame. Each of these products is tailor made and the market for financial reinsurance is large and financially extremely secure. One should not leave this subject without making one final obvious point. Unlike conventional insurance and reinsurance products, financial reinsurance contain a very important element. Unlike the conventional insurance risk transfer mechanism, it is important to bear in mind that, at the end of the contract period, the insured or the captive receives most of the premium it has paid to the financial reinsurer plus investment income (less any losses) back from the company to whom it has ceded business, an important benefit for the company with high quality risk management capability.

Summary

Looking at the captive scene today it is difficult to predict future developments precisely, but there are some themes which seem likely to develop.

First, we can see the potential for major diversifications of the captive from its own business to the business of others and the potential for captives to provide a significant amount of the world's insurance capacity, and indeed for some of these captives to become major world insurers. However, developments in recent years have shown that a large number of captives that have followed this route have suffered very considerable underwriting losses, and it seems unlikely that they will in the short term expand rapidly into these uncontrolled areas in order to make the same mistake twice. However, unrelated business expansion is likely to progress on two fronts. The development of reciprocity between captives is now well established and is likely to continue on a growing basis. The getting together of major insurance buyers to form their own insurance companies to develop new capacity was accelerated by the capacity crisis in the United States in 1986 and these vehicles have become a feature of the market and may even expand into areas other than those for which they were originally established. This is already the case with early vehicles such as ACE and XL which have become an accepted sector within the worldwide insurance market place.

Secondly, the response of the insurance and reinsurance market to the growth of captives and other risk financing mechanisms will become much more positive as they recognise that a future in the corporate insurance sector has to take account of the growing and more sophisticated needs of the buyers. This response will clearly take the form of offering alternative solutions to the captive concept and this is developing as we see major insurers offering cross-class combined corporate asset protection programmes which operate over a long time cycle and provide a relatively simple mechanism for insuring all of a corporation's risks and avoiding the complexities of traditional insurance class segmentation that many insurance technicians have attempted to maintain. For the very large company these deals could operate over a twenty year cycle with the insurance markets responding in the event of catastrophe or other event which affects profitability or the company's balance sheet. This in itself will extend the risk financing concept into areas other than the traditional insurable risk area and cover business risk in its widest form.

Apart from new concepts in risk financing, which will involve integrated products develops together by insurance companies and banks, the trend towards insurance companies separating or unbundling the services that they provide will continue. There has already been a major move away from paying commissions to brokers and employing them on a fee basis related to the work they carry out. For insurance companies, the insurance element is now increasingly split away from loss control, claims handling, actuarial and other services all of which can be purchased individually in relation to the needs of the client and the quality of services available. These developments enable the buyer to put together a programme that fits their needs and integrates into one package, the best quality and range of services that are available. Whilst there is a long way to go before the reliability and quality of service is at the required level, great strides are being made and it will not be long before the major buyer deals with the re-insurance market for risk transfer purposes, the financial reinsurance and banking markets for off balance sheet funding facilities and a wide range of independent service providers who can support risk management information systems, claims handling, actuarial services, taxation advice, loss control and so on.

In addition, captive strategies will change to reflect the fact that the tax advantages to their parents have either disappeared or are likely to be removed in the near future In the United States the arguments for tax deductibility have virtually been lost in respect of pure captive business, and in the United Kingdom and elsewhere the tax authorities have changed their legislation to ensure that profits made by captives offshore are taxed domestically. With the avoidance of tax no longer a motive for captive formation, real insurance and risk-financing yardsticks will become a feature of captive feasibility studies and the long-term development of the captive. This may mean a move from the offshore locations to onshore locations where it will be much easier to administer, control and develop the company and also enable it to diversify into the underwriting of domestic insurance risks. We are already seeing a move in this direction in the United States, with a number of companies moving from Bermuda to the State of Vermont as the offshore tax advantages have disappeared.

Re-location

The possibility of a new captive location or a move away from the area where the captive is currently located, will require careful decisions as to the most appropriate long term domicile and how any move should be organised. Recent years have seen the introduction of reciprocal re-domiciliation law between a number of offshore locations including Bermuda, Barbados, Isle of Man and Gibraltar and this is expected to continue. This points to greater movement of captives between one area and another in a way which will be easy to organise and help overcome many of the difficulties, previously associated with re-domiciliation, particularly transfer of loss portfolios, capital gains tax liabilities and regulatory concerns. As well as the possibility of relocation, it may be decided that additional captives should be formed to respond to particular needs. There are many arguments as to whether this is a rational strategy. Indeed the author believes it is possible to have a single captive in the right location which will address all the needs of the typical multinational corporation. However, others believe that there can be instances where it is necessary to have a multiple captive strategy to respond to organisational issues or demands within the company or take advantage of particular geographical requirements. Relocation generally provides a number of alternatives: —

- establishing a new captive and run off the existing captive
- relocate the existing captive from one jurisdiction to another
- manage and control the captive in another location leaving it incorporated in the original location

Each of these has various advantages and disadvantages and much will depend on the locations involved, the extent of outstanding liabilities that reside in the existing captive and the various regulatory/taxation concerns.

In general, however, it is becoming easier to re-locate a captive and this will increase the opportunities for corporate buyers to review their existing strategies and implement alternative approaches.

Underwriting losses and liquidation of a number of reinsurers, many of whom provided capacity for captives, also means that there will hopefully be a greater concentration on reinsurance security in the future. Captive owners, their brokers or advisers and their fronting insurers will be more ruthless in rejecting reinsurers where there is any doubt at all about their financial security or their attitude towards claims payments.

Another factor that has been missing in the soft market conditions is the concentration on improving loss control. In hard market conditions increased cost and reduced reinsurance capacity tend to concentrate the mind of companies on improving risk management capability throughout the organisation. It is to be hoped that this can be maintained even when market conditions alter because of the greater role that captives and their parents have in ensuring both underwriting profitability and reduced losses.

The growth of captives and the increased experience in managing insurance companies is also likely to see a decline in the number of captive managers. In Bermuda many of the smaller companies have, in recent years, either sold out or merged with the bigger operations. This development will improve the quality of captive management services, particularly in the areas of management accounting insurance documentation and premium collection which in many cases have been poorly administered. More skill, particularly in insurance technicalities rather than bookkeeping, will be required All of these developments are being emphasised and supported by changing insurance business legislation in many of the captive insurance domiciles.

These developments will not harm the growth of the captive business, and we can predict steady growth and development throughout most parts of the world, including those where currently it is difficult, for legislative reasons, for captives to be established. Insurers, reinsurers and brokers will continue to show interest in the captive idea. For the insurance industry they usually offer business which is often more profitable than that provided on a general portfolio. Whether we will see the banks showing an interest in the provision of risk-financing services is more difficult to predict, but certainly if it does occur it will improve the competitive nature of risk-financing facilities and add a new and interesting dimension to the choice of strategies for financing risk.

We are already seeing a development of a significant financial insurance and reinsurance market, a large sector of which is operating from Bermuda, which in addition to providing risk-financing facilities for insurance buyers and reinsurance companies is available to assist captive insurance companies. Of particular interest to captives and perhaps one of the more significant developments has been the extension of financial insurance to companies outside of the insurance and reinsurance industry and in particular to international corporations with uninsurable exposures. It is possible that this development, linked to captive insurance companies, could herald a change in the way major corporations finance their risk and provide a complementary risk-financing service to captives by assisting with loss spreading and capitalisation requirements, enabling captives to write greater levels of risk and also become involved in difficult risk areas.

Although the concept of financial insurance is simple and has been with us for many years in the form of time and distance policies, portfolio transfers, spread loss covers and similar facilities, the policies and structures, premium calculations and underwriting criteria are complex. The two key issues are taxation and security.

Taxation with financial insurance structures continues to be an obstacle, with attitudes of revenue authorities throughout the world varying considerably. However, it remains difficult to structure a programme which is tax-deductible to the payer of the premium where the insurer's objective is to provide what is to them a 'risk-free' insurance facility.

So far as security is concerned, financial insurance transactions often involve very substantial premium payments. The security of the financial insurer or reinsurer is therefore critical. There is, however, a growing market which now includes substantial companies, most of which have well-known and highly-regarded parentage.

In the captive insurance area these facilities are increasingly used to provide capital relief for captives underwriting difficult and high-limit exposures, and in particular are being utilised to provide funding mechanisms for longer-term pollution exposures where the captive is perhaps issuing the policies to its parent on a direct basis and buying specific financial reinsurance which enables it to spread losses over a long period of time or to obtain substantial returns of premium should the loss not occur, thereby developing what is in effect an 'off-balance-sheet' risk-financing mechanism.

We can expect to see this new area of risk-financing developing, becoming more sophisticated and linking with captives to provide new solutions for large insurance buyers. There is little doubt that new products will be developed in this and other areas over coming years, all of which are aimed at developing the ability of large insurance buyers to retain greater levels of risk within their own operations, reducing their reliance on the direct and reinsurance markets and as a consequence Using the captive insurance company mechanism as a facility to decide or influence their own destiny in the risk-financing element of the overall risk management process.

There seems little doubt that the changes in the captive scene will increase over the next five years, and certainly before the fifth edition of this book is published. There will be considerable growth in captive numbers as the concept spreads to developing economies and the grip of domestic and often nationalised insurance corporations diminishes. Existing captives will grow but their role will increasingly be questioned as new and more sophisticated risk financing mechanisms become more user friendly and popular amongst a wider band of insurance buyers. The modern captive will reflect the changing trend in risk management and risk financing concepts which are expanding into wider business risk areas and not limiting themselves to the traditional insurance exposures. This will produce challenges for the insurance and reinsurance industry, opportunities for the investment and banking industry and provide attractive solutions to corporations who wish to have greater control over volatility in earnings and the impact of unexpected events on their balance sheet. There will certainly be situations where the captive will find it difficult to compete with innovative, risk financing structures which address wider risk issues. There is the likelihood that some captives will disappear and be replaced by these new concepts. Whatever happens, we should not forget that the captive initiated the trend away from conventional insurance buying, focused the attention of management on controlling losses, reduced the grip of the insurance and reinsurance market on the pricing of insurance and the capacity they were willing to provide. We should remember that without the captive, the efficiencies now inherent in the insurance industry would not have occurred and that the new concepts which are now becoming available would never have got to the conception stage without the strong influence of the captive insurance company.

APPENDIX I

LIST OF MAJOR CORPORATIONS
AND THEIR CAPTIVES

SINGLE PARENT CAPTIVES

Parent	Name of Captive	Location	Country of Parent
Airlines of Britain Holdings	Diamond Insurance Co. Ltd	Isle of Man	United Kingdom
Alcan Aluminium	Champlain Ins. Co.	Bermuda	Canada
Aluminium Co. of America	Three Rivers Ins. Co.	Vermont	United States
All Nippon Airways	Nippon Insurance Co.	Guernsey	Japan
Amatil Ltd	Matila Insurance Pte	Singapore	Australia
America Can	Mirasure Insurance Co.	Bermuda	United States
American Home Products	AHP Assurance Ltd	Bermuda	United States
Amersham International	Amersham International Insurance Services	Guernsey	United Kingdom
Amfac Inc.	Amber Insurance Co.	Bermuda	United States
Archer Daniels Midland	ADM Ltd	Cayman Islands	United States
Arianspace	Space Related Risk Reinsurance	France	France
Arthur D. Little	Acorn Insurance Co.	Bermuda	United States
ASG	ASG Reinsurance	Luxembourg	Sweden
Ashland Oil	Bluegrass Insurance Co.	Bermuda	United States
Asko Oil	Asko Insurance	Guernsey	Finland
Assi	Assi Reinsurance	Luxembourg	Sweden
Associated British Food	Talisman Guersey Ltd	Guernsey	United Kingdom
Associated British Ports	ABP Insurance	Isle of Man	United Kingdom
Associated Dairies	Asda Group Insurance Co.	Bermuda	United Kingdom
Astra Pharmaceutical	Copthorne Insurance	Bermuda	Sweden
AT&T	American Ridge Insurance	Vermont	United States
Atlas Copco	Atlas Copco Reinsurance	Luxembourg	Sweden

CAPTIVE INSURANCE COMPANIES

SINGLE PARENT CAPTIVES (cont'd)

Parent	Name of Captive	Location	Country of Parent
Australia and New Zealand Banking Group	Anzcover Pte	Singapore	Australia
Avery Products	Cardinal Insurance Co.	Bermuda	United States
Avon Products	Stratford Insurance Co.	Bermuda	United States
Avon Tyre & Rubber	Nova Insurance Co.	Guernsey	United Kingdom
Bass plc	White Shield Insurance	Gibraltar	United Kingdom
Conoco	Danube Insurance Ltd	Bermuda	United States
Control Data	Cavalier Insurance Corp.	Maryland	United States
Cookson Group	Mainsale Insurance Co.	Bermuda	United Kingdom
Coopers & Lybrand	Abacus Insurance Co.	Cayman Islands	United Kingdom
Courtaulds	Windsor Ltd	Guernsey	United Kingdom
CRA Ltd	Metals& Minerals Insurance	Singapore	Australia
Credit Suisse	Inreska Ltd	Guernsey	Switzerland
CRH PLC	Pembroke Insurance Co.	Isle of Man	Ireland
Credit Lyonais	Corelyon	Luxembourg	
Croda International	Cowick Insurance Services	Guernsey	Switzerland
CSR Ltd	CSR Insurance	Singapore	Australia
CSX Ltd	CSX Insurance	Vermont	United States
Dana Corp.	Astro Insurance Co.	Bermuda	United States
De La Rue PLC	Burnhill Insurance Co.	Guernsey	United Kingdom
Diamond Shamrock	Colonnade Assurance Ltd	Bermuda	United States
Distillers-Seagrams Ltd	Gulf Stream Insurance	Bermuda	Canada
Dixons Group	Dixon Insurance Services	Isle of Man	United Kingdom
Dow Chemical Co.	Dorinco Reinsurance	Michigan	United States
Dow Schlumberger	Tower Assurance Co.	Bermuda	United States
Dupont de Nemours	Brandywine Assurance Co.	Bermuda	United States
Electrolux	Electrolux Reinsurance	Luxembourg	Sweden
Eli Lilley	Elco Insurance Co.	Bermuda	United States
EMI Ltd	Shaftesbury Insurance Co.	Bermuda	United Kingdom
LM Ericsson	Ericsson Reinsurance	Luxembourg	Sweden
Euroc Cement	Euroc Reinsurance	Luxembourg	Sweden
Exxon Corp.	Ancon Insurance	Vermont	United States
Fauldings & Co.	Fauldinsure Pte	Singapore	Australia
Fermenta	Fermenta Re	Luxembourg	Sweden
Figgie International	Figgie Insurance Co.	Bermuda	United States
Fletcher Challenge	Terrace Insurances	Guernsey	New Zealand
Ford Motor Company	Transcon Insurance	Bermuda	United States
Foseco PLC	Long Acre Insurance	Guernsey	United Kingdom
GEC	Mgnet Insurance Co.	Guernsey	United Kingdom
Gallaher Ltd	Galleon Insurance Co.	Isle of Man	United Kingdom
Gallo Wine Corp.	Bergundy Reinsurance	Bermuda	United States
General Motors	General Insurance Ltd	Bermuda	United States
George Wimpey	Glenthorne Insurance Ltd	Isle of Man	United States

SINGLE PARENT CAPTIVES (cont'd)

Parent	Name of Captive	Location	Country of Parent
Gillette Co.	Chancery Company Ltd	Bermuda	United States
Glaxo Group	Glaxo Insurance (Guernsey)	Guernsey	United Kingdom
Goodyear Tyre	Wingfoot Insurance Co.	Bermuda	United States
Gotenborgs Hann	Scanport Insurance	Guernsey	Sweden
Grand Metropolitan	Stag Insurance	Bermuda	United Kingdom
Great Universal Stores	All Counties Insurance Co.	United Kingdom	United Kingdom
GTE	GTE Reinsurance	Bermuda	United States
Guinness	AGS Insurance Co.	Guernsey	United Kingdom
Gulf Canada	Maple Insurance Ltd	Bermuda	Canada
Halliburton Co	Highland Ltd	Bermuda	United States
Hanna Mining	Erieview Insurance	Bermuda	United States
Henkel	Henkel Insurance	Luxembourg	Germany
Hillsdown Holdings	Citadel Insurance	Isle of Man	United Kingdom
Hilton Hotels	Hilton Insurance Corp.	Vermont	United States
Hoechst Celanese Corp.	Elwood Insurance	Bermuda	United States
Hoffman-LaRoche	Intertrade Insurance & Reinsurance	Bermuda	Switzerland
IBM	WTC Insurance Co.	Bermuda	Switzerland
ICI	I.C. Insurance	United Kingdom	United Kingdom
Ikea	Dutch American Insurance	Netherlands Antilles	Denmark
Ingersoll Rand Corp.	Woodcliff Insurance	Bermuda	United States
International Thomson Org.	Highland Fidelity	Bermuda	United Kingdom
International Minerals & Chemicals	Carnforth Ltd	Bermuda	United States
James Hardie	Harflex Insurance Pte	Singapore	Australia
Johnson Matthey	Argent Insurance Co.	Bermuda	United Kingdom
Kaiser Aluminium	Stromgbus International Insurance	Bermuda	United States
Kellogg	Trafford Park Insurance	Bermuda	United States
Kema Nobel	Frej Insurance Co.	Bermuda	Sweden
Kimberley Clark	Ridgeway Insurance Co.	Bermuda	Sweden
Krupp GmbH	Wako GmbH	Germany	Germany
Kvaerner	Kvaerner Re	Ireland	Norway
Levis Strauss	Zenith International Insurance	Bermuda	United States
London International Group	Tiercel Insurance Co.	Isle of Man	United Kingdom
Louis Dreyfus	Osiris Marine & General	Isle of Man	United Kingdom/France
Lucas Industries	Les Minquiers Ltd	Guernsey	United Kingdom
Lufthansa	Delwag	Germany	Germany
Marks& Spencer	MS Insurance Ltd	Guernsey	United Kingdom
Marriott Corp.	CL International Insurance	Bermuda	United States
Midland Bank	Griffin Insurance Co.	Guernsey	United Kingdom

SINGLE PARENT CAPTIVES (cont'd)

Parent	Name of Captive	Location	Country of Parent
Mitsubishi	New Century Insurance	Bermuda	Japan
Mobil Oil	Bluefield International	Bermuda	United States
Monsanto Co.	Mongard Ltd	Bermuda	United States
National Australia Bank	Nautilus Insurance Pte	Singapore	Australia
National Westminster Bank	Lothbury Insurance	Guernsey	United Kingdom
Neste Oy	Neste Insurances	Guensey	Finland
Nokia	North European Insurance Co.	Bermuda	Finland
Norsk Hydro	Industriforsikring AS	Norway	Norway
Occidental Petroleum	Piper Indemnity Ltd	Bermuda	United States
Ocean Transport	Odyssey Insurance	Bermuda	United Kingdom
Oreal	Real Re	Luxembourg	France
Pechiney	SOFIRI	Luxembourg	France
Pepsi Co.	Andersen-Hill Insurance	Bermuda	United States
Petrofina	Brittany Insurance	Bermuda	Belgium
Pharmacia	Pharmacia Reinsurance	Luxembourg	France
Phillips	Heldor Insurance	Bermuda	The Netherlands
PLM	PLM Reinsurance	Luxembourg	France
Promotion	Nordic Reinsurance	Luxembourg	Sweden
Qantas Airways	Southern Cross Insurance	Singapore	Australia
Railtrack	Railtrack Insurance	Guernsey	United Kingdom
Rank Xerox	Bessemer Insurance	Bermuda	United Kingdom
Ready Mixed Concrete	Bedfont Insurance	Isle of Man	United Kingdom
Reckitt & Coleman	Suffolk Insurance	Bermuda	United Kingdom
Redland plc	Redland Insurance	Guernsey	United Kingdom
Revlon Inc.	Promethean Insurance	Bermuda	United States
Rexam plc	Archer Insurance	Guernsey	United Kingdom
Rhône Inc.	Sorias	Luxembourg	France
RTZ	Three Crowns	Bermuda	United Kingdom
Rothmans International	belaire Insurance	Guernsey	United Kingdom
Saab-Scania	Saab-Scania Reinsurance	Luxembourg	Sweden
Securicor	Crosskeys Ltd	Bermuda	United Kingdom
Shell	Petroleum Insurance	Bermuda	United Kingdom
Siemens	Risico AG	Germany	Germany
SKF	SKF Reinsurance	Sweden	Sweden
SmithKline Beecham	SB Insurance	Guernsey	United Kingdom
Smiths Industries	Romulus Ltd	Guernsey	United Kingdom
Sony Corp.	PMG Assurance	Bermuda	Japan
Sothebus	Fine Arts Insurance	Bermuda	United Kingdom
Spillers Ltd	Gannet Indemnity	Guernsey	United Kingdom
Standard Chartered Bank	Standard Chartered Insurance	Isle of Man	United Kingdom
Statoil	Statoil Forsikring	Norway	Norway
Stora	Stora Kopparberg Re	Luxembourg	Sweden
Suntory	Suntory Overseas	Bermuda	Japan

SINGLE PARENT CAPTIVES (cont'd)

Parent	Name of Captive	Location	Country of Parent
Superfos	Superfos Reinsurance	Luxembourg	Denmark
Tate & Lyle	Tate & Lyle Reinsurance	Bermuda	United Kingdom
Tenneco	Eastern Insurance Co.	Bermuda	United States
Tesco	Tesco Insurance	Guernsey	United Kingdom
Tetra Alfa	Tetra Laval Insurance	Ireland	Sweden
Texaco	Heddington Insurance	Bermuda	United States
Tomkins plc	Tomkins Insurance Ltd	Isle of Man	United Kingdom
Transamerica Corp.	Pyramid Insurance	Bermuda	United States
TRW Inc.	Inlake Insurance	Bermuda	United States
Turner & Newall	Curzon Insurance	Guernsey	United Kingdom
Unilever	Blackfriars Insurance	United Kingdom	United Kingdom
Volvo	Volve Group Reinsurance	Luxembourg	Sweden

APPENDIX II

THE BAHAMAS

REGULATION OF THE OFFSHORE INDUSTRY

An offshore insurer is an insurance company which is either incorporated in The Bahamas under The Companies Act, 1866, or incorporated elsewhere but registered under The Bahamas Foreign Companies Act and

    (a) is registered under the Insurance Laws of The Bahamas;
    (b) insures only risks located outside The Bahamas;
    (c) manages its business from within The Bahamas.

There are many forms of offshore insurer giving rise to various types of captive activity; the more common forms being pure captives, association captives, rental captives and broad captives.

The activities of offshore companies operating out of The Bahamas are regulated either by the original Insurance Act of 1969, or the more recent External Insurance Act of 1983.

To qualify for registration as an external insurer under the External Insurance Act of 1983, it is necessary to demonstrate inter-alia that the offshore or captive insurer would be accepting not less than $500,000 in insurance premiums from an affiliated company (related business).

All other applicants would be accommodated under the Insurance Act 1969 as 'non-resident' insurers.

Whichever legislation is considered appropriate, the application process and subsequent ongoing statutory requirements are very similar.

Under both Insurance Acts, insurers are registered to accept life/long term business or other than life business/other than long term business or both.

CAPTIVE INSURANCE COMPANIES

Once registered in The Bahamas, an offshore insurer may only carry on the particular business described in the business plan submitted at the time of application.

APPLICATION AND REGISTRATION

It is recommended that wherever possible, the applicant should meet with the Registrar of Insurance Companies prior to submitting formal application for registration. This will enable the regulator and applicant to resolve any potential problems, having been acquainted with the proposed business plan and the identity of all key parties involved. Additionally, the Registrar needs to be satisfied with

- The fitness of those key parties to engage in the proposed operation.
- The business ethics involved.
- The feasibility of the planned business.
- The security of any outward reinsurance.

Given a satisfactory application, a positive recommendation will be made by the Registrar to the Minister of Finance.

FINANCIAL REQUIREMENTS

Insurance Act 1969
Life business

Any registered insurer shall have a paid up capital of no less than $300,000.
It should be noted that the assets of the Life Insurance Fund of a registered insurer

(a) shall be as absolutely the security of the life policy-holders as though the insurer carried on no other business other than life assurance business;
(b) shall not be liable for contracts of the registered life assurer carrying on other business or insurance business for which it would not have been liable had the business of the insurer been only that of life insurance;
(c) shall not be applied, directly or indirectly, for any purposes other than those to which the fund is applicable.

Other than life business

Any registered insurer newly incorporated in The Bahamas shall have assets that exceed all liabilities by an amount of no less than $140,000.

External Insurance Act – 1983
Long term business

A registered external insurer shall have a paid-up share capital of $200,000 or such other amount as may be prescribed.

Other than long term business

A registered external insurer shall in the current year have a net worth of $100,000 if the premium income in the last preceding year did not exceed $500,000.

If the premium income in the last preceding year exceeded $500,000 but did not exceed $7,000,000, then a net worth of one fifth of the premium income is required.

If the premium income in the last preceding year exceeded $7,000,000 then a net worth of $1,400,000 plus one tenth of the excess over $7,000,000 is required.

General

Applicants should be realistic in their determination of a suitable financial base for operations; the Registrar would not normally expect to see any application with less than $250,000 initial capital, and in any event the proposed amount should be more than adequate to support the proposed volume of business.

Likewise, working ratios should be established in the light of current market thinking and practice; a net premium to capital and surplus ratio of not wider than 3:1 being considered an acceptable initial ratio. Capitalization, certainly to the statutory minimum, should be by way of cash. Companies planning to act as direct insurers may be required by the Registrar to place deposits locally.

The Bahamian registered insurer is expected to conform to the insurance regulations in force in any jurisdiction where the subject risks are located.

REPORTING REQUIREMENTS

Ongoing reporting requirements are minimal, but their importance cannot be overstated. Basically the requirements are that the insurer should continue to carry on its business in the manner described in the business plan, and that an audited financial statement should be filed annually, within six months of the close of the financial year (which may be set by the company).

Companies registered under the External Insurance Act are also required to furnish certain statutory statements indicating compliance with terms of registration.

These are

(a) Auditor's Statement of Confirmation;
(b) Director's Statement of Confirmation;
(c) Confirmatory Statement of Directors and Underwriting Managers.

REPRESENTATION

(a) Insurance Act, 1969

The Act provides that a registered insurer must have a principal office in The Bahamas and appoint a principal representative in The Bahamas. This representative should be an insurance agent as defined in the Act.

CAPTIVE INSURANCE COMPANIES

(b) External Insurance Act 1983 – underwriting manager

An underwriting manager as defined means a company incorporated in The Bahamas which operates in or from within The Bahamas as a manager or consultant providing underwriting and insurance expertise for one or more external insurers.

To obtain a licence it is necessary for an underwriting manager to demonstrate to the Registrar of Insurance that the company is able to deliver the services expected by the client, and demonstrate an acceptable level of underwriting and insurance expertise. The fee for application is $25.00, and registration and subsequent renewals are $650.00 (in effect as at 1 January 1989).

IMMIGRATION

Government does recognize that it may be necessary to import certain specialist staff; given demonstration of the need, the requisite permits should be readily available.

APPLICATION AND REGISTRATION FEES
(in effect 1 January 1989)

(a) Insurance Act, 1969

Initial registration fee	$1,000.00
Annual renewal of registration (minimum)	$ 500.00

It should be noted that the renewal fees are payable upon the anniversary date of the registration.

(b) External Insurance Act, 1983

Application fee	$ 25.00
Initial registration fee	$2,500.00
Annual renewal of registration	$2,500.00

It should be noted that the annual renewal fees are payable on the 1st of January.

THE ANNUAL FEES PAYABLE UNDER BOTH ACTS MAY BE REDUCED BY THE AMOUNT PAYABLE ($1,000.00 AS AT 1/1/89) TO THE REGISTRAR GENERAL FOR ANNUAL CORPORATE REGISTRATION UNDER THE COMPANIES ACT OF 1866.

STAMP DUTY

Stamp duty is payable on authorized capital at the rate of $60.00 flat on the first $5,000 and, thereafter, at $3 per $1,000.

EXTERNAL INSURER, NON-RESIDENT STATUS

Registration as an external insurer requires that the applicant submit with the application for registration a statement from the Central Bank of The

Bahamas to the effect that the applicant is regarded as a non-resident company for the purpose of the Exchange Control Regulations Act.

CONFIDENTIALITY

All information handled by the Office of the Registrar of Insurance is treated in confidence (but it should be noted that the share register held by the Registrar General may be inspected by the public).

THE BAHAMAS

REGISTRATION OF A NON-RESIDENT OR EXTERNAL INSURANCE COMPANY

Suggested steps in application process

1. Conduct a feasibility study with particular reference to tax considerations, reinsurance and/or retrocession availability and cost, and any fronting arrangements that may be required.
2. Familiarize yourself with requirements of the Insurance Act 1969 and the External Insurance Act 1983 and attendant regulations.
3. Contact the Registrar of Insurance Companies and the Insurance Adviser in Nassau to discuss the proposed venture. They may have some helpful advice based upon their experience with prior applications.
4. Prepare a comprehensive business plan in accordance with Sections 12–19 of Part A of the First Schedule of the Insurance Act 1969 or Sections 12(a)–(h) of Part A of the First Schedule of the External Insurance Act 1983. These sections should be looked upon as the minimum information required.
5. Collect c.v.s and three references for each director, officer and shareholder, one each from an insurer and a broker, together with a character reference. In addition, evidence of the lack of a criminal record is required.
6. Visit the Bahamas to select an underwriting manager, lawyer, auditor and banker. During this visit, arrange to visit the Registrar of Insurance Companies and Adviser to discuss the proposed application.
7. Provide local lawyer with all the requisite application material together with three alternative corporate names.
8. Lawyer will then commence the procedures necessary to incorporate the Company and submit the application for registration to the Registrar.

If the application material is in good order, a decision regarding registration should be made within three weeks.

Note it is emphasized that the above are only suggestions and that the procedures and requirements may be varied to suit individual circumstances.

THE OFFICE OF THE
REGISTRAR OF INSURANCE COMPANIES

CAPTIVE INSURANCE COMPANIES

THE BAHAMAS

SYNOPSIS OF THE BAHAMAS INSURANCE LAW AS RELATING TO OFFSHORE (CAPTIVE) INSURERS

An offshore insurance company is an insurance company which is either incorporated in The Bahamas or registered under The Bahamas Foreign Companies Act, is licensed under The Bahamas insurance legislation, manages its business from The Bahamas but insures only risks located outside The Bahamas. The subject risks may or may not be related to the parent/s of the insurer.

Offshore insurers are licensed under one or two heads ('life' and 'other than life') under one or other of the two insurance laws dealing with offshore insurance. Single parent captives, or association owned captives which insure the risks of their parent/members to the extent of at least $500,000 premium, will be accommodated under the External Insurance Act of 1983. All others will fall under the Insurance Act of 1969. Under the 1983 Act they will be known as the 'external' insurers and under the 1969 Act as 'non-resident'. Once licensed in The Bahamas an offshore insurer may only carry on the particular business described in its business plan at the time of application.

An offshore insurer may therefore be constructed in any way which may be considered appropriate by its principals or sponsors, and may plan to transact any sort of business anywhere. To obtain a licence in The Bahamas the principals/sponsors must satisfy the Registrar of Insurance Companies that the proposal is viable, that the parties concerned are all of the utmost integrity and that the reinsurance programme (if in force) is as secure as can reasonably be expected.

Furthermore, if local or national regulations are in force which may concern the conduct or placement of insurance where the subject risks are located, the Bahamian licensed insurer will be expected to conform. This may be particularly pertinent to insurers wishing to write business directly in the U.S.A., for instance under state excess and surplus line regulations.

It follows that the Registrar will look upon each individual applicant in the light of its business plan, applying such criteria as may be appropriate in that particular instance, and come to a determination as to the advisability or otherwise of issuing a licence only after fully assessing all the relevant aspects.

Some examples will demonstrate the diversity of construction and business of modern day offshore insurers:

Single parent	(a) captive insurer writing the parents' risk; workers compensation, products liability; (b) captive writing both parent and unrelated (parentally) business but similar in nature; (c) insurer writing only unrelated business (say a reinsurance of a controlled line of business from a single production source).
Multiple owned (corporations, with common interests)	captive insurer writing risks of members (trade associations for example) and covering such hard to place lines as Professional Liability, E.O. malpractice, etc.

| Multiple owned (corporations or individuals) | insurer writing unrelated business, i.e. usually reinsurance of others, general or specific in nature. |

(The term captive insurer is usually used where there is some element of the parents' risks included in the business of the offshore insurer.)

The attached table summarizes the main provisions under each of the laws with a note of the Registrar's expectations or special requirements which may be necessary on a case by case basis.

OFFICE OF THE REGISTRAR OF INSURANCE COMPANIES

CAPTIVE INSURANCE COMPANIES

THE BAHAMAS

PROVISIONS RELATIVE TO OFFSHORE INSURERS

	1969 ACT	1983 ACT	REGISTRAR
FORMATION/APPLICATION			
Minimum capital: — general — life — both	$140,000 $300,000 Not specified	$100,000 $200,000 Not specified	Minimum must be cash, and working (exposed) capital must be cash or very liquid. Letters of credit may be accepted in respect of unexposed element. Preferred initial ratio 3:1.
Net Premium — capital surplus (general business)	5:1 on N.P. to $7m 10:1 on N.P. in excess of $7m	As 1969 Act	
Shareholders, Directors and Officers:	Names addresses and referees	As 1969 Act	Names, addresses, c.v.s — three references on each police clearance certificates. Corporate shareholders — full financial details.
Local Representation both	Appoint principal representative	No specific reference but 'Regulations' may imply use of a local underwriting manager	Expects all insurers Acts, to use local underwriting managers or show good reason for not doing so.
Lawyer	Not mandatory	As 1969 Act	Use of a local lawyer for in-corporation and application process strongly recommended.
Accountant	Independent Accountant	Independent and local	Recommends local in each case.
Actuary (Life Co.)	Triennial Valuation	No provision	May impose special requirements depending on circumstances.
ONGOING REQUIREMENTS			
Books and Records	Must be available for inspection by Registrar	As 1969 Act	Will require full books and records to be kept locally.
Financial Reporting (Financial year optional)	Audited accounts to be filed within 6 months of close of financial year	As 1969 Act	May require interim reports especially from newly licensed insurers.
	Life Cos. triennial actuarial valuation	No provision	May require more frequent actuarial reports.
Other Reporting	None	Confirmatory certificates from Directors and Auditors regarding records and compliance with business plan.	

THE BAHAMAS

PROVISIONS RELATIVE TO OFFSHORE INSURERS *(contd.)*

	1969 ACT	1983 ACT	REGISTRAR
PENALTIES			
Failure to comply with statutory or Registrar's requirements may lead to	prohibition of further business and eventual cancellation. Company must make suitable arrangements for orderly disposition of business. Registrar may petition for winding-up.	suspension and eventual cancellation. No provision for disposition of business. Registrar may petition for winding-up.	
CONFIDENTIALITY	No specific provision but Registrar's office is subject to the broader provisions of the Official Secrets Act.	Express prohibition of disclosure, penalties for contravention.	

APPENDIX III

BARBADOS

INTRODUCTION

In 1983 the Government of Barbados introduced the Exempt Insurance Act 1983-9 to establish Barbados as a domicile for captive insurance activities. This Act, which is both modern and flexible, is tailored to meet the specific requirements of the parent-owned captive as well as the changing requirements of the developing international insurance market. Prior to the passing of this Act Barbados had a well-developed domestic insurance industry supervised by the Supervisor of Insurance, who is responsible to the Minister of Finance for the regulation of the Act. Since 1983 many prestigious business have come to appreciate our supportive environment and have taken steps to incorporate their captive insurance subsidiaries in Barbados.

ELIGIBILITY

To be eligible an exempt insurer must:

    i) be a body corporate whose risks and premiums originate outside of Barbados, and on whose liquidation monies payable to shareholders are payable to or for the benefit of persons resident outside the Caribbean Community;

    ii) be a body corporate incorporated under the Barbados Companies Act as a company limited by shares or as a mutual insurance company;

    iii) be a company whose paid-up capital, or in the case of an approved mutual insurance company, contributed reserves of not less than US$125,000 (BDA$250,000). Paid-up capital or contributed reserves may be in the form of valid and irrevocable letters of credit drawn on or confirmed by a bank licensed to carry on business in Barbados, and representing a stated capital account of not less than US$125,000 or such other amount as may be approved by the Minister; and

iv) have a valid licence issued by the Minister of Finance to engage in exempt insurance business from within Barbados.

The Act also makes provision for:

i) shelf or inactive companies to facilitate ease of movement between jurisdictions, and the incorporation of companies which do not propose to commence activities on formation;

ii) management companies whose main object is the provision of management services to licensees and

iii) holding companies whose sole object is to hold shares in an exempt insurance company

FINANCIAL OBLIGATIONS

An exempt insurance company shall:

i) six months after the close of the financial year or such longer period as the Minister allows, submit to the Supervisor of Insurance two copies of its audited financial statements in a form that complies with generally accepted accounting principles and such other related information as may be prescribed.

ii) submit to the Supervisor the certificate of an auditor stating whether the licensee has complied with the solvency criteria as prescribed by the Act, and

iii) in the case of a licensee engaged in long-term insurance business, submit to the Supervisor of Insurance a certificate of an actuary approved by the Supervisor, stating that the licensee's reserves are adequate to meet its liabilities.

TAX AND OTHER EXEMPTIONS

Exempt insurance companies and management companies are exempted from:

i) the payment of Barbadian tax on their profits, and gains on the transfer of all or any of their assets or securities

ii) withholding tax on any dividend, interest or return payable to any person in respect of shares or other securities of the licensee;

iii) the provisions of the Exchange Control Act.

The Minister of Finance may by agreement give assurances or guarantees to an applicant company that all or any part of the benefits contained in the Exempt Insurance Act will apply to that company for a period of 15 years.

INSURANCE SUPERVISORY DIVISION
MINISTRY OF FINANCE AND ECONOMIC AFFAIRS
BARBADOS

Steps in Licensing an Exempt Insurance Company in Barbados

1. Submit to the Supervisor of Insurance a preliminary application on the prescribed form along with a business plan, the draft articles of incorporation of the proposed company and the names and CV's of the directors. This service can be provided by an attorney-at-law.

2. The application is thoroughly analysed with particular attention being paid to –

   (a) the source of business;
   (b) the projected premium income;
   (c) the level of capitalisation;
   (d) the loss experience of similar lines of business;
   (e) the reinsurance arrangements where applicable; and
   (f) actuarial projections, where necessary.

3. If preliminary approval is given for the incorporation of the company and the issuance of a licence, the Supervisor will return the approved draft articles incorporation to the agent of the applicant for submission to the Corporate Affairs Intellectual Property Office, where the incorporation will be effected.

4. After incorporation, the company should be capitalised and a certificate obtained from the auditors in respect of the paid-up capital or contributed reserves. The auditors should also certify the balance sheet after incorporation and capitalisation.

5. The formal application can now be submitted to the Supervisor of Insurance accompanied by the supporting documents listed on the application form, an application fee of Bds $500.00 and the licence fee of Bds $5,000.00. Provided the details on the formal application, when compared with the preliminary application, do not vary so as to be unacceptable, the exempt insurance licence will be issued immediately.

BERMUDA*

1. INTRODUCTION

The principal piece of legislation governing the insurance activities of insurance companies is the Insurance Act, 1978. References herein to the the Insurance Act are to the Insurance Act, 1978 as amended by the Insurance Amendment Acts, 1981, 1983 and 1985. The principal regulations are as follows:

1. The Insurance Applications Regulations 1980 (as amended by the Amendment Regulations 1981);
2. The Insurance Accounts Regulations 1980 (as amended by the Amendment Regulations 1981 and 1989); and
3. The Insurance Returns and Solvency Regulations 1980 (as amended by the Amendment Regulations 1981 and 1989).
4. insurance Amendment Act 1995

The contents of these regulations are quite complex and we recommend that they be considered in detail before proceeding with the incorporation of an insurance company.

2. REGULATORY FRAMEWORK

Scope

The Insurance Act applies to any person carrying on insurance business in or from within Bermuda. This includes local companies, exempted companies, non-resident insurance undertakings (which sell policies through Bermudian

*This appendix is reproduced from material supplied by Conyers, Dill and Pearman.

agents on Bermudian lives and property) and overseas companies carrying on non-domestic insurance business from an office in Bermuda under a permit. Insurance agents, managers, brokers, intermediaries and salesmen not specifically employed by a registered insurance company also fall within the scope of the Insurance Act. It is essential to note that no person can carry on insurance business unless he is registered under the Insurance Act. The fundamental purpose of the Insurance Act and the Regulations is to protect the public interest.

The Insurance Act distinguishes between long-term business and general business. Long-term business consists of life, annuity or accident and disability contracts in effect for not less than five years. General business is any insurance which is not long-term business. The other distinction under the Insurance Act is between domestic and non-domestic business; non-domestic business being that underwritten by an exempted company or overseas company registered in Bermuda, carried out abroad or between such companies. The Insurance Act does not draw distinctions between captives, mutuals or any other similar types of insurance company which exist in Bermuda.

An insurance company is incorporated in the same manner as any other Bermuda company and subject generally to Bermuda company law. In addition to the material supplied with the application for incorporation, prescribed information and a copy of the proposed insurance plan must be submitted.

Part XII of the Companies Act makes specific provision for the incorporation of mutual companies. Such companies are defined as a company, other than a company limited by shares, which is authorised to engage in or carry on as its principal object insurance or re-insurance business of all kinds on the mutual principle. A mutual company is deemed to engage in or carry on insurance or re-insurance business on the mutual principle where the members who are exposed to some contingency associate themselves together by contributing by way of premiums on the basis that if the contemplated contingency befalls any member he shall receive a compensatory payment.

A mutual company is required to create and maintain a reserve capital fund of not less than $250,000. The liability of the members of a mutual company is limited to premiums or the undischarged portion thereof due to the company by any member. 'Premiums' is defined to include retrospective premiums, adjustments and calls.

Government policy

It is the Government's policy that the insurance industry he self-regulating. The Insurance Act and the Regulations are therefore drawn to require certification by the appropriate officers and professionals connected with each company on compliance with the statutory standards applicable to that company. For example, the question of the interpretation of the pro forma categories on the statutory balance sheet in respect of the admissibility of a particular asset will be left to the certifying auditor of the insurer concerned (save where there is specific requirement for the applicants for registration as insurance managers, brokers and intermediaries without underwriting powers. However, as with insurers the Minister must have regard to whether the applicant is a fit and proper person and whether he has adequate knowledge of insurance business to enable him to act in the capacity for which he has applied for registration.

Registration once granted remains in force until cancelled by the Minister on any grounds specified in Part VIII of the Insurance Act but an appeal lies to the Supreme Court within twenty-one days of the service of the cancellation order.

Products liability, professional indemnity and medical malpractice business

Certain additional information is required where the insurance company proposes to write any of the above businesses and there are guidelines published by the Insurance Advisory Committee and its subcommittee, the Insurers Admissions Committee, which are to be followed when compiling the application and business programme. The Government will permit the incorporation of insurance companies for the purpose of writing medical malpractice liability risks of groups of individual medical practitioners who are members of a recognised medical association. The guidelines require information so as to determine that:

(a) the applicants are of good standing;
(b) the proposal is based on sound insurance principles and practices,
(c) there is a strong emphasis on loss prevention and good claims handling;
(d) adequate reinsurance protection has been obtained with acceptable security;
(e) arrangements have been made to comply with insurance regulations of other jurisdictions; and
(f) there are proper management controls.

Principal representatives and principal office

The Insurance Act requires every insurer to appoint a principal representative resident in Bermuda and to maintain a principal office in Bermuda. The principal representative must be a person or body knowledgeable in insurance, who will be responsible for arranging for the maintenance and retaining custody of the statutory accounting records and for making the annual Statutory Financial Return. The principal representative may be a salaried director or manager normally resident in Bermuda who is approved by the Minister of Finance or a Bermuda registered insurance management company. The principal office required by the Insurance Act can be the office of that director or manager, or the office of the management company, and will normally be distinct from the registered office of the company where the share register, minute book, seal, etc. are kept by the company secretary.

The Insurance Act imposes various obligations on the principal representative. Amongst these, the principal representative must report to the Minister of Finance when it considers that there is a likelihood of the insurer becoming insolvent or on it becoming aware or having reason to believe that the insurer has failed or defaulted in various matters set out in the Insurance Act. Further, neither the insurer nor the principal representative may terminate the principal representative's appointment with less than thirty days' notice to the Minister of Finance or such shorter notice as he may permit.

Auditors, accountants, actuary and loss reserve specialist

Every registered insurer must appoint an independent approved auditor who will report on the Statutory Financial Return filed with the Registrar of Companies. The auditor may be the same person or firm which reports to the shareholders.

An insurer carrying on long-term business must maintain its accounts in respect of that long-term business separate from any accounts kept in respect of any other business. The Insurance Act imposes certain restrictions on payments made from the insurer's long-term business account which must be established with respect to its long-term business.

Every insurer carrying on long-term business must appoint an approved actuary and notify the Registrar of Companies of such appointment within one month after being registered or after commencing long-term business, whichever is the later (it should be noted that present policy is for the actuary to be approved as part of the pre-incorporation process of an insurer intending to carry on long-term business). The actuary is required to certify the amount of the insurer's liabilities outstanding on its long-term business.

Where the gross premiums from products and/or professional liability insurance constitute more than 30 per cent of the gross premiums written by an insurer during the relevant year, the insurer must appoint an approved loss reserve specialist for the purpose of certifying reserves, losses and loss expenses. Requirements for an applicant to qualify as an approved loss reserve specialist, include the applicant must be either an individual or partnership firm and possess adequate professional qualifications as a casualty actuary and/or possess adequate experience to assess the sufficiency of insurance reserves.

An insurer carrying on general business will need to appoint an approved loss reserve specialist where loss reserves are discounted (i.e. reducing the amount of loss reserves by discounting the time value of money), but the insurer has not met its general business solvency margin on an undiscounted basis. In such case, the discounting of loss reserves must be certified by the loss reserve specialist.

REGULATION OF INSURANCE COMPANIES

General

The Insurance Act makes no attempt to restrict the nature of the risks underwritten by an insurer, although the Minister of Finance may from time to time impose conditions relating to the writing of certain types of insurance business at the time of application to register under the Insurance Act.

The Statutory Financial Statement

The Insurance Act requires every insurer to prepare annual Statutory Financial Statements and file a Statutory Financial Return. The rules for preparing these statements are set out in the Regulations and include a uniform format of the Balance Sheet, Income Statement, Statement of Capital and Surplus and rules for valuation of assets and determination of the liabilities. These statements are not prepared in accordance with the Generally Accepted Accounting Principles (GAAP) and will therefore be distinct from financial statements prepared for presentation to the shareholders.

The Insurance Act and the Regulations do not set out to define the type of assets in which an insurer may invest, but merely the level of liquidity that must be maintained.

Except where an insurer has discounted loss reserves, neither the Statutory Financial Statements nor the GAAP Statements are required to be filed with any regulatory body, but the Minister of Finance may call for a confidential inspection of the former. Where reserves have been discounted, the Statutory Financial Statements and the Notes thereto form part of the Statutory Financial Return. In any event, the Minister of Finance has a general power under the Companies Act to inspect the affairs of all companies. The Statutory Financial Statements must be maintained at the principal office of the insurer for a period of five years.

Minimum share capital

The Insurance Amendment Act 1995 mentioned above made provision for different classes of insurance licence depending on the type of captive or insurance company and the amount of related and unrelated premium written

Class 1   Generally for single parent captives writing solely related business

Class 2   Generally for association captives and those captives writing up to 20% unrelated business

Class 3   Generally those captives writing in excess of 20% unrelated business or a captive that does not qualify as Class 1, 2 or 4

Class 4   Generally for large excess liability and catastrophe insurance companies with a minimum capital of $100 million

The Amendment also provides for minimum share capital as follows:

Class 1, 2 or 3	$120,000
Long-term business	$250,000
Class 1, 2 or 3 and long-term business	$370,000
Class 4	$1,000,000
Class 4 and long-term business	$1,250,000

The Amendment further provides for minimum capital and surplus as follows:

Class 1	$120,000
Class 2	$250,000
Class 3	$1,000,000
Class 4	$100,000,000

Minimum liquidity ratio

In general, an insurer carrying on general business is required to maintain the value of its 'relevant assets' at not less than seventy-five per cent of the amount of its 'relevant liabilities'.

'Relevant assets' is defined as certain items contained in the insurer's statutory balance sheet for general business. These items include:

(a) cash and time deposits;
(b) quoted investments;
(c) unquoted bonds and debentures;
(d) investments in first mortgage loans on real estate;
(e) investment income due and accrued;
(f) accounts and premiums receivable;
(g) reinsurance balances receivable; and
(h) funds held by ceding reinsurers.

It should be noted that unquoted equities, investments in and advances to affiliates, real estate and collateral loans are not included for this purpose.

The 'relevant liabilities' are total general business insurance reserves and total other liabilities less deferred income tax, sundry liabilities (i.e. those not specifically defined) and letters of credit and guarantees.

Annual return

Every insurer is required to file a Statutory Financial Return within twenty-one days of the Statutory Financial Statements becoming available but, in any event, no later than six months from the insurer's financial year end. The Statutory Financial Return consists of the following:

(a) a cover sheet;
(b) an auditor's report on the Statutory Financial Statements of the insurer;
(c) a declaration of the statutory ratios; and
(d) (i) in the case of an insurer carrying on general business, a general business solvency certificate and also, where loss reserves have been discounted, a loss reserve certificate (where required), the Statutory Financial Statements and the Notes to those statements; or
(ii) in the case of an insurer carrying on long-term business, a long-term business solvency certificate and actuary's certificate is the prescribed form as to the amount of the insurer's liabilities outstanding on account of its long-term business.

The declaration of statutory ratios referred to in (c) above sets forth the following ratios:

(a) the premiums to statutory and surplus ratio:
(b) the five-year operating ratio; and
(c) the change in statutory surplus ratio.

The contents of the various documents referred to above and the means of calculating the statutory ratios are set nut in the Insurance Returns and Solvency Regulations.

The business solvency certificates and the declaration of statutory ratios must be signed by at least two directors of the insurer (of whom one must be a director resident in Bermuda if the insurer has a director so resident) and the insurer's principal representative in Bermuda. In signing the business solvency certificate, the directors and the principal representative are required to state whether the business solvency margin and the minimum liquidity ratio have been met. Further, the auditor is required to state whether in his opinion, it was reasonable for them to do so and whether the declaration of statutory ratios complies with the requirements of the regulations.

The loss reserve certificate is required where an insurer, carrying on general business, discounts loss reserves but fails to meet the minimum general business solvency margin on an undiscounted basis. The loss reserve certificate, signed by an approved loss reserve specialist, must state to what extent the insurer has complied with the regulations on discounting loss reserves.

Any statement in the Statutory Financial Returns indicating that the insurer has failed to meet the various statutory criteria or any adverse opinion or inability to certify that they have been met, is not of itself a statutory offence, but is likely to trigger an enquiry by the Registrar of Companies. The statutory records themselves, as stated above are not required to be filed and will not be open to public scrutiny in any event.

It should also be noted that where the insurer's accounts have been audited for any purpose other than compliance with the Regulations (for example, purusant to the Bye-laws on behalf of the shareholders) a statement to that effect must be filed with the Statutory Financial Return

Exemptions

Section 56 of the Insurance Act provides that the Minister of Finance may direct that certain provisions of the Insurance Act shall not apply to a particular insurer or shall apply to it subject to such modifications as may be specified in the direction. In general, the provisions to which Section 56 apply are those dealing with the margin of solvency, the solvency certificate, statutory financial statements and the statutory financial returns.

By virtue of Section 56, the Minister of Finance has the power to exempt an insurer or portions of that insurer's business from compliance with some or all of the statutory accounting provisions. It is recognised that certain types of companies, such as protection and indemnity clubs, which are only insuring member's risk, may not be able to meet such requirements and companies writing substantially or exclusively the risks of their parent and/or affiliated companies may find it inconvenient to do so and that both, in effect, are generally outside the 'public interest' which the Act seeks to protect.

5. TAXATION CONVENTION BETWEEN BERMUDA AND THE UNITED STATES

The taxation convention (the 'Treaty') which became effective on 2nd December, 1988 covers, among other things, federal income taxes and excise taxes in relation to insurance business. The tax exemptions only apply for certain Bermuda insurance companies which meet various criteria; such as being beneficially owned, directly or indirectly, more than 50 per cent by a combination of individuals resident in Bermuda or the United States or citizens of the United States. For further information, this Firm has prepared a separate memorandum on the Treaty which may be made available on request.

6. TAXATION, GOVERNMENT, FEES, STAMP DUTY AND EXCHANGE CONTROL

Taxation

At the date of this memorandum, there is no Bermuda income, corporation or profits tax, withholding tax, capital gains tax, capital transfer tax, estate duty or inheritance tax payable by an insurance company or its shareholders, other than shareholders ordinarily resident in Bermuda.

An insurance company may apply for and is likely to receive from the Minister of Finance of Bermuda under the Exempted Undertakings Tax Protection Act, 1966 an undertaking that, in the event of there being enacted in Bermuda any legislation imposing tax computed on profits or income, or computed on any capital assets, gain or appreciation, or any tax in the nature of estate duty or inheritance tax, such tax shall not until 28th March, 2016 be applicable to such company or to any of its operations or to the shares, debentures or other obligations of such company except in so far as such tax applies to persons ordinarily resident in Bermuda and holding such shares, debenture or other obligations of the company or to any land leased or let to the company.

Government fees

An insurance company, like all other companies incorporated or carrying on business in Bermuda, is required to pay an annual government fee based on authorised share capital and share premium as follows:

Paid up Capital less than $120,000	$3,360
Paid up Capital between $120,001 and $1,200,000	$5,040
Paid up Capital between $1,200,001 and $12,000,000	$6,720
Paid up Capital between $12,000,001 and $100,000,000	$8,400
Paid up Capital between $100,000,001 and $500,000,000	$15,000
Paid up Capital $500,000,001 or more	$25,000
Business fee	$2,205

An annual declaration is submitted each year at the time of payment of the annual fee. This declaration states only the type of business carried on by the company.

Stamp duty

Generally as of 1st April, 1990, stamp duty is no longer payable by, or in respect of matters concerning, exempted and permit companies, whether in respect of share capital or otherwise.

Exchange Control

Bermuda is independent for the purposes of exchange control which is operated under the Exchange Control Act 1972 and related regulations. Exempted and permit companies are designated non-resident for exchange control purposes. The non-resident designation allows these companies to operate free of exchange control regulations and enables them to make payments of dividends, to distribute capital, to open and maintain foreign bank accounts and to purchase securities, etc. without reference to the exchange control authorities.

APPENDIX V

BRITISH COLUMBIA

British Columbia's Insurance (Captive Company) Act provides for three types of captives.

- Pure captive – owned by and insuring a single parent or group of related companies.
- Association captive – owned by and insuring the members of an association, usually an industry or trade association or their directors and officers.
- Sophisticated insured captive – owned by and insuring a group of related or unrelated companies spending a certain amount on insurance premiums and demonstrating certain expertise in insurance matters.

  British Columbia does not itself offer direct tax incentives, but tax-related financial advantages to locating a captive in British Columbia are listed below.

- Most insurance premiums paid to off-shore insurers are subject to a 10 per cent federal excise tax. Although many companies avoid this tax by paying their premiums to a licensed Canadian insurer which then reinsures direct to the captive (fronting), there is still a substantial fronting fee ranging from 7 per cent to 12 per cent or more of gross premiums. Having a British Columbia captive rules out federal excise tax and may reduce or eliminate fronting fees.
- Foreign accrued property income (FAPI) tax provisions are not applicable to a B.C. captive.
- Federal withholding tax (FWT) does not apply since payments are not made out of the country.

CAPTIVE INSURANCE COMPANIES

REGULATORY REQUIREMENT

The objective of the Insurance (Captive Company) Act is to create a balanced regulatory environment. On the one hand, it is competitive with other jurisdictions and does not impose high compliance costs. On the other hand, it provides a framework within which the companies can operate while maintaining an appropriate level of public protection. Key features of the new legislation are explained as follows:

I. APPROXIMATE CAPTIVE INCORPORATION FEES AND EXPENSES IN CANADIAN DOLLARS

	British Columbia	Bermuda	Barbados
1. Attorney's fees (basic incorporation)	$ 500	$ 3,300	$ 3,300
2. Corporate equipment and miscellaneous seals	125	330	—
3. Advertising costs	—	165	—
4. Government fee	250	2,970	—
5. Application fee for permit to incorporate	—	165	530
6. Stamp duty on minimum authorized capital (1/4 of one per cent)	—	400	—
7. Filing fee	—	50	—
8. Insurance application for registration	500	130	330
9. Insurance registration fee	2,500	2,640	3,300
10. Audit certification or initial capital and opening balance sheet/actuarial review	—	—	1,320
	$ 3,875	$10,150	$ 8,780

In addition to these estimated start-up and operating costs, it must be remembered the expense of doing business off-shore is high. Airfares, hotel bills and travelling time should be taken into account.

II. ESTIMATED ANNUAL ADMINISTRATION FEE AND EXPENSES

	British Columbia	Bermuda	Barbados
1. Management fee	$20,000	$26,400	$26,400
2. Attorney's fees (basic)	200	3,960	3,960
3. Government fee	—	1,980	1,980
4. Insurance registration fee	2,500	2,970	3,300
5. Accounts/audit	10,000	13,200	13,200
6. Miscellaneous expenses	1,000	1,320	1,320
	$33,700	$49,830	$50,160

---

1. *Incorporation and registration*

A captive insurance company must be incorporated under the British Columbia Company Act.

Given an acceptable corporation business plan and application form, the superintendent of financial institutions will process registration in approximately two weeks. The plan must provide the requisite information about the company's owners, managers, operating plan and financial projections in the prescribed format.

2. Capital requirements

Sufficient capital will be required to support the insurance program being undertaken.

Minimum capital is $200,000

3. Permitted classes of business include

- property;
- casualty;
- liability including products, directors and officers;
- errors and omissions; and
- marine.

Not permitted is insurance of the general public:

- personal lines;
- life, health, sickness and accident; and
- motor vehicle insurance.

4. Reporting requirements

Annual reports primarily comprising audited financial statements and an actuarial report prepared by an approved actuary will be required.

The superintendent has the authority to request additional or more frequent reports if necessary.

5. Enforcement

Government will not interfere on a day-to-day basis unless necessary to protect the public, especially if a captive attempts to circumvent the intent of the act and insure the general public.

6. Directors, officers and managers

The directors and officers of both the captive insurance company and, if appointed, the independent captive management company are required to establish competence and integrity.

Failure to comply will be grounds for suspension or cancellation of registration.

7. Investments

No specific rules are imposed; however, investments will be reviewed with the audited financial statements.

Having demonstrated prudent behaviour, a captive insurance company will have complete flexibility.

8. Fees

- Initial application $500.
- Initial registration $2,500.
- Renewal of registration $2,500.

CAPTIVE INSURANCE COMPANIES

INSTRUCTIONS FOR APPLYING TO REGISTER A CAPTIVE INSURANCE COMPANY

General

This information kit contains the application for registration as a captive insurance company, a biographical profile form and applications for approval to act as an auditor or actuary of a British Columbia captive insurance company.

All sections of the application form must be filled in and submitted together with all other material requested and the application fee of $500 (Cdn.).

Copies of the biographical profiles form should be submitted as requested by the application. All sections of the profile must be filled in. No substitute for the biographical profile form will be accepted.

Ownership

The name of every person owning shares in the organization of the applicant, the type and extent of ownership and the voting power exercised by that ownership must be provided to the superintendent.

Business plan

A business plan for the proposed captive insurance company must be submitted.

Projected premium revenue and types of risk

A statement projecting contemplated premium revenue from insurance and reinsurance for at least three years must be attached. The types of risks to be insured must also be described. This statement must distinguish projected premium revenue for each class of insurance and must include estimates for low, best estimate and high claims scenarios

Letters of credit

If letters of credit are to be used in financing the captive insurance company, they must be previously approved as to form by the superintendent and submitted with the business plan.

Guarantee or indemnity

Where a captive insurance company enters into a guarantee or an indemnity under which a parent, sophisticated insured, member organization or affiliated corporation may incur liability for the benefit of the captive insurance company, a copy of the guarantee or indemnity agreement must be filed with registration materials.

Approval of the superintendent

All applications for registration will be reviewed by the Superintendent of Financial Institutions and/or staff. Final approval or disapproval will be made by the superintendent, on whatever terms and conditions he may require pursuant to Section 6 of the Insurance (Captive Company) Act.

Location of records of captive insurance company

All books and records necessary for statutory inspection of the captive insurance company must be located in British Columbia at all times.

STEPS IN FORMING A CAPTIVE INSURANCE COMPANY

The steps below should be followed in the process of incorporating and applying for registration of a captive insurance company in British Columbia.

1. Arrange a meeting with the Superintendent of Financial Institutions and/or staff to discuss the proposed captive insurance company. In the case of association captives, the superintendent will wish to meet with key officers of the association before registration.
2. Arrange to have the captive insurance company incorporated under the British Columbia Company Act.
3. Prepare the application for registration and other documents required for registration (see Application for Registration as a Captive Insurance Company for a list of required documents).
4. Submit five copies of all incorporation and registration materials (2 and 3 above) to the Superintendent of Financial Institutions for review, together with the $500 (Cdn.) non-refundable application fee.
5. The superintendent may require further information before completing registration.
6. If the application is accepted and approved, registration will be issued.

APPENDIX VI

BRITISH VIRGIN ISLANDS

A Summary

The Government of the British Virgin Islands passed the Insurance Act 1994 on November 21, 1994. The new legislation became effective on February 1, 1995. Significant provisions follow:

Licensing:

The insurance legislation embodied in the Insurance Business (Special Provisions) Act of 1991 has bee repealed.

The Act contains a number of parts which are common to many offshore insurance jurisdictions, but others are innovative.

Administration of the Act is the responsibility of the Commission of Insurance who shall report to the Minister of Finance.

All insurers carrying on Insurance Business in or from within the Territory shall be licensed under the Act. Such licences are renewable annually with effect from January 1st.

All insurance managers, agents, brokers and loss adjusters carrying on such business in or from within the Territory shall be so authorised under the Act.

Capital

The minimum fully paid capital requirements are US$100,000 in respect of general business, US$200,000 in respect of long term business and US$300,000 in respect of insurers writing both general and long term business.

Every insurer licensed under the Act shall:

    a. Maintain a principal office in the Territory

    b. Maintain an Insurance Manager resident in the Territory
    c. Where required, appoint an approved Actuary for its general business
    d. Appoint an approved auditor who will prepare a statement of affairs to be submitted within three months of the close of each financial year

Such statement and exhibits shall be in the form and content prescribed by the Regulations.

Prohibited Investments Include:

    1. Unpaid balances due by agents or other insurers that are more than six months overdue.
    2. Investments in office furniture or equipment.
    3. Unpaid capital.
    4. Other investments prohibited by the Act or Regulations.

Insurance Managers, Agents and Brokers:

Insurance Managers, Agents and Brokers are required to hold a Certificate of Authority in order to act as such in or from within the Territory. Such certificates will be issued provided the Governor satisfied that the resident applicant has the insurance knowledge and expertise required to act in the capacity applied for.

Insurance Managers:

Insurance Managers are specifically obliged to report to the Commissioner when they acquire knowledge that an insurer:

    a. Risks becoming insolvent.
    b. Is not in compliance with the Act.
    c. Has defaulted on the payment of liabilities.
    d. Is experiencing a serious state of affairs prejudicial to policy holders.
    e. Is a defendant in criminal proceedings in any Country.
    f. Has ceased to carry on business.

Auditors and Actuaries:

Auditors and Actuaries have similar reporting responsibilities similar to those of Insurance Managers and such reports to the Commissioner shall not constitute a breach of confidentiality.

Insurance Brokers:

Insurance Brokers are required to produce any form or type of security acceptable to the Minister.

Confidentiality

All documents and records relating to the *incorporation* of an Insurer, Insurance Manager, Broker or Agent as maintained by the Registrar of Companies are a matter of *public record*.

    All documents and records submitted to or information disclosed to the Office of the Commissioner of Insurance are absolutely privileged but the restriction on disclosure does not apply when such disclosures are made to the Governor or to any person for the purpose of discharging any duty under the Insurance Act or upon the order of Court of competent jurisdiction for the purposes of criminal or civil proceedings.

The Governor may also sanction the release of information to a recognised international organisation or a law enforcement office in a foreign country for the purposes of legal assistance in the investigation of any criminal activity. The Governor may also sanction the release of information to assist foreign insurance regulators in the discharge of their duties.

Unadmitted Insurance

The prohibition of dealing with unlicensed insurers does not apply to:

a. Reinsurance Contracts
b. Domestic Insurance, provided such contracts are authorised by the Minister.
c. Contracts placed with Lloyd's of London.

Exemptions

Acting upon the recommendation of the Commission of Insurance, the Governor may grant any insurer exemption from any or all of the provisions of the Act or Regulations or may grant such exemption subject to certain limitations or conditions.

INSURANCE REGULATIONS – 1995
INSURANCE COMPANIES

A Summary

a. Licenses
   To be licensed utilising the application form prescribed in the regulations.

b. Annual Statements
   Every annual statement shall be in the form specified in the regulations and shall be supported by the report of the approved auditor

c. The Certificate of the Actuary
   The Certificate of the approved Actuary shall be in the form specified in the Regulations

d. Solvency Margins
   Insurers should maintain a minimum margin of solvency. (The amount by which the total value of an insurer's assets exceed the total amount of its liabilities).

   1. General Business

   (i) Where the net retained annual premium of the insurer does not exceed $1,000,000, the prescribed amount is $200,000.

(ii) Where the net retained annual premium of the insurer exceeds $1,000,000, but does not exceed $5,000,000, the prescribed amount is twenty percent of said net retained annual premium;

(iii) Where the net retained annual premium of the insurer exceeds $5,000,000, the prescribed amount is $1,200,000 plus ten percent of the amount by which the said net retained annual premium exceeds $5,000,000.

2. Long-Term Business

In the case of an insurer carrying on long-term business only, the prescribed amount is two hundred and fifty thousand dollars.

3. General and Long-Term Business

In case of an insurer carrying on both general business and long-term business, the prescribed amount is two hundred and fifty thousand dollars plus the amounts required for general business.

Note:

"Net retained annual premium" means the gross premium income earned in respect of general business during any financial year of the insurer reduced by any premiums paid by the insurer for approved reinsurance during such financial year.

e. Allowable Assets

(a) Cash in hand or on deposit with financial institutions approved by the Commission;

(b) Bonds, debentures or other evidence of indebtedness issued or guaranteed by

(i) The government of the United Kingdom or of any Dependent Territory thereof;

(ii) The government of the United States of America or of any state thereof;

(iii) The government of Canada or of any province thereof; or

(iv) Any other government approved by the Commissioner;

(c) Bonds, debentures or other evidence of indebtedness issued or guaranteed by any municipal corporation and secured by rates or taxes levied and collectable by such municipal corporation under the authority of any of the governments mentioned in sub-paragraphs (i), (ii), (iii) or (iv) of paragraph (b);

(d) Other securities quoted on an appointed stock exchange not exceeding twenty percent of the total assets of the insurer;

(e) Premiums receivable;

(f) Reinsurance balances receivable;

(g) Accounts receivable not of provision for bad and doubtful debt;

(h) Irrevocable letters of credit issued by financial institutions approved by the Commissioner.

f. Non Allowable Assets
  (a) Investments in and advances to the insurer's Parent Company or any of the insurer's subsidiaries or affiliates unless specifically approved by the Commission.
  (b) Real Property or mortgages on real property; and
  (c) Securities which are not quoted on an appointed stock exchange

g. Valuation of Assets
  The value shall be determined by the market value or if not ascertainable, valued in accordance with G.A.A.P. practices acceptable by the approved auditor, and acceptable to the Commissioner.

h. Calculation of Liabilities
  The amount of total liabilities shall he determined in accordance with G.A.A.P. practices considered appropriate by the approved auditor, an acceptable to the Commissioner.

i. Books and Records
  Every insurer shall maintain at its principal office such books of accounts and records of its insurance business and financial affairs. Such books and records shall enable the Commissioner of Insurance to conduct an examination into the affairs of the Insurer and must include such information as specified in the regulations. In the event that the Commissioner considers the books and records of an Insurer have been maintained in an improper fashion, he shall appoint a competent accountant to conduct by examination at a cost not exceeding $2,000 per day which shall be born by the delinquent insurer.

j. Fees Payable to the Government
  Fees payable by an insurer:
  (a) Application fee to carry on business in or from within the Territory $ 500.00
  (b) Issue and Annual Renewal fee of licence $2,000.00

  Fees payable by Insurance Managers, Insurance Brokers and Insurance Agents:
  (a) Application for Certificate of Authority $ 250.00
  (b) Issue and Annual renewal of Certificate of Authority $ 500.00

  Fees Payable by persons wishing to inspect the Register of Licensed Insurers, authorised Insurance Managers, Insurance Agents, Brokers and Loss Adjusters. $ 50.00

  N.B. All licenses are Certificates of Authority expire on December 31st. The fee for those issued on or prior to June 30th shall be the Annual fee. Those issued on or after July 1st, the fee shall be fifty percent of the Annual fee.

  Note: We are grateful to Caribbean Insurance Management Ltd, Tortlola., D.V.I. for permission to publish the above which is extracted from one of their brochures.

APPENDIX VII

CAYMAN ISLANDS

THE INSURANCE LAW, 1979 AND REGULATIONS

Licencees

The Insurance Law, 1975 (the 'Law') requires that any person transacting insurance business in or from within the Cayman Islands must be licensed and must comply with the provisions of the Law and Regulations. A person under the Law includes an insurance company, a mutual insurance office, an association of underwriters, an insurance agent, broker, sub-agent and, finally, an underwriting manager.

Categories of insurer

The Law establishes four categories of insurers subject to varying requirements, as follows:

1. Class A (under section 4(7)) –
   an external insurer with its principal or registered office located outside the Caymans and where legislation for the regulation and supervision of insurers is acceptable and is approved by the Government.
2. Class A (under section 4(4)) –
   either an external or a local insurer carrying on business in or from within the Caymans.
3. Unrestricted Class B (under section 4(5)) –
   an 'exempted insurer' carrying on other than domestic business from within the Caymans.

4. Restricted Class B (under section 4(6)) –
an 'exempted insurer' which accepts insurance business, other than domestic business, from its shareholders, members or such other persons as may be specifically approved by the Governor.

Exempted insurer

An 'exempted insurer' means an insurer which is either:

- An exempted company incorporated under the Companies Law. To be so incorporated, the company must not trade in the Cayman Islands except in the furtherance of its business carried on outside the Caymans.
- A non-resident company registered as a foreign company under the Companies Law. This allows companies incorporated outside the Cayman Islands, who do not wish to establish a subsidiary company, to register a branch as their place of business.
- A non-resident company incorporated under the Companies Law.
- A partnership, shareholding or other acceptable mutual association of one or more members having a common interest.

The Superintendent of Insurance (the 'Superintendent') has indicated that it is preferred that new applicants for an insurer's licence be incorporated as an 'exempted company' under the Companies Law.

Domestic business

The Class A categories of insurers are permitted to write domestic business within the Cayman Islands. In this context, it should be noted that reinsurance is specifically excluded from the definition of 'domestic business'.

Net worth

The principal advantage for a captive being licensed as a Restricted Class B insurer is that it need not comply with minimum 'net worth' requirements, although the Law requires the Superintendent to be satisfied at all times as to the soundness of each licensee's operation. To assist in such assessment, the Superintendent will require annual duly audited financial statements for all Class B licensees. Restricted Class B licensees should note that although there is no specific net worth requirement, the Superintendent will take particular interest in the relationship between their actual net worth and their premium income.

Net worth means the excess of assets (including any properly secured contingent or reserve fund) over liabilities, excluding liabilities to partners or shareholders. Section 4(8) of the Law stipulates that no insurer (other than a Restricted Class B insurer) may operate with a net worth of less than:

(a) $100,000 C.I. for an insurer effecting general business but not long-term business;
(b) $200,000 C.I. for an insurer effecting long-term business but not general business;

(c) $300,000 C.I. for an insurer effecting both general and long-term business.

(One Cayman dollar equals approximately $1.20 U.S.)

Licence application

There are two methods under the Law for making application for a licence. The first is for those insurers already carrying on business at the date of commencement of the Law and who, under section 3(3), may apply for the appropriate licence within six months of the Law's enactment. Such a licence is valid for twelve months retroactive to June 17, 1980 when the Law commenced, and must be applied for by December 16, 1980. This method of application is transitional in nature to allow existing insurers up to twelve months to arrange for an application for a permanent licence under section 4(2). It would appear that the twelve month licence will be given automatically on application and payment of the appropriate fee. Although the Law does not require it, the Superintendent has indicated that application for twelve month licences should be made using the prescribed forms as sufficient information is required to ensure that each licensee is in a sound financial position and is carrying on business in a satisfactory manner.

The second method of application is under section 4(2) and must be made by:

(a) all new insurers;
(b) existing insurers who choose not to apply for a temporary licence under section 3(3):
(c) existing insurers who have not applied under section 3(3) by December 16, 1980; or
(d) existing insurers licensed under section 3(3) prior to their temporary licence expiring on June 16, 1981.

Those companies who apply for an indefinite licence (under section 4(2)) prior to the expiry of their twelve month licence (under section 3(3)) will be given the pro-rata benefit for the unexpired portion of the licence fee. As a precautionary measure, any new insurer should, prior to incorporation, apply to the Superintendent for approval in principle for the issue of a licence.

There are two types of application forms for insurers. Included in Appendix B is a copy of the Insurance (Forms) Regulations, 1980, which includes in Schedule 1, 'form 1' for Class A insurers and 'form 2' for Class B insurers. Recognizing the considerable diversity of insurers in the Cayman Islands, the application forms have been drafted to allow some degree of flexibility to provide additional information or comment where the detail sought may not be appropriate.

Application information

Information required on application includes the following principal requirements:

353

- The name of the applicant. In this regard, the Superintendent has indicated that there should be no confusion arising from the use of names which may indicate that a company licensed under one category is doing business under another; also the term 'Insurance Company' should be restricted to companies which are true insurers.
- The address of the designated office in the Caymans where full business records will be kept; in certain circumstances approval may be obtained for such records to be maintained outside the Cayman Islands. It should also be noted that separate accounts are to be kept for insurance business (segregated between general and long-term insurance business for a Class A insurer) and other business; in addition, the respective assets and liabilities must also be segregated.
- Where an agent or service company is to be used, details of such companies including evidence of their agreement to provide such services.
- Name of person resident in the Cayman Islands authorized to accept notices and service of process in legal proceedings on behalf of the applicant.
- Names, addresses and nationalities of shareholders, directors, managers and officers with evidence that none of these persons has a criminal record. In the event that nominee shareholders are used, details of the principals are to be given and where a shareholding is through a chain of companies, the link to the ultimate owner should be disclosed. Also resumes of management with particular emphasis on their experience of the insurance industry, together with three references including one from an insurer or reinsurer and one from a bank. It should be emphasized that the information filed with the Cayman Islands authorities pursuant to the Law is not a matter of public record. The strict requirements of section 11 of the Insurance Law ensure the maintenance of confidentiality.
- Various instruments (or proposed instruments) of constitution verified by statutory declaration and duly authenticated.
- Details of auditors and, for a Class A insurer where the application includes long-term business, an actuary together with an acknowledgement from each of these parties accepting appointment. Also the insurer's financial year-end together with the country whose generally accepted accounting principles are to apply.
- For an existing insurer, the annual accounts for the previous three years are to be attached. For a new applicant, a written undertaking is to be attached to disclose minimum net worth together with a statement as to how the net worth is to be provided.
- A business plan is required from all applicants except a Class A approved external insurer. The Superintendent has requested that this plan should give as much detail as possible covering the ensuing three year period for the following:
  - classes of business to be written;
  - premium volumes;
  - proportion of business to be reinsured;

- nature of reinsurance program;
- retention of net premiums and maximum liability per risk and catastrophe.

- The business plan is by far the most important part of the application and sets the limits on the nature of future business. If the annual certificate of compliance is to be signed by the auditor, it is recommended that the business plan be discussed with the auditor prior to submission of the application for licence.

Change in business

Any change in the nature of an insurer's business from that stated in the business plan requires prior approval from the Superintendent. Any change in other information filed with the application requires to be notifed immediately to the Superintendent, but does not require prior approval.

Annual reporting

All licensed insurers are required to make an annual report to the Superintendent within six months of the end of their financial year. The purpose of the report is to assure the Superintendent that business continues to be conducted in accordance with the licence application.

Discretionary powers

The Law allows the Cayman Islands authorities, through the office of the Superintendent of Insurance, certain discretionary powers including the following:

- The power to revoke the licence of an insurer;
- The power to exempt any insurer from any provision of the Law;
- The power to prescribe that investments of a specified class require prior approval and that any investments of such class already made be realized within a specified period (this does not apply to Restricted Class B insurers);
- The power by regulation to prescribe, establish and vary
  - capital and liquidity margins and ratios;
  - forms to be used.
  - the format for any returns.

Regulations

To date, the only regulation enacted relates to the forms to be used (refer Appendix B). No specific solvency ratios have been set other than the 'net worth' requirements under section 4(8)1 and there is no indication that the authorities intend to introduce regulations in this area in the near future.

Underwriting manager

The majority of captive insurers in the Cayman Islands are managed by an 'underwriting manager', defined in the Law as a person operating in or from within the Islands who, as manager or consultant (but not as a bona-fide employee), provides underwriting and insurance expertise for insurers.

Licence

An underwriting manager is required to make application for a licence within six months of the Law becoming effective. The prescribed application form is included in Appendix B (Form 6 of Schedule 1) and must be filed with the Superintendent by December 16, 1980 together with a licence fee of $5,000 C.I. Such licence may be either temporary (expiring June 16, 1981) or for an indefinite period and requires payment of an annual fee of $5,000 C.I. by January 15 of each year.

Annual information

Within six months of the end of each financial year, an underwriting manager is required to submit the following information:

- A list of all insurers for whom the underwriting manager is acting, and
- Written confirmation that the information included in the licence application remains correct and gives a full and fair picture of his activities.

Integrity

The underwriting manager is required by Law to use his best endeavors to carry on insurance and reinsurance business only with insurers of sound reputation and if he ever has cause for concern regarding the integrity or soundness of an insurer, he must report the fact forthwith to the authorities.

ACCOUNTING AND AUDIT REQUIREMENTS

Appointment of auditor

The Law requires that every licensed insurer, other than an approved external insurer, must appoint 'an independent auditor' who shall audit the insurer's annual financial statements which are to be prepared 'in accordance with generally accepted accounting principles' (section 7(3)).

Written acceptance

Insurers subject to this requirement must appoint an independent auditor and receive the auditor's acceptance in writing prior to making application for a licence under section 4(2). Existing insurers who have already applied under section 3(3), or intend to so apply prior to the December 16, 1980 deadline, have twelve months from June 17, 1980 to appoint an auditor.

Auditing standards

Coopers & Lybrand, as well as the other international accounting firms whose partners are members of the Cayman Islands Society Professional

Accountants, adhere to generally accepted auditing standards which are not less than those used in Canada, the United States and the United Kingdom and abide by the standards set by the International Accounting Standards Committee.

Accounting principles

The Law requires that generally accepted accounting principles (GAAP) be used in the preparation of annual audited financial statements. Although the insurer may choose the GAAP to be used, the Superintendent has indicated that Canadian, United States or United Kingdom generally accepted accounting principles should be used and that statutory accounting principles which differ from GAAP will not normally be permitted.

Choice of auditor

The Law does not stipulate that the appointed auditor must be a local firm although the Superintendent of Insurance has indicated that the appointment of a local firm is recommended to facilitate communication with the regulatory authority. In addition, all records must be maintained at the insurer's designated office in the Cayman Islands unless the proper approval has been obtained to hold them elsewhere.

Additional audit requirements

In addition to auditing the annual financial statements and confirming in writing compliance with section 9 of the Law, the Superintendent has recommended that the independent auditor reports on the opening balance sheet for new insurers and the annual accounts for the previous three years for existing insurers, at the time an application for licence under section 4(2) is prepared.

This information is based on a document produced by Coopers & Lybrand, Cayman Islands.

APPENDIX VIII

COLORADO

Colorado became the leader of the US captive movement when in 1972 the Colorado General Assembly enacted the 'Colorado Captive Insurance Company Act' making Colorado the first state which authorized and encouraged the formation of domestic captives.

Colorado has a long and successful history of captive operations. In 1987, in recognition of the changing market and the need for flexibility and innovation to provide viable and reliable alternatives to the commercial liability insurance market, the Commissioner, Division Staff and representatives of the Rocky Mountain Chapter of the Risk Insurance Management Society sought to modernize and revitalize Colorado's Captive law. As a result the Colorado General Assembly enacted House Bill 1232 which amended the previous Act to eliminate certain hindrances to captive formation and to make it possible to form a Risk Retention Act company as a Colorado captive.

The exciting possibilities for Colorado, which is actively promoting the State as a regional and national insurance headquarters, are now uniquely reflected in its amended Captive Insurance Company Act, streamlined Division procedures, and a resurgence of interest in new captive formations or redomestications of other states' or off-shore captives to Colorado.

DISTINCTIVE CHARACTERISTICS OR REQUIREMENTS FOR VARIOUS CAPTIVE TYPES

The Colorado Captive Act distinguishes pure, association or industrial insured captives. Of particular significance, please note the following information.

359

CAPTIVE INSURANCE COMPANIES

Pure captive insurance company

A pure captive insurance company is formed to insure the risks of its parent organization along with subsidiaries, affiliates and associates of its parent.

Any pure captive insurance company applying for a certificate of authority to engage in the insurance business in the state of Colorado must demonstrate to the satisfaction of the Commissioner that the total insurance coverage necessary to insure all risks, hazards, and liabilities of the parent and companies to be insured would develop in the aggregate, gross annual premiums of at least $500,000; except that a pure captive insurance company may be organized to underwrite professional liability or errors and omissions combined with comprehensive general liability insurance without regard to the limitation on gross annual premiums.

The pure captive must have a minimum capital of $300,000 plus a minimum surplus of $200,000.

A pure captive is *not* subject to any restrictions on allowable investments. However, it should be noted that the Commissioner may prohibit or limit any investment which threatens the solvency or liquidity of the captive.

Association captive insurance company

An association captive insures the risks, hazards, and liabilities of their members, subsidiary companies of the members and affiliated companies of the members or the organizations of the association.

Any association captive insurance company applying for a certificate of authority to engage in the insurance business in the state of Colorado must demonstrate to the satisfaction of the Commissioner that the total insurance coverage necessary to insure all risks, hazards and liabilities of the association would develop, in the aggregate, gross annual premiums of at least $1,000,000.

An association captive insurance company must have a minimum capital or guaranty fund of $400,000 plus a minimum surplus of $350,000.

The investments of an association captive are subject to all of the investment limitations imposed on allowable investments of commercial insurance carriers.

Industrial insured captive insurance company
or industrial insured group

An industrial insured captive insurance company is a company that insures risks of the industrial insureds that comprise the industrial insured group, their affiliated companies, and subsidiaries of either. An industrial insured group is: 1. a group of industrial insureds (see requirements below) who own and/or control the captive; or, 2. a group formed under the Federal Liability Risk Retention Act of 1986.

To qualify as an industrial insured an entity must meet the following criteria:

(a) must obtain insurance by the use of the services of a full time employee acting as a risk manager or equivalent; and

(b) must employ a minimum of 25 full time employees; and

(c) must have a minimum aggregate annual insurance premium for all risks of $25,000.

An industrial insured group may include a group formed under the Federal Liability Risk Retention Act of 1986 or any group of industrial insureds that collectively owns, controls, or holds with power to vote all of the outstanding voting securities of an industrial insured captive insurance company incorporated as a stock insurer; or has complete voting control over an industrial insured captive insurance company incorporated as a mutual insurer.

An industrial insured captive insurance company must have a minimum capital or guaranty fund of $300,000 plus a minimum surplus of $200,000.

Any industrial insured captive insurance company applying for a certificate of authority to engage in the insurance business in the state of Colorado must demonstrate to the satisfaction of the Commissioner that the total insurance coverage necessary to insure all risks, hazards, and liabilities of the industrial insured group and its member organizations would develop in the aggregate, gross annual premiums of at least $1,000,000.

An industrial insured captive is *not* subject to any restrictions on allowable investments. However, it should be noted that the Commissioner may prohibit or limit any investment which threatens the solvency or liquidity of the captive.

GENERAL PROVISIONS APPLICABLE TO ALL CAPTIVES

1. The capital/guaranty fund and surplus requirements may be satisfied by letters of credit approved by the Commissioner.
2. All applications for a Certificate of Authority for a Colorado captive must be processed within 60 days from receipt of the complete application (Section 10–6-113 (2), C.R.S.).
3. All captives pay a 1 per cent annual premium tax to the Division.
4. Captive insurance companies are exempted from participating in the Colorado Guaranty Fund Association.
5. The principal and home office of every captive insurance company shall be within the State of Colorado (Section 10–6-1–7(4), C.R.S.).
6. After a Certificate of Authority is issued subsequent rate changes must simply be filed with the Division prior to or concurrent with their use.
7. Any claims made policies are subject to the requirements of Section 10–4–419 C.R.S. (see Appendix D), but all or part of these requirements may be waived by the Commissioner.
8. All Colorado captives will be required to file financial information on the National Association of Insurance Commissioner's format on an annual basis with the Insurance Division and will be subject to periodic examinations.
9. The cash, securities and/or letter of credit representing the minimum capital/guaranty fund for a captive is to be placed on deposit with the Commissioner for the protection of its policyholders. Such deposit

is to be in the vault of a trust company, safe deposit company or bank in the City and County of Denver, acceptable to the Commissioner. The cash or securities held shall be considered the property of the captive and any interest or dividends earned thereon will be for the benefit of the captive.

BASIC STEPS AND REQUIREMENTS FOR THE FORMATION OF A COLORADO CAPTIVE

The following outline is designed to provide a quick reference to the basic steps and requirements for the formation of a Colorado captive.

1. Informal assessment

The Commissioner and his staff encourage interested parties to contact them and, if desired or appropriate, to schedule an informal conference to discuss the proposed captive and to provide an opportunity to address any particular questions or issues to facilitate the formal application and formation process. This process has greatly assisted the involved principals by expediting the processing of an application and reducing costs to a person or entity seeking to form a captive in, or redomesticate a captive to, Colorado.

2. Application for a certificate

Any person seeking to form a Colorado captive should submit the Application for a Certificate of Authority for a Colorado Captive Insurance Company, which is contained in the attached Forms for Formation of a Colorado Captive, as well as the required fee and supporting information described in the following paragraphs.

3. Articles of incorporation or association and bylaws

The proposed articles of incorporation or association must be submitted, in triplicate, for review. In the case of a corporation the articles of incorporation must be approved by the Commissioner and the Attorney General and then filed and recorded in the office of the Secretary of State. A certified copy of the articles of incorporation must then be filed with the Commissioner.
A copy of any proposed bylaws for the captive should also be submitted.

4. Description of organizational structure

The application must describe the type of captive structure – whether a pure, association, or industrial insured – which includes a Group formed under the Federal Risk Retention Act – and should include an organizational chart and any other information needed to identify the membership or ownership of the proposed captive.

5. Plan of Operations

The application should include a Plan of Operations which briefly describes:

(a) The risks, hazards or liabilities to be insured

(b) Risk exposure
The proposed limits of liability, captive retention, named-insured deductibles, or other aspects of the insurance plan should be described in detail.

(c) Policy forms
The forms should be included or summarized.

Note: If a claims made policy is to be used the provisions of Section 10–4–419, C.R.S. apply. Upon request all or part of the requirements may be waived by the Commissioner.

(d) Rates
Proposed rates must be filed as part of the application. The application should include supporting documentation such as previous loss history actuarial studies, reserve requirements, etc., to justify the rates.

(e) Reinsurance
Proposed reinsurance should be described and agreements provided in draft or final, if possible.

Note for Risk Retention Act Captive. In the event the application is for a Risk Retention Act Group as a Colorado Industrial Insured Captive the Plan should be in a form to satisfy the feasibility study requirements of the Federal law.

Capitalization and financial projections

(a) Capitalization
Provide details of proposed capitalization, including an explanation of how funds are to be obtained. If an irrevocable letter of credit is to be utilized for initial capital, surplus, or both, such letter must conform to Colorado Regulation 73–1.

(b) Financial projections
Provide a detailed five year projection of financial conditions and operational results of the captive. (A sample format is enclosed in the attached Forms for Formation of a Colorado Captive).

Management

(a) Board of directors
Give information on number of members; election; etc., and provide a biographical affidavit (using the NAIC form which is enclosed in Forms for Formulation) for each. When appropriate, a brief resume of the directors should be provided.

(b) Officers
Name all officers and briefly describe their authority and relevant information on elections and/or appointments. Submit biographical affidavits, on the same form as used for directors, for all officers and, where appropriate, résumés of prior experience.

(c) Management and administration

Provide basic information on the proposed management and administration of the captive (see also item VI. *infra*). Management or other administrative services may be performed by qualified contractors or outside consultants. A copy of any such proposed contract(s) should be included.

(d) Organizational Minutes

Following formal incorporation of the company, an executed copy of the Organizational Minutes of the Board of Directors, along with all resolutions, must be submitted.

(e) Other

Additionally, any other information pertinent to the formation of the proposed captive should be submitted.

Fidelity bond coverage

Submit a fidelity bond covering all directors, officers, and employees of the captive company who will have access to company funds. The bond is to meet the requirements of Colorado Insurance Regulation 74-17 (see Appendix C) and be issued by a company licensed in the State of Colorado.

Miscellaneous

Provide any and all other information pertinent to the application.

Fees

$200.00 NONREFUNDABLE – to be submitted with initial filing of the application.

$300.00 Licensing fee – to be submitted upon issuance of Certificate of Authority.

$50.00 Filing Fee – to be submitted upon filing certified copy of Articles of Incorporation or other organizational document.

GUIDELINES FOR ADMINISTRATION OF A CAPTIVE INSURANCE COMPANY

The following guidelines are to be observed in the operation and management of Colorado Captive Insurance Companies.

1. Management, administration and records

It is a statutory requirement that the principal and home office of a captive be located in the State of Colorado (see Section 10-6-107(4), C.R.S.). If management or administrative services are to be performed in whole or part by contractors or outside consultants the entities or individuals must be properly qualified to perform the involved functions. Any contract or agreement must include a provision providing for advance notice to the Colorado Division of Insurance in the event of termination. The essential management and administrative functions must be performed in Colorado to satisfy the headquarters in Colorado requirement. Knowledgeable personnel and adequate records must be available to conduct a regular financial examination in the State. Records of the proceedings and deliberations of the captive and its management, such as authorizations or ratifications, minutes, and all financial accounting, or other business records, including claims files, must be maintained in the headquarters office.

2. Investment functions

Colorado statutes (Section 10-3-234, C.R.S.) require prior approval of investments by the Board of Directors, or of a committee appointed by the Board and charged with duty of making such investments, or of an officer charged with such duty. A permanent written record shall be maintained by the Company. This record shall be ratified at the next regular meeting of the Board of Directors.

Although in many instances the investment function will be exercised by the parent company, it is incumbent upon the resident officer to be aware of all investment transactions in order that they will be promptly recorded on the books of the Company. In the case of an association captive the resident officer is further charged with the responsibility to ascertain that all investments fall within the authorized investments permitted by statute.

Investment portfolios should be carefully planned and properly diversified to provide for necessary reserves, stability and liquidity to meet the projected financial needs and future claims. Although investment return is important, it is secondary to the importance of assuring the captive can properly and timely pay claims.

3. Safe deposit boxes

At least two persons in the resident officer's office should be authorized to enter the Captive's safe deposit boxes. This can be done without losing necessary controls and will facilitate access.

4. Securities – custodial agreements

Securities comprising the Captive's investments must be in possession of the captive manager or held in safekeeping pursuant to a custodial agreement in accordance with the requirements of Colorado Insurance Regulation 78-15 (see Appendix E).

Subsidiary ledgers must be maintained for bonds and stocks. These records must include a detailed history of each investment.

5. Accounting system

Pursuant to Section 10-1-108 (2), the accounts and records of the Companies are to be maintained in a manner which will facilitate preparation and verification of the annual statement.

The following are considered basic essentials of an acceptable accounting system:

(a) the general records are to be maintained on a modified cash basis (statutory).
(b) subsidiary records supporting ledger controls are to be in a form clearly supporting those controls.
(c) additional work papers supporting the annual statement figures, along with source documentation, must be maintained and readily available for review by the examiners.

The resident officers must be fully active in the accounting phase of the operation, possessing an understanding of the system and the ability to assist during the periodic examination. The general accounting records of the Captives must be physically located and maintained at all times in the Captive's office.

Checks

In the interest of internal control each Captive should set a nominal amount, such as $500.00, for which checks can be issued on one signature. For checks issued above the nominal amount established by the Board, two signatures will be required, of which one must be the authorized signature of the Colorado resident corporate officer of the Captive. It is advisable to authorize at least two signatures from the resident officer's office.

Loss and loss adjustment expenses

The loss reporting system must provide accurate detail readily supporting both paid and unpaid claims as shown in the annual statement. The system must be capable of developing unpaid losses on a case basis for any given period.

The liability for unpaid loss adjustment expense as shown in the annual statement shall be supported by a worksheet showing the detailed calculation. The reserve shall be projected in order to adequately cover the cost of claims settlements for both allocated and unallocated expenses.

Other liabilities

Detail for all other liabilities shall be maintained to support annual statement figures and must include reference to source documentation. An adequate reserve for any liabilities shall be established. Such liabilities would be items incurred or ordered for which bills have not yet been received.

APPLICATION FOR CERTIFICATE OF AUTHORITY
FOR A COLORADO CAPTIVE INSURANCE COMPANY

Commissioner of Insurance   Date: _____
Division of Insurance
State of Colorado
303 West Colfax Avenue, Suite 500
Denver, Colorado 80204

On behalf of the _____

(Name of Company or Association)

organized under the laws of the State of _____, with Home

Office address at _____

(give full address)

and Mailing address at _____

(give full address)

application is hereby made for a license authorizing and empowering this company to transact business in the State of Colorado, under and in compliance with the laws thereof, during the license year beginning March 1, as a:

Captive Insurance Company

_____ Pure   _____ Association   _____ Industrial Insured

_____ Industrial Insured Group under the Risk Retention Act

Indicate specifically the lines of insurance which you desire to transact in this State by placing a check in the appropriate boxes alongside the lines to be transacted. THE AUTHORITY UNDER THE COLORADO LICENSE INCLUDES ON THOSE LINES INDICATED IN THIS APPLICATION.

CASUALTY	FIRE
21 ☐ Plate Glass	41 ☐ Fire & Lightning
22 ☐ Steam Boiler Machinery	42 ☐ Extended Coverage
23 ☐ Burglary and Theft	43 ☐ Hail on Growing Crops
24 ☐ Fidelity and Surety	44 ☐ Earthquake
25 ☐ Motor Vehicle – Full Coverage	45 ☐ Motor Vehicle – Full Coverage
26 ☐ Workmen's Compensation	46 ☐ Aircraft
27 ☐ Liability	47 ☐ Inland Marine
33 ☐ Professional Malpractice	48 ☐ Ocean Marine
35 ☐	50 ☐
36 ☐	51 ☐
37 ☐	52 ☐
38 ☐	53 ☐
39 ☐	
40 ☐	55 ☐ Commercial Mutiple Peril

As a condition precedent to and as a consideration for the issuance of the Certificate of Authority, hereby declares acceptance of the terms and provisions of the laws of the State of Colorado applicable to said Company.

_____

(Name of Company or Association)

_____

(President or Manager)

FINANCIAL PROJECTION

	199	199	199	199	199
ASSETS					
Liquid:					
Fixed					
Other					
Total					
LIABILITIES					
Policy Obligations:					
General					
Other					
Total Liabilities					
Capital					
Paid in Surplus					
Unassigned Surplus					
Total					

OPERATIONS PROJECTION

	199	199	199	199	199	199
Income						
Premiums Earned						
Investment Income						
Other _____						
Total Income						
Deductions:						
Claims paid						
Other policy benefits paid						
Administrative Salaries						
Plan Management Fees						
Other Administrative:						
Taxes, License and Fees						
Other:						
Total deductions						
Gain or Loss						
Beginning Surplus (Equity)						
Gain or Loss from above						
Ending Surplus (Equity)						

APPENDIX IX

GIBRALTAR

LEGISLATION

The conduct of insurance business in Gibraltar is regulated by the Insurance Companies Ordinance 1987 and its subsidiary legislation.

Insurance business is licensed and controlled by the Commissioner of Insurance who is charged with the administration of the Ordinance and its Regulations. The Ordinance lays down a basic framework for the setting of Gibraltar insurance companies, both 3rd party insurers and captive insurance companies. It also provides for the licensing of foreign insurance companies wishing to carry on business in Gibraltar. This framework is fully consistent with EU Non-Life and Life Directives but leaves the detail of the regulatory regime to be covered by regulations and rules.

During the course of 1995 the following legislation was implemented.

- Legal notice No. 42 of 1995 cited as the Insurance Companies Ordinance (General Insurance and Long Term Insurance Directives) Regulations 1995.
- Legal notice No. 50 of 1995, cited as the Insurance Companies Ordinance (General Insurance and Long Term Insurance Directives) (No. 2) Regulations 1995.
- Legal notice No. 51 of 1995 cited as Notice of Corrigendum to the Insurance Companies Ordinance (General and Long Term Insurance Directives) Regulations 1995.

These Regulations did not fully implement all of the outstanding insurance supervisory directives and accordingly on 13th June 1996 the following regulations were issued to come into effect on 1st July 1996: –

- Insurance Companies Ordinance (General Insurance and Long Term Insurance Directives) Regulations 1996 (Legal Notice No. 63 of 1996) – further amendments which were necessary to the Insurance Companies Ordinance 1987.
- Insurance Companies (Conduct of Business) Regulations 1996 (Legal Notice No. 64 of 1996) an entirely new set of regulations and provide for certain matters and words to be included in insurance advertisements and also for certain information to be given by an intermediary to a person whom he invites to enter into certain insurance contracts.
- Insurance Companies (Deposit) Regulations 1996 (Legal Notice No. 65 of 1996) – these regulations replace the Insurance Companies (Deposits) Regulations 1987 (Legal Notice No. 104 of 1987) and the Insurance Companies (Deposit)(Amendment) Regulations 1991 (Legal Notice No. 27 of 1991) and contain only minor changes to regulations 3 and 4.
- Insurance Companies (Prescribed Particulars) Regulations 1996 (Legal Notice No. 66 of 1996) – these regulations replace the Insurance Companies (Prescribed Particulars) Regulations 1987 (Legal Notice No. 102 of 1987) and the Insurance Companies (Prescribed Particulars) (Amendment) Regulations 1992 (Legal Notice No. 55 of 1992) and covers the information to be submitted by an applicant for authorisation and specify the particulars which have to be notified in connection with a change of director, controller, manager etc.
- Insurance Companies (Solvency) Margins and Guarantee Funds) Regulations 1996 (Legal Notice No. 67 of 1996) – these regulations replace the Insurance Companies (Solvency Margins and Guarantee Funds) Regulations 1996 and contain amendments to regulations 3, 4, 5, 9 and Schedule 4.
- Insurance Companies (Valuation of Assets and Liabilities) Regulations 1996 (Legal Notice No. 68 of 1996) – these are an entirely new set of regulations and are necessary to meet the terms of the Directives. The 3rd Life and Non-Life Directives introduced detailed rules on what assets covering technical provisions are admissible for covering insurers' technical provisions and solvency margins and how these should be valued. The broad purpose of the regulations are to establish standards for the valuation of assets in evaluating compliance with statutory requirements and to ensure that companies maintain a prudent spread of investments. The Valuation of Assets is covered in Part II and the Determination of Liabilities which is covered in Part III lays down the principles for the determination of liabilities.
- Insurance Companies (Forms) Regulations 1996 (Legal Notice No. 69 of 1996) – these regulations replace the Insurance Companies (Forms) Regulations 1987 (Legal Notice No. 105 of 1987) and the Insurance Companies (Forms) (Amendment) Regulations 1991 (Legal Notice No. 26 of 1991) and detail the statutory notice required by section 72 of the Ordinance and the exemptions. The regulations also detail certain statistical information which now has to be supplied.

- Insurance Companies (Accounts and Statements) Regulations 1996 (Legal Notice No. 70 of 1996) – these are an entirely new set of regulations. These Annual Returns are required to demonstrate that the required solvency margin is covered and have to be affirmed by certificates by the Directors, the Auditors and for long term business by the Actuary. Member States require every insurance undertaking whose head office is situated in its territory to produce an annual account together with statistical documents which are necessary for the purposes of supervision.

All of the above regulations have implemented the following insurance Directives: –

78/473/EEC	Community co-insurance Directive
84/641/EEC	Tourist assistance Directive
87/343/EEC	Credit insurance and suretyship insurance Directive
87/344/EEC	Legal expenses insurance Directive
88/357/EEC	2nd non-life Directive
90/618/EEC	Motor vehicle liability insurance Directive
90/619/EEC	2nd life directive
91/371/EEC	EEC Swiss agreement Directive
92/49/EEC	3rd non-life Directive
92/96/EEC	3rd life Directive

The effect of this is that Gibraltar has now implemented all outstanding insurance supervisory Directives apart from the Insurance Accounts Directive which is, however, at an advanced stage, and should have been published at the time of reading.

3RD INSURANCE DIRECTIVES

The 3rd Life and Non-Life Insurance Directives complete the single European market for insurance by establishing the "single passport". The passport will enable insurance companies established within the EEA to cover risks situated within the EEA on the basis of the authorisation they receive from the member State where they have their head office (in our situation, Gibraltar). The Directives also give consumers, irrespective of their size and the nature of the risks to be insured the freedom to choose to buy an insurance policy from any insurer in the EEA.

Under the single passport, the financial supervision with a head office in an an EEA State will be carried out by the home Member State alone. Accordingly, the supervisory authorities in an EEA State in which such companies sell insurance through a branch or on a service basis (the "host State") will have no power to intervene unilaterally in the financial supervision of the company. However, the "host State" authorities will retain powers under the Directives to prevent persons entering into contracts and to prohibit advertising if it is considered to be in the "general good" to do so.

"General good" is not defined but the European Court of Justice has determined that any measure imposed in the interest of the general good must: –

- be objectively necessary
- be in proportion to the objective
- not duplicate a restriction with which the insurer must comply in its home State
- not discriminate between insurance companies operating in an EEA States

MAIN FEATURES OF THE NEW REGULATIONS

Greater emphasis is now placed on the overall financial supervision and fitness matters. The Commissioner is required to ensure that he has all the powers and means necessary to supervise effectively the activities of Gibralter insurance companies both in Gibralter and in EEA States.

The main features are: –

- sound and prudent management – requires a company to have sound and prudent management at the authorisation stage and provide for the effect on the soundness and prudence of management to be taken into account when considering fitness of proposed controllers.
- notifiable persons – person now has a notifiable holding if he exercises 10% or more of the voting power at a shareholders meeting. Consent required to become any category or to move up from one category to a higher category.
- investment principles – an insurance company must invest in assets that are appropriate to cover its liabilities. The company must have regard to the safety, yield and marketablility of its investments which must be diversified and adequately spread both in relation to the category of investment and the investment market.
- hybrid capital/subordinated debt – legislation introduces new ways in which insurance companies can raise capital. Insurance companies can now have some borrowed capital and this can count towards part of the solvency margin.
- currency matching and localisation – liabilities expressed in a particular currency have to be matched, to the extent provided for, by assets in that currency. Assets can be localised anywhere within the EEA.
- disclosure of information to policyholders – legislation has now extended the information which is requested to be given to policyholders for both life and non-life business.
- conduct of business – Article 14 both 3rd life and non-file Directives prevent member States from stopping EEA insurers from advertising their products in their territory subject to any rules which they may maintain in the general good.

PASSPORTING

Implementation of the Directives, is the first important stage in the process which will eventually enable Gibraltar insurance companies to write business into the EEA States without the problem of establishing an insurance presence in each of the individual territories where the risks are to be written.

This will eventually mean that an insurance company licensed in Gibraltar, with the approval of the Commissioner of Insurance, will be free to do business in EEA States either by setting up a branch there or by providing insurance on a services basis.

A company wishing to carry on business through a branch in an EEA State or provide insurance into an EEA State will have to submit to the Commissioner a notification containing information about the risks to be covered. Once the Commissioner is satisfied that the notification is in order and that the solvency position is satisfactory, he will notify the supervisory authorities in the host state of the company's intention, providing a dossier of information including a certificate of solvency.

FUTURE DEVELOPMENTS

Under the Financial Services Commission Ordinance, Gibraltar has to establish and implement standard required by legislation and supervisory practice in the United Kingdom. In this connection on the subject of legislation some further amendments to the Insurance Companies Ordinance will need to be made to deal with matters which go beyond the requirements of the Directives.

It may also be necessary to make amendments to the Insurance Companies (Valuation of Assets and Liabilities) Regulations and also the Insurance Companies (Accounts and Statements) Regulations to take account of recent changes in the United Kingdom.

Furthermore, consideration is being given to the implementation of the "Post BCCI Directive" in the areas of insurance, banking and investment services.

As yet Gibraltar companies are not in a position to passport throughout the EEA. With the appointment of an Insurance Supervisor, it is hoped that Gibraltar will complete implementation of the necessary standards with regards to the supervision of insurance companies during the first part of 1997.

The Commission will over the coming months be issuing a series of guidance notes aimed at assisting interested parties in understanding various regulatory requirements. The topics which the guidance notes will cover will be wide ranging and cover notes for applicants for authorisation and interpretation of the rules on valuation of assets. There will also be some which deal with the adequacy of a company's system of control over certain aspects of its business which will be a significant consideration in the company's compliance with the new regulatory requirement of "sound and prudent management". These "system of control" guidance notes will set out performance standards which companies systems will be expected to achieve.

RE-DOMICILIATION

On 29th February 1996, the Companies (Re-domiciliation) Regulations 1996 (Legal Notice No 24 of 1996) were published. These Regulations came into effect on the 1st March 1996. The regulations mean that a company domiciled outside Gibraltar may, if permitted to do so by its constitution and by the applicable laws in the jurisdiction of its incorporation and, if the company is domiciled in a jurisdiction other than that in which it is incorporated apply to establish a domicile in Gibraltar. The Government is expected to make a minor amendment to the regulations in order to put beyond doubt the ability of insurance companies, if licensed by the Commissioner, to take full advantage of re-domiciliation in Gibraltar.

Information supplied by Norman T. J. Ritchie assistant Insurance Supervisor – Financial Services Commission/Gibraltar.

APPENDIX X

GUERNSEY

FORMING A COMPANY

The only form of company recognised and registered in Guernsey is that with limited liability by shares and there is no distinction between public or private companies. There are two types of company (resident and exempt) but only resident companies may be formed as insurers.

How to incorporate and register a company

Companies incorporated in Guernsey or Alderney must comply with the Companies (Guernsey) Laws 1908 to 1973 and the Companies (Alderney) Laws 1894 to 1973 respectively. Incorporation is effected by registration with the Royal Court in Guernsey or Alderney and requires the services of a local Advocate.

The Advocate will undertake the following steps:

1. Obtain approval from the Greffe (which acts as the local companies' registry) for the company's name. In the case of an insurer, the Superintendent of Insurance Business must also approve the proposed name.
2. Arrange for the Memorandum and Articles of Association to be prepared, which must specify amongst other things:
   (a) name of the company;
   (b) objects of the company;
   (c) the amount of authorised share capital for which stamp duty is payable at the rate of $\frac{1}{2}\%$ subject to a minimum of £50.
3. The company must have seven shareholders, who need not be resident. It is common practice for professional firms to provide nominee shareholders to make up the number required.

4. In addition, certain other information including ultimate beneficial ownership is disclosed to the Financial Services Commission and the Crown Officer on an application form for registration which is completed and signed by an Advocate and submitted for inspection. In order for a company to be registered it requires the consent of the States Advisory and Finance Committee for the issue of the founder shares and the Crown Officers' visa. In practice this can be accomplished in conjunction with the Insurance Registration application. The Financial Services Commission scrutinises applications on behalf of the Advisory and Finance Committee to ensure that no undesirable activities are to be carried on through the legal persona of a Guernsey company whilst the Crown Officers are concerned with avoidance of UK tax. For this purpose the names of the beneficial owners have to be disclosed; this information is not available to anyone but the officials mentioned.

Public information

The only information available for public record under the Companies Law is the nominal and issued share capital, the registered office, the names and addresses of directors, secretary, and shareholders. Accounts of companies are not filed for public record but must be produced if requested by the shareholders and, in the case of resident companies, to the Income Tax office to support its tax return. The companies must also be audited.

The Insurance Law makes certain other information available to the public.

Costs

The cost of forming a new company in addition to the stamp duty, and the £100 filing fee (which is payable annually) is upwards of £400 depending on the complexity of the Memorandum and Articles of Association to be drafted. Insurance Companies are subject to additional costs.

Administration

Day-to-day administration and secretarial duties can be carried on by local professional firms and organisations on behalf of non-resident beneficial owners. All prospective captive insurers must be managed by authorised insurance managers unless the insurers themselves have permanent, physical expertise in Guernsey.

APPLICATION FOR REGISTRATION UNDER THE INSURANCE BUSINESS (GUERNSEY) LAW, 1986

Submission and processing the application

1. Complete the application form with the help of the General Representative or other local adviser.

2. There are two ways of processing an application:
   (a) application for full registration immediately
   (b) application for approval-in-principle pending incorporation and placement of the share capital.
3. Ask your local adviser to check the application and submit, together with the fee of £1,000, to:

> The Superintendant of Insurance Business
> The Guernsey Financial Services Commission
> Weighbridge House
> Lower Pollet
> St. Peter Port
> Guernsey, Channel Islands
> Telephone 0481 712801
> Telefacsimile 0481 712010

The Commission normally meets monthly to consider applications but the Superintendent of Insurance Business has discretionary powers to approve applications prior to taking to the Commission.

4. Where the application is for approval-in-principle the Registration Certificate will be issued upon receipt, by the Superintendent of Insurance Business, of the documents of incorporation (Memorandum and Articles of Association and Certificate of Incorporation), evidence of placement of the share capital, and any other items which he deems to be necessary.

Fees and costs

Registration

On applying to the Guernsey Financial Services Commission for registration of an offshore insurance company, a fee of £1,000 is payable.

Additionally there is a filing fee of £100 payable on incorporation and annually to the Greffier.

Document duty is set at £50 for a company with an authorised share capital of up to £10,000; over this amount duty is payable at a rate of ½ per cent authorised capital. The total costs for a company incorporated with standard Memorandum and Articles and a share capital of £100,000 would be approximately £1,000, inclusive of legal fees and stamp duty. For a more complex formation the costs would increase.

Annual

Each year, at the same time as the registered offshore insurer deposits its annual return and accounts, a fee of £1,000 is payable to the Guernsey Financial Services Commission.

The annual costs for a medium sized captive would be somewhere in the region of £25,000, taking into account management, audit and directors' fees, as well as secretarial, travelling and general expenses.

CAPTIVE INSURANCE COMPANIES

THE INSURANCE BUSINESS (GUERNSEY) LAW, 1986

A SHORT SUMMARY FOR OFFSHORE INSURERS WRITING GENERAL BUSINESS

Minimum share capital

£100,000 or equivalent in another currency.

Minimum margin of solvency

18 per cent of first £5 million of net premium income and 16 per cent thereafter. (Long term — the greater of £50,000 or 2½ per cent of the long term fund).

Net premium income

Gross premium income less rebates, refunds, reinsurance commissions and reinsurance ceded.

Approved assets

75 per cent of the assets required to maintain the minimum margin of solvency must be approved assets The approved assets are:

  (a) cash in hand and at banks;
  (b) bank certificates of deposit;
  (c) eurobonds rated by Standard & Poor at BBB and above at market value;
  (d) quoted securities (on a recognised stock exchange);
  (e) net investment income receivable in relation to any of the above;
  (f) premiums receivable;
  (g) reinsurance balances receivable;
  (h) net accounts receivable;
  (i) irrevocable letters of credit.

Non-approved assets include

Related party balances (unless specifically approved by the Commission).

Guernsey representative

Each registered insurer must appoint a general representative who is either:

  (a) both
      (i) Guernsey resident executive director, or if not, a Guernsey resident employee, and
      (ii) fit and proper, or
  (b) an authorised insurance manager.

Annual return

Includes the audited accounts (audited financial statements), a declaration by the General Representative, and amended business plan and an actuary's report (if applicable) together with the supplementary information outlined in information circular 2/87. It must be submitted within 4 months of the insurer's financial year end.

UK FINANCIAL SERVICES ACT
SECTION 130 DESIGNATION

On 5th April 1988 Guernsey gained designation for the purposes of section 130 of the Financial Services Act 1986 by the UK Secretary of State for Trade and Industry. Guernsey Offshore Life Companies may now market their products in the UK.

Bacon & Woodrow have been appointed as consulting actuaries to help the Commission with the supervision of the life companies. They will initially look at past actuarial valuations, product literature, underlying investments and the business plan. After this they will rely on certificates from the company's actuary who will monitor whether the policyholder's reasonable expectations will be fulfilled. They will continue to check on aspects such as solvency, mismatching of assets against liabilities and mode of operation. There will be an additional fee on application to cover the cost of the work done by Bacon & Woodrow, but this will be no more than that charged in the UK (£5,000).

The Commission must be notified of any material changes to the business plan and require the company's audited accounts and an actuarial certificate to be submitted annually. It is also a requirement that assets representing 90 per cent of the company's liabilities be placed with an approved custodian trustee.

Guernsey has also gained FSA Section 87 designation relating to collective investment schemes.

THE STATES OF GUERNSEY
THE INSURANCE BUSINESS (GUERNSEY) LAW, 1986

APPLICATION FORM REGISTRATION UNDER SECTION 10

Company writing business in or from within Guernsey

Please complete all sections as fully as possible giving reasons for non compliance if any, and attaching appendices where appropriate.

If any question is inapplicable for your type of business, please clearly indicate by marking 'N/A'.

1. Name of proposed name of applicant _____

2. Registered Office _____

3. Address on the Islands where full business records will be kept _____

_____

_____

4. List all names (including any previous names) addresses and nationalities of all beneficial shareholders and ultimate beneficial shareholders, together with the number and class of shares (to be) held directly or on their behalf (large publicly held corporations need only list those beneficial shareholders owning over 10 per cent of their shares)

_____

_____

_____

_____

_____

_____

_____

5. What is the authorised and issued share capital and how is it to be subscribed?

_____

6. Name and address of the proposed general representative (S19(1)) _____

_____

_____

7. In those cases where shares are beneficially owned by a corporate body or bodies, or the company is part of a group, the chain of connection (group organisation chart showing all associates and affiliated companies) to the ultimate beneficial owners must be shown _____

_____

_____

_____

_____

_____

_____

8. Please provide the latest audited financial statements of the immediate parent, and if applicable the consolidated accounts of the group.

9. Provide a list of all directors, officers, managers, consultants and administrators showing their respective positions with the insurer.

10. If the above individuals in the answers to questions 4, 6, 7 and 9 hold positions in any nationally known publicly held corporation or other corporation already known to the Commission, please outline those positions and provide a short résumé of each individual.

11. In all other cases except Guernsey (including Alderney, Herm and Jethou) residents already known to the Commission, please provide a full particulars form (available

from the Superintendent of Insurance Business) and two references (one of which should be a bank reference).

12. Attach evidence of auditors' acceptance of the appointment of their willingness to act. Details of their professional indemnity insurance and insurance auditing experience may also be required if the proposed auditors is not known to the Commission.

13. Date on which applicant commenced or intends to commence carrying on business. _____

14. Whether business being, or proposed to be, transacted is 'general' or 'long term' or both. _____

15. If long term please give the name and address of the appointed actuary and attach evidence of their willingness to act. Details of their professional indemnity insurance may also be required if the proposed actuary is not known to the Commission. _____

_____

_____

16. For an existing insurer attach the latest audited accounts of the company and where appropriate the latest actuarial report.

17. Attach a business plan. The Superintendent of Insurance Business may indicate that any part of the information included in the business shall not form part of this application for the purposes of the certificate provided by the General Representative included within the Annual Insurance Return.

18. Have any of the parties connected with this application ever applied, either individually or in conjunction with others for authority to transact insurance business in any other jurisdiction? If so, please give details.

_____

_____

_____

19. If incorporated attach Memorandum and Articles of Association and Certificate of Incorporation. If not incorporated these items will be required before the registration certificate is issued.

20. Are you also applying under Section 7 to carry on insurance business, as outlined, in a country outside Guernsey?

_____

_____

21. Are you applying to write domestic insurance business, offshore insurance business, or both?

_____

22. For new companies, to what date will the company make up its first set of audited accounts, and what date will it use annually thereafter? _____

23. What country's generally accepted accounting policies will apply? _____

24. It is preferred that the insurer will use the accruals method of a country (rather than the three year method of underwriting accounts). If any other method is to be used, please give reasons _____

25. Who will underwrite the business? _____

26. Who will handle the claims? _____

27. If the company is not fully funded in the formative years what provision is there in effect if there are early heavy losses? _____

28. All information relative to this application is treated in confidence except that which must be disclosed by the Law (S17). However in order to promote Guernsey as an offshore insurance centre and to inform the market of its legitimacy, will you let the Superintendent of Insurance Business disclose ON ENQUIRY:

    (a) Owners? _____ Yes/No

    (b) Latest figures of Capital, Surplus, Total Assets and Gross Premiums?

    Yes/No

    (c) Classes of Business? _____ Yes/No

29. Are there any other parties and/or intermediaries involved? _____

30. Is the fact that there is coverage by the company used publicly (e.g. for marketing, etc.) or known to third parties in any way (e.g. contractors bonds certified to developers or product liability) advertised?

31. What local (Guernsey) resources will be required during the formative years in the way of staff and accommodation (office and personnel) – direct and indirect (additional staff required by managers, etc.)?

32. Assuming this application is successful, what economic benefit will Guernsey gain from the company? Please quantify if possible.

I/We hereby apply for registration under Section 10 of the Insurance Business (Guernsey) Law 1986.

*I/We hereby apply for the consent of the Commission under Section 7(1)(b) of the Law to carry on business, as outlined above, outside Guernsey.

DECLARATION

We certify that the information given in answer to the questions is complete and correct to the best of our knowledge and belief, and there are no other facts of which the Superintendent of Insurance Business should be aware.

We undertake to inform the Superintendent of Insurance Business of any changes material to the application which arise while the application is being considered.

We further undertake that, if and for as long as the institution is registered under the Insurance Business (Guernsey) Law, 1986 or under any subsequent legislation, we will notify the Commission of any material changes in the answers to the questions above within a period of 21 days of these changes coming to our nonce.

We are aware that it is an offence under Section 59(4) of the Insurance Business (Guernsey) Law, 1986 to furnish information or make a statement which we know to be false or misleading in a material particular or recklessly to furnish information make a statement which is false or misleading in a material particular in connection with an application for registration/authorisation.

We also apply for the appropriate consents under the Control of Borrowing and the Protection of Depositors, Companies and Prevention of Fraud legislations.

Date _____ Signed _____ Name in Block Capitals _____

      (Duly authorised office)   Position held _____

Date _____ Signed _____ Name in Block Capitals _____

                                  Position held _____

Section 59(4) of the Law provides that any person who is guilty of any offence as stated shall be liable.

(a) on conviction on indictment to imprisonment for a term not exceeding two years or to a fine or to both.

(b) on summary conviction to a fine not exceeding £1,000.

*Delete if inappropriate.

APPENDIX XI

HAWAII

OUTLINE OF HAWAII CAPTIVE INSURANCE LAW

I. Chapter 431, Article 19

A. Definitions (431: 19–101, 102)

1. Pure: insures risk of parent and affiliated companies
2. Association: insures risks of member organizations of the association and affiliated companies

B. Captive Requirements (431: 19–102(b))

1. Obtain a license to do insurance business from commissioner
2. Hold at least one board of directors meeting each year in the State
3. Maintain its principal place of business in Hawaii
4. Appoint a resident agent to act on its behalf
5. Appoint Director of Department of Commerce and Consumer Affairs for receipt of service

C. Filings with commissioner (431: 19–102(c) and (d))

1. Certified copy of charter and by-laws
2. Statement under oath of president and secretary re: financial conditions
3. Evidence of amount and liquidity of assets relative to risks assumed
4. Evidence of adequacy, expertise, experience and character of manager
5. Evidence of overall soundness of business plan
6. Evidence adequacy of loss control program
7. Other statements, documentation and information deemed relevant by commissioner

D. Fees (431: 19–102(e))

1. Application fee (non-refundable): $1,000
2. License fee and renewal fee: $300

E. Lines of business

1. Permitted (431: 19–102(g))
   casualty
   marine and transportation
   marine protection and indemnity
   wet marine and transportation insurance
   – vessels, crafts, hulls and interests therein
   – insurance on freights and disbursements
   – insurance on personal property and interests therein
   import/export
   property
   surety
   title
2. Limitations (431: 19–102(a)(3) and (a)(4)
   Prohibited from providing personal motor vehicle or homeowners
   Reinsurance must conform w/431: 19–111

F. Company name (431: 19–103)
Must not be deceptively similar, or likely to be confused with, or mistaken for any other existing business name registered in the State

G. Capital and surplus (431: 19–104 and 105)
In form and amount deemed appropriate by insurance commissioner. Form may include cash, letter of credit, approved security

H. Form of business (431: 19–106(a) and (b))

1. Pure: must be incorporated as a stock insurer
2. Association: may be incorporated as a) stock insurer with capital shares held by stockholders, or b) mutual insurer with governing body elected by members

I. Incorporators (431: 19–106(c))
Minimum of three incorporators
At least 2 incorporators must be Hawaii residents

J. Certificate of public good (431: 19–106(d))
Captive to petition commissioner for certificate before filing incorporation papers with DCCA

K. Stock (431: 19–106(f))
Capital stock shall not be issued at less than par value

L. Board of Directors (431: 19–106(g))
At least one member must be Hawaii resident

M. Investments (431: 19–110)
To be governed by Article 6 of insurance code

N. Reinsurance (431: 19–111)

1. Assumption of: no restrictions
2. Ceding to another insurer: commissioner's prior approval of insurer required. Insurer also required to file with commissioner.
   (a) power of attorney accepting reinsurance and appointing director DCCA for service of process;
   (b) $100 fee (reinsurance renewal fee of $100/year);
   (c) certified copy of charter and by-laws;
   (d) statement re: financial condition made under oath of president and secretary of reinsurer;
   (e) additional info deemed relevant by commissioner.

O. Application of laws

1. Insurance code: not applicable except where specified (431 :19–115)
2. Corporation laws: apply unless in conflict with captive insurance law (431: 19–106(h))

II. H.B. No. 2035, Proposed Amendments Being Considered by State Legislature

A. Taxation (New)

1. Pure captives: 0.25 per cent of gross premiums received from all risks or property resident, situated, or located in State, and on risks situated elsewhere if not tax paid.

B. Definition (431: 19–101 and 102)
Adds 'risk retention captive insurance company', and limits provision of insurance by risk retention captive to members of the risk retention group

C. Captive requirements (431: 19–102(b)(4))
Appoint insurance commissioner for service of process (instead of DCCA director)

D. Captive advisors (new)
Requires commissioner to establish list of qualified advisors to review applications. Advisors' fees limited to $3,500 and $7,500 for pure and association/risk group captives respectively. Section is repealed in 2 years.

E. Lines of business

1. Permitted (431: 19–102(h))
   Adds credit life and credit disability insurances

F. Financial statements and reports (431: 19–107)

1. Statement of financial condition must be written according to GAAP

2. In addition, association and risk group captives must submit annual statements in accordance with SAP, under oath of at least two of the captive's principal officers

G. Investments (431: 19–110)
Pure captives may obtain approval from commissioner for investments not specified in insurance code.

H. Reinsurance
Both assuming and ceding of reinsurance require commissioner approval

INSURANCE DIVISION
STATE OF HAWAII
STEPS IN FORMING A HAWAII CAPTIVE INSURANCE COMPANY

These steps will generally be followed in the process of incorporating a captive insurer in Hawaii and applying for a license from the Insurance Division, Department of Commerce and Consumer Affairs:

1. Arrange a meeting with the Insurance Division staff to make introductions and to briefly explain the who, what, where and how of the proposed captive. In the case of association captives, the staff will want to meet with key officials of the organization.
2. Prepare documents necessary for incorporation. The services of a local lawyer may be desirable.
3. Prepare documents necessary for application to the Division (see Application for Admission for list of documentation requirements). Remember to include applications for authorization as independent CPA, as analyst of loss reserves and loss expense reserves, and as captive insurance manager.
4. Submit three (3) copies of all documentation required in items 2 and 3 above to the Insurance Commissioner, Insurance Division, Department of Commerce and Consumer Affairs, for initial review. Include $1,000 non-refundable application fee.
5. Two (2) copies of application documentation will be sent to the appointed Approved Advisor by the Insurance Commissioner. The Approved Advisor will review the entire submission and submit recommendations to the Insurance Commissioner for further action by the Insurance Commissioner.
6. Petition the Insurance Commissioner to issue a Certificate of Public Good. The factors to be addressed are outlined in Section 431: 19–1–106 of the Hawaii Captive Law. In addition, a statement of the benefits to Hawaii must be included.
7. After the Insurance Commissioner has issued the Certificate of Public Good, present this and the documentation required in item (2) above to the Business Registration Division of the State Department of Commerce and Consumer Affairs along with the appropriate fee, to incorporate the captive.

8. After incorporation, apply to the Insurance Commissioner for a Certificate of Authority and enclose the Service of Process form, and a statement of the President and Secretary as to the Captive's financial condition.
9. An organization exam will be performed by the Insurance Division, at its discretion, after issuance of the Certificate of Authority and capitilization of the captive. The costs of this examination will be borne by the applicant.

INSURANCE DIVISION
STATE OF HAWAII
INSTRUCTIONS FOR CAPTIVE INSURANCE COMPANY
APPLICATION

General

Enclosed is the Application for Admission as a Captive Insurance Company together with a sample Letter of Credit form and Biographical Affidavit form.

The Application form must be filled out in its entirety and when submitted should include all material requested (3 copies of each), together with a non-refundable application fee of $1,000. No incomplete package of material will be accepted. If Letters of Credit are used to meet capital and surplus requirements the enclosed form must be adhered to by the institution issuing the Letter of Credit.

One Biographical Affidavit form is enclosed. Copies should be made and enclosed as required by the application. Each Affidavit must be filled out entirely and no substitute for the enclosed form will be accepted.

Financial regulations

Financial Regulations will require that an Independent certified Public Accountant, approved by the Insurance Commissioner, audit the Captive annually. It is incumbent upon the applicant to select an accountant who is authorized as an independent Certified Public Accountant with knowledge of the captive insurance business. Please include the CPA's application for authorization as a part of the application of the proposed captive.

INSURANCE DIVISION
STATE OF HAWAII
CAPTIVE INSURANCE COMPANY
APPLICATION FOR ADMISSION

1. Name of Proposed Captive: _____

2. Type of Proposed Captive:
   ☐ Pure   ☐ Association

3. Date of Incorporation and Address (if applicable): _____

4. Principal Office of Proposed Captive: _____

_____

5. Location of Books and Records: _____

_____

6. Capitalization if Stock Company:
   a. Amount of Paid-In-Capital $ _____
   b. Type of Stock(s) to be Authorized: Number of Shares
      i. _____   _____
      ii. _____   _____
   c. Par Value of Each Share by Type: Selling Price
      i. _____ $ _____
      ii. _____ $ _____
   d. Location of Shares of Stock
      i. _____   _____
      ii. _____   _____

7. Free surplus if mutual company $ _____

8. Has Parent Prepared Resolutions for Authorizing Establishment of Captive. Designating Individual(s) to:
   a. Vote the Stock of Shareholders? _____
   b. Negotiate Letter of Credit, The Repayment Agreement and/or Continuing Guaranty Agreement? _____

9. Contributed Surplus $ _____
   a. Name(s) and Address(es) of   Percent of
      Beneficial Owners   Ownership
      i. _____   _____

        _____
      ii. _____   _____
      iii. _____   _____

        _____

   (use separate sheet if needed)

10. Explain relationship among Beneficial Owners: _____

_____

_____

11. Enclose Annual Report and Form 1OK of each Beneficial Owner, or Federal Income Tax Return for individual owners. Please describe what has been enclosed:

_____

_____

12. If Letter(s) of Credit Is (Are) to be Used:
   Name and Address of Bank   Issue in Favor of: Amount
   _____   _____   _____

   Form CIC–N(3/88) (enclosed) must be used

13. Name and Address of Lawyer: _____

_____

14. Name and Address of Certified Public Accountant: _____

_____

15. Name and Address of Management Firm: _____

(include biographical affidavits on officers and directors)

_____

16. Name and Address of Actuary or Loss Reserve Advisor: _____

_____

(include biographical affidavit)

17. Name and Address of Risk Management Advisor for Captive Application: _____

_____

_____

18. Name and Address of registered Resident Agent: _____

_____

19. Is Audit Committee to be Formed?: _____
    If Yes, Name the Members: _____

_____

20. Is Executive Committee to be Formed?: _____
    If Yes, Name the Members: _____

_____

_____

21. Name Members of Investment Committee: _____

_____

_____

22. Names and Residence Addresses of all Directors of the Captive:

_____

_____

_____

_____

_____

Résumés of each Director must be prepared and include all past and present affiliations. (Please use biographical affidavit enclosed.)

23. Names and Residence Addresses of Officers of the Captive:
    Chairman _____
    President _____
    Vice President & Secretary _____

Vice President _____

Vice President _____

Assistant Secretary _____

Assistant Secretary _____

(Résumés of each Officer must be prepared on biographical affidavit enclosed).

24. Include the following with this application. (See administrative guidelines fo Business Plan, Pro-Forma Financial Projections, Actuarial Assumption Disclosure).

   a. Name, address, telephone number of the individual to be contacted regarding application.

   b. Copy of Captive's Charter and Bylaws (Certified).

   c. A non-refundable Fee of $1,000.

   d. An Economic Feasibility study by an Actuary.

   e. If Applicant is Association Captive, give history, purposes, size and other details of parent association.

   f. Detailed Business Plan of Operations with supporting data, including:

      i. Risks to be Insured – Direct, Assumed and Ceded – By Line of Business.

      ii. Fronting Company if Operating as a Reinsurer.

      iii. Expected net Annual Premium Income.

      iv. Maximum Retained Risk (Per Loss and Annual Aggregate).

      v. Rating Program.

      vi. Reinsurance Program.

      vii. Organization and Responsibility for Loss Prevention and Safety Including the Main Procedures Followed and Steps Taken to Deal with Events Prior to Possible Claims.

      viii. Loss Experience for Past Five Years Together with Projections for the Ensuring Five Years.

      ix. Organization Chart.

      x. Financial Plan (pro-forma).

   Items i., iii., iv., and x. above should be projected for a five year period.

NOTE: Submit three (3) complete copies of all documents required by this Application. All material requested will be sent to an Approved Advisor upon direction of this Department for review and recommendations to this Department. Fees for review by Approved Advisors are to be paid by Proposed Captive.

I CERTIFY THAT TO THE BEST OF MY KNOWLEDGE AND BELIEF ALL OF THE INFORMATION GIVEN IN THIS APPLICATION IS TRUE AND CORRECT AND THAT ALL ESTIMATES GIVEN ARE TRUE ESTIMATES BASED UPON FACTS WHICH HAVE BEEN CAREFULLY CONSIDERED AND ASSESSED.

Name _____ Date _____

Signature _____

(Director)

INSURANCE DIVISION

STATE OF HAWAII

GUIDELINES FOR BUSINESS PLAN FOR CAPTIVE FORMATION

To properly evaluate applications for a license to do business as a captive insurance company in the State of Hawaii, the submission of a five-year Business Plan is required, including an economic feasibility study prepared by the accredited actuary.

The overall Business Plan must, at a minimum, address each of the three following issues. Because it is possible that there will be overlaps of information between the Application Form, other resources and the Business Plan, it will be acceptable to cite the document, page, and paragraph where needed information is to be found.

Business Plan Issues:

1. Parent (or Sponsor), Subsidiaries and Affiliates (Pure 'captive'), E-1 or Supplementary Application (Association Captive), F-1.
2. Five Year Captive Strategic Plan, G-1
3. Economic Feasibility Study, I-1.

INSURANCE DIVISION

STATE OF HAWAII

PARENT (OR SPONSOR), SUBSIDIARIES AND AFFILIATES

('Pure' Captive)

Supplementary Data

1. Provide operating names of parent, subsidiaries and affiliates.
2. Is the parent (or sponsor) owned or controlled by another?
3. Legal status.
4. Legal domicile.
5. States and countries in which the parent (or sponsor), subsidiaries and affiliates do business.
6. Combined annual gross revenues.
7. Number of employees.
8. Type of Business.
9. Describe your primary exposures to loss.
10. Attach a copy of your Risk Control program.
11. Describe long range (five years) plans with respect to:
    (a) Mergers/Acquisitions by parent (sponsor).
    (b) Spin-offs.
    (c) Reorganization.
12. Attach a schedule of current corporate insurance coverages.
13. What is your objective in forming a captive insurance company?

INSURANCE DIVISION
STATE OF HAWAII
SUPPLEMENT TO APPLICATION
TO FORM ASSOCIATION CAPTIVE INSURANCE COMPANY

1. ACCOUNT INFORMATION
   (a) Is the sponsor of the captive:
   _____ Trade Association   _____ Pool   _____ Professional Group
   _____ Franchise   _____ Other _____
   (b) Individual representing sponsor:
   Name _____ Title _____
   Address _____ Phone _____
   (c) Geographic area covered by sponsor:
   (d) Number of members currently in Association: _____
   Percentage of members expected to participate in insurance program:
   _____ % first year   _____ % second year   _____ % third year
   (e) Briefly describe purpose/goals/services of sponsor:
   (f) Are there other sponsors competing for the members? _____
   Do they have an insurance program? _____
   (g) Describe insurance programs presently in force for members:

2. AGENT/BROKER INFORMATION
   (a) Has the agent/broker had previous experience with mass marketing
   accounts? _____
   (b) Number of sales people to be assigned to this account: _____
   (c) Does the producer currently write any of the members? _____
   (d) Describe the producer's marketing strategies: _____

3. PREMIUM: BY LINE OF BUSINESS (Repeat for multiple lines)

4. RATING INFORMATION:
   (a) Explain in detail recommended rating plans:

5. PARTICIPATION:
   (a) What are requirements to qualify for program regarding safety program
   for members?
   (b) What are financial requirements for members to qualify for the program?

6. EXIT:
   (a) Describe exit procedures including financial arrangements for members
   leaving the program.

INSURANCE DIVISION
STATE OF HAWAII
CAPTIVE STRATEGIC PLAN
(FIVE-YEAR)

1. Give proposed name for captive insurance company. You should also have an alternative name in the event that your original choice cannot be registered. The word 'Insurance' should appear in your name.
2. What is the proposed date of commencement of business?
3. State end of financial/fiscal year.
4. Will there be any guarantees? If so, please provide the amount and the names and addresses of the guarantors.
5. Give particulars of any business other than insurance underwriting which the captive carries on, or proposes to carry on.
6. Give names and locations of banking arrangement which the captive will use.
7. Indicate by check mark which of the following will be located in Hawaii:
   (a) general ledger.
   (b) general journal.
   (c) subsidiary ledgers (referred to in the general ledger).
   (d) cash books – receipts and disbursements
   (e) premium registers.
   (f) loss registers.
   (g) reinsurance reports.
   (h) daily reports of claim files.
   (i) copies of policies.
   (j) copies of reinsurance treaties and agreements.
8. What lines of business are to be written by the captive insurance company?
9. Does the parent own or have an investment in any other captives? If yes, list names and domiciles. Will the proposed Hawaii captive accept or cede any business to this captive(s)?
10. Describe reinsurance arrangements above your proposed net retentions, up to policy limits. Separately describe excess of loss and aggregate stop loss arrangements.
    Will any portion of the limits above the net retention be unreinsured?
    Provide the names of reinsurance brokers or reinsurance intermediaries on the reinsurance program.
11. Does the captive intend to assume reinsurance from unrelated sources? Describe your procedures for underwriting the ceding companies and the risks involved.
12. The Reinsurance Contract.
    Who will prepare the reinsurance contract?
    In addition to the usual clauses certain special clauses are needed.
    Indicate if the contract wording includes such clauses as follows:
    (a) Cancellation clause with period of notice which exceeds by 30 days that period stipulated in the original policy.
    (b) Prompt reimbursement clause of losses paid which exceed the re-insurance premium due.

(c) Authority clause to the company to pay and settle claims without approval of the reinsurer who shall be obligated for its part of such losses.

(d) Indemnification of the company clause.

(e) Empowerment clause for the company to immediately draw upon Letters of Credit in the event of breach of any of the provisions of the reinsurance contract.

(f) Reinsurers liability surviving cancellation clause with respect to claims presented thereafter.

(g) Clause providing that the reinsurance agreement follows in full conformity the original policy, except as to cancellation, premium, and limits of liability.

(h) Solvency clause as required under Section 77 of the New York Insurance Law.

13. Have your cash flow projections taken into account the possibility of negative cash flow in the event of claim payments exceeding the premium retained in the captive?

14. How do you propose to correct any deficiencies in required capital which may occur in the future?

15. State the method by which business will be obtained (i.e. by the captive's own employees, by brokers or agents, or by both methods).

16. Do you intend to issue policies on a cash flow basis (paid loss) or retrospectively rated plan? If yes, provide formula for the captive's retention, timing of payments, and timing of interim and final retrospective determination.

17. Please describe methods, including formulae and time frames, contemplated in the return of premiums to policyholders in the form of dividends, or of distribution of profits to shareholders.

18. Give details of any loans which the captive has made, or proposes to make, to any director, officer, shareholder, or employee of the captive and of any loans or investments to or in any subsidiary or associated company.

19. Attach a specimen copy of each policy form and all endorsements to be used for each line of coverage.

20. Will the captive be a reinsurer for a ceding (front) company?

(a) Provide the name and domicile of the front company.

(b) How much of the risk will the fronting company retain?

(c) Provide allocation factors for premium retained by the fronting company, and the amount to be ceded to the captive.

21. The Fronting Fee: _____ % of Gross Primary Premium, or $ _____ .

22. Claims Administration.

(a) Name, address, telephone number of claims administrator.

(b) Describe claims management program.

(c) Who will develop the claims statistical and accounting experience data as may be required?

23. Do you have a contingency plan in the event you or your captive become insolvent, or if you are taken over by another company, or if you decide to voluntarily close down the captive operation?

INSURANCE DIVISION
STATE OF HAWAII
CAPTIVE INSURANCE COMPANY
ACTUARIAL ASSUMPTION DISCLOSURE

The State of Hawaii Captive Insurance Company Application for Admission Form CIC-C(3/88) requires an economic feasibility study by an Actuary, including projected expected losses and expenses for the upcoming policy period of policies that will be issued by the Captive. To evaluate such projections for appropriateness, actuarial assumptions used in the projections need to be documented, including:

1. Descriptions of data used.
2. Limits and types of coverage offered.
3. Paid and incurred losses and ALAE for at least the past 5 exposure years. Specify inclusion or exclusion of allocated loss adjustment expense (ALAE) in 'losses'.
4. Exposure data for the same-periods as losses.
5. Trend rates and their sources. Limits of losses trended.
6. Development factors and their sources. Limits of data used.
7. Methodology for establishing unallocated loss adjustment expense (ULAE) provision.
8. Expected loss ratios and expense provisions in rate make-up.
9. Cash flow considerations used in determining rates.

INSURANCE DIVISION
STATE OF HAWAII
ECONOMIC FEASIBILITY STUDY

1. What is the premise for the captive? Describe the general purpose and main objectives of the captive being created.
2. Type of Operation.
3. What limits, by line, are to be written by the captive insurance company?
4. Describe the net retentions, by line, which will be assumed by the proposed captive. How much of the underlying liability will be ceded to other reinsurers?
5. What is the initial leverage ratio of the proposed captive? Over the long term, state the expected leverage ratio of the proposed captive.
6. What will be the initial capital of the proposed captive? How will this be funded (i.e. paid up, Letter of Credit, other)?
7. Please provide a brief discussion of the assumptions underlying the determination of the premium rates and projected premium growth. Include the following items within your discussion.
   (a) basis for determining rates.
   (b) projected premium growth.
8. State your estimate of gross premium income, net premium income after reinsurance ceded, expenses and taxes for the first five years of operation.

9. While it is realized that the forecast of losses is subject to the outcome of unknown future contingent events, the underlying assumptions regarding incurred losses must be reasonable within today's economic environment. Please provide a brief discussion of the assumptions used in regard to the following:
   (a) Economic/inflationary adjustments.
   (b) Loss ratio.
   (c) Expected number of claims.
   (d) Allocated loss expense ratio.
   (e) Unallocated loss expense ratio.
   (f) Cash flow or payment pattern of losses.
   (g) Policy regarding discounting of reserves.
   (h) Method by which IBNR losses are treated.
10. Please state your expense assumptions regarding their potential growth in relation to the following:
   (a) Economic conditions – inflation.
   (b) Growth.
   (c) Economics of Scale.
11. Please provide a brief discussion and series of exhibits regarding the investment philosophy and cash flow position of the proposed captive. This discussion should include:
   (a) Cash Flow Exhibit.
   (b) Interest rate assumptions.
   (c) Portfolio assumptions.
12. Pro-forma Balance Sheet
   (a) Assets.
       (i)   Cash.
       (ii) Investments.
       (iii) Real Property.
       (iv) Other.
   (b) Liabilities
       (i)   Loss Reserves.
       (ii) Other.
       (iii) Paid Capital.
   (c) Retained Earnings.
   (d) Underwriting Profit/Loss.
   (e) Dividends (Paid or Declared).
   (f) Capital and Surplus.
   (g) Tax Status.
13. Other Actuarial Exhibits.
   (a) Presentation of Standard Premiums/Developed Losses.
   (b) Claims Payout Factors.
   (c) Projections Based on Various Assumptions (i.e. low loss, median loss, high loss).
   (d) Loss and Loss Adjustment Expense Paid.
14. The Tax Reform Act of 1986 had reforms in the tax posture of insurance companies. Your pro-formas should reflect the provisions of the TRA relative to your individual application. Some of these provisions could include:

(a) With respect to group and association captive, owners will be taxed on their share of the captive's income.
(b) Loss reserves must be discounted.
(c) A portion of unearned premium reserves must be included in income.
(d) A certain percentage of tax-exempt income goes to reduce deductible losses.
(e) Impact of 'related person's income'.

APPENDIX XII

IRELAND – DUBLIN FINANCIAL SERVICES CENTRE

THE REGULATORY SYSTEM

In Ireland the insurance industry is regulated and supervised by the Department of Insurance and Commerce. There are no specific regulations for captives. A captive insurance company writing direct insurance must be licensed in the same way as a non-captive insurance company. The primary objective of the regulators is to protect independent third parties. The special circumstances of captives may be reflected in the conditions attaching to any particular licence granted by the Department of Industry and Commerce.

An international insurance company operating from Dublin must be licensed if it is carrying out direct insurance, even if no insurance business is transacted within the Republic of Ireland.

The regulations in Ireland cover direct insurance only. Reinsurance is not subject to regulatory control, other than the requirements to notify the Department of Industry and Commerce that reinsurance activity is being carried on. There is also a requirement that annual audited accounts can be filed with the Registrar of Companies.

So captive insurance companies can elect to be either a captive reinsurance company or a captive direct insurance company in Dublin.

The requirements for establishing a direct insurance captive are set out in the memorandum from the Department of Industry and Commerce entitled 'Non-Life/1 March 1988'. These require that direct insurers:

- must be licensed
- must be incorporated and resident in Ireland

- must employ qualified staff with power to issue cover
- must have minimum paid-up share capital of IR£500,000
- must maintain a guarantee fund and a solvency margin in line with the EC guidelines of 1976.

The full text of this memorandum follows:

OUTLINE REQUIREMENTS FOR THE ESTABLISHMENT OF A NON-LIFE INSURANCE HEAD OFFICE

General requirements

Under Regulation 4 of *S.I. 115 of 1976*, it is generally illegal for a person to carry on non-life insurance business in the State without being authorised to do so by the Minister for Industry and Commerce. Non-Life insurance business must be carried on in accordance with the terms of an authorisation granted by the Minister and an undertaking must be established in the State by:

(a) having an office, the existence of which is notified to the public and which is open during normal business hours for the transaction of non-life insurance business for which it is authorised

(b) employing at such office persons duly qualified to carry on the business transacted and empowered to issue cover for the authorised classes and to settle claims.

Special requirements

For an undertaking applying for an authorisation which has or proposes to have its Head Office in the State, the following requirements must be fulfilled:

1. An Irish incorporated company limited by shares or by guarantee or unlimited, within the meaning of the Companies Act, 1963, must be established.
2. The Irish company should have a paid-up share capital of *at least* £500,000.
3. The Irish company must possess a guarantee fund defined as being equal to one third of the solvency margin required by Regulation 16 of S.I. 115, subject to the following minimum levels:
   (a) *400,000 units of account*. (Unit = IR£.778539 at 31 October, 1987) where all or any of the following classes are covered:
   10 (Motor vehicle liability)
   11 (Aircraft liability)
   12 (Liability for ships)
   13 (General liability)
   14 (Credit)
   15 (Suretyship)
   (b) *300,000 units of account*, where all or any of the following classes are covered:
   1 (Accident)
   2 (Sickness)

        3 (Land vehicles)
        4 (Railway rolling stock)
        5 (Aircraft)
        6 (Ships)
        7 (Goods in transit)
        8 (Fire and natural forces)
        16 (Miscellaneous financial loss)
        18 (Assistance)

    (c) *200,000 units of account* where all or any of the following classes are covered:
        9 (Other damage to property)
        17 (Legal expenses)

4. The business activities must be limited to insurance and to operations directly arising therefrom. In this connection, a copy of the proposed Memorandum and Articles of Association of the Irish company should be submitted.

5. Details should be submitted of the proposed directors, managers and staff; details of qualifications and experience of staff and a description of the proposed organisational arrangements should also be provided.

6. A scheme of operations must be submitted giving details of:
    (a) the classes of business proposed and including copies of the proposed policy documents;
    (b) the tariffs proposed for each class of business;
    (c) proposed reinsurance programme (draft treaties);
    (d) the items constituting the Minimum Guarantee Fund (see 3 above);
    (e) estimates of the expenses of installation and the financial resources intended to cover them; and for the first three financial years:
    (f) estimates of management expenses (other than installation expenses), particularly current general expenses and commissions; a schedule outling proposed commission rates for each class of business should be supplied;
    (g) estimates of premiums and claims;
        Note: The information required under (f) and (g) should be submitted in the form of a revenue account – gross and net of reinsurance. (See Form 1 in the Schedule to S.I. 401 of 1977.)
    (h) a forecast balance sheet:
    (i) estimates relating to the financial resources intended to cover technical reserves in respect of underwriting liabilities and the solvency margin required by Regulations 14 and 16 of S.I. 115. (Assets representing technical reserves must be valued in accordance with Regulations and a register showing the assets must be kept by the Company. Assets of an amount equivalent to the technical reserves must be localised in the State in accordance with Regulations.)

7. An application fee, which is set from time to time by Regulations, must be paid before the application can be considered.

CAPTIVE INSURANCE COMPANIES

GUIDE TO APPLICATION FOR A 10 PER CENT CORPORATION TAX CERTIFICATE UNDER THE INTERNATIONAL FINANCIAL SERVICES PROGRAMME

Introduction

Certificates guaranteeing the 10 per cent tax rate under the International Financial Services programme are issued by the Minister for Finance. Applications for certificates should be sent to the Industrial Development Authority of Ireland (IDA) which has been appointed by the Government as the marketing agency for the programme. IDA require the following information to process applications.

1. Promoters
General information on promoting company outlining its size, history, performance and the principal shareholders. Recent Profit and Loss Accounts and Balance Sheets should also be provided. In the case of individuals and start-up operations information should be provided on the promoter's track record in the proposed financial services activity.

2. Proposed International Financial Services activity
Details of the proposed activity/service including a technical description of the activity for which a 10 per cent certificate is sought.

3. Marketing information and plans
Details of the demand for this service in proposed markets and the expected growth in these markets.
Details on competitors and on the advantages the project will have over competitors.
Details on the marketing plans for the project.

4. Accommodation and facilities
Outling of office space requirements, whether this will be rented or purchased and details, where relevant, of interim arrangements for period prior to occupying the Centre. Proposed investment in equipment (office equipment/work stations) and details of any special facilities required.

5. Management and staffing
Details on organisational structure, management and special skills requirements.

6. Financial/capital structure
Details on financing requirements and how will these be funded (share capital, loans, etc.).

7. Projections
Detailed projections of Profit and Loss Accounts and Balance Sheets for the first 3 years and of the realistic full potential position of the project.

8. Displacement
In applications from Irish based organisations the following information is required:

- What effect will the proposed operation have on existing operations?
- To what extent, if any, will parent activity be transferred to the new operation?
- To what extent will movement to the Centre result in an increase of existing activity in the Company?
- Are the activities proposed new areas within the company?

9. Contribution to the Irish economy
Details on

- Contribution of the project to the development of the Centre.
- Job potential.
- Demand for local services.
- Other benefits of the proposed project.

ISLE OF MAN
INSURANCE AUTHORITY
(GUIDANCE NOTES)

INTRODUCTION

1. The Isle of Man Government is fully commited to encouraging the development of insurance carried on from within the Island provided it is properly managed and adequately financed.

2. Government control is exercised by the Insurance Supervisor who is charged with the general administration of the Insurance Act 1986 and Regulations issued thereunder but is subject to any Directions that may be issued by the Insurance Authority.

3. These notes set out the essential features of the Act, the Regulations and those Directions which are not specific to individual cases.

4. By Section 3 of the Act no one may carry on an insurance business in or from the island, and no Isle of Man company may carry on an insurance business outside the Island, unless
   (a) specifically authorised by the Insurance Supervisor, or
   (b) the holder of a permit issued under Section 25 of the Act (see para 38), or
   (c) exempted by the Regulations (see para 40).

SUBMISSION OF THE APPLICATION

5. Application for authorisation by the Insurance Supervisor may only be submitted by or on behalf of a company incorporated or to be incorporated in the Isle of Man.

6. Persons intending to apply for authorisation are advised to study the Act and Regulations before filing an application which should normally be submitted at least one month before the date on which it is desired to commence business.
7. The application should be on the form prescribed which must be signed by the promoter(s) or, in case of an authorised company, two directors, and be accompanied by the documents and information specified.
8. The Insurance Supervisor is prepared to discuss or give advice on a draft application or possible problems in completing an application and/or business plan.

REQUIREMENTS FOR AUTHORISATION

9. Before granting authorisation to a company the Insurance Supervisor must be satisfied on the basis of the application submitted and other information received that
   (a) the company has been incorporated
   (b) the memorandum and Articles of Association are appropriate for the business to be carried on
   (c) the ultimate beneficial interests in all shareholdings of the company that exceed 10 per cent of its issued capital have been disclosed.
   (d) the minimum capital or guarantee requirement (see para 16) has been paid up
   (e) the company has adequate financial resources to support the business described in the application and provide the requisite margin of solvency (see para 20) during the first three years of operation.
   (f) reinsurance support is adequate, appropriate to the class(es) of business, prudently placed and properly spread. If the applicant intends to reinsure with its holding company, details of that company's reinsurance arrangements may be required.
   (g) the net premium retention after reinsurance will not be less than 15 per cent of the total premium written, unless the Authority agrees to a lower percentage in a particular case
   (h) the company will not be operating solely or primarily as a front to earn risk-free income for itself or any connected party.
   (i) the controllers, directors, chief executive and managers of the company are fit and proper persons to hold the positions concerned and collectively have the technical competence to carry on the classes of insurance business for which authorisation is sought. It is normally a requirement that at least two of the directors of the company will be resident in the Isle of Man or that the company is managed by a body registered under the provisions of Section 27 of the Act (see paras 34 and 35)
   (j) proper records, books of account and other documents appropriate to the business will be maintained on the Island and be available for inspection and investigation by the Insurance Supervisor or his appointed agent if he so wishes

(k) the appointed auditors have experience of insurance business, carry professional indemnity insurance for not less than £10 million and have accepted the appointment.

(l) if the company is to carry on long-term business an actuary has been appointed and has agreed to the appointment.

CLASSES OF BUSINESS

10. The categories and classes of insurance business for which authorisation may be applied for are:

Category	Class	Description
Long term	1	Linked long term
	2	Long term (other than linked)
General	3	Marine, Aviation & Transport
	4	Property (other than Classes 3 or S)
	5	Motor
	6	Pecuniary Loss
	7	Liability (other than Classes 3 or 5)
	8	Credit & Suretyship
	9	Personal Miscellaneous including accident, Health Disability and such other insurance of a personal nature as is not, or is deemed by Regulations not to be, long-term business
Reinsurance	10	Reinsurance only of Classes 1 and 2
	11	Reinsurance only of Classes 3 to 9
Restricted	12	Classes 1 to 11 inclusive but restricted to contracts with related group companies or members of a common industry or association

11. Authorisation will not usually be granted to carry on both long-term and general business unless

(a) the long-term business is restricted to reinsurance under Class 10, or

(b) the general business is restricted to Class 9, or

(c) both long-term and general business are within the restrictions of Class 12.

BUSINESS PLAN

12. In deciding whether an applicant has adequate financial resources to support the business proposed the Insurance Supervisor will require to examine a 3 year Business Plan indicating:

(A) for each class of general business (including individual classes within Class 12)

(i) maximum net retention per risk or event and in aggregate after all reinsurance ceded based on

(a) policy limits, or

(b) estimated maximum loss (if applicable and less than 65 per cent of policy limits)

      (ii) reinsurance programme stating
          (a) type of reinsurance contract(s)
          (b) threshold and limit any one risk/event and in aggregate
          (c) basis of premium payable and commission receivable
          (d) names of reinsurers writing individually (or together with associated companies) 10 per cent or more of any contract and their percentage lines
    (iii) projected annual premium, gross and net of reinsurance
    (iv) projected claims, gross and net of reinsurance, showing net amounts
          (a) paid in year
          (b) outstanding at each year end (reported claims)
          (c) IBNR provisions at each year end
(B) for each class of long-term business (including business within Class 12)
     (i) estimated premium volume by product and the corresponding new business strains.
     (ii) details of reinsurance arranged or to be arranged, including names of reinsurers
(C) projected Cash Flow stating interest rate and other assumptions used including the claims 'run off' pattern by class of insurance
(D) projected Revenue or Fund Account(s) ⎫
(E) projected Profit & Loss Account (or   ⎬ giving the details
     Income & Expenditure Account for a   required in the prescribed
     company not trading for profit)   formats to the extent they
(F) projected Balance Sheet   ⎭ are relevant

13. Authorisation will be restricted to those classes for which a projected revenue or fund account has been submitted.

14. The appointed auditors are required to confirm that they consider the information provided in the Business Plan to have been properly prepared on the basis of the assumptions stated. If the company is to carry on long-term business, the appointed actuary is required to confirm that he considers the financing of the company to be sufficient to cover both technical reserves and the required margin of solvency and that he agrees with the information provided in the Business Plan in so far as it relates to long-term business.

15. When the projected claims experience for a class is more favourable than the ratio to net premium income normally expected on the basis of UK market experience supporting justification, such as actual claims statistics for the risks to be insured, should be provided.

FINANCING

16. The *minimum* requirements for paid up share capital or, in the case of a mutual, the guarantee fund depend on the classes of insurance for which authorisation is granted and are as follows:

Classes 1 and/or 2   £500,000 (but a lower amount may be admissible provided the business plan demonstrates that solvency margin is unlikely to drop below £250,000)

Classes 3 to 9   £150,000
Classes 10 and/or 11 £100,000
Class 12   £50,000

17. However, an applicant (other than a mutual) is required to have initial financial resources sufficient
    (a) to support the business proposed, allowing for projected capital expenditure investment losses, bad debts and possible variation in the projected operating results or, in the case of Life Companies, new business and expense strain, and
    (b) to provide the requisite margin of solvency during the three years following authorisation.

18. As a general rule the minimum capital requirement plus 10 per cent of the difference between that requirement and the initial requirement, as determined by the Insurance Supervisor on the basis of the Business Plan, must be paid up in cash and deposited with an Isle of Man bank authorised under the Banking Act 1975. Except for the purchase of IOM or UK Government Securities no transfer of or reduction in the required bank deposit may be made without prior written consent of the Insurance Supervisor. The balance of the said initial requirement should be represented by admissible assets which may include an irrevocable letter of credit or independent guarantee acceptable to the Supervisor in support of uncalled capital or to provide for exceptional circumstances.

19. A mutual is required to satisfy the Insurance Supervisor that its rules, membership and limits of liability are such that its members would be able to make such contributions as may be necessary to maintain or reconstitute the solvency margin requirement, inclusive of the minimum guarantee fund which is required to be held in an authorised Isle of Man bank.

SOLVENCY MARGINS

20. A company is required to maintain at all times a minimum margin of solvency calculated as follows:

Class 1   1/4 per cent of actuarial value of liabilities assumed net of reinsurance

Class 2   1 per cent but not less than £250,000

Classes 3 to 9   15 per cent of net written premium but not less than £150,000

Classes 10 and/or 11 £100,000

Class 12   £50,000
                         10 per cent of net premium written (of general business) up to £2m, and
                         5 per cent of net premium written (of general business) in excess of £2m

plus   £100,000, if long-term business written

The solvency margin requirement for a company carrying on both long-term and general business (other than by a restricted class 12 authorisation) is the sum of that required for each category.

413

21. The format for calculating the solvency margin of a company, including details of non-admissible assets, is given in Schedule 7 of the Regulations. (See Appendix A.)

STATUTORY RESERVE

22. An insurer (other than a mutual) which, in respect of general business, has during a relevant period an exposure ratio, any open contract, greater than 25 per cent is required to maintain a statutory reserve as a non-distributable part of shareholders' funds. Exposure ratio is defined as the maximum net liability any one loss or event expressed as a percentage of the adjusted net assets shown in the solvency margin calculation for the financial year end within that period. Relevant period is the period between successive annual general meetings of the insurer.

23. Any such insurer shall transfer to the statutory reserve 20 per cent of its pre-tax profits for each year until such time as the exposure does not exceed 25 per cent. If any claim, or the aggregate of all claims from any one event, exceeds 25 per cent of adjusted net assets the amount in excess of that percentage shall be charged to the statutory reserve in priority to revenue.

24. If and when the exposure ratio is agreed by the Insurance Supervisor to be less than 15 per cent the statutory reserve shall be released to profit or to undisclosed reserves (see para 26), provided this does not cause the ratio to exceed 25 per cent.

*Note: the statutory loss reserve is under review and may be changed in 1997.

ACCOUNTS

25. Every authorised insurer is required by Section 12 of the Act to submit to the Insurance Supervisor, not later than six months after each year end, a copy of its audited accounts to shareholders in the format prescribed by Regulations and supplemented as stated in para 28 below.

26. It should be noted that the disclosure exemptions available to insurance companies under the IOM Companies Act have been revoked and replaced by a specific exemption which permits authorised insurers to include undisclosed reserves in provisions for claims or in general business or long-term business insurance funds provided the existence of any such reserves is disclosed in the accounts, whether or not the reserves are included in the calculation of solvency (Regulation 6 refers).

27. If the insurer carries on long-term business the annual accounts must incorporate a certificate from the appointed actuary that in his opinion the aggregate amount of liabilities in respect of long-term business as at the balance sheet date does not exceed the amount stated in the balance sheet as representing the Long-Term Business Fund.

SUPPLEMENTARY INFORMATION FOR SUPERVISORY PURPOSES

28. The directors of a company are required to annex to its annual accounts, for submission to the Insurance Supervisor, such of the supplementary information prescribed by Regulations as may be relevant. This includes analyses of business written, claims run off, net retention, reinsurance arrangements, letters of credit and calculation of solvency margin.

    The directors are required to certify the information submitted and the auditors are required to report that, in their opinion and according to the information and explanations they have received,

    (i) all of the prescribed information as is relevant has been properly prepared and submitted, and

    (ii) it was reasonable for the persons giving the certificate to have made the statements to which it relates

29. In addition, every authorised insurer is required to submit to the Insurance Supervisor, within 3 months of each quarter end, a statement that includes the following, at or for the year to date:

    (a) premium written, gross and net of reinsurance

    (b) commission and other expenses

    (c) claims paid/benefits payable, net of reinsurance

    (d) reported claims oustanding

    (e) amounts due from reinsurers

    (f) cash balance including deposits

    (g) value of investments

    (h) details of any material change, made or projected, in business written, net retentions or reinsurance ceded from the information last provided.

    This requirement may be waived, at the Supervisor's discretion, when audited accounts have been submitted for at least 3 financial years.

FEES

30. A registration fee of £1,000 and the initial business fee, calculated pro rata from the date of authorisation to 5th April next, is payable on notification that authorisation has been granted.

31. The annual business fee payable on or before the 6th April each year is £2,500 but is reduced to £500 for any year of assessment in respect of which the company does not apply for exemption from liability to pay income tax. The business fee is inclusive of any fee payable to the Assessor for tax exemption.

CONTROL

32. The ownership and the ultimate beneficial interests in the ownership of a company must be fully disclosed to the Insurance Supervisor if not stated on the application form. This includes any person who has power to secure the affairs of the company are conducted in

accordance with his wishes or is able to control, directly or indirectly, the exercise of one third or more of the voting power at any general meeting of the company. Ownership by a discretionary trust is not acceptable.

MANAGEMENT

33. If management of a company is to be exercised solely by the directors and controllers it is normally a requirement that at least two of the directors will be resident in the Isle of Man. Staffing must be adequate and competent for the business conducted.

34. Section 27 of the Act requires any person, not being an employee of an insurer, who provides management services for one or more insurers or who holds himself out as a manager in relation to one or more insurers to apply for registration as an insurance manager unless such services are limited to the keeping of insurance business accounts for an authorised insurer or registered insurance manager.

35. If the company appoints a registered insurance manager to carry out the day to day management and that person or body is considered competent to act in such capacity for the business conducted, the Insurance Supervisor may agree to a reduction in the number of directors otherwise required to be resident in the Island.

DECISION ON THE APPLICATION

36. The Insurance Supervisor will advise the applicant in writing whether or not authorisation will be granted and, if so, the conditions if any that will be imposed. If the decision is not to grant authorisation the applicant will be told the general nature of any reason so that, if changes can be made, a new application may be submitted.

ISSUE OF AUTHORISATION

37. When the Insurance Supervisor is satisfied that the applicant has complied with all requirements the authorisation will be issued and sent by post to the applicant or the appointed manager. Receipt should be acknowledged in writing and the Insurance Supervisor should be advised of the date on which business in each class is commenced and the date on which the first financial year will end. Failure to commence a class of business within one year from the date of authorisation may result in the authorisation for that class being withdrawn.

PERMIT HOLDERS

38. An insurance company incorporated outside the Isle of Man may apply to the Insurance Supervisor under Section 25 of the Act for a permit to carry on insurance business from an establishment on the Island.

39. A permit will not be granted unless the Supervisor is satisfied that –
    (a) the company is authorised to carry on the same or equivalent class or classes of insurance in the UK, or
    (b) the company is carrying on insurance business in a country other than the Island and the UK in accordance with the laws of that country, and that the business is adequately supervised in that country, or
    (c) the company –
        (i) could be authorised under Section 6 of the Act but for its incorporation outside the Island, and
        (ii) will comply with all the provisions of the Act and the Regulations made thereunder as apply to an authorised Manx insurer (subject to such exceptions, adaptions and modifications as may be specified).

EXEMPTION BY REGULATION

40. Section 3 of the Act does not apply to –
    (a) industrial assurance business carried on by a Friendly Society registered under the enactments relating to such societies.
    (b) insurance business carried on by a trade union or employers' association and limited to the provision of provident benefits or strike benefits to its members
    (c) general business within classes 6 (pecuniary loss) or 8 (credit and suretyship) carried on solely in the course of and for the purpose of banking business
    (d) an insurer authorised by the UK/EEC that does not have a fixed place of business on the Island.

EXEMPTION FROM INCOME TAX

41. A company applying for authorisation or permission to carry on insurance business in or from the Isle of Man may apply, through the Insurance Supervisor, under the provisions of the Income Tax (Exempt Insurance Companies) Act 1981 for exemption from liability to tax on profits or income and in respect of payment to non-residents of dividends, interest, share of profit or remuneration of directors.

42. A company seeking exemption from tax will need to satisfy the Assessor that its underwriting profits and losses arise from risks outside the Island and its other profits and income arise outside the Island or from approved financial institutions or approved investment companies in the Island. A concession may be granted by the Assessor if income arises from the underwriting of risks within the Island which, in relation to the company's total business may be regarded as insignificant.

VALUE ADDED TAX

43. (a) VAT applies in the Isle of Man on the same basis as in the UK. Services by authorised or permitted insurers in the IOM are normally exempt or zero rated depending on whether the policyholder (or other client) belongs within or outside the EEC.

   (b) Services supplied to an IOM insurer by a management company in the Island or elsewhere may be partly standard rated and partly exempt whilst some specific services if performed abroad may be zero rated. Recovery by an IOM insurer of input tax is dependent on its status but is generally limited to the tax attributable to its taxable supplies, i.e. other than exempt.

   (c) Any query on VAT by an applicant should be addressed to the nominated manager, accountant or advocate.

NAME OF COMPANY

44. Application for name approval should be made to the Registrar who will refer to the Insurance Supervisor.

REGISTRATION FEE AND DUTY

45. Both charges are calculated on authorised share capital – registration fee (as at 1st January 1988) on a sliding scale up to £250; duty at the rate of 1.1 per cent plus £18, with a maximum of £50,000, but a company may issue shares at a premium.

APPENDIX A
CALCULATION OF SOLVENCY MARGIN

1. The Solvency Margin of an insurer shall be calculated in the manner specified in the following table:

(A) SHAREHOLDERS FUNDS AND GENERAL BUSINESS

Shareholders funds as shown by audited (non-consolidated) balance sheet (note i)		x
Undisclosed reserves included in:		
Provision for claims	x	
General business fund	x	
		x
Adjustment of assets to market value (note ii)		x
		x

Adjustment on restatement of assets in
accordance with Part II of Schedule 7 of the Insurance Act, 1986.

1. Investments (other than land and
   buildings)   (x)
2. Land and buildings   (x)
3. Other tangible assets   (x)
4. Assets subject to charge   (x)
5. Intangible assets   (x)
6. Deferred acquisition costs   (x)
7. Debts   (x)
8. Unpaid share capital   x
9. Letters of credit and guarantees
   (note iii)   x

Adjusted net assets   (x)
                                                           x

Required minimum margin for general business
(note iv)   (x)

Excess over required minimum margin   x

(B) LONG-TERM BUSINESS

Quantified actuarial surplus in
long-term business fund (note v)   x

Surplus from section A (note vi)   x
                                                           x

Required minimum margin for long-term
business (note iv)   (x)

Excess over required minimum margin   x

NOTES:

(i)   In the application of this Part to mutual associations, references to
      'shareholders' funds' and 'general business insurance provisions and funds'
      shall be construed as references to 'the sum of the guarantee fund and
      the reserves' and 'the fund available for outstanding and unreported
      claims' respectively.

(ii) Where investments or land and buildings are stated in the shareholders'
      accounts at an amount less than market value, an adjustment to market
      value may be included in the calculation of adjusted net assets for
      solvency margin purposes (subject to any restriction on admissibility in
      accordance with Part II of Schedule 7).

(iii) Issuing body to be specified.

(iv) Detail of calculation to be shown.

(v)   As certified by the actuary to the insurer.

(vi) The amount to be entered at this line will, in the case of a company not
      writing general business, be the amount of the net assets of the company
      (excluding those attributed to the long-term fund) adjusted in accordance
      with Part II of Schedule 7.

APPENDIX XIV

JERSEY

INSURANCE BUSINESS (JERSEY) LAW, 1983

The business of insurance and reinsurance in Jersey is regulated by the terms of the Insurance Business (Jersey) Law, 1983 ('the Law'). The Law requires that no insurance or reinsurance business may be conducted in or from Jersey by any person or company except that they be:

1. Authorised under the Insurance Companies Act 1981 to carry on business in the United Kingdom, provided the business being transacted in Jersey would be lawful in the United Kingdom, or
2. Authorised to carry on business in a member state of the European Economic Community provided the business being transacted in Jersey would be lawful in the member state, or
3. Authorised by permit granted by the Finance and Economics Committee ('the Committee') of the States of Jersey to carry on restricted insurance business.

The Law further prohibits a company incorporated in Jersey to carry on insurance or reinsurance business outside the Island unless it is authorised to do so by a permit issued by the Committee. The law does not apply, however, to Members of Lloyd's, friendly societies registered under the Acts of Parliament in the United Kingdom, trade unions or employers associations (but solely in respect of provisions for their members of provident and strike benefits) and certain other bodies which are defined in the Law.

The Law is designed to regulate insurance business within a flexible framework and there are no statutory reporting requirements. However, the Committee is empowered to impose conditions on the granting of permits and these will include requirements to file annual audited accounts, together

421

with a certificate of compliance, generally issued by auditors, to confirm that the business of the company is being carried on in accordance with the terms of the permit. In addition, companies must file annual returns, in compliance with the Companies Laws, and income tax returns in compliance with the Income Tax (Jersey) Law 1961. The Law is silent on capital requirements but the Committee is likely to require that companies have capital in excess of £100,000. Solvency requirements, based on income, will be imposed unless the company is a pure captive.

PERMIT APPLICATION PROCEDURES

Prospective applicants are encouraged to arrange a preliminary meeting with the Jersey authorities to discuss the insurance operations proposed for the captive and to present a letter detailing information on shareholders, corporate structure, nature of the business, and preliminary profit projections. If the proposals are approved in principle, a permit application with supporting documentation, and accompanied by the prescribed fee, must be directed to the Committee through the office of the Commercial Relations Officer. Once the application is approved, the captive may be incorporated and capitalised. Thereafter, copies of the incorporation documents, with proof of capitalisation, should be directed to the Committee. The captive may then commence business within the terms of its permit. Application procedures usually take from four to six weeks.

When considering a permit application, the Committee will be primarily concerned with:

(a) The standing, reputation and nature of business of the parent company and its subsidiaries and their combined level of free capital and reserves;

(b) The knowledge and expertise in insurance matters available to the applicant;

(c) The paid-up share capital of the applicant and the level of free capital and reserves compared with premium income;

(d) Arrangements made or to be made by the applicant regarding reinsurance;

(e) Whether fit and proper persons are employed by or associated with the applicant in the management, control and audit of its operations;

(f) The nature of the risks to be insured:

(g) Whether it is in the best economic interests of Jersey that the applicant be granted a permit and, in this connection, its residence for Jersey tax purposes.

PERMIT APPLICATION

An application for a permit for an insurance or reinsurance company should contain the following information:

1. The name of the proposed company ('the Company'). The name may be reserved for use until the application is approved in principle, when the Company may be incorporated.

2. Particulars of the classes of insurance business to be included in the permit.
3. The date on which business is to commence. (If the Company is to assume risks retroactively, this must be disclosed).
4. The name and address of the company, firm or partnership which is to administer or manage the business and affairs of the Company.
5. The address of the registered office of the Company within Jersey at which it must maintain its register of members, together with copies of its annual returns, to be available for inspection by the public. It is also the address for the acceptance of notices and service of process in legal proceedings.
6. Evidence of the proper incorporation of the Company pursuant to the Companies Laws of Jersey or the laws of the country in which it is incorporated.

   Notes:
   (a) In the case of a Jersey company, two copies of each of the Certificate of Incorporation and the Memorandum and Articles of Association are required. A draft of the Memorandum and Articles of Association should accompany the application.
   (b) In the case of a foreign corporation, two copies of its Charter or Certificate of Incorporation should be presented together with copies of its By-Laws or incorporation documents. The documents should be certified by a statutory declaration made by a director or the company secretary which, in turn, must be authenticated under the public seal of the country, city or place of incorporation. If the incorporation documents are not written in English, a certified translation must be furnished with the certification being sworn before a Notary Public, whose signature should be confirmed by an official of a British Embassy or Consulate.

7. Names, addresses and nationalities of all shareholder companies and the nature and scope of the activities of the group or groups to which they belong.
8. The curriculum vitae or resumé of each director, officer and manager. These should detail the name, address, nationality, date of birth, education, professional qualification and provide a brief summary of the individual's career to date with particular emphasis on any insurance activities in which that person may have been engaged.
9. Each proposed shareholder, director and officer is required to provide a banking reference.
10. Name and address of the auditors.
11. Two copies of the annual accounts of holding, parent or other companies for the three preceding years.
12. A business plan. This is a crucial part of the application and should give full details of the proposed insurance activities for at least a three year period. The plan should include the following:
    (a) A statement showing the amount of assets and a detailed analysis showing their projected excess over liabilities at the date of the permit.

(b) The sources of business and the approximate percentage expected from each source.

(c) The nature of the risks within each class to be assumed.

(d) The guiding principles as to reinsurance including the maximum retention by the Company per risk or event, exclusive of ceded reinsurance.

(e) The nature and value of the assets which represent or will represent the solvency margin.

(f) Projected profit and loss accounts and balance sheets for at least three years which should provide details of:

> Premiums receivable and payable
> Commissions receivable and payable
> Investment and other income
> Claims
> Management and administrative expenses

(g) The proposed investment policy indicating the nature of the investments which are likely to represent the capital and reserves.

(h) The residence of the Company for Jersey taxation purposes and the basis on which taxable income will be determined.

13. Particulars of any association which exists or which will exist between the directors and controllers of the Company and any person who acts or will act as an insurance broker, agent or reinsurer.

14. Copies or drafts of reinsurance treaties.

15. Copies or drafts of any agreements which the Company will have with persons (other than employees of the Company) who will manage its business.

16. Where applicable, copies or drafts of any agreements to be concluded with brokers or agents.

TAXATION

The underwriting insurance surpluses of a captive engaged in insuring or reinsuring the risks of its shareholders and their associated companies are not subject to Jersey income tax. Conversely, underwriting losses are not deductible for the purposes of calculating taxable income. Profits from the reinsurance of third party risk will attract Jersey income tax.

Income from the investment of capital, shareholder funds and reserves is assessable to income tax at the standard rate of 20 per cent but relief is granted in respect of management expenses not directly attributable to underwriting activities. Profits from the realisation of investments are not subject to income tax unless the Company is engaged in the trade of dealing in investments. Conversely, losses incurred on the realisation of investments are not deductible for tax purposes.

The burden of income tax in relation to investment income may be mitigated by interposing a Corporation Tax Company between the captive and its ultimate shareholders.

The captive may pay dividends, or effect interest-free loans, to the interposed company, provided the lending does not deplete, unreasonably, its taxable income. The income of Corporation Tax Companies is not subject to taxation in Jersey at the standard rate rather tax is paid at the flat rate of £300 per annum.

CONTINUING REGULATION

Captives may only carry on insurance business in accordance with the terms of their permits. Any change to the business requires the prior approval of the Committee.

Permits will require captives to file audited financial statements, made up to the end of their financial year, within six months of such year end. At the same time, they will also be required to file a certificate of compliance issued by an independent auditor, or such other person as the Committee may approve, confirming that the Company has carried on business in accordance with the terms of its permit.

The Law grants the Committee discretionary powers through the attachment of conditions to permits inter alia to:

Exempt permit holders from provisions of the Law

Prescribe investments

Prescribe liquidity margins and ratios

Prescribe forms and returns

The Committee also has power to revoke permits.

APPENDIX XV

LUXEMBOURG

LEGISLATION/FEES

Applicable laws and provisions

Company Law (1928); Insurance Law (1968, 1984).

Supervising authority

'Commissariat Aux Assurances'.

Local office required

Yes. The company must have an authorised resident manager. A management company incorporated in the Grand-Duchy can be the resident manager.

Is there a need for local directors? (local members)

No.

Restrictions

(a) Direct business
Yes, the captive will be considered as any other insurance company and has to follow exactly what is contained in the Law.

(b) Indirect business
If the captive company applies for a licence to write business it has to comply with what is stated in Articles 46 and 47 (see below). If licence is granted the company may write all kinds of indirect business.

CAPTIVE INSURANCE COMPANIES

Local auditor

Yes, an auditor approved by the Commissariat Aux Assurances.

Local lawyers

Only when needed for legal matters.

Fees

Initial Licence:	Lux francs 100,000,
Annual renewal of Licence:	Lux francs 50,000.

CAPITAL REQUIRED

Minimum share capital

Lux francs. 50,000,000.

Stamp duty

1 per cent on capital paid in.

Investments restrictions

Share Capital to be invested in Luxembourg.

Solvency margin

Reinsurance companies must have free assets which do not constitute technical reserves and which represent at least 10 per cent of the annual premiums net of ceded reinsurance (7 per cent if the company does not write General Liability and 5 per cent for pure captives).

Untaxed reserves

Reserve for Unearned Premiums; Reserve for Outstanding Claims; Catastrophe Provision.

Annual audited accounts

To be deposited at the Commissariat aux Assurances.

TAXES

1. General

Reinsurance companies are in principle subject to the same taxes as any other Luxembourg company:

- corporate income tax
- net worth tax
- municipal business taxes
- issued capital tax
- tax on capital brought in

(a) Corporate income tax

Any Luxembourg commercial company whose taxable income exceeds Flux 1,312,000 is subject to corporate income tax of 34 per cent (from 1 January 1989). There is also a surcharge at a rate of 2 per cent on the tax itself. The effective rate of tax will therefore be 34.68 per cent for 1989.

(b) Net worth tax

This tax is levied at a rate of 0. 5 per cent on the net worth of the company. The basis for this taxation is established every three years. However it is revised every year (new basis) when the net worth at the beginning of the year varies by more than one fifth or more than Flux 3,000,000 from the worth recorded at the last reference date.

On the other hand the catastrophe provision is tax deductible. This tax is not a deductible item in calculating the profit subject to corporate income tax.

(c) Municipal business taxes

There are two types of municipal business tax:

- The business tax on net worth is 0.2 per cent multiplied by a municipal coefficient (actual rate of tax in the City of Luxembourg: 0.5 per cent). This tax is levied on the net worth at the beginning of the financial year, increased by 40 per cent of the long-term debts and reduced by an allowance of Flux 1,800.000.
- The business tax on incomes is 4 per cent multiplied by a municipal coefficient. The amount of this income is determined after deduction of the catastrophe provision and an allowance of Flux 700,000. In the case of the City of Luxembourg the rate of tax is 10 per cent (9.9 per cent after taking into account the deductibility of this tax from its own basis).

Corporate income tax is deductible from municipal business taxes. Net worth tax and issued capital tax are not deductible in determining the income on which this tax is assessed. Payroll tax was abolished on 1 January 1987.

(d) Issued capital tax

This tax, payable quarterly (20 January, 20 April, 20 July, 20 October) at a rate of 0.36 per cent of the fair market value of the issued shares, is not deductible in calculating the profit subject to income tax.

(e) Tax on capital brought in

This tax is levied when the company is formed and when new capital is brought in. It is levied at a rate of 1 per cent.

2. Double taxation treaties

The tax legislation in Luxembourg is similar to that in the main industrialized countries. Any Luxembourg company therefore, with the exception of holding companies, benefits from a network of double taxation treaties. Luxembourg has already entered into agreements with a number of countries.

Unlike reinsurance companies operating in the tax havens which, in the absence of double taxation treaties, pay a tax at the rate applicable in the country of the parent company, reinsurance companies in Luxembourg enjoy definite advantages:

- Luxembourg does not deduct any interest at source.
  Paid dividends are however subject to a deduction of 15 per cent unless the agreements stipulate otherwise. When a foreign parent company has a significant holding in the capital of a Luxembourg company this rate is, with very few exceptions, reduced to 5 per cent (see the table in the appendix). As from 1 January 1986 Luxembourg unilateraly reduced from 25 per cent to 10 per cent the level of participation which the parent company must have in the subsidiary in order to be eligible for this reduced rate.
- Deductions at source from interest or dividends in the country of origin are reduced or reimbursed in accordance with the terms of the international double taxation treaties.
  It should also be pointed out that under certain conditions the law of 30 November 1978 incorporating unilateral measures in Luxembourg against double taxation allows for the offsetting of any residual deductions made after application of the treaties.
- Reinsurance companies are also exempt from tax on dividends received from foreign companies in which they have a significant holding.

3. Catastrophe provisions

A reinsurance company, by its very nature, has to undertake long-term commitments so it is essential that it be allowed to build up substantial financial reserves to cope with claims which might arise. In his instructions of 11 November 1985, approved by the Ministry of Finance on 13 November 1985, the Director of the Fiscal Administration set out the provisions and limits governing the creation of a tax-free catastrophe provision by reinsurance companies. This provision is meant to cover the liabilities which they might incur if any of their risks gave rise to exceptionally heavy claims.

The annual allocation to the catastrophe provision may not exceed a sum such that the result of the year's commercial operations, including due taxes other than corporate income tax, would show a deficit or be inadequate to cover losses carried forward from previous years.

The total set aside for the catastrophe provision may not be higher than a ceiling equal to a multiple of the average of the premium income in the current and four previous years, net of cancellations, commissions and reinsurance ceded.

The multiple applied depends on the risk category to which the Commissaire aux Assurances has assigned the company. In order to determine the maximum amount of the catastrophe provision, the average premium income as defined in the previous paragraph should be multiplied by a figure of not more than 12.5 for a class I risk category; 15 for a class II risk category; 17.5 for a class III risk category; 20 for a class IV risk category.

The multiple to be applied must be shown in the actuarial schedule to be submitted to the Commissaire aux Assurances when applying for authorisation. The category can be changed to take account of the evolution of the risks covered.

The catastrophe provision would only be taxable to the extent that it exceeded, on a consolidated basis, the maximum provided for by the regulations.

It is deemed to be a liability against net income provided the amount of the provision is shown in the trading balance.

If the catastrophe provision exceeds the ceiling provided for by the regulations the amount in excess of the permitted maximum would be included as income in the year in which it arose. At the time of liquidation of the company any provision not used would be included in the taxable profit.

In order to encourage reinsurance companies and captives to have a substantial level of capital the tax provisions in force apply solely to companies with a capital of at least Flux 50,000,000.

4. Loss carry-forwards

When the year's trading result shows a deficit, the catastrophe provision has to be reduced and an amount written back to the income statement. If the provision is not sufficient to eliminate the loss, the loss can be carried forward in accordance with Article 114 of the Law on income tax, i.e. the loss on any year is deductible from profits for the five following years.

5. Conclusion

(a) Based on a trading result of Nil after allocation to the Catastrophe Provision the total tax for a reinsurance company with a share capital of Flux 50,000,000 would be about Flux 880,000.

(b) If the company would show a trading profit after allocation to the Catastrophe Provision this profit will be taxed at the normal company tax mentioned under item 3 above.

EXTRACTS FROM INSURANCE LAW

Art. 46.

(Law of February 24, 1984)

1) Every reinsurance company which establishes itself in the territory of the Grand-Duchy must be authorized by the Minister before beginning its activities.

2) Luxembourg reinsurance companies may obtain authorization only if they adopt the form of a 'société anonyme' and if the fully paid up initial capital is a minimum of fifty million francs. The request for authorization must be addressed to the Minister and accompanied by the following documents and information:

- the by-laws
- the last and first names, domicile, residence, profession and nationality of the administrators and the persons responsible for the management of the company.

- proof that the minimum initial capital has been constituted and has been fully paid up.

3) Every reinsurance company which establishes itself in the territory of the Grand-Duchy shall appoint a manager who must have been appointed by the Minister before performing his functions. This appointment is given only to persons proving their good morality and a high professional knowledge in the area of reinsurance and who have their domicile and their residence in the Grand-Duchy.

4) The Minister may reduce the minimal capital required to a sum of six million francs for those reinsurance companies which limit their activity to covering risks originating in industrial and/or commercial firms which belong to the same groups as those belonging to the leading stockholder(s) of the reinsurance company.

5) A Grand Ducal regulation determines the minimal rules following which the reinsurance companies' free assets must evolve in terms of the evolution of commitments of the companies. These free assets, however, may in no case fall below the amounts alluded to in paragraphs 2 and 4 of the present article.

6) A Grand Ducal regulation fixes the amount of the fee to which the examination of a request for authorization is subjected and the contribution of the reinsurance company to the operation costs alluded to by Article 24 of the present law.

Art. 47.
(Law of February 24, 1984)

1) The Commissariat aux Assurances is competent for the supervision of the responsibilities incumbent upon reinsurance companies in accordance with Article 46, for the examination of requests for authorization from companies and managers and for the presentation of all objections and opinions to the Minister before the delivery of the authorization.

During the pursuit of operations by the reinsurance companies, the Commissariat aux Assurances shall supervise those companies to ensure that these conditions are permanently respected. It shall require each reinsurance company to submit itself to an external audit to be executed annually at the expense of the company by an independent auditing firm to be chosen from a list appointed by the Commissariat aux Assurances.

2) The Minister may withdraw the authorization granted to reinsurance companies and to the managers if they no longer fulfill the conditions of access and of operation as they are defined in the present article and in the preceding article.

It has been decreed that the withdrawal of authorization by simple request from the Commissariat aux Assurances, after an initial inquiry carried out by the Commissariat aux Assurances, the company or persons be given the opportunity of being heard in their means of defense or duly notified by registered mail.

3) The decision made by the Minister to refuse or withdraw an authorization may be deferred to the Council of State, settlements committee. The decision must be justified precisely and communicated to the company concerned.

The recourse must be introduced under pain of foreclosure within one month after the notification of the impunged decision.

For the case that the Minister has not pronounced a verdict on a request for authorization, the delay of three months foreseen by Article 32 of the law of February S, 1961, concerning the organization of the Council of State is extended to six months.

Art. 17.

In application of the Article 46, paragraph 5 of the law reinsurance undertakings' free assets must evolve in relation to the evolution of their commitments.

To this end, the reinsurance undertakings always must have their free assets at their command which do not constitute technical reserves and which represent at least 10 per cent of the annual premiums, net of ceded re-insurances.

This rate is reduced to 7 per cent for the reinsurance undertakings which do not practice the coverage of risks of general liability.

The rate is reduced to 5 per cent or reinsurance undertakings which limit their activity to taking charge of risks originative in industrial and/or commercial companies, which belong to the same groups as the stockholders holding the majority of shares of the reinsurance undertakings, as long as they do not practice the coverage of risks of general liability.

Art. 18.

In application of Article 46, Paragraph 6 of the law, the amount of the fee to which the examination of a request for authorization is subjected and the contribution of an authorized reinsurance undertaking to the operation costs of the Commissariat aux Assurances are fixed as follows:
- a single fee of one hundred thousand francs (100,000 Fr.) for the examination of each request for authorization;
- an annual fee in a lump sum of fifty thousand francs (50,000 Fr.) for each authorized reinsurance undertaking.

This fee is due from the first entire accounting period following the current period for which the first authorization was granted.

The single tax for the examination of a request for authorization is payable in the month following the authorization to the 'Administration de l'Enregistrement' in charge of collecting it.

The annual tax in a lump sum is payable in the month following the notification of payment made by the Administration de l'Enregistrement in charge of collecting it.

APPENDIX XVI

MALTA

INSURANCE OFFSHORE COMPANIES AND THE INSURANCE BUSINESS ACT, 1981

General

The Insurance Business Act, 1981 ('IBA') applies to insurance offshore companies, subject to the exemptions and amendments indicated below.

By virtue of the Malta International Business Activities Act, 1988, the Minister responsible for international business activities may, on the advice of the Authority, make rules or regulations whereby he may exempt any class of insurance offshore company from any of the provisions of the IBA, subject to such conditions as may be specified.

Notwithstanding any other provisions of the Malta International Business Activities Act, 1988:

(a) a company shall not be registered as an insurance offshore company unless the Authority is satisfied that the company is capable of properly conducting and supporting the business to be carried on, that it has the financial resources for such purpose and that it will keep such resources in assets and maintain where appropriate margins of solvency, as are normally acceptable;

(b) a company whose business is, or includes, the management of captive insurance offshore companies shall not be registered as an offshore company unless the company proves to the satisfaction of the Authority that it has sufficient special knowledge and practical experience of insurance business so to act and that it is properly and adequately insured against its liabilities for negligence and misfeasance in the conduct of its affairs.

435

CAPTIVE INSURANCE COMPANIES

Business of Insurance

The business of insurance is defined as:

the making or proposing to make, whether as principal or as agent, any contract of insurance or reinsurance, and includes any business carried on in connection therewith, or as ancillary thereto, or which is generally recognised as insurance.

Exemptions and amendments applicable to all insurance offshore companies

Grant of licences (Section 5 of the IBA)

In terms of the IBA any company desirous of commencing the business of insurance in Malta must apply in writing to the Minister of Finance for a licence.

In the case of insurance offshore companies, such applications must be channelled through the Authority, and the Minister of Finance, when considering any application, is required to act after he has received a recommendation from the Authority.

Furthermore, insurance offshore companies are exempted from the provisions whereby the Minister of Finance may subject licences granted by him to such conditions as he may deem fit.

In order to carry on business as principals, insurance offshore companies, other than oversea companies and captive companies, must have a minimum paid-up share capital of US$ 750,000 or its equivalent in any other foreign currency, and must have at all times unimpaired assets equal at least to that amount, which is in lieu of the normal capital/unimpaired assets requirement of Lm2,000,000.

In the case of captive companies, the paid-up capital/unimpaired assets must amount to at least US$250,000, or its equivalent in any foreign currency.

Insurance offshore oversea companies are exempted from the requirement of keeping within Malta, and out of their own funds, unimpaired assets as stipulated in Section 5(1)(b) of the IBA.

Matters concerning licensed companies requiring Minister's approval (Sections 6(2) and 6(4) of the IBA)

The provisions whereby insurance companies are required to obtain prior Ministerial approval before effecting share transfers, beyond a certain level, to non-residents are obviously not applicable to insurance offshore companies.

Re-insurance (Section 15 of the IBA)

In terms of Section 15 of the IBA, a licensed insurance company may only re-insure a risk with another company which is licensed to carry on the business of insurance as principal, or with a foreign company approved by the Minister of Finance. The Minister may also require a licensed company to cede to a named licensed local company up to 30 per cent of risks insured.

These restrictions do not apply to insurance offshore companies.

Financial year and publication of accounts (Section 16 of the IBA)
Insurance offshore companies need not publish annually a copy of their balance sheet and profit and loss account in two local daily newspapers, nor need they exhibit their accounts in a conspicuous position in each of their offices in Malta.

Security fund (Section 26 of the IBA)
Insurance offshore companies are exempted from making any contribution to the security fund established under Section 26 of the IBA for the payment of any claims remaining unpaid by reason of an insurance company's insolvency.

Exemptions and amendments applicable to insurance offshore 'oversea' and 'subsidiary' companies only

Matters concerning licensed companies requiring Minister's approval (Sections 6(1) and 6(3) of the IBA)
Insurance offshore oversea and subsidiary companies are exempt from the provisions of Section 6(1) of the IBA which requires an insurance company to obtain prior Ministerial approval before making any addition or alteration to its Memorandum and Articles of Association, or other instrument constituting the company.

Such companies, moreover, are not requited to obtain prior Ministerial approval before entering into any arrangement or agreement for the sale, disposal or reconstruction of their business by amalgamation or otherwise, though they are required to inform the Minister of Finance of any such sale, disposal or reconstruction.

Reserve and other funds to be kept by insurance companies (Section 8 of the IBA)
Insurance offshore subsidiary companies are exempted from the requirement of transferring at least 25 per cent of their net annual profits (before any dividends) to a reserve fund, until such fund reaches the amount of the company's paid-up share capital. (Insurance offshore oversea companies are not required by the IBA to keep such a reserve fund.)

As already indicated, insurance offshore oversea companies need not keep in Malta, and out of their own fund, unimpaired assets as stipulated in Section 5(1)(b) of the IBA. Therefore the requirement of Section 8(2) to invest these funds only in such manner as the Minister of Finance may permit also falls away.

Margin of solvency (Section 9 of the IBA)
The margin of solvency stipulated in Section 9 of the IBA does not apply to insurance offshore oversea and subsidiary companies.

Normally, a company carrying on business other than life insurance is deemed not to have a margin of solvency if the value of its assets does not exceed its liabilities by either 15 per cent of its premium income in the preceding year or Lm100,000, whichever is the greater. Insofar as life insurance business is concerned, a company is normally deemed not to have a margin of solvency if its liabilities under unmatured life policies exceed the amount of its life insurance fund.

Payment of dividends (Section 10 of the IBA)

Insurance companies may not normally declare or distribute any dividend except from profits which the auditors of the company have certified, in a statement delivered to the Minister of Finance, to be remaining on hand after retaining unimpaired the entire paid-up share capital, the margin of solvency and reserve funds required to be kept, and a sum sufficient to pay all net losses and all liabilities.

These provisions do not apply to insurance offshore oversea and subsidiary companies.

Inadmissible assets (Section 11 of the IBA)

Section 11 lists those assets which are non-admissible, and of which no account shall be taken in determining the financial position of an insurance company.

This section is not applicable to insurance offshore oversea and subsidiary companies.

Investments (Section 12 of the IBA)

Section 12 prohibits insurance companies from making certain investments or entering into certain transactions.

These prohibitions do not apply to insurance offshore oversea and subsidiary companies.

Reserves of insurance companies (Section 13 of the IBA)

Insurance offshore oversea and subsidiary companies are not required to establish their reserve liability in respect of life insurance business, or to maintain a reserve for unearned premiums on policies relating to non-life insurance business, on the basis stipulated in Section 13 of the IBA.

Limit of single risk (Section 14 of the IBA)

Insurance offshore oversea and subsidiary companies are not bound by Section 14 which, in respect of non-life business, precludes insurance companies from retaining any risk on any one subject of insurance in an amount exceeding 20 per cent of the net worth of the company.

CONDITIONS, APPLICABLE TO OFFSHORE COMPANIES

The particular conditions applicable to the different types of offshore companies are detailed below. Reference is made in these conditions to:

Private companies

In terms of the Commercial Partnerships Ordinance, Cap. 168, a private company is a company which by its Memorandum or Articles of Association.

(a) limits the number of its members to a maximum of fifty;

(b) prohibits any invitation to the public to subscribe for any shares or debentures of the company; and

(c) restricts the members' right to transfer shares.

Nominee companies

A Nominee Company is a private company, set up solely for the purpose of acting as nominee with respect to offshore companies and/or trusts, and duly authorised by the Authority to act as such. These Nominee Companies in their role as secretary/sole director of an offshore company, or as trustee of an offshore trust, are assigned the duty and the responsibility to help in upholding the reputation of Malta as a respectable business centre by ensuring that their clients carry on their activities with due respect to the laws of Malta. The share capital of a Nominee Company, and any voting or controlling power therein, may not be held by, or vested in, non-residents of Malta in an amount exceeding in the aggregate forty per cent. This percentage is increased to sixty per cent in the case of a Nominee Company formed exclusively to act as a trustee of offshore trusts, and in such cases, the Authority may exceptionally also allow non-residents to own all the shares in the Nominee Company. A Nominee Company must have not less than three directors of whom at least two are Maltese citizens, resident in Malta, and possess the qualifications and experience required by section 42(2)(f) of the Malta International Business Activities Act, 1988.

Restrictions on ownership of property in Malta

Except for banking and insurance offshore LOCAL companies, any other offshore company may only own immovable or movable property situated in Malta to a limited extent as follows:

(a) immovable property held on lease for the purpose of its operations from Malta;

(b) deposits in bank accounts;

(c) furniture, equipment, material, documents and other property reasonably required by it for its operations from Malta;

(d) in the case of an offshore company which is exclusively or mainly a holding company, it may own shares in, or debentures of, a subsidiary company, registered in Malta, which has its main objects the manufacture or processing of goods in Malta, or the ownership, management, administration or operation of ships, and which is wholly owned by persons not resident in Malta (except that one person resident in Malta may hold shares as do not exceed in the aggregate one lira in nominal value, without any special voting rights).

Note: For the purposes of the Malta International Business Activities Act 1988, shares in, and debentures of, an offshore company, and ships, even if registered in Malta, shall be deemed to be property NOT situated in Malta.

CAPTIVE INSURANCE COMPANIES

Banking and insurance offshore oversea companies

Such a company must:

- Be registered or incorporated outside Malta.
- Be a banking institution or an insurance company recognised by the Authority as being of international standing and repute.
- Establish a branch in Malta exclusively for offshore activities.
- Not own any movable or immovable property in Malta except as indicated in the preceding section.
- Be registered with the Authority as an offshore company.
- Pay the applicable registration and annual fees.

Banking and insurance offshore subsidiary companies

Such a company must:

- Be a private company registered in Malta.
- Be a subsidiary of a banking institution or of an insurance company recognised by the Authority as being of international standing and repute.
- Restrict its business exclusively to offshore banking or insurance.
- Not have any part of its capital, voting or other controlling rights owned by, or vested in, any person resident in Malta.
- Have a name which clearly identifies it as a subsidiary or an associate of a banking institution or of an insurance company, as the case may require, which is of international standing and repute, and which is accepted as such by the Authority.
- Not own any movable or immovable property in Malta except as indicated in the preceding section.
- Be registered with the Authority as an offshore company.
- Pay the applicable registration and annual fees.

Banking and insurance offshore local companies

Such a company must:

- Be a private company registered in Malta.
- Be a subsidiary of a company registered in Malta which is itself licensed to carry on the business of banking or of insurance in Malta, under the Banking Act, 1970 or the Insurance Business Act, 1981.
- Restrict its business exclusively to offshore banking or insurance.
- Not have any part of its capital, voting or other controlling rights owned by, or vested in, any other person resident in Malta EXCEPT that one person resident in Malta may, if so authorised by the Minister of Finance, hold shares up to Lm1,000 in nominal value, or 1 per cent of the Company's share capital, whichever is the lower.
- Have the permission of the Minister of Finance, for the purposes of Exchange Control, to operate as a banking offshore company or an insurance offshore company.

- Be registered with the Authority as an offshore company.
- Pay the applicable registration and annual fees when due.

REGISTRATION AND ANNUAL FEES

All offshore companies must be registered with:

- The Registrar of Partnerships, in terms of the Commercial Partnerships Ordinance, Cap. 186.
- The Malta International Business Authority in terms of the Malta International Business Activities Act, 1988.
  The certificate of Registration issued by the Registrar of Partnerships will state that the company is only capable of commencing business after it has been registered with the Authority as an offshore company.

Registration with the Registrar of Partnerships

The fees payable to the Registrar of Partnerships on registration ate charged on the Company's AUTHORISED share capital as follows:

on amounts up to the equivalent of	Lm2,000	Lm100
on amounts up to the equivalent of	Lm3,000	Lm106
on amounts up to the equivalent of	Lm4,000	Lm112
on amounts up to the equivalent of	Lm5,000	Lm118

On the equivalent of every additional Lm1,000 or
part thereof up to Lm100,000.......................... Lm 1
On the equivalent of every additional Lm1,000 or
part thereofup to Lm1 million........................ Lm0.40

No further fees are payable on capital in excess of the equivalent of Lm1 million. Effectively, therefore, the maximum fee cannot exceed Lm573.

Moreover, all offshore companies are exempt from the stamp duty which is normally payable on registration.

Note: A banking offshore company is required tv have a minimum paid-up capital of US$1,500,000 or its equivalent in any other foreign currency.

In the case of insurance offshore companies, the minimum required is US$ 250,000 or equivalent for captive insurance companies, and US$750,000 or equivalent for other insurance companies.

All other trading and non-trading companies are required to have an issued share capital of not less than the equivalent of Lm500, of which at least 20 per cent must be paid up.

Registration with the Malta International Business Authority

Registration and annual fees payable to the Authority by offshore companies are as follows:

CAPTIVE INSURANCE COMPANIES

	On registration	Annual fee
	Lm	Lm
(i) Banking offshore companies	25,000	25,000
(ii) Insurance offshore companies OTHER THAN captive Insurance offshore companies	5,000	5,000
(iii) Trading offshore companies for collective investment	5,000	5,000
(iv) Captive insurance offshore companies	1,000	1,000
(v) General trading offshore companies other than those falling under (iii) above	1,000	1,000
(vi) Non-trading offshore companies	500	500

The annual fee is payable upon each anniversary of the company's registration with the authority.

Note: With reference to (vi) above, Legal Notice 167 of 1989 has reduced the registration and annual fees from Lm500 to Lm100 in the case of non-trading offshore companies only owning a ship or ships, and/or holding shares in, or debentures of a company owning a ship or ships.

APPENDIX XVII

PANAMA

MEMORANDUM
CAPTIVE INSURANCE COMPANIES

I – Panama Corporations Law, 1927

The majority of companies in Panama are incorporated by registration under the Panama Corporations Law of 1927, this is a relatively simple process and its usually done in conjunction with a local lawyer. The article of incorporation of Insurance companies cannot be notarized or registered until the pertinent authorization is issued by the Superintendency of Insurance of Panama.

II – Captive Insurance Act, 1996

The operation of captive insurance companies in the Republic of Panama is governed by the Captive Insurance Act of 1996. The Minister of Commerce is the ultimate regulatory authority, but the issue of licenses and the supervision of licensees is the immediate responsibility of the Superintendency of Insurance of Panama.

The law requires that companies wishing to carry on captive insurance businesses or to act as a captive manager should hold a license to do so.

For the propurses of the ordinance it is necessary to distinguish between general business, which is property and casualty insurance and long term business, which is the insurance business involving the making of contracts of insurance in human life, hospitalization or contracts to pay annuities of human life.

Captive Insurance Companies may only insure or reinsure those risks authorized under the licence covering their respective activities.

443

III – Application for a Captive License

Applications for captive licenses must be made through an attorney at law before the Superintendency of Insurance accompanied by:

1 The prescribed application fee of US$ 1,000.00
2 The applicant's name and address in the Republic of Panama
3 The applicants Corporate Capital
4 The name of the company's resident representative, who may be a captive manager, or a resident of the Republic of Panama. In the latter case, he must submit his curriculum vitae, bank and personal references, experience in the matter of insurance or reinsurance and the powers of attorney or authorisations granted to him for the purpose of managing the company.
5 Financial statements of the company duly audited by an independent authorised public accountant; or, in the case of new companies, the audited initial application balance showing the amount of the paid capital. These documents may not be more than three months old with respect to the date of the licence application.
6 The names, addresses, and nationalities, of the applicants's shareholders, together with at least two references verifying the financial good standing of individual shareholders or parent company.
7 A certified copy of the corporate applicant's charter, statues, memorandum and articles of association or other similar documents, plus a certified copy of its certificate of incorporation which should include the name of the legal representative and the corporate authorized capital all verified by a statutory declaration of a director or the secretary of the applicant.
8 A brief business plan giving a projection and containing details as to type of business to be undertaken principal source(s) of income anticipated premium income.

IV – Specific requirements

1 Every insurer's license is subject to the conditions that the licensee notifies the Superintendent of Insurance of any change or proposed change in the information supplied in connection with its application; that the licensee carries on business only in accordance with such information and any changes therein as have been approved by the Superintendency of Insurance.
2 A licensed insurer is required to maintain a principal office in Panama where its license should be displayed.
3 A licensed insurer must submit to the Superintendent of Insurance, audited financial statements in the prescribed form verifying its solvency and report on the risk insured or reinsured, as the case maybe, in accordance with the format authorized by the Superintendency.
4 As a matter of policy aimed at facilitating the regulatory function of the Superintendent of Insurance, it will require a licensed insurer to be represented in Panama by an Insurance Manager, which will maintain full and proper record of the insurer's business activities.

The Insurance Manager must be a company which provides expertise to or for insurers and which has properly qualified persons in its employ,

5 Insurance Managers will pay a license fee of US$ 500,00 and will have to place a surety bond of US$100,000.00.

6 A licensed insurer must appoint a "resident representative" in Panama approved by the Superintendency of Insurance to act as his insurance manager or qualified insurance executive. The Resident Representative will be responsible for the insurer's actions and reports and submission to the Superintendency of Insurance of the required declarations and returns. Also he will have to report to the Superintendency of Insurance of any likelihood of the insurer for which he acts, becoming insolvent.

7 The minimum paid capital requirements are as follows:
In the case of property and casualty.......................US$150,000.00
In the case of long term business
or both general or long term business......................US$250,000.00
In addition the act requires that a long term business company maintain a solvency margin of six percent (6%) of its mathematical reserves. A property and casualty company is required to maintain a ratio of not more than one to five between the retained net premiums and their net worth.

8 Every insurer will have to pay US$2,000.00 annual fee. There will be no taxation at all.

9 Thirty-five percent (35%) of the reserves must be invested in Panama.

V – Incorporation and operation costs

1 Startup costs

Professional fee (incorporation)................................US$1,200.00
Notarial and public registry..US$ 200.00
Superintendency of Insurance...................................US$1,000.00
Miscellaneous expenses...US$ 75.00
Assistance in preparation of captive licence application,
liaison with the Superintendent and general advice........US$5,000.00*

.... Total: US$7,475.00

*Please note that legal fees incurred depend on the nature of the application so that a complex insurance program will involve more professional time and hence higher fees.

2 Annual operating costs

Company maintenance fee.......................................US$1,200.00
Insurance license fee...US$2,000.00

In addition to the above mentioned annual cost there will be insurance management costs which vary greatly depending on the services required, auditors fees and miscellaneous expenses (telephone, facsimile, bank charges, etc.).

PANAMA, 1996

CAPTIVE INSURANCE COMPANIES

GENERAL INFORMATION ON PANAMA CORPORATIONS

1. INCORPORATION AND REGISTRATION

Once the required information is received, it takes only three or four working days to establish and register the company, provided that the chosen names are acceptable and that our standard articles of incorporation are used.

In cases of urgency, the corporate documents will be sent by courier service which will add approximately US$60.00 to the incorporation costs.

2. SHELF CORPORATIONS

In cases of extreme urgency or for clients who for one reason or another require an "aged" company, we keep a stock of "ready-made" or "shelf" corporations, at a slightly higher cost.

For the convenience of our clients we keep a stock of these corporations with various correspondents in several countries. For further information in this regard, please contact us directly so that we can refer you to the correspondent in your country.

3. MAIN OBJECTS OF THE CORPORATION

The company may engage in any lawful business even though the nature of such business is not actually specified in the Articles of Incorporation.

4. DIRECTORS AND OFFICERS

(1) The Directors/Officers may be of any nationality and residents of any country. This is particularly important as nominee directors can be employed while the beneficial owners may remain anonymous and still control all the shares of the company and its assets. Members of our firm may be appointed as nominee directors, acting upon the instructions of the owners.

(2) There may be any number of directors provided there is a minimum of three.

(3) There will be a President, Secretary and Treasurer, and any other officers as determined by the Board of Directors. Each officer may hold two or more positions however it is advisable that the President does not also hold the position of Secretary.

(4) The meetings of the Board of Directors may be held in any country and may be attended by the Directors in person or by proxy.

5. CAPITAL

There is no paid-in capital requirement which means that the corporation can exist without unnecessarily tying up funds until they are actually needed.

There is no requirement insofar as a correlation between the corporation's paid in capital and the value of its assets, therefore the assets may well be considerably greater than the paid in capital.

6. CAPITAL STOCK

Under Panamanian law, a corporation may have any number of share-holders, it thus being possible for it to be owned by a single person.

The company shares may be issued to the bearer, in which case there is no record of the shareholder's identity.

7. SHAREHOLDERS MEETINGS

The meetings of the shareholders may be held in any country and may be attend by the shareholders in person or by proxy.

8. POWERS OF ATTORNEY

If nominee directors are employed, upon request, they will provide the beneficial owners with a power of attorney authorising them to operate the company, open and operate bank accounts and in general conduct the company's affairs as they wish.

For the purposes of issuing the general power of attorney, we would require the full name (no abbreviations permitted) city of residence and nationality of the person or persons in whose favour the power of attorney should be issued. This may be in the name of one or more persons and is sworn before a Notary. Only one copy is issued which is sent to the person or persons named in it

According to law, powers of attorney should be registered but in practice they are almost universally accepted without this formality, thus there being nothing on public record to indicate that any power of attorney has ever been issued.

9. TAXATION

Those Panamanian companies that do not operate within the territory of Panama (off-shore companies) are exempt from the payment of income tax, need not present tax declarations or financial statements in Panama and may keep their accounting books outside Panama.

The only annual fee charged by the government of Panama to all offshore Panama registered companies, is the sum of USD150.00, payable at the time of the company's incorporation and each year thereafter, within three months following the anniversary of the company's inscription date. A fine of USD30.00 will be imposed by the government for late payment.

We notify annually the due date for such payments and effect payment upon receipt of funds, the official receipt for which is then forwarded to the client.

Taxation in Panama is based on the "source of income" principle. Profits arising from activities outside Panama are not subject to taxation by Panama even though the corporate office and staff may be resident in Panama and transactions flow through the Panama office.

Article 694 of the Tax Laws provides:

"Income derived from the following activities shall not be considered as produced within the territory of the Republic of Panama:

a) Invoicing from an office established in Panama, the sale of merchandise or products for a sum higher than that at which said products or merchandise had been invoiced to the offices established in Panama, provided that said merchandise or products are handled exclusively abroad.

b) Directing from an office established in Panama, operations which are completed consummated or take effect abroad and

c) Corporate dividends or participations when said dividends or participations are derived from income not produced within the territory of the Republic of Panama including the income derived from activities mentioned in subsections a) and b) hereof."

10. ANNUAL FEES

Once the company is established, there is only one annuity payable to us as Resident Agent of the company in the Republic of Panama. (It is a legal requirement that all Panama corporations must have a Panamanian attorney as its resident agent.)

In the event of a client requesting our personnel to act as Nominee Directors/Officers, as previously mentioned, an additional yearly fee per Director/Officer, will be payable.

11. AMENDMENTS TO THE ARTICLES OF INCORPORATION

Any change to the articles of incorporation, be it the name of the company, members of the board of Directors or Officers, authorised capital, issue of additional shares, the granting of general or specific powers of attorney, requested by our clients, will generate additional fees.

12. STABILITY

The acceptability of Panama corporations in banks and commercial centres worldwide is owed partly to the fact that the law governing them was passed more than half a century ago and has never been reformed, but only supplemented by law No.9 of 3rd July, 1966, and a decree of 4th May 1966

13. LIMITED ADMINISTRATIVE SERVICES

Many clients find it convenient to avail themselves of our limited administrative services, which entail receipt and forwarding of correspondence, the use of our telephone and telex numbers on the company's letterhead, opening and management of bank accounts on the company's behalf, invoicing minutes of Board meetings, etc. The fees for these services would be calculated depending upon the extent of the work involved.

Note: We acknowledge permission from Arias, Arias & Associates, Panama to reprint the above.

APPENDIX XVIII

SINGAPORE

SINGAPORE AS A DOMICILE FOR CAPTIVE INSURANCE COMPANIES

Policy

1. Singapore is keen to promote itself as a domicile for pure captives established by large reputable and financially sound multinationals with a commitment to the long term of a captive for risk management purposes.

2. Proposals to set up 'rent-a-captive' operations in Singapore will also be considered, especially when they are needed to facilitate the set up of insurance captives eventually. We are also prepared to consider proposals for 'mutual' captives where the need for their proposed establishment can be properly justified.

3. Captive insurers are not allowed to operate as commercial insurers. They are allowed only to write the in-house risks of their parents and related companies within the group.

4. The proposed captive operation should be economically viable and generate a significant premium volume. As a start, it should have premiums of at least around S$1 million with good prospects for growth in future years.

Requirements for captive insurers

The major financial requirements captives would have to comply with are outlined below:

    (a) *Minimum paid-up capital* a capital of S$1 million is required;

(b) *Solvency margin* a surplus of assets over liabilities of S$1 million is to be maintained; and

(c) *Annual fees* annual fees of S$5,000 are payable.

Investment

5. A captive insurer is given a great deal of freedom in the investment of its funds. As part of the Authority's efforts to promote fund management activities in Singapore, captive insurers are encouraged to utilise fund management services available in Singapore where they find it advantageous to do so.

Taxation

6. The corporate tax rate in Singapore is currently 33 per cent. Taxation in Singapore is governed by the Singapore Income Tax Act (Cap 141). Like commercial insurers, captives would be able to enjoy a concessionary tax rate of 10 per cent on profits from offshore business. Details on the concessionary tax rate are contained in the Income Tax (Concessionary Rate of Tax for Income from Insuring and Reinsuring Offshore Risks) Regulations 1980. A copy of the regulations is attached at Annex 1. (It should be noted that the present 10 per cent concessionary tax does not extend to investment income derived from the shareholders' capital funds.)

Procedures to set up a captive insurer in Singapore

7. A company that wishes to set up a captive insurer in Singapore should apply formally to the Authority using the application form in Annex 2. The Authority would normally want to meet with senior representatives of the company before a formal application is submitted. The meeting is to assist the Authority in the assessment of the company's long-term commitment towards a captive operation. The company will be briefed on the Authority's admission policy and expectations during the meeting.

8. The Authority would give a decision on the application *within a month* from the submission of a complete, formal application. To prevent delays, applicants should ensure that all information required in the application form is provided.

9. Where the application is approved, the Authority will issue a letter of in-principle approval. This letter specifies the conditions that the company must accept before its captive can be registered to carry on insurance business in Singapore. The company is given *one month* to indicate acceptance of these conditions.

10. It is also given *6 months* to complete the following registration requirements and commence business. These requirements are
   i) registration under the Companies Act (Cap 185); and
   ii) payment of the annual fee of S$5,000.

11. On completion of the registration requirements, the captive insurer would be formally registered to carry on insurance business.

Management of captive insurers

12. Captives should be well managed and run on sound insurance principles. Companies with in-house insurance expertise may manage

their captive insurers themselves. Where the company wishes to utilise the services of a captive insurance management company, it should obtain the approval of the Authority. Approval would normally be granted where the Authority is satisfied with the capability of the captive management company, to manage the captive.

INSURANCE COMMISSIONER'S DEPARTMENT
THE MONETARY AUTHORITY OF SINGAPORE
NOVEMBER 1987

ANNEX 1

THE INCOME TAX ACT
(CHAPTER 141)

THE INCOME TAX (CONCESSIONARY RATE OF TAX FOR INCOME FROM INSURING AND REINSURING OFFSHORE RISKS) REGULATIONS, 1990

In exercise of the powers conferred by section 43C of the Income Tax Act, the Minister for Finance hereby makes the following regulations:

1. These Regulations may be cited as the Income Tax (Concessionary Rate of Tax for Income from Insuring and Reinsuring Offshore Risks) Regulations, 1980, and shall have effect for the year of assessment 1980 and subsequent years of assessment.

2. Tax shall be payable at the rate of 10 per cent on –
    (a) the income of an insurance company derived by it from accepting –
       (i) general insurance covering offshore risks;
       (ii) general reinsurance covering offshore risks; and
    (b) the dividends and interest derived by the insurance company from the investment of its income arising from its business of insuring and reinsuring offshore risks.

3. (1) The following provisions shall apply to an insurance company carrying on the business (other than the business of life insurance) of insuring and reinsuring offshore risks.

   (2) The income in respect of dividends and interest attributable to the business of insuring and reinsuring offshore risks referred to in paragraph (b) of regulation 2 for a basis period for any year of assessment shall be ascertained by the formula: $\dfrac{A - B - C}{D} \times I$

   where A is the total of –
   (a) the relevant profits; and
   (b) the reserve for unexpired risks and provision for outstanding claims as at the end of that basis period, relating to the business of insuring and reinsuring offshore risks;

   B is –
   (a) where the company is resident in Singapore, the total amount of the dividends deemed to have been paid by the company, during the relevant period, out of the profits of the business of insuring and reinsuring offshore risks; and the amount of such dividends deemed to have been paid in each year within the relevant period shall be determined as follows:

$$\text{Total amount of dividends paid by the company during each year} \times \frac{A}{D} \text{ and}$$
within the relevant period

(b) Where the company is not resident in Singapore, the total amount of the income deemed to have been remitted out of Singapore, during the relevant period, out of the profits of the business of insuring and reinsuring offshore risk; and the amount of the income deemed to have been so remitted in each year within the relevant period shall be determined as follows:

$$\text{Total amount of income remitted out of Singapore during each year within the relevant period} \times \frac{A}{D}$$

C is the total amount of losses attributable to the business of insuring and reinsuring offshore risks from the realisation or disposal of any assets of the company during the period;
    (a) in the case of the business of reinsuring offshore risks, commencing with the basis period for the years of assessment 1978; and
    (b) in the case of the business of insuring offshore risks; commencing with the basis period for the year of assessment 1980,
    and ending with the basis period for the year of assessment in question; and the amount of such losses (if any) in each basis period shall be determined as follows:

$$\text{The total losses from the realisation or disposal of any assets of the company during that particular basis period} \times \frac{A}{D}$$

D is the difference between the original value of the total assets before deduction for depreciation and provision or reserve for doubtful debts (excluding asset producing rental income) and the current liabilities (excluding provision for outstanding claims and reserves for unexpired risks) of the company ascertained from the balance-sheet of the company as at the end of the basis period for the year of assessment in question;

I is the total amount of interest and dividend income derived by the company, during the basis period for the year of assessment in question, less any expenses allowable under the Act.

(3) Any item of expenditure not directly attributable to the business of finsuring and reinsuring offshore risks and capital allowances allowable under the Act shall be apportioned between such business and the other general insurance business; and the portion attributable to such business shall be determined by the formula:

$$\frac{X}{X + Y} \times Z$$

where X is the amount of the gross premiums received or receivable in Singapore from the business of insuring and re-insuring offshore risks:

Y is the amount of the gross premiums received or receivable in Singapore from the other general insurance business; and Z is the total of

(a) the common expenses which may be attributable to both the business of insuring and reinsuring offshore risks and to the other general insurance business; and

(b) capital allowances allowable under the Act.

4. For the purposes of regulation 3 –

'relevant period' means

(a) in the case of the business of reinsuring offshore risks, the period commencing on or after the 1st day of January 1977; and

(b) in the case of the business of insuring offshore risks, the period commencing on or after the 1st day of January, 1979,

and ending on the 31st day of December of the year immediately preceding the year of assessment in question; 'relevant profits' means the excess of the total profits over total losses (as computed in accordance with the provisions of the Act) relating to the business of insuring and reinsuring offshore risks for the period –

(a) in the case of the business of reinsuring offshore risks, commencing with the basis period for the year of assessment 1978; and

(b) in the case of the business of insuring offshore risks, commencing with the basis period for the year of assessment 1980;

and ending with the basis period for the year of assessment in question; and for this purpose any losses disregarded under subsection (5) of section 37 of the Act shall be taken into account.

5. The Income Tax Act (Concessionary Rate of Tax for Income from Reinsuring Offshore Risks) Regulations, 1979, are hereby revoked.

Made this 17th day of June, 1980

J Y M PILLAY
Permanent Secretary
Ministry of Finance
Singapore

ANNEX 2

THE MONETARY AUTHORITY OF SINGAPORE

INFORMATION REQUIRED IN RESPECT OF APPLICATION TO SET UP A CAPTIVE INSURANCE COMPANY IN SINGAPORE

I Information on Parent Company of Proposed Captive

1. Name.
2. Date and place of incorporation.
3. Brief history of the company.
4. Names and addresses of shareholders owning 10 per cent or more of the shares in the company and their respective shareholdings.
5. Names of insurance and reinsurance companies and insurance intermediaries in Singapore or elsewhere in which the company or any of its subsidiaries have an equity interest.
6. Description of the company's business and activities and details on its areas of specialisation.
7. Details on the company's international network of branches and subsidiaries.
8. Ranking of the company in its home country in terms of income, total assets or other indicators, if available. Please supply 1 copy of the Annual Report and Financial Statements of the company for each of the last five years.
9. What was the total cost of insurance incurred by the company and its subsidiaries for each of the last five years?
10. How are the insurance needs of the company and its subsidiaries presently being met? (E.g. insurance with conventional insurers, self-insurance, etc.)
11. Does the company or any of its subsidiaries already own a captive insurer? If so, please give reasons why it is necessary to set up another captive insurer in Singapore and supply 1 copy of the Annual Report and financial statements of the captive insurer for the last five years.
12. Details on the expertise that the company has (or has access to) in the following areas:
    (i) insurance underwriting
    (ii) loss prevention and risk management

(Note The information required in Part 1 above relates to the ultimate parent company. Where it is proposed to use another company in the group to own the shares in the captive, the Annual Report and financial statements of this company should also be supplied.)

II Proposed Operations in Singapore

1. Name of proposed captive.
2. Authorised and paid-up capital of proposed captive.
3. Names and addresses of shareholders and their shareholdings in proposed captive.

4. Names, addresses, occupation and nationality of directors of proposed captive. (Please include Identity Card Numbers for proposed Singaporean directors.)
5. Outline the objectives of your proposed captive in Singapore and elaborate how it would be of economic benefit to Singapore and contribute to the development of the Singapore insurance industry.
6. If the company had considered other locations for its proposed captive before selecting Singapore, please explain why Singapore was selected.
7. Details on the tax benefits that would accrue to the company if its captives were located in Singapore. Would the proposed captive be able to take advantage of the 10 per cent concessionary tax rate on offshore business?
8. Details on the classes of business which the proposed captive would write and the estimated volume of business (gross and net premiums) for the first 5 years of operations for these classes. Please indicate the source of each business.
9. Details on the management of the proposed captive in Singapore. If the proposed captive is to be managed by a captive management company give the name and address of the management company. If the proposed captive is to be managed by the company's own executives, provide details on the insurance expertise, qualifications and experience of such persons.
10. Supply a copy of the organisation chart of the proposed captive in Singapore.
11. Would the proposed captive handle all of the insurance requirements of the parent company and its subsidiaries? If not, please explain why
12. Details on the reinsurance arrangement that would be made for the proposed captive.
13. Details on the investment policy for the proposed captive.
14. Supply a copy of the report on the feasibility of the company forming a captive in Singapore or elsewhere.
15. Name and address of proposed auditor in Singapore for the captive insurer. (The proposed auditor is subject to the approval of the Authority.)

III Others

1. Name and address of senior officer of the company to whom queries on the application can be directed.
2. The application should be accompanied by certified copies of letters from the relevant home authorities approving the company's plan to set up a captive in Singapore. Where such approval is not required, a statement to this effect should be given by the applicant.
3. The application should be signed by a director of the company. This director should also certify that the information given in the application is true and complete.
4. Applications should be submitted to:
   The Insurance Commissioner and Actuary
   Insurance Commissioner's Department
   Monetary Authority of Singapore
   10 Shenton Way, MAS Building
   Singapore 0207

APPENDIX XIX

SWITZERLAND

A. INCORPORATION

1. Primary Data and Positions of Authority
- ☐ Name of the captive
- ☐ Address
  If a captive management organisation is used, a declaration of the parent's acceptance of domicile ("Domizilannahmeerklärung") is required.
- ☐ Board members
  Names, addresses, and citizenship of all board members; the majority must be Swiss citizens.
- ☐ Appointed chairman of the board
  Name, address, and citizenship.
- ☐ Signatures
  Swiss citizens and foreigners in Switzerland: certified signature by Notary Public (Notariat). Foreigners abroad: Notary Public and Ministry of Foreign Affairs or the Swiss Embassy.

2. Incorporation Documents
To be written in any of the official languages of Switzerland.
- ☐ Articles of incorporation
- ☐ Minutes of Founders Meeting/Deed of Foundation ("Gründungsversammlung/Öffentliche Urkunde")
- ☐ List of founders
  There must be at least three shareholders, who shall all be present in person or through proxies, at the incorporation, and each shareholder represents at least one share.

457

☐ Appointed Auditor
His acceptance letter in original must be submitted to the Founders Meeting.

☐ Managing Director
The person in charge must be permanently living in Switzerland, be an insurance professional and as such approved by the Insurance Commissioner. A managing director is included in the captive management agreement with Nordic Mutual.

☐ Equity
Share capital: To be calculated as 20% of net retained premium (minimum CHF 1 million). Bank Certifcate of receipt and amount hold in custody is required.

☐ Organisation fund
CHF 200,000. Bank Certificate of receipt and amount hold in custody is required for subsequent application of licence.

B. APPLICATION OF LICENCE TO THE INSURANCE COMMISSIONER

1. Documents to be submitted

☐ Minutes of Founders Meeting/Deed of Foundation ("Gründungsversammlung/Öffentliche Urkunde")
☐ Articles of incorporation ("Statuten")
☐ Extract from the Commercial Register ("Handelsregisteramt")
☐ List of shareholders

2. Organisation

☐ The names of all the board members
☐ An organisational chart
☐ Name, address, and domicile of the captive management organisation
☐ The names of other employees (if any)

3. Business Plan

☐ Underwriting policy and principles for investment of reserves and funds
☐ Reserving rules
☐ Opening balance
☐ Business forecast for the next three years

4. Equity

☐ Amount of share capital and adjustment ruling
☐ Amount of the organisation fund
CHF 200,000. Bank Certificate of receipt and amount hold in custody is required.

5. Insurance Policies

☐ Ceding agreements (preliminary)
☐ Retrocession agreement (preliminary)
☐ Flow chart for each insurance class

C. APPLICATION FOR TAX REDUCTION

Application for tax reduction to the Tax Commissioner. Short description of the mother company and the captive including the business plan, business forecast, and an organisational chart as well as management agreement.

CONDITIONS FOR CAPTIVES IN ZURICH

Incorporation

The establishment of a captive in Zurich includes registration at

- Register of Trade (Handelsregister des Kantons Zürich)
- Resolution of tax pre-ruling of company privileges (Steueramt Kanton Zürich)
- Operation licence granted by the Federal Ministry of Justice (through the Swiss Insurance Commissioner, BPV)

The share capital shall be 20% of net premium held for own account and at least CHF 1 million to be paid before establishment. In addition, an amount of CHF 200,000 shall be held in a so called "organisation fund". This fund is to cover costs for establishment, including stamp duty and a possible financial loss. One third of the share capital can be lent back to the parent company.

Stamp duty is 2% of the share capital plus organisation fund.

For the incorporation, the company name, address, names of board members, managing director, signatories of the company, and an auditor have to be submitted with the registration application. Articles of association and list of shareholder(s) have to be submitted to the Register of Trade.

For the application of the insurance license, a Business Plan together with a three year business forecast, underwriting guidelines and reserving rules, a presentation of the parent company (annual report), and the incorporation documents have to be submitted to the Insurance Commissioner.

Administration

Management of the captive can be handled through a captive management organisation (CMO) with terms and conditions according to a management agreement. The CMO will provide a managing director, who has to reside in Switzerland and whose qualifications must have been approved by the Insurance Commissioner. It is not necessary for the captive to employ its own staff when an approved CMO is appointed. The board must have a majority of Swiss citizens in a company with a foreign owner, authority and obligations may thus be regulated via a mandate agreement, whereby an executive committee, formed with representatives of owners, instructs the board.

Technical reserves

Principles of technical reserving are generally drawn up for each individual captive and approved by the Insurance Commissioner who will retrospectively check that sufficient technical reserves have been set aside. Approved reserves are:

Claims reserve	In accordance with ceding agreement.
IBNR	Provision for a cautious estimation of claims development in respect of class of insurance, area and ceding practice.
Special technical reserves	Provision for a cautious estimation of potential catastrophes and fluctuations in respect of exposure of class of insurance and area.

Reserving from a taxation viewpoint

In a Master Ruling for Captive Companies, Zurich tax authorities accept the special reserving requirements for captive business but do not set any rigid limits of these technical reserves. For tax purposes, any such reserving amount is accepted as long as their creation does not lead to insufficient profits. A minimum profit shall be the average Swiss bond yield plus 2% return on equity (ROE).

Accordingly, the general guidelines and master ruling allow for much flexibility and possibilities for reserving.

Taxation

Profit and capital are taxed separately. Furthermore, state and canton have different tax rates. Summarised, these are as follows.

Federal tax

a) Tax on profit
The rate is decided in respect of the relation between profit after tax deduction and capital (profitability). The lowest rate is 3.63% (at 4% profitability) and the highest 9.8% (at 23.15% profitability) and is applied to the net profit, i.e. after deduction of all taxes.

b) Tax on capital
Tax on capital is paid yearly at a fixed rate of 0.0825% of taxable equity.

Communal and canton tax

a) Tax on profit
The rate is decided in the same way as for federal tax. In 1993 in Zurich the minimum rate was 9.5% (at 4% profitability) and maximum 28.5% (from 28% profitability)

b) Tax on capital
Tax on capital is 0.37% of taxable equity.

Stamp duty

On establishment, a special stamp duty tax of 2% of the capital (share capital plus organisation fund) is paid

Tax on dividend

Switzerland has double taxation agreements with most industrialised countries in the world. There are tax rates on dividend between 0% to 32.5% to be paid in Switzerland The treaty withholding tax rates on dividends are:

0% for *Denmark, Luxembourg, the Netherlands and Sweden*
5% for *Austria, Egypt, Finland, France, Germany, Greece, Malaysia, Norway, UK, Poland and the USA*
10% for *Belgium, China, Hungary, Indonesia, Ireland, Japan, Korea, Portugal, Singapore, Spain, Sri Lanka and Trinidad*

Tax on foreign-owned captives

Administration privilege (Verwaltungsprivileg) granted by the tax authorities makes it possible to reduce the communal and canton tax on companies which do not operate in the Swiss market.

Net tax, federal, canton and community tax combined on profit varies therefore between 4.0 and 12.4%.

Note: We are grateful to Nordic Mutual of Zurich for permission to print an edited version of a document issued by them in 1996.

APPENDIX XX

TURKS AND CAICOS

INSURANCE

An insurance company wishing to be licensed in the Turks and Caicos Islands must show that those persons who control its affairs are competent, with evidence of ability, integrity and experience. The insurance regulations in force are flexible and have been designed to accommodate a wide variety of insurance business. The Superintendent of Insurance may recommend that certain companies with particular characteristics be allowed to operate under modified regulatory requirements after he has assessed the nature of the risk and, in particular, the risk that insureds, wherever they reside, may have if their legitimate claims are not met in full.

Fundamental to an application for an insurer's, broker's or manager's licence is the submission of a Business Plan which will (I) be a major factor in determining whether or not a licence is issued and (2) if so, define and thereby control the modus operandi of the licensee. The Business Plan must include, where appropriate:

1. A five years projection including anticipated risk exposure and asset base at the end of each year during the period.
2. The type and source of business contemplated, specifically categorised.
3. Anticipated premium income, properly categorised.
4. The reasons for choosing the Islands as a base for operations.
5. An overall assessment of the risk factors and, if appropriate, an analysis of proposed reinsurances. Companies which require to furnish details of reinsurance and net risk retained will provide such information as determined in consultation with the Superintendent. The prime concern is to ensure that where reinsurances are used to

463

reduce substantially the potential liabilities outstanding, the policies should be taken out with only reputable well-reserved companies.

6. An assessment of the expected ratio of claims to premiums for each category of business written with a statement explaining the rationale applied.

The name of the insurance company should reflect the type of insurance being written. It is now unlawful for a company to use in its name the word insurance or any other word which connotes insurance business unless the Financial Secretary's consent has been obtained.

Capital requirements for insurers will vary, but those companies engaged in reinsurance, life or general (domestic or international) business should expect to have a minimum paid-up capital of US$100,000. Capital levels will be determined on the following criteria (projected or actual):

1. The size of the company as measured by its assets, capital and/or surplus, reserves, premium writings and insurance in force.
2. The kinds of business written, the company's net exposure and the degree of diversification of lines of insurance.
3. The past and anticipated trend in the size of the company's capital and consideration of premium growth, operating history, loss and expense ratios.

Solvency ratios will be established on the basis of the risk assessment in each particular case. As a guideline, the minimum net worth requirement will be calculated as follows:

Business	Net Premium Income	Net Worth
A. General only	up to $5,000,000	20% of premiums
	over $5,000,000	10% of premiums plus $100,000
B. Long term only		$180,000
C. Long term and general	up to $5,000,000	20% of premiums
	over $5,000,000	10% of premiums plus $180,000

Net worth is defined as the excess of assets (including any contingent or reserve fund) over liabilities other than liabilities to partners or shareholders. The assets readily available must be sufficient to meet liabilities at all times and therefore the net worth must comprise assets which are acceptable to the Superintendent. The range of permitted assets will be as broad as possible but will depend upon the type of business to be written. Companies must satisfy the Superintendent that the maturity dates of relevant assets are planned to correspond with maturing liabilities.

Permitted assets will include:

1. Cash and time deposits with acceptable financial institutions.
2. Fixed interest securities and blue-chip equities traded on recognised stock exchanges.
3. Eurobonds rated at BBB or above by Standard & Poor.

4. Premiums receivable.
5. Irrevocable Letters of Credit issued by acceptable financial institutions.

All assets should be valued at market value and no amounts receivable from related parties may be included without approval from the Superintendent.

Prohibited assets will include:

1. Yachts, aeroplanes, motor vehicles and livestock.
2. Loans to group or connected companies and individuals.
3. Investments in options, futures or forward contracts.

There are, at present, six categories of licence covering:

1. Insurers
2. Agents
3. Brokers
4. Managers
5. Principal Representatives
6. Sub-agents

Further categories of licence may be added when circumstances dictate.

Branches/subsidiaries of leading international insurance companies will receive every assistance when applying for a licence; parent companies, however, may be requested to provide a suitable guarantee covering the liabilities of any subsidiary applying for a licence. Approval from the insurance supervisor in the company's country of domicile and copies, periodically, of statutory filings made in the home jurisdiction may be requested.

The application fee is $500 for an insurer's licence and $300 for all other licences, half the fee is refundable if the application is not approved. Annual fees for the licensees are as follows:

1. Insurers
   (a) General (local & offshore) $2,500
   (b) Non-domestic $2,000
   (c) Restricted non-domestic $1,750
   (d) Other $2,000
2. Agents $ 100
3. Brokers $ 750
4. Managers $3,500
5. Principal Representatives $ 300
6. Sub-agents $ 50

When a licence is first granted, the annual fee shall be reduced by one-twelfth for every completed month from the 31st day of March last preceding the date of the grant.

The Superintendent is particularly anxious to encourage the licensing of Insurance Managers – companies with insurance experience and expertise capable of managing the affairs of insurers. Insurance companies wishing to be licensed in the Islands which do not appoint a professional Insurance Manager will be required to demonstrate that the necessary expertise is readily available at all times.

Profit and loss statements and balance sheets must be prepared and audited. Such accounts may be required annually or every six months, at the discretion of the Superintendent, and subject to the type of business written. In any event, a full set of accounts will be required annually.

The auditors of insurance companies must be approved in terms of the Insurance Ordinance ('the Ordinance'). In addition to being suitably professionally qualified, auditors must satisfy the Superintendent that they have adequate knowledge of the insurance industry to be relied upon to conduct a proper audit. The auditor is required to provide the necessary annual confirmations (accounts/business plan compliance) to the Superintendent. Residence on the Islands is not a prerequisite to obtaining approved-auditor status. The Superintendent will seek agreement from insurers that an open dialogue between his department and the auditors is maintained. This practice should be extended to Insurance Managers as well.

Unless an insurer is owned by non-insurance companies and is insuring its own or its group's assets (and the Superintendent considers it unnecessary) actuarial valuations will be required from insurers. The actuary must hold an appropriate professional qualification and, unless otherwise specified, all valuations prepared must be sent direct to the Superintendent.

APPENDIX XXI

VERMONT

CAPTIVE INSURANCE FINANCIAL REGULATION

Section 1: Purpose and authority

The purpose of this regulation is to set forth the financial and reporting requirements which the commissioner deems necessary for the regulation of captive insurance companies, as authorized by the Captive Insurance Company Act, 8 V.S.A., Section 6015. Reference hereunder to 'company' shall mean captive insurance company or companies, unless otherwise specified.

Section 2: Annual reporting requirements

An association captive insurance company doing business in this state shall annually submit to the commissioner a report of its financial condition, verified by oath of two of its executive officers. The report shall be that required by 8 V.S.A., Section 3561.

A pure or industrial insured captive insurance company doing business in this state shall annually submit to the commissioner with a report of its financial condition, verified by oath of two of its executive officers. The report shall be that prescribed by the commissioner as 'Captive Annual Statement: Pure or Industrial Insured'.

Section 3: Annual audit

All companies shall have an annual audit by an independent certified public accountant, authorized by the commissioner, and shall file such audited financial report with the commissioner on or before June 30 for the year ending December 31 immediately preceding.

The annual audit report shall be considered part of the company's annual report of financial condition except with respect to the date by which it must be filed with the commissioner.

The annual audit shall consist of the following:

(A) Opinion of independent certified public accountant

Financial statements furnished pursuant to this section shall be examined by independent certified public accountants in accordance with generally accepted auditing standards as determined by the American Institute of Certified Public Accountants.

The opinion of the independent certified public accountant shall cover all years presented.

The opinion shall be addressed to the company on stationery of the accountant showing the address of issuance, shall bear original manual signatures and shall be dated.

(B) Report of evaluation of internal controls

This report shall include an evaluation of the internal controls of the company relating to the methods and procedures used in the securing of assets and the reliability of the financial records, including but not limited to such controls as the system of authorization and approval and the separation of duties.

The review shall be conducted in accordance with generally accepted auditing standards and the report filed with the commissioner.

(C) Accountant's letter

The accountant shall furnish the company, for inclusion in the filing of the audited annual report, a letter stating:

(a) That he is independent with respect to the company and conforms to the standards of his profession as contained in the Code of Professional Ethics and pronouncements of the American Institute of Certified Public Accountants and pronouncements of the Financial Accounting Standards Board.

(b) The general background and experience of the staff engaged in audit including the experience in auditing captives or other insurance companies.

(c) That the accountant understands that the audited annual report and his opinions thereon will be filed in compliance with this regulation with the Department of Banking and Insurance.

(d) That the accountant consents to the requirements of Section 6 of this regulation and that the accountant consents and agrees to make available for review by the commissioner, his designee or his appointed agent the work papers as defined in Section 6.

(e) That the accountant is properly licensed by an appropriate state licensing authority and that he is a member in good standing in the American Institute of Certified Public Accountants.

(D) Financial statements

Statements required shall be as follows:

(a) Balance sheet

(b) Statement of gain or loss from operations
(c) Statement of changes in financial position
(d) Statement of changes in capital paid up, gross paid in and contributed surplus and unassigned funds (surplus)
(e) Notes to financial statements.

The notes to financial statements shall be those required by generally accepted accounting principles, and shall include:

1. A reconciliation of differences, if any, between the audited financial report and the statement or form filed with the commissioner.
2. A summary of ownership and relationship of the company and all affiliated corporations or companies insured by the captive.
3. A narrative explanation of all material transactions and balances with the company.

(E) Certification of loss reserves and loss expense reserves
The annual audit shall include an opinion as to the adequacy of the company's loss reserves and loss expense reserves. The individual who certifies as to the adequacy of reserves shall be approved by the commissioner and shall be a Fellow of the Casualty Actuarial Society, a member in good standing of the American Academy of Actuaries, or an individual who has demonstrated his competence in loss reserve evaluation to the commissioner.

Certification shall be in such form as the commissioner deems appropriate.

Section 4: Designation of independent certified public accountant

Companies, after becoming subject to this regulation, shall within ninety days report to the commissioner, in writing, the name and address of the independent certified public accountant retained to conduct the annual audit set forth in this regulation.

Section 5: Notification of adverse financial condition

A company shall require the certified public accountant to immediately notify in writing an officer and all members of the Board of Directors of the company of any determination by the independent certified public accountant that the company has materially misstated its financial condition in its report to the commissioner as required in Section 6007 of 8 V.S.A. The company shall furnish such notification to the commissioner within five working days of receipt thereof.

Section 6: Availability and maintenace of working papers of the independent certified public accountant

Each company shall require the independent certified public accountant to make available for review by the commissioner or his appointed agent the work papers prepared in the conduct of the audit of the company. The company shall require that the accountant retain the audit work papers for a period of not less than five years after the period reported upon.

The aforementioned review by the commissioner shall be considered investigations and all working papers obtained during the course of such investigations shall be confidential. The company shall require that the independent certified public accountant provide photocopies of any of the working papers which the Department of Banking and Insurance considers relevant. Such working papers may be retained by the Department.

'Work Papers' as referred to in this section include, but are not necessarily limited to, schedules, analyses, reconciliations, abstracts, memoranda, narratives, flow charts, copies of company records or other documents prepared or obtained by the accountant and his employees in the conduct of their examination of the company.

Section 7: Deposit requirement

Whenever the commissioner deems that the financial condition of the company warrants additional security, he may require a company to deposit with the Treasurer of this state cash or securities approved by the commissioner or, alternatively, to furnish the commissioner a clean irrevocable letter of credit issued by a bank chartered by the State of Vermont or a member bank of the Federal Reserve System and approved by the commissioner.

The company may receive interest or dividends from said deposit or exchange the deposits for others of equal value with the approval of the commissioner.

If such company discontinues business, the commissioner shall return such deposit only after being satisfied that all obligations of the company have been discharged.

Section 8: Organizational examination

In addition to processing of the application, an organizational investigation or examination may be performed before an applicant is licensed. Such investigation or examination shall consist of a general survey of the company's corporate records, including charter, bylaws and minute-books; verification of capital and surplus; verification of principal place of business; determination of assets and liabilities; and a review of such other factors as the commissioner deems necessary.

Section 9: Reinsurance

Any captive insurance company authorized to do business in this state may take credit for reserves on risks ceded to a reinsurer subject to the following limitations:

(a) No credit shall be allowed for reinsurance where the reinsurance contract does not result in the complete transfer of the risk or liability to the reinsurer.

(b) No credit shall be allowed, as an asset or a deduction from liability, to any ceding insurer for reinsurance unless the reinsurance is payable by the assuming insurer on the basis of the liability of the ceding insurer under the contract reinsured without diminution because of the insolvency of the ceding insurer.

Reinsurance under this section shall be effected through a written agreement of reinsurance setting forth the terms, provisions and conditions governing such reinsurance.

The commissioner in his discretion may require that complete copies of all reinsurance treaties and contracts be filed and/or approved by him.

Section 10: Insurance managers and intermediaries

No person shall, in or from within this state, act as an insurance manager, broker, agent, salesman, or reinsurance intermediary for captive business without the authorization of the commissioner. Application for such authorization must be on a form prescribed by the commissioner.

Section 11: Directors

Every company shall report to the commissioner within thirty days after any change in its executive officers or directors, including in its report a statement of the business and professional affiliations of any new executive officer or director.

No director, officer, or employee of a company shall, except on behalf of the company, accept, or be the beneficiary of, any fee, brokerage, gift, or other emolument because of any investment, loan, deposit, purchase, sale, payment or exchange made by or for the company in his or her usual private, professional or business capacity.

Any profit or gain received by or on behalf of any person in violation of this section shall inure to and be recoverable by the company.

Section 12: Conflict of interest

In addition to the investment of funds in Section 11 of this regulation, each company chartered in this stage is required to adopt a conflict of interest statement from officers, directors and key employees. Such statement shall disclose that the individual has not outside commitments, personal or otherwise, that would divert him from his duty to further the interests of the company he represents but this shall not preclude such person from being a director or officer in more than one insurance company.

Each officer, director, and key employee shall file such disclosure with the Board of Directors yearly.

Section 13: Rescission of captive license

The commissioner may, subject to the provisions of this section, by order rescind the license of the company:

(a) if the company has not commenced business according to its plan of operation within two years of being licensed; or

(b) if the company ceases to carry on insurance business in or from within Vermont;

(c) at the request of the company; or

(d) for any reason provided in 8 V.S.A., Section 6009.

Before the commissioner rescinds the license of a company under (a) or (b), the commissioner shall give the company notice in writing of the grounds on which he proposed to cancel the license, and shall afford the company an opportunity to make objection in writing within the period of thirty days after receipt of notice. The commissioner shall take into consideration any objection received by him within that period and, if he decides to cancel the license, cause the order of cancellation to be served on the company.

Section 14: Acquisition of control or of merger with domestic company

No person other than the issuer shall make a tender offer for or a request or invitation for tenders of, or enter into any agreement to exchange securities for, seek to acquire, or acquire in the open market or otherwise, any voting security of a domestic company if, after the consummation thereof, such person would, directly or indirectly (or by conversion or by exercise of any right to acquire) be in control of such company; and no person shall enter into an agreement to merge with or otherwise to acquire control of a domestic company without the prior written approval of the commissioner. In considering any application for acquisition of control or merger with a domestic company, the commissioner shall consider all of the facts and circumstances surrounding the application as well as the criteria for establishment of a company set out in this chapter.

Section 15: Change of business

Any change in the nature of the captive business from that stated in the company's plan of operation filed with the commissioner upon application requires prior approval from the commissioner.

Any change in any other information filed with the application must be filed with the commissioner but toes not require prior approval.

George A. Chafee
Commissioner of Banking and Insurance
October 7 1981

STEPS IN FORMING A VERMONT CAPTIVE

Generally the following steps will be followed in the process of incorporating a captive insurer in Vermont and applying for a license from the Department of Banking and Insurance:

1. Arrange a meeting with the commissioner and staff to discuss the proposed captive and obtain initial reactions from the Department. In the case of association or risk retention captives, the commissioner will want to meet with key officers prior to licensing. Risk retention captives should have a feasibility study for this meeting.
2. Prepare documents necessary for incorporation. The services of a local lawyer may be desirable.

3. Prepare documents necessary for application to the department (see captive application for a list of these items).
4. Submit one copy of all materials in numbers (2) and (3) above to the Commissioner of Banking and Insurance for review. Include a $200.00 nonrefundable application fee.
5. Submit one additional copy of the application material to the assigned review firm together with a check in the amount of $1,200.00 when instructed to do so by the commissioner.
6. Submit the application summary form to each member and alternate of the Captive Advisory Committee.
7. Petition the commissioner to issue a Certificate of Public Good. The factors to be addressed are outlined in 8 V.S.A. S6006(d). In addition, a statement of the benefit to Vermont should be included.
8. After the commissioner has issued the Certificate of Public Good, present this and the documents in number (2) above to the Secretary of State's office along with the appropriate fee in order to incorporate the captive (see 11 V.S.A. S2201).
9. After incorporation, apply to the commissioner for a Certificate of Authority and enclose the Power of Attorney form along with a $300.00 license fee.
10. Other requirements:
    (a) Have your CPA firm complete the necessary form for authorization to perform audits.
    (b) Have your actuary complete the necessary form for authorization to render the opinion on reserves.

Instructions for captive insurance company application

General

Enclosed is the application for admission as a captive insurance company together with a sample letter of credit form and biographical affidavit form.

The application form must be filled out in its entirety and when submitted should include all material requested together with a non-refundable application fee of $200.00. No incomplete package of material will be accepted.

If letters of credit are used to meet capital and surplus requirements Form E-702 enclosed must be adhered to by the institution issuing the letter of credit.

One biographical affidavit form in enclosed. Copies should be made and enclosed as required by the application. Each affidavit must be filled out entirely and no substitute for the enclosed form will be accepted.

Financial Regulation

Financial Regulation 81-2 will require that an independent certified public accountant, approved by the commissioner, audit the captive annually. It is incumbent upon the applicant to select an accountant who meets the requirements of Regulation 81-2.

Certification of reserves

Financial Regulation 81-2 requires that loss reserves and loss expense reserves be certified by a Fellow of the Casualty Actuarial Society, a member in good standing of the American Academy of Actuaries or an individual who has demonstrated his competence in loss reserve evaluation and has been approved by the commissioner. It is incumbent upon the applicant to select a member or individual who meets the requirements of this regulation.

Review committee
All applications will be reviewed by one of the five review firms appointed by the commissioner. The firms' duties are of an advisory nature only and final approval or disapproval of an application will be made by the commissioner only.

Captive blank
Pure Industrial Insured and Risk Retention captives will file an annual statement on a Vermont Captive Insurance Company blank established by the commissioner.

Association captives will file an annual statement on the NAIC blank currently in use by the insurance industry.

Location of captive records
All books, records, and other information necessary for a statutory examination must be located in Vermont.

APPLICATION FOR ADMISSION

1. Name of Proposed Captive _____

2. Indicate Type of Proposed Captive

   ☐ Pure   ☐ Association   ☐ Industrial Insured   ☐ Risk Retention

3. Address of Incorporation and Date _____

   _____

4. Principal Office of Proposed Captive _____

   _____

5. Location of Books and Records

   _____

6. Capitalization if Stock Company
   (a) Amount of Paid-In Capital $ _____
   (b) Type of Stock(s) to be Authorized   Number of Shares

   (1) _____   _____

   (2) _____   _____

   (c) Par Value of Each Share by Type   Selling Price

   (1) $ _____ $ _____

   (2) $ _____ $ _____

   (d) Location of Shares of Stock

   (1) _____

   (2) _____

7. Has Parent Prepared Resolutions for Authorizing Establishment of Captive, Designating Individual(s) to

   (a) Vote the Stock of Shareholders? _____

   (b) Negotiate Letter of Credit, The Repayment Agreement and/or Continuing Guaranty Agreement? _____

8. Contributed Surplus $ _____
   (a) Name(s) and Address(es) of Beneficial Owners   Percent of Ownership

   (1) _____   _____
       _____

   (2) _____   _____
       _____

   (3) _____   _____
       _____

9. Explain Relationship Among Beneficial Owners _____

_____

_____

_____

10. Enclose Annual Report or 10K's of Beneficial Owners.

11. If Letter(s) of Credit Is (Are) to be Used

Name and Address of Bank	Issued in Favor Of	Amount
_____	_____	$ _____
_____	_____	$ _____

Form E-702 (enclosed) must be used.

12. Name and Address of Lawyer _____

_____

13. Name and Address of Certified Public Accountant _____

_____

14. Name and Address of Management Firm _____

_____

15. Name and Address of Registered Resident Agent _____

_____

16. Is Audit Committee to be Formed?
    If Yes, Name the Members

_____

_____

_____

17. Is Executive Committee to be Formed? _____
    If Yes, Name the Members

_____

_____

_____

18. Name Members of Investment Committee

_____

_____

_____

19. Names and Residence Addresses of Directors of the Captive (at least three)

_____

_____

_____

_____

Résumées of each Director must be prepared and include all past and present business affiliations.
(Please use biographical affidavit enclosed.)

20. Names and Residence Addresses of Officers of the Captive

Chairman _____

President _____

Vice President and Secretary _____

Vice President/Treasurer _____

Vice President _____

Vice President _____

Assistant Secretary _____

Assistant Secretary _____

Résumés of each Officer must be prepared on biographical affidavit form enclosed.

21. If Applicant is an Industrial Insured Captive, answer the following:
    (a) Name and address of each full-time employee acting as an Insurance Manager or Buyer

    _____

    (b) Aggregate annual premium $ _____
    (c) Number of full-time employees   _____

22. Include the following with this application:
    (a) Name, address and telephone number of the individual to be contacted regarding this application
    (b) Certified copy of Captive's certificate of incorporation, articles of association and bylaws (to be filed before issuance of license)
    (c) A non-refundable fee of $200.00
    (d) A feasibility study by an actuary
    (e) Application Summary Form (Form E-703)
    (f) Statement of benefit to Vermont
    (g) Biographical affidavits on officers and directors
    (h) If applicant is Association Captive, give history, purpose, size and other details of parent association
    (i) List all other providers and their responsibilities together with how fees for services rendered are to be charged
    (j) Detailed Plan of Operation with supporting data including:
        (1) Risks to be insured – direct, assumed and ceded – by line of business
        (2) Fronting company if operating as a reinsurer
        (3) Expected net annual premium income
        (4) Maximum retained risk (per loss and annual aggregate)
        (5) Rating program

    (6) Reinsurance program

    (7) Organization and responsibility for loss prevention and safety including the main procedures followed and steps taken to deal with events prior to possible claims.

    (8) Loss experience for past five years together with projections for the ensuing five years

    (9) Organization chart

    (10) Financial plan

Items 1,3,4 and 10 above should be projected for a five year period.

NOTE: Prepare one extra copy of all documents required by this application to be sent to the assigned Captive Review Firm upon direction of this Department together with the appropriate fee.

I CERTIFY THAT TO THE BEST OF MY KNOWLEDGE AND BELIEF ALL OF THE INFORMATION GIVEN IN THIS APPLICATION IS TRUE AND CORRECT AND THAT ALL ESTIMATES GIVEN ARE TRUE ESTIMATES BASED UPON FACTS WHICH HAVE BEEN CAREFULLY CONSIDERED AND ASSESSED.

Name _____ Date _____

Signature _____

                                        (Director)

VERMONT CAPTIVE APPLICATION SUMMARY

1. Name of Captive _____

2. Parent(s) _____

3. Type of Captive   4. Organization Form

   _____ Pure/Single Parent   _____ Stock

   _____ Industrial Insured   _____ Mutual

   _____ Association

   _____ Risk Retention Captive

5. Purpose of Captive (describe) _____

   _____

   _____

6. Capitalization Amount _____

7. Initial Premiums

                                                    Assumed
                                                    Growth
   Annual Gross Premiums $ _____   _____%

   Reinsurance Ceded $ _____   _____%

   Net Premium Retained $ _____   _____%

8. Minimum Participation   Yes/No   Years _____

9. Mandated Loss Control Program Yes/No

For 10 through 16, List Firm and Key Contact

10. Captive Manager _____

    _____

11. Feasibility Study by _____

    _____

12. Insurance Broker Involved _____

    _____

13. Reinsurance Broker Involved _____

    _____

14. Claims Handler _____

    _____

15. Accountants for Captive _____

    _____

16. Law Firm _____

_____

17. Coverage/limits/reinsurance

Coverage	Direct or reinsurance	Policy limits per occ.agg.	Excess of amount and form

Claims made or occurrence	Assessable-rateable policy	Amount reinsured	Reinsurance by

18. Biographical Information for Officers and Directors

Name	Position with Captive	Employer and Position

19. Other information to Review Application

Prepared By _____

Date _____

N.B. For pure/single parent captives where the parent is public, please attach the current annual report with financials. For all others, attach appropriate information to describe the business nature of the parent(s) or association group.